C000181071

THE SUNDAY TIMES GUIDE TO THE WORLD'S BEST FOOD

THE SUNDAY TIMES GUIDE TO THE WORLD'S BEST FOOD

Michael Bateman, Caroline Conran,
Oliver Gillie

Illustrations by Susan J. Curtis

Photography by Christine Hanscomb

Hutchinson
London Melbourne Sydney Auckland Johannesburg

Hutchinson & Co. (Publishers) Ltd
An imprint of the Hutchinson Publishing Group
3 Fitzroy Square, London W1P 6JD
Hutchinson Group (Australia) Pty Ltd
30–32 Cremorne Street, Richmond South, Victoria 3121
PO Box 151, Broadway, New South Wales 2007
Hutchinson Group (NZ) Ltd
32–34 View Road, PO Box 40-086, Glenfield, Auckland 10
Hutchinson Group (SA) (Pty) Ltd
PO Box 337, Bergvlei 2012, South Africa
First published 1981
© Michael Bateman, Caroline Conran, Oliver Gillie 1981
Illustrations © Hutchinson Publishing Group
Set in VIP Sabon by D. P. Media Limited
Hitchin, Hertfordshire
Printed in Great Britain by
The Anchor Press Ltd
and bound by Wm Brendon & Son Ltd,
both of Tiptree, Essex
British Library Cataloguing in Publication Data
Bateman, Michael
The Sunday Times guide to the world's best food
1. Cookery (Natural foods)
I. Title II. Conran, Caroline
III. Gillie, Oliver
641.5'63 TX741
ISBN 0 09 143890 X

CONTENTS

Acknowledgements 6
Introduction 7

1 South-West Europe 16
2 The Balkans 52
3 The Middle East 82
4 Japan and South-East Asia 112
5 Latin America and the Caribbean 148
6 The Vegetarians 182
7 Breads of the World 208

Knowing Your Cooking Oils 227
Choosing the Right Rice 231

Glossary: Flavours and Foodstuffs 234
Indexes
Recipe titles 239
General 240

ACKNOWLEDGEMENTS

Contributors and consultants
Alan Davidson, consultant *The Far East*
Rose Elliot, contributor *Vegetarian food*
Moira Hodgson, contributor *Latin America*
Robin Howe, contributor *The Balkans*
Maria Johnson, consultant and contributor *The Balkans* (for the recipes for Bulgur Pilâvı, Köfte, Şiş Kebap, Mousaka s Patladzhani, Pechena Tikva, Pogača, Popara, Punjeni Paprike i Paradajz, Savanyú Káposzta, Trahana, Tyropitta, Türlü Guveç and Yoghurt)
Julie Jordan, contributor *The Vegetarians*
Anna MacMiadhacháin, contributor *Spain and Portugal*
Elisabeth Lambert Ortiz, contributor *The Caribbean and Japan*
Sri Owen, contributor *Indonesia*
Rachael Pacray, consultant *The Philippines*
Claudia Roden, consultant and contributor *The Middle East*
Momoko Williams, consultant *Japan*

Photographer
Christine Hanscomb

Illustrator
Susan J. Curtis

Recipes for photography
Dinah Morrison

Recipe testers
Sarah Kelly
Judy Lister
Rosamund Wallinger

Production team
Editor Heather Maisner
Chief sub-editor Judith Taylor
Special contributors Susan Campbell (Rice), Katy Franklin (Central America)
Writers/researchers Julia Blackburn, Sue Ramus, Rosemary Atkins

The authors are particularly grateful for special assistance from the following people and organisations: Maria Lourdes Nichols, exclusive recipe for *tortillas* (p. 155); Evelyn Williams, advice on Malaysia; Elisabeth Lambert Ortiz for additional Japanese and Latin American recipes; Prospect Books for permission to adapt recipes from *Indonesian Cookery* by Sri Owen (pp. 138, 139, 141, 144). The authors also would like to acknowledge their indebtedness to the following publications: Fu Pei-Mei, *Pei Mei's Chinese Cook Book* (Taiwan, 1969), for recipes adapted on pp. 140, 143; Ellen Schrecker with John Schrecker, *Mrs Chiang's Szechwan Cookbook* (Harper & Row, 1976), for the adapted recipes on pp. 132, 135; Hsiang Lin and Tsuifeng Lin, *Chinese Gastronomy* (Hastings House, New York, 1969), for the adapted recipe on p. 136.

Our special thanks for permission to use the following locations for photography: Julie's Restaurant, 136 Portland Road, London W11, and Suntori Japanese Restaurant, 72 St James's Street, London W1.

INTRODUCTION

The best food in the world is found not in the richest countries of the West but in a few favoured areas where climate and agriculture have combined to provide man with the sort of diet to which he has been adapted by millions of years of natural selection. People in these countries are stronger and healthier and live longer – when differences resulting from inferior health services and greater prevalence of infectious disease are allowed for. In these countries people eat more grains – rice, bread or pasta – and much less meat and fat than in the West. They also eat more beans, nuts, fruit and vegetables.

This is much nearer to the sort of diet which man ate before he turned to settled agriculture some 10,000 years ago than is the usual diet in Britain or America. We are not descended, as many people think, from cave-men who ate a diet consisting mostly of meat from large animals, but from hunter-gatherers who lived in small groups moving from place to place eating fruits, seeds and berries as they came into season, with relatively little meat.

In this book we provide recipes from the countries of the world where disease caused through diet is least. The food has been chosen because it is eaten daily in these countries. The recipes take their inspiration from local ingredients and have been tested by daily use in families for hundreds of years: in other words, they are not in the least monotonous; they have stood the test of time – and they have style.

Recent years have seen a multitude of theories about the relationship between the food we eat and the diseases we suffer from – for instance that heart disease is caused by too much cholesterol, too much fat, too much meat, too little fibre (roughage), etc. These theories may be partly or even wholly correct, but in practical terms it is very difficult to reconcile them all. And it is difficult to produce food which conforms to them all and is enjoyable.

In this book we have taken a pragmatic approach which sidesteps the confusion resulting from strict adherence to different dietary theories. Our approach is based on our observations of the diets of other countries where dietary disease is less common. Our overriding aim has been to produce well-tried and tested recipes for dishes which are not only healthy but also attractive and enjoyable to eat.

Dietary diseases in the Western world

More then half of all deaths in Western countries can be directly attributed to diseases caused by the food we eat. In nearly every case heart disease is caused by atherosclerosis, a furring up of the arteries, which is caused by our Western diet. Almost half the deaths from cancer are probably caused by the food we choose to eat. Even breast cancer, a major killer of women in middle age, seems to be caused by diet. High blood pressure and stroke appear to be caused by excess salt in the diet. And the commonest form of diabetes, which occurs in middle age, seems to be caused by excessive fat or sugar in the diet. These diseases are often the cause of premature death. For example, one in three deaths in men aged 35 to 54 is caused by heart disease or diabetes.

Our Western diet also causes a great deal of ill-health which does not lead to death: constipation, haemorrhoids, varicose veins, gallstones, kidney stones, diverticular disease, tooth and gum disease, peptic ulcers, overweight and birth defects. A change in diet can delay or prevent these diseases from occurring, or may even reverse them in some cases.

These diseases do not occur among people in parts of Africa where they have not yet changed to the Western industrialized type of diet. As people take to a Western diet so our Western diseases begin to be found, although the incidence of these diseases varies greatly in different developed countries. In Spain, for example, heart disease and the dietary cancers are rare compared with Britain or the United States, and the same is true of Japan. This is not because the Japanese or Spanish people have inherited a different constitution from people in the vulnerable countries – when Japanese emigrate to the United States and eat American food they soon start to suffer from Western diseases.

Countries which have a low incidence of heart disease also tend to have a low incidence of certain cancers, diabetes and other Western diseases. This suggests that there may be a common dietary cause of some of these diseases and that a consistent change in diet might rid us of them all, and even reduce the incidence of birth defects such as spina bifida.

Deaths from birth defects are lower in Japan and Spain than in other industrialized countries of the world, suggesting that a diet which is good at preventing heart disease and cancer in later life is also good for babies in the womb. This conclusion is reinforced by studies of different socio-economic groups of women in Britain which show that risks of cancer and heart disease are closely correlated with risks of malformation and infant mortality. We therefore believe that the diet recommended in this book is suitable for minimizing the risks of heart disease and cancer and should also prove excellent in pregnancy.

How we chose the countries with the best diet for health

We have identified the countries of the world with the best diet for health in a systematic way using published research figures from the World Health Organization and other international sources to find those countries which have the lowest mortality or incidence of heart disease and certain cancers. From these sources we were able to compile a list of countries where the incidence of mortality from heart disease and certain cancers was not more than half that of Britain or America and sometimes it was one third or even one quarter. This method can of course only identify countries with a healthy diet when the necessary statistics are available. Other evidence points to the healthy diet of people living, for example, in Africa. However we have not attempted to gather information about this sort of diet because of the uncertainties involved.

It is not possible to select countries with the healthiest diet simply on the basis of the longevity of their inhabitants because longevity is also dependent on medical services, sanitation and the ability to pay for drugs. In fact the life expectancy of Greek or Spanish people *at birth* is very similar to our own in Britain or the United States and in some good-diet countries it is less. In Spain males can expect to live until they are about 69 and females until 74 or 75. However, in Spain deaths of men aged 55 to 64 are about

20 per cent less than in England or the United States, showing that Spaniards are much healthier in middle age. This is because their diet makes them much less vulnerable to heart disease and cancer, as statistics for these diseases show.

There are distinct regional patterns of mortality. Countries such as Spain, Italy and Greece have a relatively high mortality at birth and during infancy up to age five. Children in these countries are particularly exposed to diseases such as severe diarrhoea, which are common because of the warm climate, relatively poor sanitation, and contaminated water supplies. Health services have not been so well developed until fairly recently and problems of communications make it difficult to get emergencies to hospital. In some countries mortality increases sharply after the age of 50 or 60 because people at this age become vulnerable again to infectious and parasitic diseases, especially when sanitation and health services are poor.

For this reason we cannot use life expectancy alone to choose countries with the healthiest diet. Heart disease and cancer are the major killers in Western countries and examination of accumulated evidence implicates our diet. To find the healthiest food in the world we have therefore gone to those countries and cultures where these killer diseases are known to be least common.

How we chose the recipes

Some of the countries such as Spain or Greece with outstanding health today are changing quite rapidly and within a decade their health may have deteriorated noticeably. Their good record in recent years has been determined by their diet over the last 25. Therefore in choosing recipes for the book we have selected traditional dishes which for many years have been the everyday fare of ordinary people. These use local ingredients and combine them skilfully in ways which have gained from the experience of years. And in providing information about the quantities of various foods eaten we have relied on the UN Food and Agriculture Organization Food Balance Sheets compiled for the years 1964–66. These are more appropriate than more recent figures because the illnesses of today are caused, in part, by the food of yesterday.

Wherever possible we have sought to give recipes for food produced as it would be in the authentic local manner. Sometimes it is possible to suggest alternative ingredients which would be acceptable locally, or which are very close to the locally used ingredient. Spinach is not the same as *malunggay* leaves used by Filipinos to make their traditional *Sinigang*, but it is an alternative they might use themselves. Anchovy sauce is not exactly the same as the Filipino *bagoong* used in so many of their dishes but they find it a satisfactory alternative and from the nutritional point of view it is much the same. In the glossary we suggest alternatives for some ingredients.

Some of our countries use a certain amount of butter, sour cream, peanut oil or coconut in their dishes and we have included recipes for these although we do not recommend these ingredients for everyday use in large quantities. Butter, sour cream and peanut oil each have their own characteristic flavour which is important to the dish and they also serve each in their own way to enhance certain flavours. In seeking inspiration from the healthy cuisines of the world we have avoided changing recipes to conform with dietary theories. Our aim has been to provide authentic recipes for the everyday food eaten in countries with the best health record.

The new food wisdom

Our studies of the food and cooking of countries selected for their good health records have enabled us to distil a new food wisdom which goes beyond the guidelines to be found in many reports limited to preventing heart disease or high blood pressure, or reducing weight. All these are desirable objectives which we believe can be attained – together with all-round health – by following the recipes and principles set down in this book.

Rules of eating

The eating styles represented in this book are very varied. Nevertheless certain basic principles of healthy eating are common to them all. We have used this great variation in styles to derive guidelines and define limits which should help you to eat wisely.

These rules take account of current medical thinking but they have not been specially devised to cover any one particular aspect of health. They are simply based on the customs of millions of people who have been eating well and eating healthily for many hundreds of years. Our rules can be applied to everyday eating both when you are cooking at home and when you are looking over the menu in a restaurant.

Meat: eat less, particularly less beef and lamb; they are rich in saturated fats

Most of the recipes in this book use meat economically, mainly because they come from countries where meat is expensive.

Beef and lamb contain more saturated fat than pork and chicken. All meat, even the leanest, contains 20 per cent fat.

The ideal serving portion of meat in a dish is 2 ounces per person; any protein surplus to this is broken down by the body to form energy or may actually be converted into fat and stored in the body, thereby contributing to overweight.

Meat is a major source of protein, but if you eat less there is no need to fear a deficiency of protein in the diet. Bread and potatoes are excellent sources: so are fish, eggs, milk, cheese, pasta, rice and corn (maize).

Eat free-range chickens when you can get them. Chickens which are intensively reared may be often fed on hydrogenated fish meals, which contain saturated fats.

Eat game, which is lean, when you can get it. Cook it in its own juices or using a vegetable oil like olive oil. Don't cook it with animal fats, and turn it into a heart hazard.

Fish: eat more; it's one of the best sources of protein, vitamins and minerals

Fish is rich in polyunsaturated fats which protect the heart against blood-clotting. It is a good source of protein, vitamins and minerals – particularly phosphorus and iodine.

Keep the water in which you cook the fish for stock: in this way you conserve vitamins and minerals.

The good health of Japanese and Eskimos may have much to do with the abundance of fish in their diet. Do not be put off eating fish by reports of methyl mercury poisoning. You would have to eat more than a pound of fish a day for this to be of any importance.

Eggs: a good source of protein and vitamins

Eat free-range eggs when you can get them. They contain more folic acid, vitamin B12 and vitamin D (because free-range hens have a more varied diet than battery hens).

People have been frightened off eggs, because they contain cholesterol. But in Spain they eat three or four eggs a week and are apparently none the worse for it.

Eggs are indeed rich in cholesterol, and high cholesterol in the blood is linked with heart disease. But high cholesterol in the blood may reflect a diet high in fat rather than in cholesterol itself. If you eat too much animal fat you stimulate the body's own production of cholesterol.

There are, however, sometimes medical reasons for a low cholesterol diet: after a heart attack for example, or because of trouble with gallstones.

Milk and milk products: use less milk, butter and cream; instead use low-fat cheese, and yoghurt

We drink more cow's milk than is good for us. Half a pint a day as part of a varied diet provides us with as much calcium as we need; milk is also a useful source of vitamin B2, minerals, energy and protein but these can be obtained from other sources, for example bread.

Adolescents and women who are pregnant may drink more but it should be skimmed.

Yoghurt is a good alternative to milk and cream. It's an important part of Balkan and Middle East eating where it is not only eaten plain, but also used in cooking. It is made from milk which is soured with lactic bacteria which break down the milk sugars to make lactic acid; and the bacteria it contains are said to have a beneficial effect if you have an upset stomach.

Natural, live yoghurt is better than the processed product which may contain refined starchy thickeners.

Allergy to cow's milk is common, particularly in children. Do not be afraid to dispense with it in your diet, but make sure you have alternative sources of calcium, e.g. white bread and dark green vegetables.

Vegetables and fruit: eat plenty every day

Vegetables and fruit are a useful source of vitamins and minerals as well as providing bulk fibre and energy.

The vitamin C and vitamin A content of vegetables provides an important protection against cancer. Vitamin A in the diet may even protect against lung cancer, which is important because vitamin A cannot easily be provided in pill form.

Cabbage, Brussels sprouts, broccoli, lettuce, tomatoes, peppers and citrus fruits are all good sources of vitamin C. Vegetables and fruit which are yellow-orange in colour – carrots, peaches, apricots, yellow melons – are a good source of vitamin A. So are dark-green vegetables such as spinach and broccoli.

Eat fresh or frozen fruits and vegetables. Canning and drying tend to destroy vitamins. Cook by quick methods such as stir-frying. Or use only a little cooking water. When possible use the cooking water for stock, as it will contain some vitamins.

Eat whole fruit and vegetables rather than juices as a general rule – otherwise the valuable fibre is lost.

Eat plenty of onions and garlic. Folk medicine and modern science agree on their healthy properties. They contain substances which delay blood clotting, and may reduce the risk of heart attacks.

Eat plenty of potatoes. As well as energy they provide good quality protein, and in northern climates are an important source of vitamin C as well as other vitamins and iron. They contain a lot of bulk and water and so are filling. They only become a cause of overweight when they are fried or roasted in fat, or served with masses of butter. (People who mistakenly cut out potatoes to help reduce weight would achieve greater effect by cutting out 7 or 8 teaspoons of sugar a day instead.)

Fats and oils: use less animal fat and more vegetable oils, especially olive, soya or corn oil

Eat less fat, particularly animal fat and hard margarines. The people represented in this book use half the fat we use in the West, or even less. Butter is used very little.

Try to cut down on butter and margarine. Use vegetable oils like soya, maize (corn) or olive oil for salads and cooking. Use other oils and butter sparingly for dishes which require their special flavours.

Vegetable oils contain essential fatty acids (polyunsaturated) which control blood clotting and regulate cholesterol in the blood. These fatty acids cannot be produced by the body so vegetable oils containing them are important. Animal fats contain relatively little of these precious fatty acids.

Soft margarines high in polyunsaturates may not be as valuable as we have been led to believe. They may contain dubious 'trans-fatty acids' created during the process of hydrogenation or saturated fats used to solidify the margarine. We recommend that you eat the food of the countries in this book and then you will seldom need to use a spreading fat such as margarine.

Avoid commercial cakes, pastries and ice-cream: they are usually made with saturated fats. See the chapter on cooking oils.

Bread, pasta, rice and corn (maize): eat much more of them

Eating more bread and other grain foods is the healthy way to make up for the calories you drop when you cut down on meat, animal fats, and sugar, so always have good bread on the table at mealtimes. See Chapter 7 for details of the world's healthiest breads.

Wholemeal (wholewheat) bread is particularly interesting because it contains bran – which doctors refer to as dietary fibre. This fibre is that part of vegetables, seeds and fruits which the system does not actually digest. It used to be thought that this fibre was useless but in the last ten years it has been increasingly recognized that it is important for health. Fibre eases the passage of food through the body and slows absorption of sugars which otherwise assault the system.

Fibre is removed in the process of refining starch and sugar. When white flour is made, the bran and germ are removed, leaving the polished grain. (The bran and germ go to make animal feed – so they benefit from what we lose.) Bran contains much of the fibre, and the germ much of the vitamins.

The polished grain is ground into flour which contains about one third of the fibre in wholewheat flour.

Lack of fibre in the diet is a cause not only of overweight, but other horrors like diabetes, constipation, diverticular disease, varicose veins, and even piles.

The everyday food of the people in this book provides much more fibre than the standard Western diet because it includes much more bread, pasta, rice and other cereals. The bread eaten in these countries is often white or brown rather than wholemeal – nevertheless they eat more fibre than we do because they eat more of it. If you do not eat much bread then it is more important to eat wholemeal bread to be sure that you get the fibre you need. However, white bread is a better source of calcium than wholemeal bread, so there is something to be said for both types.

If you eat a lot of rice it is a good idea to eat a substantial proportion of brown rice. See p. 232.

Sugar: eat less; it provides unwanted calories and has no food value

Teach your palate to enjoy more subtle, savoury flavours. If you give up sweet drinks and stop taking sugar in coffee and tea you will find that your palate adjusts to it within a few weeks.

To sweeten dishes use whole fresh fruit or dried fruit. Brown sugar is slightly less refined than white but is just as bad when used excessively. Honey contains different types of sugars and also minerals but still should not be used regularly in large quantities. Artificial sweeteners may not be the best way of satisfying a craving which to many is as desperate as an addiction. Saccharin is suspected of causing bladder cancer – though the risk is slight compared with the other risks of bad diet.

Sugar is a serious health hazard in the West because our bodies are simply not adapted to dealing with the huge amount of sugar we eat (twice as much as most of the peoples in this book).

It used to be said that all the starchy foods we eat turn into sugars when they have been digested so that ultimately it makes no difference whether you eat sugar or starch. This is misleading because there is a difference. The body absorbs sugar more quickly than starch. The result is that the body may overreact and remove too much sugar from the blood – inducing a feeling of hunger about an hour after you've eaten. This inevitably leads to over-eating, overweight and sometimes diabetes.

Sugar is also associated with the illnesses caused by lack of fibre in the diet. But it's a long story and we'll spare the grim tale. Sugar is also the villain which hurries you to the dentist, of course.

Salt: cut it to the minimum

Use less salt and cut down on salty foods.

Salt is believed to cause high blood pres-

The chart below shows a breakdown of the calorie value of foods eaten in the UK and USA, and compares these figures with representative countries in the five main geographical areas described in the book. The information is based on UN Food and Agriculture Organization food balance sheets, 1964–66. It shows how much more vegetables produce, particularly cereals, is eaten in countries with a relatively low incidence of heart disease and certain cancers. It also shows the high consumption of meat, milk products, sugar and animal fats in the UK and USA compared with these countries.

	Cereals including bread	*Potatoes and starchy roots*	*Sugars*	*Pulses nuts seeds*	*Vegetables*	*Fruit*	*Meat*	*Eggs*	*Milk products*	*Fish*	*Oils and fats*	TOTAL	*Total calories from veg. sources*	*Total calories from animal sources*
United Kingdom	770	196	530	68	44	79	526	62	378	29	551	**3233**	1859	1374
United States	649	95	513	103	73	101	598	71	397	26	530	**3156**	1885	1271
Latin America (Colombia)	778	290	504	41	28	61	182	15	173	5	115	**2192**	1795	397
Japan	1397	134	197	146	90	40	53	38	62	85	174	**2416**	2135	281
Middle East (Jordan)	1287	25	320	115	90	162	53	11	82	5	247	**2397**	2229	168
Balkans (Greece)	1287	91	191	148	87	145	152	36	272	41	451	**2901**	2368	533
South-West Europe (Spain)	1018	239	231	131	95	132	168	38	145	49	560	**2806**	2294	512

sure which in turn causes strokes. Never add salt to food without tasting it first. People who add salt automatically without tasting are more prone to high blood pressure.

Many processed foods, particularly bacon and canned meats and pickles, are highly salted. About two-thirds of the salt in our diet comes from processed food – so if you want to cut down on salt you will have to start doing more of your own cooking. Processed foods are also preserved by the use of nitrates and nitrites which are readily changed into cancer-causing nitrosamines. If you are eating these foods, make sure you have them with vegetables rich in vitamin C which reduces the formation of nitrosamines.

Measurements are given in imperial, metric and US cup units. Precise conversions are not practicable. To avoid error never mix measurements. Use either imperial or metric or US measurements for each recipe.

REFERENCES

Main sources of information used in identifying the good-diet countries of the world are as follows:

American Cancer Society and National Cancer Institute, 'Nutrition in the Causation of cancer', *Cancer Research*, 1975 vol. 35.

Armstrong, Bruce, and Richard Doll, 'Environmental factors and cancer incidence and mortality in different countries with special reference to dietary practices', *International Journal of Cancer*, 1975, vol. 15, pp. 617–31.

Doll, Richard, Calum Muir and John Waterhouse, *Cancer Incidence in Five Continents*, vol. II, Springer Verlag, 1970.

Dunham, Lucia J., and John C. Bailar III, 'World maps of cancer mortality rates and frequency ratios', *Journal of the National Cancer Institute*, July 1968, vol. 41, p. 155.

Keyes, Ancel, *Seven Countries: A multivariate analysis of death and coronary disease*, Harvard, 1980.

Knox, E. G., 'Foods and diseases', *British Journal of Preventive and Social Medicine*, 31 June 1977.

MacLennan R., and F. Meyer, 'Food and mortality in France', *The Lancet*, 16 July 1977.

Masironi, R., 'Dietary factors and coronary heart disease', *Bulletin of the World Health Organization*, 1970, vol. 42, pp. 103–14.

McGill, H. D. Jr (ed.), *Geographic Pathology of Atherosclerosis*, Williams and Wilkins, 1968

Waterhouse, John, Calum Muir, Pelayo Correa, Jean Powell, *Cancer Incidence in Five Continents*, International Agency for Research in Cancer, Lyon, 1976.

Yano, Katsuhiko *et al.*, 'Dietary intake and the risk of coronary heart disease in Japanese men living in Hawaii', *American Journal of Clinical Nutrition*, July 1978, Vol. 31, p. 1270.

CHAPTER 1

SOUTH-WEST

The millions of visitors to Spain every year would hardly expect its food to be among the healthiest in the world. But the food of the tourist resorts and the food of the majority of the people are two different things. Spain, Portugal, Southern Italy, and a narrow stretch of the South of France have eating habits which serve as a model to the Western world.

The peoples of these four areas have marked cultural differences: they speak different languages and they prepare food differently, for example. But what they do have in common is a climate which encourages the same crops: olives; wheat; many kinds of beans; vegetables such as aubergines (eggplants), green peppers and tomatoes; and a wide range of fruit including oranges, lemons and grapes. The land supports the same kind of animals, not cattle, since the quality of the grass is poor, but sheep and goats. Every farm has pigs, rabbits and chickens. The coasts produce fish in plentiful supply. The terrain is often rugged, but wild game thrives.

Mediterranean food is nearly always delicious and the choice is wide-ranging. It first developed under the influence of the Greeks and Romans, and then the Moors from North Africa introduced their skills in irrigation and cultivation, which led to better quality crops in larger supply. Later, Mediterranean food reached a new level of sophistication when Italian traders introduced the spices of the Far East. The quality of the region's cooking is hardly surprising: what may not be expected is that it is among the healthiest in the world, despite some long-held and misplaced prejudices against oiliness and garlic.

EUROPE

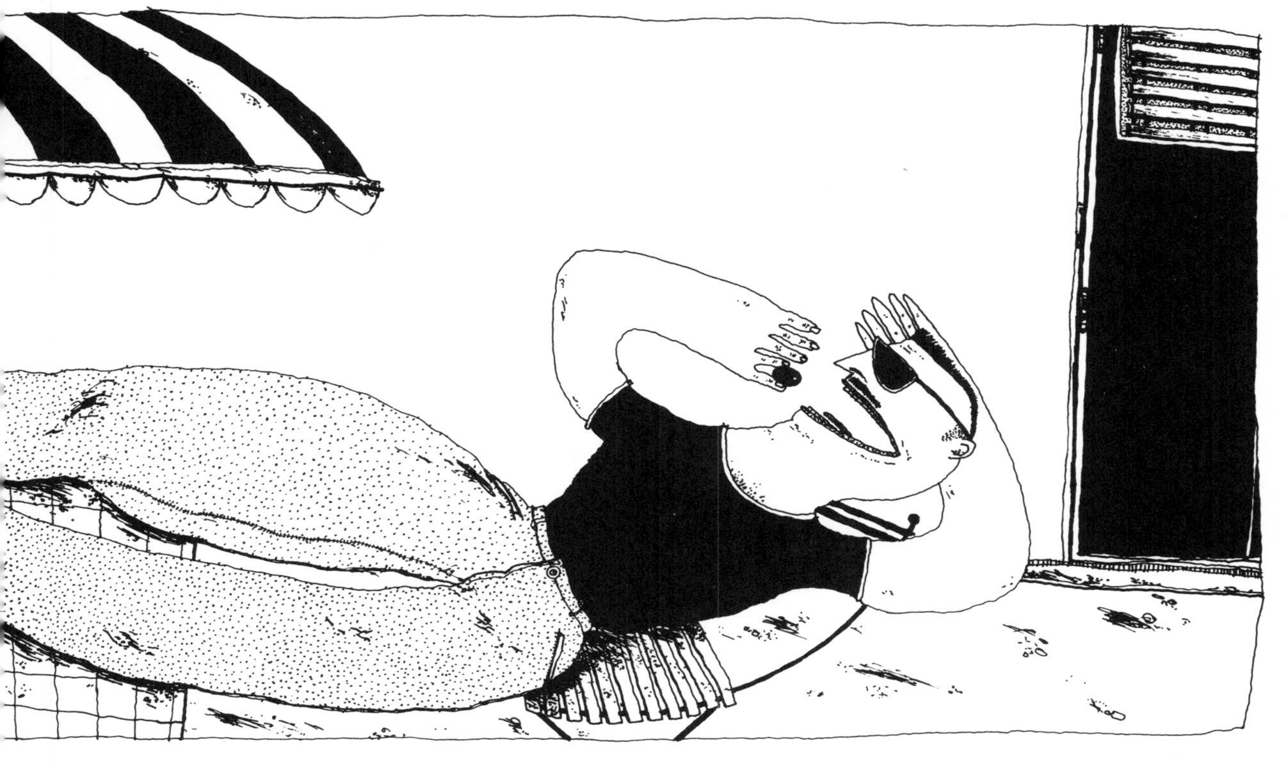

The Spanish, in particular, have an outstandingly low incidence of heart disease, among the lowest in the Western world, and they are also much less likely to be afflicted by the various diet-related cancers. It seems that wherever they have settled, from Mexico to Peru, to the Philippines, and even to the meat-eating state of Texas in the USA, they have taken their good health with them. Southern Italy, Southern France and Portugal all boast records of good health which are far superior to those of Great Britain or the USA.

The Portuguese have relatively high blood pressure, which is associated with eating a lot of salt. However, this is a health risk which is readily avoided. The Portuguese have developed a liking for a lot of salt, partly due to the important place which salt cod (*bacalhau*) has in their diet. We have included recipes for this dish in the book because it is nutritious, so typical of Portugal, and need not contribute to any risk of high blood pressure if carefully prepared by lengthy soaking of the fish to remove salt.

So what is it that gives these people such an enviable record? Perhaps their most important shared assets are the beautiful groves of olive trees which have graced the southern landscape for the past 2000 years. Olive oil adds its distinctive flavour to countless traditional recipes, and dairy produce, whether it is cheese, butter or milk, is noticeable only in its scarcity. The people of South-West Europe consume about the same total quantity of fats and oils as people in the USA or the UK. However, three-quarters of this is vegetable oil, and most of it is olive oil which has now become increasingly expensive. Even when a substitute is used, however, it is always a vegetable oil, such as sunflower or corn oil, and never butter. Indeed, no ordinary family would think of using butter in lavish quantities – it is very rarely eaten on bread. Only the most persevering and knowledgeable tourist will be able to enjoy the true South-West European cuisines, since the expensive hotels and the cheap cafés too often give the wrong impression. You can be offered the international, bland imitations of English, French and German cooking – such as the ubiquitous steak and chips – or else you may try a famous dish which, despite its cook's efforts at authenticity, ends up as something quite different from what is eaten in local homes. The paella in a Spanish restaurant tends to be a visually stunning display of bright yellow rice, red peppers, enormous bewhiskered prawns, chicken legs, mussels and lemon slices. In contrast, a family from Valencia would sit down to a simple dish containing bits of rabbit, lamb, squid, octopus, cod and whatever else had been saved up to make this traditional Sunday afternoon feast. The quantity of meat might be quite small but the combination of flavours and textures would be much more interesting.

South-West Europe has only recently emerged from a long period of poverty. This has largely shaped its attitude towards food and sharpened local ingenuity in producing varied dishes from limited ingredients. Farming peoples, who are concerned with producing the foods that they eat, put every scrap to use. Meat and fish are the luxury ingredients, which give flavour to quantities of rice, pasta, beans and potatoes. All forms of offal, especially tripe, brains and trotters, are held in high favour; as meat is in such relatively short supply, no part of the animal is wasted. Because of the good climate, a wide variety of fruit and vegetables is available all year. The poorest country family can muster up a green salad or tomato salad or a dish of marinated aubergines (eggplants) as well as a dish of cooked greens. These, together with a variety of freshly picked herbs and the pungency of the well-loved garlic, can transform the most simple of dishes. Sweet cakes and puddings very rarely follow as dessert but there is the rich luxury of grapes, melon and figs. Even in the bleakest winter months, and they can be very cold indeed, oranges, lemons, limes and grapefruit will ripen in the more southerly districts.

Fresh fruit and vegetables cannot entirely satisfy the pangs of real hunger. The main dish at a meal is always supplemented by a generous quantity of bread. South-West Europeans eat about 40 per cent more of it than we do. In most farming communities it is made in local bakeries, and is a pale-coloured bread with a strong hard crust and a delicious wheaty-tasting crumb. Dark breads are not very popular, but a fine maize (corn) bread is made in Galicia and Northern Portugal and rye flour gives a flavoursome bread in the central areas of Portugal.

Abruzzi in Italy is especially famous for its wheat, which is used to make a very light wholewheat bread called *pan integrale*. Throughout Southern France and in Italy, a hefty *pain de campagne*, based on a sourdough recipe, is the most usual accompaniment to meals. These enormous loaves can be kept for at least two weeks. (For more information about bread, see Chapter 7.)

Dried peas and beans – especially white beans and chick peas – are used a lot and many families eat them every day. They are a useful source of protein which is used to supplement the small amounts of meat in stews or soups.

Rice is eaten widely and usually with small quantities of meat, chicken, rabbit or fish; the paella of Spain is a classic example, as are the risottos of Italy. Sometimes rice is cooked plainly, but perfumed with the strong scent of saffron, and served as an accompaniment to a meat or fish dish.

Pasta is used a lot in Portugal and Spain, though less often as a main dish than in Italy. However, cannelloni has been adopted by the Spanish, and in both Portugal and Spain small quantities of pasta are added to give body and interest to soups.

The food of South-West Europe needs far more chewing than we are accustomed to. Salads are crunchy, sausages and salamis are sometimes so tough that when eaten with a slab of bread they make your jaws ache. The dried fish that the Portuguese like never loses its leathery quality; nor does octopus, unless it is overcooked. Although the South-West Europeans do have a sweet tooth their sugar intake is about half that of Britain or America. Puddings and cakes are not nearly so popular and their dessert is usually fresh fruit, and a local cheese eaten with bread or a hard biscuit. A meal is a leisurely affair, and mealtimes tend to be more relaxed and convivial events than in the UK or the USA.

South-West Europeans in general follow a rather unsatisfactory daily pattern by North European standards, with very little to eat from the time of getting up, usually with the dawn, until lunch at about 2 p.m. Supper tends to be the heaviest meal of the day, and it is eaten late at night.

Breakfast is always simple: a cup of milky coffee with a sweetened bun or a hunk of bread rubbed with a large raw tomato and sprinkled with olive oil or perhaps spread with whole fried green peppers or, in some regions, home-made fruit preserve, but no butter. In some of the really poor areas of Spain, they might rub the bread with garlic, while in Provence they flavour bread with *anchoïade*, a pungent mixture of anchovies and garlic. Some working people shock themselves into the new day with a glass of wine or spirits such as grappa or cognac, accompanied, of course, by a small, sweet and powerful cup of black coffee. Such a start is effective on a winter morning. Tea is not often drunk but tisanes, medicinal herb teas, are popular.

The first main meal of the day begins between 1 and 2 p.m. The Spanish and Portuguese often start with a soup such as garlic soup which can be rather watery by North European standards. The Southern Italians and French favour thick bean, fish or vegetable soups. There is always a wide variety of local hors d'oeuvres from salamis and home-cured hams to black or green olives. The main midday dish is most likely to be soup or a pasta with a tomato sauce in Italy. In the other three countries it could be a stew of beans or a seasoned rice dish. Some areas, notably Calabria in Italy, are almost totally vegetarian in their everyday diet. Even the most carnivorous family will eat only a quarter of our regular meat intake. When meat is served at lunchtime, even if it appears only in very small pieces among the beans and vegetables, it is unlikely to make a second appearance later in the day. Generous quantities of bread and wine accompany the meal. And cheese, fresh or dried fruit and coffee follow the main course.

Supper follows a similar pattern, although the main dish is probably more substantial and the atmosphere more leisurely. Neither at lunch nor dinner is the food served hot – it is always at a lukewarm temperature.

The evening might well be rounded off with a glass of grappa or cognac and possibly something very sweet. In Spain and Portugal caramel custard known as *flan* is popular all the year round; in Italy ice-cream or pastries may be bought from the shops; but throughout the whole of South-West Europe there is always a wonderful choice of fresh fruit and locally made cheeses.

Everybody wants to nibble on something in between the main meals of the day. This is especially true if you wait until ten, eleven or even twelve at night for supper. Whereas our snacks consist of cakes and biscuits, chocolate and salty crisps, the people of South-West Europe are more sensible. Spain is famous for its *tapas*, highly spiced and delicious hors d'oeuvre dishes served in bars. The Portuguese might choose a *pasteis de bacalhau*† with a glass of wine or a cup of coffee, or freshly caught sardines grilled over an open charcoal fire, or sticks of crisply fried batter dipped in sugar. But, on the whole, the Portuguese are not such determined snack eaters as the Spanish. The Italians might well buy or make a pizza at any time of the day, just as we would eat a sandwich, while the Provençals eat *pissaladière* – freshly cooked bread dough, covered with onions softened in olive oil, and dotted with black olives and anchovies. Throughout the area every home at all times has a supply of olives, salamis and other sausages, as well as cheeses – sometimes home-made fresh white cheese made with soured milk – all of which can be eaten at any time with a slice of bread, often slightly moistened with a few drops of olive oil. For more simple palates, the same bread rubbed with a clove of garlic, sprinkled with some strong olive oil and a little coarse salt, makes a wonderful snack – simple and remarkably delicious.

Caldo Verde
Cabbage soup

This warming soup from the wet North of Portugal is almost a meal in itself. The Portuguese use a strong cabbage called *couve*, but kale or any other dark green cabbage is just as good.

serves 4–6

3 medium potatoes, peeled and sliced
2 pints/1.1 litres/5 cups water
salt
2 tablespoons olive oil
1 lb/450 g/4½ cups cabbage or kale, very finely shredded
4–6 slices *chouriço* sausage

Boil the potatoes in the lightly salted water until tender, then lift them out with a slotted spoon and mash well. Stir back into the water, together with the oil. Add the cabbage and boil briskly for about 3 minutes, then add the sausage and simmer for about 5 minutes. Season to taste. Put a slice of the sausage in each bowl before serving.

Minestra di Pasta e Ceci
Chick pea and pasta soup

Chick peas and pasta complement each other from the nutritional point of view in this dish from Apulia in Italy, and the *pancetta* (or bacon) and parsley provide a rich and fresh flavour.

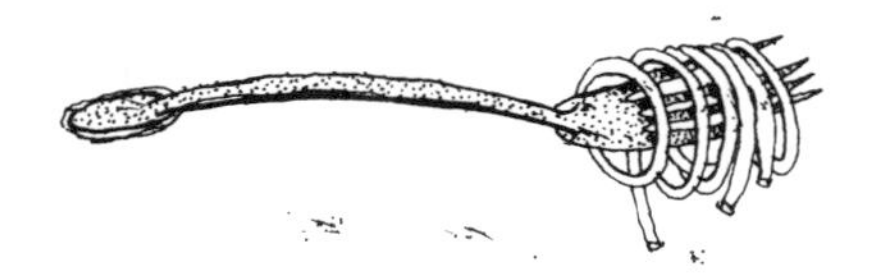

serves 4–6

8 oz/225 g/1 cup chick peas
2–3 slices *pancetta* or streaky bacon
2 cloves garlic
4 tablespoons chopped parsley
4 tablespoons olive oil
salt and pepper
12 oz/350 g/3 cups *gramigna* (short, curled macaroni)
freshly grated Parmesan or Pecorino cheese

Soak the chick peas in cold water for 8 hours or overnight and then drain. Bring to the boil in 4 pints (2.3 litres/2½ quarts) of water, partially cover with a tilted lid and simmer until tender. The exact time needed will depend on the quality of the chick peas, but it should be about 2 hours.

When the chick peas are cooked, spoon out about half of them, reduce to a purée in a food mill and return this to the pan.

Chop the *pancetta* and garlic finely and fry with the parsley in the oil until cooked through. Add this mixture, known as the *soffrito*, to the chick peas, bring the mixture to the boil and season with salt and freshly ground pepper. Add the *gramigna* and cook until just tender. The soup should thicken considerably during this last cooking.

Serve with a liberal grinding of fresh pepper on top and with the cheese to sprinkle over the soup.

Bouillabaisse
Fish soup

All along the Mediterranean coast of France, each fishing port has its own *bouillabaisse*. Saffron is characteristic, while other ingredients vary a good deal. Choose as widely as you can from fish with firm flesh, such as cod, haddock, eel, and more delicate fish such as red mullet, bass or hake, and add shrimps, prawns and tiny crabs.

serves 4–6

- 3–4 fl oz/100 ml/⅓–½ cup olive oil
- 2 onions, roughly chopped
- 3 cloves garlic, peeled
- 4 large tomatoes, peeled and quartered
- 1 tablespoon flour
- 2 pints/1.1 litres/4 cups water
- salt
- 2 sticks fennel
- 1 sprig thyme
- 1 strip orange peel
- ½ teaspoon saffron strands
- 2 large potatoes, cut into pieces
- 2 lb/900 g assorted fish, cut into suitable pieces

Heat the oil in a large, heavy pan and gently cook the onion and garlic in it until soft but not browned and add the tomatoes. When they are bubbling add a paste made with the flour and some of the water. Pour in the remaining water, season well with salt and put in the fennel, thyme, orange peel and saffron. Add the potatoes and continue to simmer until they are almost tender.

Put in the fish, the coarse and thick pieces first, letting them cook for about 2 minutes before adding any delicate or thin pieces of fish and the shellfish. Boil furiously, covered, for the shortest possible time – only 2–3 minutes after the shellfish have been put in; stick a knife into several pieces to make sure everything is cooked.

You can serve the fish and liquid together, with a round of toasted French bread and a spoonful of *rouille*† for each person; or you can drain off the broth into soup bowls, float a piece of toast in each and drop a spoonful of *rouille* on to it, and serve the fish on separate plates with more *rouille*.

Rouille
Garlic mayonnaise

No bouillabaisse is complete without *rouille*, a smooth sauce made fiery with Tabasco and mustard – a bouillabaisse of peas† or fish is enlivened by it.

serves 4

- 1 raw egg
- 1 teaspoon Dijon mustard
- salt
- 5 fl oz/150 ml/⅔ cup olive oil
- 1 hard-boiled egg yolk
- pinch powdered saffron
- 3 large cloves garlic, peeled
- 2 teaspoons tomato paste
- generous dash of Tabasco
- squeeze of lemon juice

Mix the raw egg yolk and mustard in a bowl with a pinch of salt, then gradually add the oil, slowly at first and whisking vigorously all the time.

Pound the hard-boiled egg yolk, saffron and garlic with the tomato paste, Tabasco and lemon juice to make a smooth paste, or reduce them to a paste in a blender. Stir the paste into the mayonnaise.

Taste: the *rouille* should be hot and fierce. Add a little more salt or Tabasco as necessary.

Sopa de Ajo
Garlic soup

This very ancient Spanish dish from the central plains of Spain, which was no doubt invented when times were particularly hard, is surprisingly delicious. There are many regional variations to the recipe: in Madrid paprika is used, some areas use tomatoes, and others add a beaten egg immediately before serving to form golden threads in the soup.

serves 4

4–6 stale rolls, or ½ a small crusty white loaf
6 tablespoons olive oil
4 large cloves garlic, peeled and chopped
2 teaspoons paprika
about 2 pints/1.1 litres/5 cups boiling water
½ teaspoon salt
½ a chilli pepper, chopped (optional)

Break up the bread into walnut-sized pieces. Heat the oil gently in a large saucepan. Cook the garlic in it for a minute or two without letting it brown too much. Put in the bread, a few pieces at a time, turning them in the oil with a wooden spoon. Sprinkle on the paprika and add the water, salt and chilli pepper if used.

Simmer gently for about 15 minutes. The bread will swell, soften and disintegrate. If the soup gets too thick, add more hot water.

Sopa de Lentejas
Madrid lentil soup

Every country has its own version of lentil soup. In this version from Madrid the *chorizo* gives a special Spanish flavour.

serves 4

1 lb/450 g/2 cups brown lentils
3 tablespoons olive oil
2 onions, sliced
1 red or green pepper, deseeded and sliced
1 tablespoon flour
1 ham bone
4 slices *chorizo* sausage, chopped
1 bay leaf
6 tomatoes, peeled and chopped
2 carrots, chopped
2 cloves garlic, peeled and chopped
2½ pints/1.4 litres/6 cups water
salt and black pepper

Carefully pick over the lentils to remove all stones and grit. You can do this most easily by spreading out a handful at a time on a white plate. Put them into a fine colander or sieve and rinse well under a running tap.

Heat the oil in a large saucepan and gently cook the onions and peppers for a few minutes with the lid on the pan. When they start to soften, stir in the flour and cook briefly, then put in the lentils and stir well. Add the bone, *chorizo*, bay leaf, tomatoes, carrots, garlic and water. Season well with salt. Partially cover the pan and simmer very gently for about 1¾ hours. If the soup becomes too thick, add a little hot water. Remove the bone.

For the best texture, put the soup through a food mill, but reserve some of the meat and vegetables to stir back into it. Grind some black pepper over the top at the last moment and serve with plenty of crusty bread.

Panzarella
Cold tomato soup with bread

serves 4

6 generous slices home-made bread
1 bunch spring onions (scallions). or 1 medium onion, finely chopped
4 large ripe tomatoes, sliced
1 small cucumber, peeled and sliced
12 or more leaves of basil, shredded
salt and freshly ground pepper
a wine-glass of olive oil
1 tablespoon wine vinegar

Combinations of bread and raw salad vegetables make several rustic dishes, halfway between soup and salad. Authentic versions use the large oval or round Italian country bread, which is made from sour-dough or natural yeasts and baked in a wood-fired brick oven. As a good substitute, use home-made bread of a round shape, preferably made with a mixture of wholewheat and a little rye flour.

Soak the bread in water for 30 minutes and then squeeze it dry in your hands. Put it in a salad bowl with the onions and tomatoes. Add the cucumber and the basil. Sprinkle everything with salt and pepper, oil and vinegar. Mix thoroughly and serve the dish just as it is.

To make a similar, but hot, dish called *pancotto*, cook the tomatoes with garlic and parsley in olive oil, add water and simmer for 30 minutes. Add toasted bread at the last minute and serve the soup with grated Pecorino cheese.

Petits Pois en Bouillabaisse
Pea soup with eggs

This soup-cum-stew from Provence has an attractive appearance: green peas and creamy potatoes gilded by the saffron and poached eggs. It makes an ample lunch dish.

serves 4–6

2 lb/900 g fresh peas in the pod, or 1 lb/450 g/2 cups frozen peas
5–6 large new potatoes, waxy yellow ones if possible
1 onion, chopped
3 tablespoons olive oil
1¾ pints/950 ml/4½ cups boiling water
3 cloves garlic, peeled and crushed
bouquet of bay, thyme, fennel and parsley
salt and pepper
pinch of saffron
6 eggs
6 slices French bread

Shell the fresh peas and scrape the potatoes. Put the onion to soften over a gentle heat in the oil, without browning. Add the potatoes, cut into slices about ½ in/1.25 cm thick, and stir them round for a minute or two without letting them brown. Add the boiling water and the peas, the garlic and the bouquet of herbs. Season with salt, pepper and the saffron. Cover the pan and let it simmer away slowly.

When the potatoes and peas are cooked after 20–30 minutes, carefully break the eggs into the pan one at a time. Poach in the bubbling liquid for 3–4 minutes.

To serve, put a slice of bread in each soup plate and carefully spoon on to it an egg and some soup. You can serve the bread separately if you prefer. Add a spoonful of *rouille* † or *all-i-olli* † if you like.

Xató
Curly endive salad in hot dressing

Magnificent curly endives are grown throughout the winter months in South-West Europe and provide a welcome source of fresh greenery. Chilli peppers give a hot pungency to this Catalonian dressing.

serves 4

- 1 large head curly endive
- 6 blanched almonds, toasted
- 4 cloves garlic, peeled
- ½ small fresh chilli pepper, or cayenne pepper to taste
- 6 tablespoons olive oil
- 2 tablespoons wine vinegar
- ½ teaspoon salt

Wash and thoroughly drain the endive, break it up and put into a large bowl.

To make the dressing, crush the almonds, garlic and chilli pepper together thoroughly, using a pestle and mortar. Work in the oil gradually; the dressing will thicken and become opaque. Stir in the vinegar and salt. Alternatively you can make the dressing very easily by putting all the ingredients in a blender and blending until smooth.

Pour the dressing over the endive and toss well. Leave to stand for about an hour in a cool place before serving.

Xató is usually eaten as a first course with various sliced sausages, such as *chorizo* or *salchichón*. Serrano ham is also a popular accompaniment, but other well-flavoured cold meats are equally suitable. Marinated fish† also go well with the piquant flavour.

Caponata alla Marinara
Anchovy and bread salad

The intense richness of anchovy is much liked by the people of Sicily and the coastal regions of Italy.

serves 4

- 1 slice stale white bread, about 1 in/2.5 cm thick
- 3 tablespoons olive oil
- 10 black olives
- 3 canned anchovy fillets
- ½ teaspoon oregano
- 1 small clove garlic, chopped

Soak the bread in water for about 30 minutes, then squeeze it well in your hands and break it into pieces. Put it in a dish, cover it with the oil and mix in the olives, anchovies, oregano and garlic. Leave until the oil has been absorbed and serve as a first course.

Pan Bagnato
Egg salad with bread

serves 4

8 round slices stale home-made bread
2 tablespoons wine vinegar
1 small onion, sliced
4 ripe tomatoes, sliced
a few chopped basil leaves
salt and freshly ground pepper
8 tablespoons olive oil
5 hard-boiled eggs, halved

This dish probably originated as a farm-workers' lunch, when the ingredients were slapped between two thick slices of bread.

Cut the slices of bread in half, lay them in a wide earthenware dish and sprinkle with vinegar. Arrange the onion and tomatoes on top. Scatter on the basil, season with salt and pepper and then sprinkle everything copiously with the oil. Place the eggs on top and serve.

Ensalada de Tomate y Cebolla
Tomato and onion salad

serves 4

10 small, firm, dark red tomatoes, quartered
4 small Spanish onions or shallots, sliced
a few fresh mint leaves, chopped
4 tablespoons olive oil
1 tablespoon vinegar
1 small clove garlic, peeled and crushed
pinch of salt
pinch of sugar

The success of this Spanish salad depends upon a judicious blend of ripe Mediterranean tomatoes and mild sweet onions.

Put the tomatoes and onions into an earthenware dish and sprinkle on the mint. Beat together the oil, vinegar, garlic, salt and sugar and pour over the salad.

Serve the salad in individual earthenware bowls so the diners can mop up all the dressing with bread.

Insalata di Verdure
Fresh vegetable salad from Sicily

serves 4

4 oz/110 g/1 cup freshly-cooked green beans
2–3 ripe tomatoes
2 boiled new potatoes, sliced
1 cucumber, sliced
2–3 oz/50–75 g/½ cup black olives
salt and freshly ground pepper
5 tablespoons olive oil
1 tablespoon wine vinegar

A simple light lunch for a summer's day. Serve it on its own or with salami.

Arrange the beans, tomatoes, potatoes, cucumber and black olives in separate piles on a large flat dish. Season with coarse salt and plenty of very coarsely ground black pepper. Sprinkle with the olive oil and vinegar, and serve with bread.

Aubergines Farcies
Stuffed aubergines (eggplants)

The handsome glossy aubergine has been cultivated in the South of France since the early 1600s. The use of olive oil and onions enhances the health value and flavour of this simple vegetable. Serve for lunch or as a first course.

serves 4

- 4 aubergines (eggplants)
- salt and pepper
- 2 tablespoons olive oil for frying
- 2 onions, finely sliced
- 2–3 cloves garlic, peeled and crushed
- 1½ lb/700 g tomatoes, peeled and chopped
- 3–4 leaves of fresh basil or ⅔ teaspoon dried basil
- 5 fl oz/150 ml/⅔ cup oil
- 15 fl oz/450 ml/1¾ cups water
- juice of ½ lemon

Cut the aubergines in half lengthways. Scoop out, chop and reserve the middle flesh and sprinkle the hollowed-out shells with salt. Stand them round the sides of a colander and leave to drain for ½–1 hour.

To make the filling, heat the olive oil in a saucepan and gently cook the onions until soft. Add the garlic, tomatoes, and the reserved chopped aubergine flesh. Season with salt and pepper, add the basil and simmer until everything is soft and sauce-like.

Rinse the aubergine shells under the cold tap and spoon in the filling. Put in an earthenware gratin dish with the oil, water and lemon juice and sprinkle lightly with salt. Cook in a pre-heated oven at 300° F/150° C/gas mark 2 for 1 hour. Eat hot or cold with bread.

Caponata alla Siciliana
Sweet-sour aubergines (eggplants)

This Sicilian dish has a sweet-sour flavour – a legacy of Roman times, when dates were used instead of tomatoes and sugar. There are many variations: in Palermo pine nuts are added and sometimes green tomatoes are used instead of ripe ones.

serves 4

- 2 medium aubergines (eggplants)
- 5 fl oz/150 ml/⅔ cup olive oil
- 4 sticks celery, thinly sliced
- 2 onions, thinly sliced
- 1 lb/450 g tomatoes, peeled and chopped, or 6 canned Italian tomatoes, drained and chopped
- 2 tablespoons drained capers
- 1 tablespoon pine nuts
- 10 black olives, halved and stoned
- 2 tablespoons sugar
- 4 tablespoons wine vinegar
- salt and freshly ground pepper

Cut the aubergines into 1 in/2.5 cm cubes, sprinkle with salt and leave to drain for ½–1 hour. Heat half the oil in a deep frying pan and fry the cubes a few at a time until browned and soft, adding more oil as necessary. Put the cubes in the pan with the celery, onions and tomatoes. Simmer for 15–20 minutes and then add the capers, pine nuts and olives. Dissolve the sugar in the vinegar and add it to the pan. Season with salt and pepper and simmer very gently for a further 20 minutes. Taste and add a little more vinegar if necessary. Cool and leave for several hours for the flavours to blend and mellow.

For a first course serve cold with Italian bread. Serve with hard-boiled eggs or fried octopus for a substantial lunch or supper dish.

Melanzane al Funghetto
Aubergines (eggplants) cooked like mushrooms

Aubergines are one of the principal vegetables of Southern Italy and this is an easy way of cooking them.

serves 4

- 2 lb/900 g aubergines (eggplants)
- 6 tablespoons olive oil
- 2 cloves garlic, peeled and chopped
- salt and pepper
- 6 leaves of fresh basil, shredded
- 1 teaspoon chopped fresh oregano, or ½ teaspoon dried oregano

Cut the aubergines into 1 in/2.5 cm cubes, sprinkle them with salt and leave them draining in a colander for 1 hour to lose some of their bitter liquid. Drain them well.

Heat the oil in a large pan, put in the pieces of aubergine and cook quite gently for 5 minutes, turning them frequently. Add the garlic and a little salt and pepper and cook 5 minutes more until the aubergine cubes are nicely browned, adding a little more oil if necessary. Add the basil and oregano, turn down the heat and cook until the aubergines are tender – about 20 minutes more.

To vary the dish you can add tomatoes, anchovies, capers, black olives or a combination of any of these. Serve with bread as a first course.

Melanzane Sott'Olio
Aubergines (eggplants) in oil

Aubergines are delicious in a marinade of oil and vinegar. Prepared the Calabrian way, a full harvest provides a nutritious vegetable throughout the winter months.

Slice the aubergines, put them in a colander and sprinkle with salt. Leave to drain for 1 hour and then pat dry. Finely chop the garlic, basil and chilli and mix them together.

Heat 2–3 tablespoons of oil in a large pan and fry the aubergine slices until golden brown on both sides. Transfer them to a dish without draining off the oil. Put a layer of aubergine slices into a wide jar and sprinkle with some of the garlic, basil and chilli. Continue to fill the jar with layers of aubergine and flavourings.

Put in the wine vinegar and leave for 1 hour.

Close the jar with a lid, turn it upside down and leave for 3 hours for the vinegar to be absorbed. Reopen the jar and fill to the top with olive oil. Cover tightly with an airtight lid and put in a cool place.

After a few days, check to see if all the olive oil has been absorbed and fill with more if necessary. The aubergines will keep perfectly for at least 2 months, if stored in a cool place. Serve them in their oil with plenty of bread as a first course. Make sure that those left in the jar are still covered by oil.

serves 4

3 lb/1.4 kg aubergines
salt
3 cloves garlic, peeled
6 sprigs fresh basil
1 chilli pepper
5 fl oz/150 ml/⅔ cup wine vinegar
olive oil

Anchoïade
Anchovy spread

This is often the first mouthful of food eaten in the morning by people of the Midi region; anchovies certainly do seem to give an appetite for the day to come.

Pound the anchovy fillets with some of their oil and the vinegar. Spread on the pieces of bread and arrange a few slices of egg and onion on each. Trickle some oil over each piece and put them under the grill (broiler), or into a hot oven, to toast for a minute. Serve them piping hot as soon as they are golden.

For an alternative version, without egg or onion, wash and pat the anchovy fillets dry and then crush them with a fork. Mix a pounded clove of garlic and a little freshly ground pepper with the vinegar and olive oil. Combine with the anchovies and spread firmly on to the pieces of bread, so that the paste penetrates. Brown the pieces under a grill, or in the oven, and serve at once.

serves 4

1 can of anchovy fillets in oil
½ teaspoon wine vinegar
2 lengths French bread, split in half
1 hard-boiled egg, sliced
1 small onion, very thinly sliced
1 tablespoon olive oil

Pescado en Escabeche
Marinated fish

serves 4–8

8 herrings or large fresh sardines or mackerel
seasoned flour
olive oil for frying
2 onions, cut into rings
2 carrots, cut into rounds
4 peppercorns
4 cloves
handful of chopped parsley
2 cloves garlic, peeled and chopped
½ teaspoon salt
2 bay leaves
½ pint/300 ml/1¼ cups vinegar
½ pint/300 ml/1¼ cups white wine
½ pint/300 ml/1¼ cups water
3 lemon slices
a few olives

After a good catch, this spicy marinade provides a good way of preserving the smaller local fish along the coasts of the Iberian peninsula.

Cut the heads off the fish, gut them and open them out flat. Remove the backbone and cut each fish in half lengthways. Dip in the seasoned flour and fry in the oil. Drain and place in a shallow serving dish (preferably earthenware).

Put the onions and carrots in a saucepan with the spices, herbs and seasonings, pour in the vinegar, wine and water and simmer for about 15 minutes. Allow to get completely cold and then pour over the fish. Add the slices of lemon and the olives. Leave in a cool place overnight, or for up to 24 hours.

Serve with crusty white rolls and a salad. *Xató*† goes particularly well with this dish.

Pissaladière
Olive and anchovy tart

serves 4

for the pastry:
6 oz/175 g/1½ cups flour
1½ oz/40 g/3 tablespoons lard
1½ oz/40 g/3 tablespoons butter
pinch salt

for the filling:
6 medium onions (preferably Spanish), sliced
7 tablespoons olive oil
salt and pepper
4 large red tomatoes, the riper the better (optional)
1 can of anchovy fillets in oil
4 oz/110 g/¾ cup small black olives
olive oil for sprinkling

Some of the biggest and best anchovies come from the waters off Nice and Catalonia. Combined with onions and olives they make a delicious tart, sold as a snack in the pastry shops of Provence.

To prepare the pastry, put the flour into a bowl, cut up the fats into cubes and put them with the flour and sprinkle in the salt. Rub in the fats until they are the size of small cornflakes, then add a few tablespoons of cold water – just enough for you to work the ingredients together to form a mass. Gather together in a ball, place in a plastic bag and chill for at least 1 hour.

To make the filling, cook the onions gently in the oil in a heavy saucepan for about 30 minutes. Turn them from time to time and when they are soft, golden and translucent, season them with salt and pepper.

Roll out the pastry thinly to line a small roasting tin and bank up the edges well to hold in the filling. Cover with the onions in a thick layer and cover this with the tomatoes, if you are using them; press them down lightly. Lay a lattice of anchovy fillets on top and put an olive in each diamond.

Sprinkle with more oil and bake in a pre-heated oven at 425° F/220° C/gas mark 7 for 15 minutes, then at 375° F/190° C/gas mark 5 for a further 15–20 minutes.

Serve hot or cold with a green salad to follow.

Bacalhau com Pimentos e Tomates
Salt cod with green peppers and tomatoes

For many centuries salt cod has been a major source of protein in the Portuguese diet. It has been honoured with hundreds of methods of preparation and this recipe from Alentejo is one of the most popular. It is important to soak the fish well to remove the salt.

serves 4

- 1 lb/450 g *bacalhau* (salt cod)
- 3 tablespoons olive oil
- 1 lb/450 g potatoes, unpeeled but sliced thinly
- 1 lb/450 g tomatoes, sliced thinly
- 4 green peppers, deseeded and cut in rings
- 2 handfuls fresh coriander leaves, chopped
- black olives for garnish

N.B.Use no salt as the fish is salty.

Soak the fish in cold water for at least 12 hours in several changes of water. Then rinse it well and poach it gently in very little water for about 15 minutes. Drain it, discard the skin and bones and break the flesh into pieces.

Put the oil in a large, heavy casserole. Arrange a layer of potato slices in the bottom, then tomato, then peppers and then fish. Sprinkle with coriander and continue filling the pot with these layers until all the ingredients are used up. Cover and cook on a low heat, shaking the pot gently from time to time. The liquid from the vegetables should prevent sticking. Cook for about 30 minutes or until the potatoes are done.

Garnish with a few black olives and serve straight from the casserole with plenty of bread.

If you cannot obtain coriander leaves, you can substitute fresh parsley. This will give the dish the same appearance, but the flavour will be different.

Pasteis de Bacalhau
Salt cod croquettes

Ever since Columbus introduced potatoes to the Portuguese in the fifteenth century they have been a staple of the local diet. They are frequently cooked with salt cod as in this recipe: the cod must be well soaked to remove as much salt as possible.

The croquettes are made in neat oval shapes by moulding between two tablespoons. You can make them more simply by dropping the mixture straight from a spoon.

serves 4

8 oz/225 g *bacalhau* (salt cod)
1 bay leaf
1 lb/450 g potatoes, peeled and coarsely chopped
2 eggs
1 onion, finely chopped
2 tablespoons finely chopped parsley
olive oil for frying

N.B. Use no salt as the fish is salty.

Soak the cod for at least 12 hours, in several changes of water, to drain off the salt. Then rinse well.

Simmer the fish in water with the bay leaf and potatoes until the potatoes are done. Drain off the water, discard the bay leaf and flake the fish, removing the skin and bones. Mash the fish and potato together.

Separate the eggs and beat the yolks one at a time into the fish mixture, adding the onion and parsley at the same time. Beat the egg whites until stiff and fold in.

Pour olive oil into a saucepan to a depth of about 1 in/2.5 cm. Heat until a light haze appears above it and then drop in separate spoonfuls of the mixture, cooking just a few at a time. When golden brown and puffed up, remove and drain on paper towels. Serve hot or cold as a snack with drinks or coffee, or as part of a meal.

Calamares a la Plancha
Tiny squid cooked on a hotplate

Cooking *a la plancha*, a favourite way of cooking in Spanish bars, is perhaps the best way to capture the delicate flavour of squid and other small fish and prawns (shrimp). The *plancha* is a large hotplate or griddle on which the food is cooked directly over an open fire; but a large, heavy frying pan can be used instead.

Serve the squid as *tapas* (appetizers) sizzling hot in their juices on individual small plates with a wedge of lemon, a crusty roll and a small glass of wine.

serves 4

12 small fresh or frozen squid or cuttlefish, with bodies about 2 in/5 cm long
3 cloves garlic, peeled and finely chopped
3 tablespoons finely chopped parsley
3 teaspoons paprika
1 teaspoon salt
olive oil for frying
1 lemon, cut in quarters

To prepare the squid, stretch them out and gently pull out the head section. Snip off the tentacles with scissors and reserve. Discard the head section, including the eyes. Remove and discard the contents of the body sac, including the transparent central bone. Wash the sac under running water, rubbing off the outer membrane with your fingers. Pat dry.

Mix together the garlic, parsley, paprika and salt. Pour a little oil into the frying pan and heat gently. Put in 6 of the squid, including their tentacles, and sprinkle with half the garlic mixture. Cook gently for 8–10 minutes, turning them over once. Remove and keep hot while you cook the remaining squid.

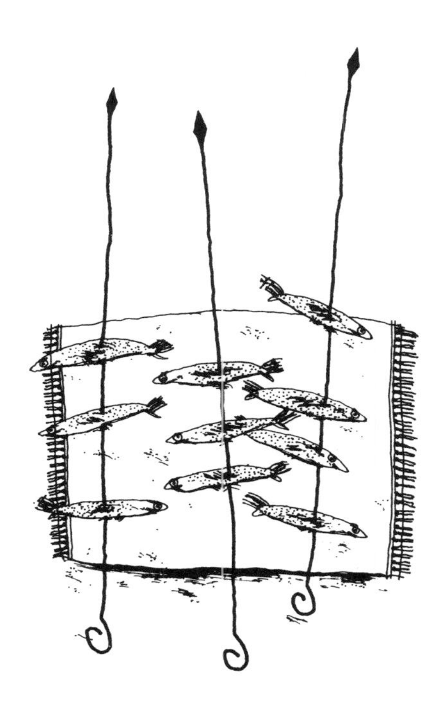

Almendras Tostadas
Toasted almonds

Toasted nuts are especially good with a dry sherry, as served in Andalusia.

serves 4

6 oz/175 g/1½ cups blanched split almonds
1 tablespoon olive oil

Spread the almonds over a piece of foil in the bottom of the grill pan (broiler). Sprinkle on the oil and toast for a few minutes until lightly browned. Turn them over once with a metal spatula.

Alternatively, you can spread the almonds in an ovenproof dish, sprinkle them with the oil and roast them in a pre-heated oven at 275° F/140° C/gas mark 1 for 15–20 minutes. Shake the dish occasionally to turn the nuts. You can roast hazelnuts in the same way, but leave on their skins.

A third method is to fry the almonds briefly in the fairly hot oil. Pine nuts can be fried in the same way.

Pasticcio di Spaghetti e Peperoni
Spaghetti and pepper gratin

All the flavours of the Mediterranean echo through this dish from Calabria. Anchovies, olives and capers penetrate the pasta filling.

serves 4

4 large red or yellow peppers
8 tablespoons olive oil
2 cloves garlic
4 canned anchovy fillets
8 stoned black olives, cut in pieces
1 tablespoon capers
8 oz/225 g spaghetti
2 tablespoons dried breadcrumbs
salt and freshly ground pepper

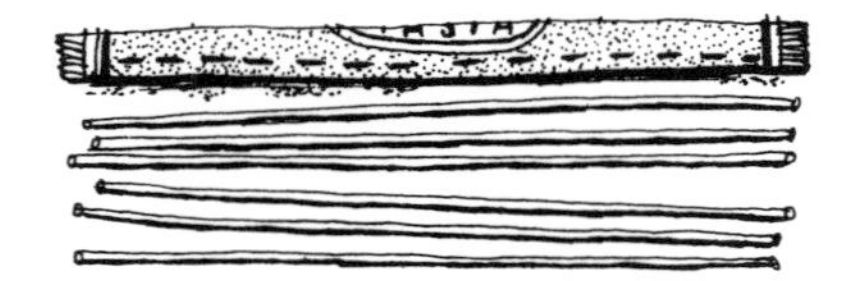

Cook the peppers under a hot grill (broiler) or in the flames of a gas ring – or even better, over a wood fire – until the skin has blistered and blackened all over. Peel the peppers, discard the seeds and stalks and cut the flesh into strips.

Heat 4 tablespoons of the oil in a medium frying pan and fry the strips of pepper with the garlic for 2–3 minutes. Remove the peppers to a dish and fry the anchovies, capers and olives in the same pan for 1–2 minutes. Discard the garlic.

Cook the spaghetti for 10–15 minutes in a large pan of boiling salted water. Drain and return to the pan with 2 tablespoons of the oil.

Oil a deep ovenproof dish and sprinkle half the breadcrumbs over the bottom. Cover with a layer of peppers, season with salt and pepper and scatter on half the anchovy, olive and caper mixture. Fill the dish with the pasta, spread on the rest of the peppers, season and scatter the remaining anchovy mixture over the top. Sprinkle on the remaining breadcrumbs and the rest of the oil. Bake in the pre-heated oven at 375°F/190°C/gas mark 5 for 20 minutes.

Serve very hot followed by a green salad or fresh fruit.

Orecchiette
Little ears of pasta

This type of pasta, made from relatively unrefined flour, retains some natural fibre and wheatgerm with its vitamins. Shape it into 'little ears' the Sicilian way or cut it into other shapes, and serve with a simple tomato sauce† and grated cheese, or with broccoli as in the next recipe.

serves 4

12 oz/350 g/3 cups unbleached strong white flour
4 oz/110 g/1 cup wholewheat flour
½ teaspoon salt
about 5 fl oz/150 ml/⅔ cup warm water

Mix the flours together in a bowl and make a well in the centre. Dissolve the salt in the water and pour into the well. Mix to work up a dough, adding a little more flour or water if necessary. Knead thoroughly until the dough is no longer sticky but smooth, springy and pleasant to handle.

Roll the dough with your hands into short cylinders about 1 in/2.5 cm across. Cover with a damp cloth and leave to rest for 30 minutes. Slice into thin rounds and press each round over your thumb to make a tiny cup. Spread the cups out to dry for 2–3 hours. Cook them for about 5 minutes in boiling salted water and serve very hot.

Orecchiette al Cavolfiore
Little ears with broccoli

In this light pasta dish the 'little ears' of pasta are cooked in the water from the broccoli, so absorbing nutrients and the delicious flavour from it.

serves 4

- 1 lb/450 g/5 cups Calabrese broccoli or purple-headed cauliflower
- 12 oz/350 g *orecchiette*, pasta shells or other small, hollow pasta shapes
- 6 tablespoons olive oil
- 2–3 slices *pancetta* or streaky bacon
- 1 clove garlic
- salt and pepper
- grated Pecorino cheese

Wash the broccoli or cauliflower and cut it downwards into separate heads. Cook in a large pan of boiling salted water for 5 minutes, then lift out with a slotted spoon.

Put the *orecchiette* in the same pan of boiling water to cook for 5–10 minutes. Meanwhile heat the oil in a frying pan and add the *pancetta*, cut in strips, and the garlic. When the garlic is brown, add the broccoli and stir it round but do not let it brown. Season with pepper.

Drain the *orecchiette* and tip into a wide bowl. Pour the broccoli and *pancetta* on top, discarding the garlic, and sprinkle with cheese.

Maccheroni alla Pastora
Country macaroni

Ricotta alone is somewhat tasteless, but it acts as a marvellous vehicle for other flavours as in this country dish.

serves 4

- 6 oz/175 g/¾ packed cup *salsicce* or coarse-cut pork sausage
- 1 tablespoon olive oil
- 8 oz/225 g/2 cups ricotta cheese
- salt and freshly ground black pepper
- 2 oz/50 g/½ cup grated Pecorino cheese
- 14 oz/400 g/3½ cups macaroni

Crumble the sausage into a frying pan, stir in the oil and cook over a moderate heat until the meat is lightly browned. Mix the ricotta cheese in a large bowl with salt and pepper and half the Pecorino cheese.

Cook the macaroni in a large pan of boiling salted water until just tender. Ladle a spoonful of the cooking water into the ricotta mixture and stir it in. Drain the pasta, mix it with the ricotta and stir in the sausage with its fat. Serve at once with the remaining Pecorino cheese.

Salsicce
Sausage meat

serves 4

- 1 lb/450 g boneless pork shoulder
- 8 oz/225 g *pancetta* or streaky bacon
- 2 teaspoons salt
- 1 teaspoon freshly ground coarse black pepper

The rather coarse and countrified Italian sausages are excellent – solid meat all the way through. You can use this mixture in a pasta sauce, or shape it into sausages for frying or grilling. Authentically the mixture would be put into skins, which somewhat alters the texture, but the flavour is just as good in this skinless version.

Mince (grind) the meats coarsely and mix with the seasonings. Leave in the refrigerator overnight for the flavours to blend and mellow before use.

Maccarones a la Catalana
Catalonian macaroni

serves 4

- 4 oz/110 g/½ cup shelled peas
- 4 oz/110 g/½ cup shelled broad beans (*fava*) or large lima beans
- 2 courgettes (zucchini), sliced
- 1 small aubergine (eggplant), sliced
- salt and freshly ground black pepper
- 1 lb/450 g/4 cups macaroni
- olive oil for frying
- 2 onions, chopped
- 2 cloves garlic, peeled and chopped
- 1 red or green pepper, deseeded and chopped
- 6 tomatoes, peeled and chopped
- 1 tablespoon almonds, peeled and toasted
- 1 tablespoon pine nuts
- 2 tablespoons chopped parsley
- 3 tablespoons grated cheese

Pasta, so firmly associated with Italy, is eaten frequently in Spain, too. It is added to soups and stews or combined with mixed vegetables to make a nourishing main dish. You can replace the peas, beans, courgettes and aubergine with any vegetables in season. Grate goat's milk cheese on top for the authentic Spanish dish.

Put the peas, beans, courgettes and aubergine (or other chosen mixed vegetables) to boil in a little salted water for 8–10 minutes, or until just tender. Drain and set aside, reserving the liquid. Meanwhile, in another pan, boil the macaroni in plenty of lightly salted water for 10 minutes or until tender, and then drain.

Heat a little olive oil in a flameproof casserole and gently fry the onion, garlic and pepper. When they start to soften, add the tomatoes and the cooked mixed vegetables and stir well. Cook gently for a few minutes, then add the almonds, pine nuts and parsley. Stir in some of the reserved cooking liquid to make a thick sauce.

Put the cooked macaroni into this sauce, stir well and season to taste with salt and pepper. Sprinkle the top with the cheese and a little more pepper. Brown the top under the grill (broiler) or in a pre-heated oven at 400° F/200° C/gas mark 6.

Serve straight from the casserole accompanied by a green salad, bread and wine.

Maccheroni al Funghi
Macaroni with mushrooms

This recipe demonstrates the economical use of meat, typical of Mediterranean cooking. The amount of veal at first seems unusually large for an Italian country dish, but the cook gets double value from it: it makes the stock for this dish and provides the meat for another meal.

serves 4

1 onion
2 small carrots
3 sticks celery
4 oz/110 g/½ cup *salsicce* (sausage mixture†) or coarse-cut pork sausage
2 tablespoons olive oil
salt and pepper
1–2 lb/450–900 g shin (shank) of veal on the bone
1 tablespoon flour
4 tablespoons tomato paste
1 oz/25 g/2 tablespoons *funghi porcini* (dried mushrooms)
1 small cabbage (optional)
12 oz/350 g macaroni
4 tablespoons grated Parmesan cheese

Chop the onion, carrots, celery and *salsicce* finely and put them in a large pan or flameproof casserole with the oil. Season lightly with salt and pepper and put the veal on top. Fry everything, turning it over with a wooden spoon, until the meat is browned. Sprinkle on the flour and add the tomato paste diluted with 4 tablespoons of water.

Cover the pan and stew gently for 2½–3 hours until the veal is tender. Add more water from time to time if necessary. Towards the end of this cooking time, cover the mushrooms with warm water and soak for 20 minutes.

When the veal is cooked, lift it out and set aside for another meal. Add the mushrooms to the sauce, together with the water in which they were soaked, and continue to simmer for about 20 minutes.

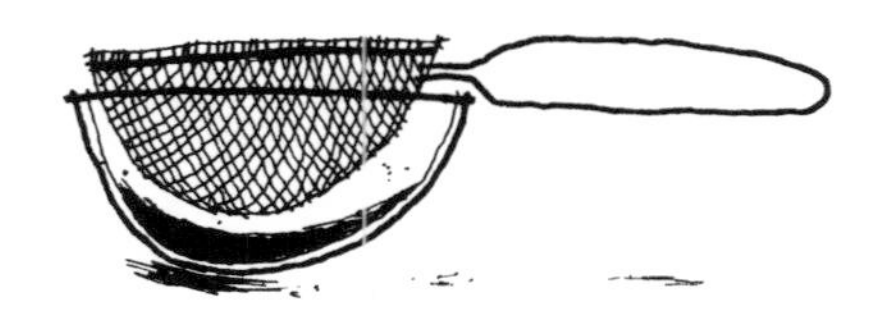

A quarter of an hour before you are ready to serve the meal chop the cabbage and put into a large pan of fast-boiling salted water. When it comes back to the boil, add the macaroni and cook rapidly until just tender. Drain the macaroni and cabbage well and put in a deep dish. Add the Parmesan cheese to the sauce at the last moment, and then mix the sauce with the macaroni and cabbage.

To serve the veal, slice it and reheat it thoroughly in a little tomato sauce† and arrange on a serving dish in a ring of boiled potatoes.

Torta di Vermicelli e Pomodori
Vermicelli and tomato gratin

A little-known baked pasta dish from Naples – the home of pasta. Serve as a main lunch or as a starter in the evening.

serves 4

1½ lb/700 g fresh tomatoes
5 tablespoons olive oil
2 tablespoons dried breadcrumbs
1 clove garlic, finely chopped
8 leaves of basil, shredded, or
 1 teaspoon dried oregano
salt and freshly ground pepper
8 oz/225 g/2 cups vermicelli

Skin the tomatoes and cut across into four slices. Brush the inside of an ovenproof dish with 1 tablespoon olive oil and sprinkle with 1 tablespoon breadcrumbs. Cover with a layer of inner slices of tomato (reserving the round outer slices for the top). Sprinkle with some of the garlic and basil and season with salt and plenty of pepper.

Drop the vermicelli into a large pan of salted water and boil rapidly for 2 minutes. Drain, return to the pan and toss with 3 tablespoons of oil. Tip the vermicelli into the oven dish and cover with the remaining slices of tomato, laying the outer slices on top with their round sides upwards. Sprinkle on the remaining garlic, basil and breadcrumbs and season with salt and pepper.

Pour on the remaining tablespoon of oil and bake in a pre-heated oven at 400° F/200° C/gas mark 6 for 20 minutes. Serve very hot with bread and salad, and fruit to follow.

Pizza Calabrese
Calabrian pizza

Pizza really means a pie – a title faithfully interpreted in this robust version where light, crisp dough, top and bottom, holds the moist tuna and tomato filling.

serves 4

for the filling:
2 lb/900 g can of Italian tomatoes,
 drained
1 generous tablespoon olive oil
1 tablespoon chopped fresh basil,
 or 1 teaspoon dried basil
2 cloves garlic, peeled, crushed
 and chopped
salt
½ red chilli pepper, deseeded and
 flaked or chopped
4 oz/110 g/½ cup canned tuna,
 crushed
12 black olives, halved and stoned
2–3 tablespoons chopped, canned
 anchovy fillets

Start the filling first. Put the tomatoes in a wide pan with the oil, basil and garlic and season with salt. Add the chilli pepper and bring to the boil. Simmer until the mixture is thick and the juices have all but evaporated, stirring from time to time to prevent sticking. Then stir in the tuna, olives and anchovies and cook for about 5 minutes. Allow to cool.

To make the dough, mix the yeast with 2–3 tablespoons of the warm water. Put the flour in a large bowl, make a well in the centre and sprinkle the salt round the edge. When the yeast froths, pour it into the well, add the remaining water and mix to a dough. Knead for 5 minutes, then set on a board, cover with a damp cloth and leave to rise until doubled in size.

If you are using the egg yolks and lard, add them now; punch the dough to make a well in the centre, put in the egg yolks and lard and knead thoroughly into the dough. This will make the dough very sticky, so allow it to rest for a few minutes to make it easier to handle, and add a little more flour if necessary.

Now divide the dough into two and roll out each piece on a well-floured board into a large rectangle about 12 × 8 in/35.5 × 20 cm. Place one in a well-greased roasting tin and spread the filling over it, leaving a margin of ¾ in/2 cm round the edge. Lift the other rectangle on a rolling pin and place it very carefully over the top.

Press the edges together well and roll them, pinching all the way round to make a tight seal. Brush the top with melted lard and bake in a pre-heated oven at 425° F/220° C/gas mark 7 for 30–35 minutes, until golden and crisp.

Serve hot with a green salad and fruit afterwards.

for the dough:
- ½ oz/15 g/1½ teaspoons fresh yeast
- 10 fl oz/300 ml/1¼ cups water, hot to the hand
- 1 lb/450 g/4 cups unbleached strong white bread flour
- 1 teaspoon salt
- 2 egg yolks (optional)
- 2 oz/50 g/¼ cup softened lard (optional)
- melted lard for brushing over

Pipérade
Scrambled eggs with sweet peppers

Creamy eggs marbled with strips of sweet pepper and tomato make one of the most familiar Basque dishes. It is traditionally eaten with Bayonne ham. Pipérade makes a filling lunch dish – as a first course for dinner it would serve six.

Gently cook the onions in the oil in a heavy pan. After about 15 minutes when they are soft but not browned, add the peppers and simmer until they are tender; it should take about 10 minutes. Add the tomatoes and season with salt and pepper and the sugar if you wish. Let this stew simmer until it thickens.

Now take the pan off the heat. Beat the eggs in a bowl and stir them into the vegetables with a wooden spoon. Put the pan on a gentle heat and keep stirring until the eggs become creamy. Do not overcook or the eggs will separate. Serve at once with plenty of bread.

You can use one red pepper and one green for extra colour, and add two crushed cloves of garlic for a stronger flavour.

serves 4–6

- 2 large onions (preferably Spanish), sliced
- 3–4 tablespoons olive oil
- 2 red peppers, deseeded and sliced thinly
- 1 lb/450 g sweet, ripe tomatoes, peeled and chopped
- salt and pepper
- pinch of sugar (optional)
- 6 eggs

Tortilla Española
Spanish omelette

Spaniards eat as many eggs as Britons and Americans, but they usually make better use of them. This favourite family dish provides a perfectly balanced meal: the plainness of the potatoes complements the richness of the eggs, and the onion provides flavour.

serves 4

6 tablespoons olive oil
2 large onions, peeled and diced
2 large potatoes, diced
½ teaspoon salt
3 eggs

Heat the oil in a frying pan without letting it smoke. Stir in the vegetables, mixing them well together and turning them in the oil with a wooden spatula. Sprinkle on the salt and cover the pan with a lid. Cook very gently for about 15 minutes, turning often so that they do not brown or stick to the pan.

Beat the eggs in a large bowl. When the vegetables are tender, remove the pan from the heat and lift the vegetables carefully with a slotted spoon into the egg mixture, leaving as much oil as possible in the pan. Stir the mixture quickly.

Make sure there are no bits sticking in the pan and return it to the heat. When the oil starts to smoke, pour in the mixture. Flatten it down evenly right to the edges of the pan and shake to settle the mixture and prevent sticking. Cook over a medium heat for about 5 minutes, shaking often until the mixture sets and begins to shrink from the sides of the pan.

You can cook the top most easily by putting the pan under a hot grill (broiler) for a few minutes until the *tortilla*, is golden brown. Spanish cooks invert a plate over the pan, turn out the *tortilla*, then slide it back from the plate into the pan to cook the other side.

The finished *tortilla* should be like a solid, flat cake. It is good eaten hot or cold. Add other vegetables, such as peas, beans or green peppers, for variation. A tomato and onion salad† goes well with a *tortilla*.

Arroz con Carne de Cerdo
Rice with pork

In Spain pork is a favourite meat and many people keep their own pigs. This substantial dish from Murcia is enhanced by the warm, pervasive flavour of saffron. Note the modest amount of meat.

Gently heat the oil in a flameproof casserole on top of the stove. Stir in the pieces of pork, turning them constantly until lightly browned all over. Remove and set aside. Brown the whole garlic cloves in the casserole, then remove and set aside. Put in the tomatoes and peppers and cook gently. Meanwhile crush the garlic, saffron and parsley thoroughly in a mortar.

When the tomatoes and peppers have softened slightly, replace the pork, stir well and add the garlic mixture. Add a little cold water, stir and cover. Cook for about 5 minutes until most of the liquid has been absorbed.

Stir in the rice, cook for a minute or two and add the boiling water. Season with plenty of salt and pepper. Cover the casserole and cook in a pre-heated oven at 350° F/180° C/gas mark 4 for about 20 minutes.

Take the dish straight to the table and serve with bread and a green salad.

serves 4

6 tablespoons olive oil
1 lb/450 g lean pork, trimmed and chopped
6 cloves garlic, peeled
1 lb/450 g tomatoes, peeled and chopped
4 red peppers, deseeded and cut in strips
2 pinches saffron strands, toasted
1 handful chopped parsley
14 oz/400 g/1⅔ cups medium grain (Spanish or Italian) rice
2 pints/1.1 litres/5 cups boiling water
salt and freshly ground black pepper

Arroz com Grelos
Rice with turnip tops

Treated with a proper respect turnip tops are a valuable addition to the winter diet. They give colour, flavour and nutritional balance to this Portuguese rice dish from Minho.

Heat half the oil in a large saucepan and cook the onion, carrots and potato gently for about 5 minutes. Add the rice and turn it well in the oil. Continue to cook for another 5 minutes, stirring often. Add the boiling stock, cover the pan and simmer for about 20 minutes, or until the rice is swollen and the liquid absorbed.

In another saucepan heat the rest of the oil, cook the garlic in it for a minute or two without letting it burn and then add the turnip tops. Turn them well until coated with oil, then add very little water, season with salt and cover the pan. Cook briskly for 10–15 minutes, or until the vegetable is tender. Drain and stir into the rice mixture.

This is served as a main course with perhaps some *Vinho Verde*.

serves 4

5 tablespoons olive oil
1 onion, sliced
2 carrots, sliced thinly
1 potato, peeled and diced
8 oz/225 g/1 cup medium grain rice
1 pint/575 ml/2½ cups well-seasoned stock, preferably chicken
2 cloves garlic, peeled and chopped
8 oz/225 g/2 cups prepared turnip tops (or Brussels sprout tops)
salt

Bar (ou Mulet) Grillé au Fenouil Sea-bass (or grey mullet) grilled with fennel

One of the most prevalent scents of the coastal towns of Provence is of fish being grilled (broiled) on dried fennel twigs over charcoal. This recipe uses fennel bulbs to give a similar but more delicate flavour.

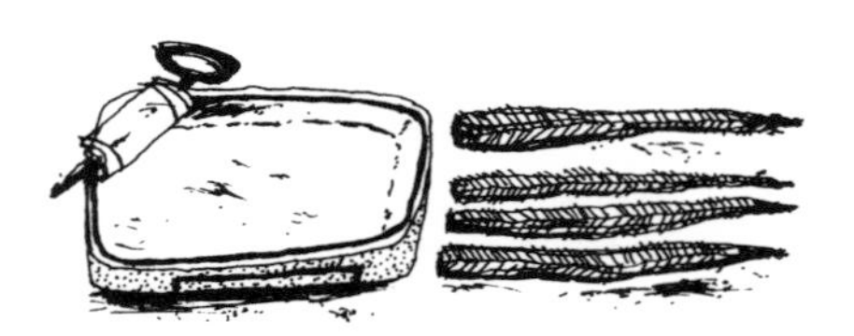

serves 4

1 sea-bass or grey mullet (striped mullet), weighing about 3 lb/1.4 kg
2 fennel bulbs, washed and trimmed
salt and pepper
2 tablespoons olive oil
3 canned anchovy fillets, chopped
2–3 tablespoons melted butter

Clean and scale the fish and make 2 cuts in each side. Cut the fennel into thin slices and lay these over the bottom of a large, oval gratin dish. Sprinkle them with salt, pepper and most of the oil.

Put the fish in the grill (broiler) pan, sprinkle with the remaining oil and grill until it is half cooked. Then lay it on the bed of fennel and finish cooking it in a pre-heated oven at 400° F/200° C/gas mark 6 for 10–15 minutes. Baste it frequently with the juices.

Meanwhile, put the anchovies and butter in a small pan over a low heat and warm through to serve as a sauce with the fish. Alternatively, serve the fish with pats of chilled anchovy butter, or with plain melted butter.

Giraboix Salt cod with vegetables and *all-i-oli* sauce

A simple dish from Valencia to serve in two stages: a warming broth followed by fish and vegetable bathed in the unmistakably Spanish *all-i-oli* sauce†. Use the version of *all-i-oli* thickened with egg yolks to give a pleasing contrast of textures. Soak the salt cod well to remove the salt.

serves 4

1 lb/450 g *bacalao* (salt cod)
1 lb/450 g onions, sliced
1 lb/450 g potatoes, sliced
8 oz/225 g/1½ cups dwarf green beans, sliced
½ small cabbage, finely sliced
1 small dried chilli pepper, deseeded
1 clove garlic, peeled and crushed
2 thin slices bread
red pepper, blanched and cut into strips for garnish
all-i-oli sauce

Soak the fish for 12 hours, changing the water several times. Rinse thoroughly, remove the skin and as many bones as possible, and break the flesh into pieces. Put in a saucepan with the onions, potatoes and a little water.

Bring to the boil, then simmer for about 10 minutes. Add the beans, cabbage, chilli pepper and garlic. Add a little boiling water to cover, and cook for another 15 minutes.

Just before the cooking is finished, toast the bread and crumble into a soup tureen. Drain the liquid from the pan into the tureen; lift out and chop the chilli pepper finely and sprinkle it over the broth.

Serve this broth first, with the fish and vegetables as a second course. Arrange them on a large hot dish garnished with the strips of red pepper, and serve them with the *all-i-oli* sauce and plenty of bread.

Caldeirada de Peixe
Fish stew

This is a real fisherman's stew, dependent on whatever the boats have brought in. The spices and herbs give the dish its special Portuguese identity.

serves 4–6

8 oz/225 g each of fresh sardine, fresh tuna, eel and whiting, or any other available fish including shellfish
2 pinches sea salt
4 tablespoons olive oil
2 onions, chopped
8 tomatoes, peeled and chopped
1 green pepper, deseeded and chopped
4 large cloves garlic, peeled and well crushed
a little grated nutmeg
½ teaspoon ground allspice
3 teaspoons *piri-piri* sauce†
1 small glass dry white wine
1 handful coriander leaves, chopped
3–4 slices of bread, with crusts cut off

Clean the fish and cut into fairly small pieces, removing as many bones as possible. Sprinkle the salt over the fish and leave while you make the following sauce.

Heat 2–3 tablespoons of the oil in a saucepan and stir in the onions, tomatoes and pepper. Cook gently until they start to soften, then put in the garlic, nutmeg, allspice and *piri-piri* sauce. Add the wine and a little water. Cook for about 5 minutes, stirring frequently, then remove from the heat.

Lightly oil the bottom of a shallow, ovenproof dish (preferably earthenware). Put in a layer of fish followed by a layer of sauce and sprinkle with coriander. Continue with these layers until the ingredients are used up. Cover the top with the bread and sprinkle well with the remaining oil or dot with a little butter. Cook in a pre-heated oven at 350° F/180° C/gas mark 4 for about 30 minutes or until the fish is tender.

Serve with boiled or sliced and fried potatoes, bread and a salad to make a substantial main meal.

If you cannot obtain coriander leaves, you can use fresh parsley instead, but this will alter the flavour of the dish.

Mero al Jerez
Grouper cooked in sherry

The delicate flavour and firm flesh of the grouper are much prized in the Mediterranean. In Andalusia it is baked with local sherry and almonds. You can also cook halibut in this way.

serves 4

4 large steaks of fresh grouper or halibut
2 tablespoons olive oil
salt and pepper
24 blanched almonds, cut in slivers
1 clove garlic, very finely chopped
1 large glass sherry
2 tablespoons chopped parsley

Lightly oil a shallow ovenproof serving dish and lay in the unskinned fish steaks. Sprinkle with the oil and season lightly with salt and pepper. Scatter the almonds and garlic evenly over the fish and pour on the sherry.

Bake uncovered in a pre-heated oven at 350° F/180° C/gas mark 4 for about 30 minutes. Baste the fish frequently. Just before the cooking is finished, scatter the parsley on the steaks. Serve straight from the cooking dish. Bread and a glass of white wine are the usual accompaniments.

Faves con Butifarrones
Broad beans with *butifarron* sausage

Butifarrones are pork sausages from Catalonia and Majorca, flavoured with cumin, cinnamon and pine nuts. Their distinctive flavour is used for many local dishes. Fresh young broad beans in their pods give extra character to this dish. If you cannot obtain *butifarrones*, you can substitute garlic sausage, but the dish will not have quite the authentic flavour.

serves 4

4 tablespoons olive oil
12 spring onions or scallions, chopped
4 tomatoes, peeled and chopped
2 cloves garlic, peeled and chopped
1 tablespoon paprika
2 oz/50 g/¼ cup *tocino* (salted pork fat), diced
a few raisins
2 *butifarrones*, sliced
2¼ lb/1 kg/5 cups small, freshly picked broad (*fava*) beans or lima beans in their pods, sliced
salt and pepper

Heat the oil, in a large earthenware casserole for the authentic method, but otherwise in a saucepan. Stir in the onions, tomatoes and garlic and cook gently until softened. Stir in the paprika, *tocino* and raisins and add the sausage and beans. Pour in a very little water, season with salt and pepper, cover and cook gently for about 30 minutes.

Take the dish straight to the table and serve as a main course. If you have used a saucepan, transfer the dish to a heated bowl to serve.

Cocido Madrileño
Madrid stew

Spain's national dish is a whole meal in itself – served as three courses. It uses small amounts of several everyday ingredients in a really delicious combination. If you are short of one or two ingredients, simply leave them out.

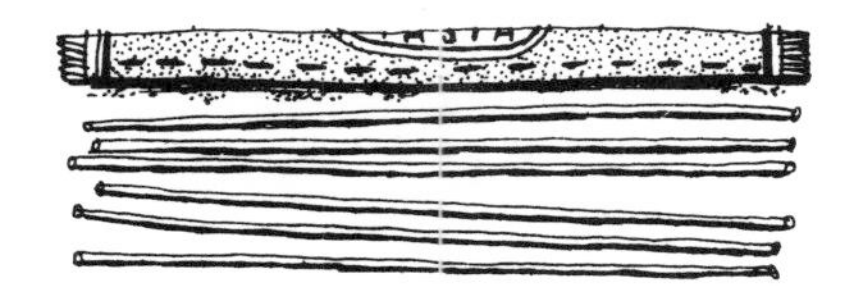

serves 4

8 oz/225 g/1 cup chick peas
1 salted pig's foot, soaked overnight
½ boiling fowl
4 oz/110 g/½ cup *tocino* (salted pork fat), diced
4 oz/110 g *morcilla* sausage
4 oz/110 g *chorizo* sausage
4 oz/110 g smoked bacon, in one piece
4 oz/110 g stewing beef, in one piece
2 bay leaves
1 onion, roughly chopped
½ small cabbage, coarsely shredded
2 carrots, cut up
½ head of garlic in one unpeeled piece
4 potatoes, cut in chunks
any other vegetables as available
salt and pepper
8 oz/225 g/1 cup small pasta

Soak the chick peas for at least 8 hours or overnight in cold water, then drain. Choose a very large, flameproof pot – earthenware is traditional, but you can use any heavy vessel. Half fill it with water and put in the chick peas; if you tie them up loosely in a muslin (cheesecloth) bag, you can lift them out more easily when they are done. Put in the pig's foot, fowl, *tocino*, *morcilla*, *chorizo*, smoked bacon, beef and bay leaves. Add more water if necessary to cover. Bring to the boil and skim.

Lower the heat and simmer very gently for about 2 hours. Add the onion, cabbage, carrots, garlic, potatoes and any other vegetables and continue to cook for another 30 minutes or so, adding more hot water if the dish becomes too dry. Taste and season as necessary. When all the meats and the chick peas are tender, the *cocido* is ready.

Cook the pasta and drain. Pour off the broth from the *cocido* and stir in the hot pasta. Serve as a soup. Next, lift out the chick peas and turn on to a large, heated dish. Spoon out the other vegetables with a slotted spoon and arrange on the dish. Cut up the meats and arrange on a large, heated plate. Serve the vegetables and meats at the same time with a home-made tomato sauce (similar to Italian tomato sauce†).

Serve lavish amounts of bread for mopping up the juices. A red wine usually accompanies this meal.

Puchero
Canary Island stew

serves 4–6

1 lb/450 g stewing beef, cubed
ham bone
4 oz/110 g/½ cup *tocino* (salted pork fat), diced
4 oz/110 g/½ cup *chorizo* sausage, sliced
8 oz/225g/1 cup chick peas, soaked overnight, then drained
bay leaf
2 corn on the cob, each cut into 4 pieces
4 potatoes, peeled and cut up
1 onion, chopped
2 pears, peeled and cut in half
½ small cabbage, sliced
1 aubergine (eggplant), peeled and cut up
2 courgettes (zucchini), cut up
4 oz/110 g/¾ cup green beans, sliced
4 tomatoes, chopped
small piece of pumpkin or squash, cut up (optional)
1 sweet potato, peeled and cut up (optional)
2 cloves garlic, peeled
pinch of saffron threads
2 cloves
salt and pepper

This colourful stew, full of vegetables that grow so abundantly in the warmth of the Canary Islands, makes a pleasant main meal.

Put the beef, bone, *tocino*, *chorizo*, chick peas and bay leaf into a large saucepan. Cover with plenty of water and bring to the boil. Skim, then simmer very gently for about 2 hours. If the corn seems rather dry and hard, put it in at the start of cooking, otherwise add it after about 1 hour.

When the chick peas are almost tender, add the potatoes, onion, pears, cabbage, aubergine, courgettes, beans and tomatoes. Add the pumpkin and sweet potato if available. Pour in more hot water if necessary, to cover the vegetables, and simmer for a further ½–1 hour until everything is tender.

Just before serving, crush the garlic, saffron and cloves together, using a pestle and mortar, and add to the *puchero*. Taste and season with salt and pepper as necessary, remove the bone and serve at once. Serve with bread and wine.

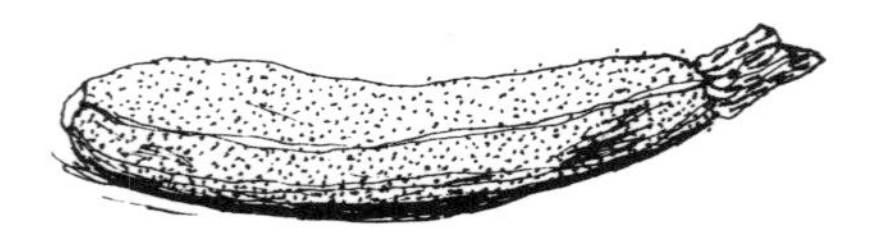

Caldo Gallego
Galician stew

serves 4–6

1 lb/450 g/2 cups haricot (dried white) beans
½ in/1.25 cm thick slice of *unto* (aged fat bacon)
1 lb/450 g potatoes, peeled and sliced
1 large bunch turnip tops, washed and coarsely cut up
salt

This is a real peasant dish, cheap but filling and nutritious. Characteristic of Galicia, it uses local fat bacon to give a distinct flavour to the otherwise bland beans and potatoes.

Soak the beans overnight in cold water, then drain. Put them in a large, flameproof casserole half filled with water and bring to the boil. Add the *unto* and simmer for about 1½ hours. Add the potatoes and turnip tops and continue cooking until everything is tender, after about another hour; the exact time will depend on the quality of the beans. Add a little salt and more hot water if necessary. Cut up the meat before serving.

Unto is an acquired taste and often a piece of ham or pork, or some *chorizo* sausage, is added to mellow the flavour. If you like, you can substitute smoked fat bacon with its rind for the *unto*.

Porco com Feijao
Pork and beans

A classic farmers' dish throughout the Western world. Olive oil makes it better for health than the more familiar pork and baked bean dish of New England. The flavouring with cumin shows the strong Moorish influence in Southern Portugal.

serves 4

8 oz/225 g/1 packed cup salt pork
4 oz/110 g/½ cup haricot (dried white) beans
2 tablespoons olive oil
1 onion, finely chopped
4 oz/110 g *morcela* sausage
1 teaspoon cumin seeds, bruised
4 oz/110 g/1 cup macaroni
1 small cabbage

Soak the pork and beans together in cold water overnight, and then drain. Cut the pork into cubes and put it into a large flameproof pot with the beans, oil, onion, sausage and cumin. Just cover with water and bring to the boil, skimming when necessary.

Cover and simmer for 1–1½ hours or until the beans are almost tender, and then add the macaroni. Shred the cabbage and add it to the pot. Pour in some hot water if the dish is becoming dry, cover again and simmer for 15–20 minutes. The beans and macaroni should be tender and the cabbage still fairly crisp.

Serve from the cooking pot with plenty of crusty white bread.

Agnello al Forno
Roast lamb

Lamb is the favourite meat in Southern Italy; in this Sicilian dish it is larded with bacon and rosemary and then coated in cheese and breadcrumbs to seal in the flavours.

serves 4

3 lb/1.4 kg shoulder of lamb
3 oz/75 g *pancetta* or streaky bacon, cut into strips
2 sprigs rosemary
1 oz/25 g/2 tablespoons lard or chicken fat
1 oz/25 g/4 tablespoons grated Pecorino or Parmesan cheese
2 oz/50 g/1 cup fresh breadcrumbs
salt and freshly ground pepper

Make small cuts in the meat and push a strip of *pancetta* and a rosemary leaf into each one. Spread the lard over the meat. Mix the cheese and breadcrumbs together and sprinkle them over the meat, patting the mixture on firmly. Season with salt and pepper.

Roast in a pre-heated oven at 375° F/190° C/gas mark 5 for 1½ hours.

Serve in thick slices with bread, with an aubergine (eggplant) salad to start with and fresh fruit afterwards.

Agnello con Finocchi e Pomodori
Lamb with fennel and tomato

Fennel, which grows wild over much of Southern Italy, gives a delicate perfume to this dish. Serve the melting slices of lamb very hot with a spoonful or so of the rich tomato jam and a few potatoes. A meat dish like this is eaten only seldom.

serves 4

2 tablespoons olive oil
2 large onions
half a shoulder of lamb (the fillet end rather than the shank end), or 3 lb/1.4 kg neck of lamb
6 tomatoes
2 tablespoons tomato paste
large bunch of fennel twigs, fresh or dried, or 1 fennel bulb
salt and pepper
1 lb/450 g potatoes, halved (quartered if very large)

Heat the oil in a flameproof casserole, brown the sliced onions in it, then add the meat and brown it. If you are using a fennel bulb, slice it and add it to the meat.

When everything is a deep brown, add the peeled, sliced tomatoes and the tomato paste, with a wine-glass of water. Add the fennel twigs and season with salt and pepper. Arrange the potatoes round the meat, cover the casserole and braise in a pre-heated oven at 325° F/170° C/gas mark 3 for 1½ – 1¾ hours. Remove the meat and potatoes to a serving plate and pour or spoon the excess oil from the sauce, which should be almost like jam now.

Follow with a green or mixed salad.

Coelho em Vinho Verde
Rabbit in *Vinho Verde*

Vinho Verde is a sparkling wine from the northern district of Portugal. In this recipe from Tras-os-Montes it is used to cook wild mountain rabbits that have their own special flavour. The Spanish and Portuguese eat a fair amount of wild game, which has less fat than most domestic animals.

serves 4

1 wild rabbit, cut into joints
1 clove garlic, cut in half
2–3 tablespoons seasoned flour
1 oz/25 g/2 tablespoons lard
½ bottle *Vinho Verde* or any dry white wine
1 tablespoon chopped fresh coriander leaves (or parsley)
small bunch fresh herbs, such as thyme, oregano, or rosemary
2 bay leaves
salt and pepper

Rub the rabbit pieces well with the garlic and coat them with the seasoned flour. Heat the lard in a large flameproof casserole and brown the pieces of rabbit lightly in it. Pour in enough wine just to cover them. Add the coriander and the bunch of herbs and the bay leaves, tied together with string. Season with salt to taste and a few grindings of pepper.

Cover and simmer very gently until the rabbit is tender; this will take 1–2 hours depending on the toughness of the meat. The dish improves with keeping and is even better the next day.

The Portuguese often serve it with potatoes, which are parboiled, then sliced thickly and fried in shallow olive oil. Potatoes boiled in their skins are just as good with it. Serve bread as well and some more *Vinho Verde*.

Piri-Piri
Piri-piri sauce

Ready-made *piri-piri* can be bought by the Portuguese, who use it a good deal as a spicy condiment on pasta, fish or meat and also to flavour stews.

serves 4

10 fl oz/300 ml/1¼ cups olive oil
about 8 chilli peppers with tops removed
1 bay leaf
1 small piece lemon rind

Pour the oil into a small, screw-top jar and add the chilli peppers, bay leaf and lemon rind. Screw on the top and shake. Leave to stand in a warm place for at least 24 hours before use. It will keep at room temperature indefinitely.

All-i-oli
Garlic and oil sauce

Garlic, as well as providing a robust flavour, is good for the heart. This garlic sauce from Catalonia is the Spanish equivalent of the classic French *aïoli*, but as it is made without eggs it is less rich.

serves 4

4–6 large cloves garlic, peeled
pinch of salt
7 fl oz/200 ml/⅞ cup olive oil
1 teaspoon lemon juice

Have all the ingredients and utensils at room temperature so that the sauce will thicken properly.

Crush the garlic thoroughly with the salt, using a pestle and mortar. When it is thoroughly pulped, add the oil little by little, stirring constantly. Add the lemon juice a drop or two at a time. The finished sauce should be thick and opaque. Traditionally it is served in the mortar in which it has been made.

You can make *all-i-oli* very easily by putting all the ingredients in a blender for a few seconds. This is the classic recipe, but in many places an egg yolk or two is incorporated at the beginning with the garlic. This produces a sauce much more like a mayonnaise.

The sauce is served with fish dishes, hot or cold vegetables, meat, and, in Valencia, even with paella.

Salsa di Pomodori
Very plain tomato sauce

serves 4

- 2 lb/900 g fully ripe or canned tomatoes
- 2 large cloves garlic
- 4 tablespoons olive oil
- 1 heaped tablespoon chopped flat-leaved parsley
- salt
- 1 tablespoon fresh basil leaves, shredded, or 1 heaped teaspoon dried oregano

Sweet, full-flavoured tomatoes from Italy make this straightforward sauce ideal for lunch-time pasta dishes. Don't feel that you are cheating by using canned tomatoes; in Italy they use canned or bottled tomatoes throughout the winter months.

Peel the tomatoes (if fresh), cut them in half and press out the seeds by squeezing each half in the palm of your hand. Discard the seeds and chop the flesh coarsely.

Peel and lightly crush the garlic and fry in the oil in a small saucepan. When the garlic is a good brown, remove and discard. Put in the tomatoes and parsley, season with salt, cover the pan and cook over a medium heat for 20 minutes. Add the basil or oregano just before the end of cooking.

Toucinho do Céu
Heavenly food

Cakes and puddings made with almonds, sugar and eggs are popular in Portugal, but they are usually only for special occasions and festivals and not for eating every day. This very sweet cake from Minho could be served after a meal. It is often eaten as an afternoon snack in the cafés of Lisbon and other towns.

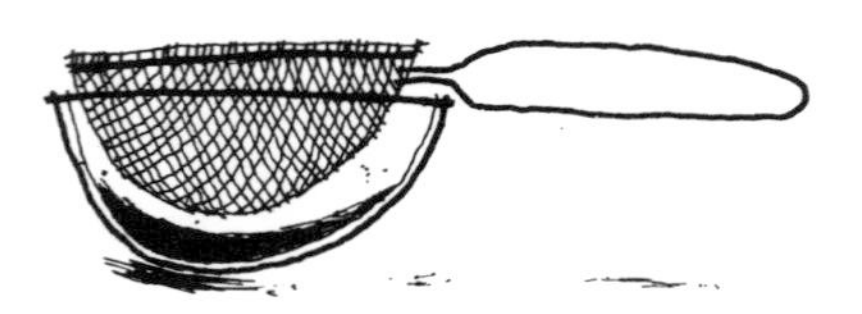

serves 4

- 9 oz/250 g/1¼ cups sugar
- 6 fl oz/175 ml/¾ cup water
- 10 oz /275 g/1¼ cups almonds, peeled and shredded
- 8 egg yolks
- sugar for sprinkling

Boil the sugar and water together, stirring, until the mixture begins to clear after about 5 minutes. Add the almonds and then remove the pan from the heat and stir in the egg yolks. Cook over a very low heat, stirring constantly, until the mixture thickens. Take care not to let it boil.

Grease a tart tin with a removable base and pour in the mixture. Sprinkle the top with sugar and bake in a pre-heated oven at 400° F/200° C/gas mark 6 for about 10 minutes or until the mixture is just set. Cut into slices when cool.

Flan de Leche
Baked caramel custard

One of the few desserts, other than fresh fruit, served in Spain – delicious, delicate but very sweet.

serves 6–8

1 pint/575 ml/2½ cups milk
1 vanilla pod (bean)
6 oz/175 g/¾ cup caster (superfine) sugar
4 oz/110 g/½ cup sugar for caramel
2 tablespoons cold water
4 eggs
pinch of salt

Put the milk, vanilla pod and sugar into a saucepan and slowly bring to the boil, stirring to dissolve the sugar. Leave to cool a little.

To prepare the caramel, put the dry sugar into a small saucepan and melt it over a moderate heat, stirring well with a wooden spoon. When the sugar turns brown, remove from the heat and add the water, taking care as it will bubble up. Stir over a low heat until it forms a smooth syrup. Pour a little into each of 4 wetted moulds.

Whisk the eggs and salt thoroughly in a bowl and stir in the slightly cooled, sweetened milk, first removing the vanilla pod. Fill each mould with this mixture. Stand in a bain-marie (or ovenproof dish) with hot water to reach halfway up the sides of the moulds. Bake in a pre-heated oven at 350° F/180° C/gas mark 4 for about 30 minutes. The custard is ready when a small knife inserted into it comes out clean.

Chill thoroughly and turn out on to small plates just before serving. You can vary the basic custard by adding coffee, cinnamon, orange, or other flavourings.

CHAPTER 2

THE BALKAN

The people of the Balkans have long been renowned for their good health; at one time their fine record was attributed to the widespread consumption of yoghurt, but today we know that their excellent health statistics are due to a much wider pattern of eating, and a well-balanced cuisine which deserves to be better known. The low rate of heart disease and diet-related cancers in the Balkans is now attributed to the fact that they eat a lot more grain and wheat products than in the UK and US, less meat, less animal fat and fewer manufactured foods. They generally use vegetable oils as a cooking medium and they eat large quantities of fruit and vegetables, often in the raw state.

In Plato's *Republic* there is a reference to a utopian race of happy people who would be found living beyond the north wind in a valley of plenty: 'They will have olives and cheese and country stews of roots and vegetables . . . they will sip their wine . . . leading such a healthy and peaceful life they will naturally live to a good old age.'

Such a simple diet and such good health may well have been enjoyed by the majority of Greek peasants in classical times. Today it is enjoyed by the Balkan people who inhabit this vast mountainous area which stretches south of the rivers Sava and Danube, forming a huge triangle bounded on the west by the Adriatic Sea and on the east by the Aegean Sea and the Black Sea. Within its boundaries lie Albania, Bulgaria, Greece and Yugoslavia and the north-western tip of Turkey. Rumania lies north of the Danube, so although it is not part of the Balkans, historical, cultural and trade links are shared.

The people are a mixture of races. The predominant religion is Eastern Orthodox, but other groups include Muslims and Jews. At various times the Balkans have been overrun by Greeks, Turks, and most recently Germans. The Turks have left the most lasting influence on the food. All the Balkan countries were once part of the vast Turkish empire and their conquerors brought with them a Middle Eastern style of cookery, which was adopted by Turkish cooks. Into this was absorbed the cuisine of ancient Greece. Cookery has been modified in the various Balkan countries over the centuries to suit cultural tastes and religious requirements, while still based, of course, on the availability of local produce.

In the southern olive-growing belt food is cooked in olive oil. Further north sunflower oils, other seed oils and lard are used. The whole region has vineyards which produce characteristic wines and brandies. The farming lands are rich in fruit and such vegetables as peppers, aubergines, pumpkins and melons. The inland mountainous areas are unsuitable for cattle, but support great flocks of sheep which supply milk as well as wool and meat. The barren limestone of the Greek coastline also supports the hardy and tenacious goat.

The main staples are bread, along with other wheat products, and to a lesser extent dried beans such as haricots. They consume two or three times as much of these staples as we do in the UK and US. Wheat is the most commonly eaten cereal, although in Bulgaria, Rumania and Yugoslavia maize (corn) is included in the diet. Rumania is sometimes known as the Land of *Mamaliga* (bread of gold) because of their cornmeal bread which is the national dish, commonly eaten instead of or as well as wheat bread. In the past, it was not only the food of the people but also 'the delight of the upper classes'.

Before the invention of the roller mill in the second half of the nineteenth century, the ordinary loaf was coarse-grained and often a mix of any cereals available – cornmeal, barley and rye – with a high proportion of bran. This mix is not so usual today. Home-made bread is not common, since bread from the local bakeries is so good; it is made from wheat flour with a faint, almost undetectable, yellowish tint because it is not bleached. Warm, flat bread enriched with eggs and sunflower seed oil might be made at home as a special treat.

Yoghurt, of course, makes a special contribution to the Balkan diet. At the turn of the century Professor Elie Metchnikoff of the Pasteur Institute in Paris recommended the consumption of yoghurt, declaring that the live bacteria in it drove out harmful 'putrefactive' bacteria which weaken the resistance of the higher elements of the body. Yoghurt then became a health fad in the West, gaining world-wide acceptance during the last two decades following the production of commercial yoghurts, which often contain added sugar and highly refined starch.

True yoghurt is made from ewe's milk and the very best is said to come from Bulgaria, the namesake of one of the two active bacteria (*Lactobacillus bulgaricus* and *Streptococcus thermophilus*) which combine to coagulate the milk and produce the characteristic mildly acid taste. A true yoghurt is sufficiently thick to be cut with a knife. It is pure white in colour with a rich yellowish cream layer on top, much coveted by both children and adults. Originally it was made and often sold in huge earthenware pots or enamel bowls, but now it is usually packed in plastic containers. Its distinctive tangy flavour is added to salads and soups and it is often served as a main dish for supper with bread and sometimes with whole peeled garlic cloves.

There are only a few desserts made with yoghurt, but it is sometimes added to a cake mix so that its acidity strengthens the baking powder, to a bread or biscuit mixture, or to a soda bread. In summer, yoghurt is sometimes diluted with water and served as a long iced drink called *ayran* in Turkish – it is known under this name throughout the Balkans.

Fruit and vegetables are a vital part of the Balkan diet. They are plentiful and eaten fresh in season, bottled in winter and nowadays sold frozen. They are not considered as an accompaniment to meat, but are featured in special dishes on their own, or in combinations. There's a Greek country saying of aubergines: 'We pickle them as babies, roast them when they are getting big and fat and, when they are old, we fry them. What would we do without our friend the aubergine?'

White cabbages are a great favourite. In October they are bought by the cartload, pickled whole in wooden tubs, or shredded and prepared as sauerkraut, serving as a standby all winter, and as a continuing source of vitamin C. Peppers, tomatoes, leeks, spinach, onions, spring onions and spring garlic (especially good with yoghurt) are abundant in the markets. Celeriac is an important winter vegetable, served in stews or on its own with a dressing of olive oil and lemon. Potatoes appear in many guises and as a separate vegetable.

The pumpkin is another favourite. Bulgarians call it the 'chestnut pumpkin' and Yugoslavs the 'sugar pumpkin', an indication of its sweetness and firmness. It is mostly eaten baked and served in thick slices. But it is also an ingredient in many pies.

All the Mediterranean fruits are available in the south except limes and grapefruits. Further north a surprising number of the 'old-fashioned' fruits are very popular, including medlars and quinces, mulberries and bilberries, as well as the more familiar plums and apricots, peaches and cherries. Big juicy melons and watermelons are to be found throughout the region.

The Adriatic, the Mediterranean and the Black Sea have a wealth of fish, and inland the rivers, ponds and lakes provide freshwater varieties – carp, pike, perch and trout. The Yugoslavs in fact claim that they can enjoy a different variety of fish every day of the year. Recipes are usually simple and the Greeks declare that 'most of them apply to most fish'! Fish will usually be grilled (broiled), fried, or cooked in a thick tomato sauce.

Meat has its place, but does not have the significance it has in Britain or America. Much less beef is eaten and seldom as steaks. It is usually cut into cubes for kebabs or minced (ground) and combined in stuffing. Pork is eaten mostly in the winter. Meat most often means mutton and lamb, and sometimes, in Greece, kid. On patron saints' days (such as Slava and Kourban), or to celebrate a family or community event, like the harvest gathering, a lamb will be roasted whole on a spit. Herbs are used in all cooking, and one of the most haunting smells is that of sweet oregano, 'the joy of the mountains', with spit roasted lamb, or simple salads. Lamb is used also in stews (*yahni*) which are cooked on top of the stove or baked slowly in an earthenware baking dish called a *gyuvech* or *güveç*.

Cheese is a prime source of protein in the Balkan diet and is often served with salad and bread as a light supper. Shepherds in the Balkan mountains grill cheese over charcoal. In the towns, cheese is coated with egg and breadcrumbs and fried, or mixed with eggs and stuffed into green peppers and baked or fried.

Ewe's milk is used to make a delicious soft white cheese called *feta* in Greece, *sir* in Yugoslavia, *sirene* in Bulgaria and *brinza* in Rumania, while goat's milk cheeses are a speciality of Greece.

Small amounts of cheese are used in the wonderful layered pies of the Balkans, such as the *burekakia* of Greece and the *börek* of Turkey; they are filled with ewe's cheese and baked or fried. And there are big round layered pies like the Bulgarian *banitza* and the Yugoslavian *gibanica* which are often filled with *feta* cheese or low-fat curd cheese mixed with egg. Slices of this pastry, or individual *banichka*, are sold from street stalls or bakeries in the day, and are often eaten as a snack on the way to work. These pies are quite rich and filling, but the proportion of fat to flour is one to three as opposed to one to two in the traditional British and American shortcrust pastry.

The daily eating pattern is very similar throughout the Balkans. People go to work early and start the day with a small cup of strong black coffee for breakfast, though not necessarily sweetened. There might be bread with *feta* cheese, yoghurt or salami for breakfast, or a slice of the delicious *gibanica* pie. The main meal of the day is lunch; it will probably be three courses, starting with a cheese or a savoury *meze* as appetizer, or a light soup, cold and fresh in the summer. A rich vegetable dish or a meat and vegetable dish is the likely second course. Dessert is frequently a milk pudding, such as semolina pudding, crême caramel, or *kissel* (pudding of fruit pulp or fruit juice thickened with flour). Rich or grand desserts, like the traditional Balkan *baklava*, *kadaif* or pastries soaked in syrup, are only rarely served on special occasions. Overall consumption of sugar is less than half that of Britain or the USA.

In the evenings people like to go out to a

local restaurant or grill-bar where they might have grilled *kebapche* (minced meat), or *shish kebabs*, or a mixed grill of lamb and offal with bread rolls and salad. A meal at home will consist of a vegetable dish, or bread and a bowlful of thick yoghurt, followed by fruit. Supper is always lighter than the midday meal and is always eaten early in the evening.

The Balkans contain numerous vineyards and, although the wines might not match up to the great classics of the world, they are always more than adequate and sometimes very good. Wine is served with the meal generally on special occasions, when having friends for lunch or supper, for festivities or when eating out. Sweet fruit drinks and mineral water are popular on ordinary days. Alcohol is seldom drunk on its own, but generally as an accompaniment to food.

Both the climate and the sociable temperament of the people encourages street life. There is no time of the day when you cannot buy some delicious little snack, either in a café or milk bar or from a street stall. The milk bars sell yoghurts and sweet milk puddings, as well as a variety of ice-cream, made with fresh cream or fruit pulp; but most of the favourite snacks are based on flour and cheese. In the autumn street stalls sell corn on the cob boiled in big metal vats, slices of baked pumpkin, roasted chestnuts, hot layered pies and salted popcorn.

Whenever you stop for a drink in a café-cum-pastry shop (*sladkarnitza*), you can choose from a variety of cakes, fancy petits fours, *baklava*, *tortas*, *revane* (cake soaked in milk or syrup), *kadaif*, halva or chocolate confectioneries. The choice is enormous. Drinks include fruit nectar, *boza* (a thick millet yeast drink), lemonade or black coffee.

It is not difficult to recreate many of these delicacies at home and the recipes demonstrate that one of the healthiest cooking styles in the world can also be remarkably interesting and deliciously special.

Popara
Hot milk breakfast dish

A bowl of hot bread and milk flavoured with cheese makes a well-balanced Bulgarian breakfast to sustain you through a hard morning's work – but only top quality ingredients are suited to such simple treatment. Use only *feta* cheese, unsalted butter and the best white bread you can make or buy. Decorate the creamy white *popara* with a few drops of amber paprika oil.

serves 4

- 9 oz/250 g/5 slices 2-day-old white bread (made with unbleached flour, or enriched with eggs or milk)
- 7 oz/200 g/1 cup *sirene* (*feta*) cheese, coarsely crumbled with a fork
- 2½ oz/60 g/5 tablespoons unsalted butter
- 1½–2 pints/850–1100 ml/4–5 cups milk
- 2 tablespoons sugar
- paprika oil for sprinkling (see below)

Leave the crusts on the bread and cut it into cubes. Divide them equally between four small ovenproof bowls. Sprinkle the cheese into the bowls and stir to mix. Dot the surface with flakes of butter and put the bowls in a pre-heated oven at 300° F/150° C/gas mark 2 for 10–15 minutes to warm through.

Pour the milk into a saucepan, stir in the sugar and bring to the boil. Take the bowls out of the oven and pour in the milk. Cover each bowl with a plate and leave to stand for 1–2 minutes while the bread soaks up the milk. Some people like the milk to be absorbed completely; others prefer some to be left in the bowl.

Serve the *popara* immediately with a few drops of paprika oil sprinkled on top.

You can prepare paprika oil by stirring ¼–½ teaspoon of paprika into 5–6 tablespoons heated sunflower oil or corn oil and leaving the mixture to stand until the sediment has settled. Carefully spoon or pour the clear oil into a small screw-topped bottle fitted with a plastic one-hole dropper (a soy sauce bottle serves the purpose). Store in a cool dark place and use it to decorate egg, cheese or yoghurt dishes, and in salad dressings.

Tarama Salata
Smoked cod's roe purée

This purée is made throughout the Balkans from the hard roe of the grey mullet, carp or mackerel, but you can use salted or smoked cod's roe as a substitute. It makes an ideal appetizer. Serve with pitta bread† or white bread.

serves 4

- 4 oz/110 g/2 slices 2-day-old bread
- 4 oz/110 g/¼ cup packed salted or smoked cod's roe or grey mullet roe
- 1 small mild onion, grated (such as a Spanish onion)
- about 6 fl oz/175 ml/¾ cup olive oil
- 1–2 tablespoons lemon juice

Soak the bread in water until very soft and then squeeze dry. Skin the roe and crumble it into a bowl. Mix in the bread and onion, then pound to a paste or purée in a blender. Add the oil drop by drop, as for mayonnaise, beating constantly until the mixture is thick and smooth. Work in enough lemon juice to soften the purée and beat thoroughly. It should form thick peaks firm enough to scoop up with bread.

To vary the flavour, you can add paprika to taste, or a crushed clove of garlic.

Patlıcan Salatas
Aubergine (eggplant) purée

This dish has many names: *köpoglu* in Turkey, *zelen hajver* in Bulgaria, *srpski ajvar* in Serbia. Throughout the Balkans it is regarded as 'poor man's caviare' and all who prepare it are agreed on one point – the aubergines must be roasted until the skin blackens and burns to give the purée its characteristic flavour. Some people add garlic to this Turkish version; the Rumanians garnish it with black olives; the Serbs include diced red peppers and the Bulgarians always add pounded garlic and crushed walnuts to the paste.

serves 4

- 1 lb/450 g aubergine (eggplant)
- 1 onion, finely chopped
- 1–2 teaspoons salt
- pinch pepper
- about 3 tablespoons olive oil
- 1 tablespoon chopped parsley
- 2 tablespoons lemon juice

Spear the aubergines on toasting forks or kitchen forks and roast over a coal or gas flame – or failing this under an electric grill (broiler) – for 5–10 minutes. Keep turning them so that all the skin is charred. Then put into a paper bag, seal and leave for 15 minutes. The skin can now be peeled off easily. Cut the flesh into small pieces and mash until smooth.

Add the onion and pound in a mortar or reduce in a blender until the mixture is smooth. Add the salt and pepper and beat in enough oil to produce the consistency of mayonnaise. Stir in the parsley and finally the lemon juice.

Serve with chunks of bread.

Biber Yoğurtlu
Peppers with yoghurt

On a summer's day, eat this Turkish pepper salad as an appetizer. In Bulgaria the same dish is served with a glass of *slivova rakiya* (plum brandy). Try serving it as a hot side dish. Choose fleshy peppers.

Grill (broil) the peppers until the skins blacken and crack, then wrap in paper or place in a covered saucepan for 5 minutes; this makes it easier to peel them. Pull off the skin. Cut the pepper flesh into thin strips.

Heat the oil in a frying pan and lightly sauté the peppers, then cool in a shallow bowl. Pound the garlic in a mortar with a pinch of salt, mix with the yoghurt and pour over the peppers. Sprinkle with salt to taste.

serves 4–6

- 6 large peppers, cored and seeded
- 2 tablespoons olive oil
- 1 clove garlic, peeled
- salt
- 10 fl oz/300 ml/1¼ cups plain yoghurt

Patlıcan Tavası
Aubergine (eggplant) with yoghurt

All over the Balkans this summer dish is eaten hot or cold, either on its own as a main course or as one of a selection of dishes offered before the main course.

Wipe the aubergines and, without peeling, cut across or lengthways into slices. Sprinkle generously with salt and set the slices tilted on a tray or large plate for about 1 hour, then drain. Their somewhat bitter juices will drain off, and also the slices will need less oil for frying.

Heat plenty of oil in a frying pan, add the aubergine slices and fry until brown on both sides. Drain on kitchen paper. Serve either hot or cold with the yoghurt mixed with the pounded garlic poured on top.

serves 4

- 1 lb/450 g aubergine (eggplant)
- salt
- olive oil
- 15 fl oz/450 ml/1¾ cups plain yoghurt
- 2–3 cloves garlic, peeled and very finely chopped

Tarator
Cucumber and yoghurt soup

On a hot day serve your friends *tarator* and rice and follow it with *banitza*† and *feta* cheese.

In Bulgaria every household has a *gavanka* – a wooden pestle and mortar – kept especially for pounding garlic and making *tarator*.

Pound the garlic in a mortar with a pinch of salt. Add the walnuts, reserving a few for garnish, and continue pounding. Add the bread and pound together until smooth. Dilute this very thick paste with most of the olive oil. Transfer to a soup tureen or large bowl.

Gradually add the yoghurt, beating with a wooden spoon. Stir in enough cold water to give the consistency of thin cream. Mix in the cucumber. Crush the reserved walnuts and scatter on top, then sprinkle with the dill. Float 1–2 teaspoons olive oil on top like little eyes. A few minutes before serving, add the ice cubes.

serves 6–8

- 2–3 cloves garlic, peeled
- salt
- 4 oz/110 g/1 cup shelled walnuts
- 4 oz/110 g/½ cup bread, soaked in water and squeezed
- 2–3 tablespoons olive oil
- 2 pints/1.1 litres/5 cups plain yoghurt
- 1 large cucumber, peeled and chopped fairly finely
- 2 tablespoons chopped fresh dill
- ice cubes or crushed ice

Fasolado
Bean soup

Inexpensive bean soups are served throughout the Balkans and differ only slightly from this Greek version. In Bulgaria, the dish is known as Monk's Soup. In some other parts it is known as Poor Man's Soup – and as such it is eaten at least once a week.

serves 4–6

1 lb/450 g/2 cups dried haricot (white) beans
2 slices celeriac, chopped
2 large onions, chopped
2 large carrots, chopped
2–3 tablespoons tomato paste
5 fl oz/150 ml/⅔ cup olive oil
2 tablespoons chopped flat-leaved parsley
salt and pepper

Soak the beans overnight in plenty of cold water to cover. Next day rinse well in a colander under running water. Put into a large pan with 6 pints/3.4 litres/12 cups cold water and bring to the boil. Drain off and discard this water, then pour on the same quantity of water, bring to the boil and simmer very gently over a low heat until the beans are cooked – about 1 hour.

Add the celeriac, onions, carrots, tomato paste, oil and parsley and continue to cook slowly until the beans and vegetables are tender. Season with salt and pepper to taste.

You can serve the soup as it is, but the Greeks prefer it sieved. You can also sprinkle some finely chopped parsley on top as a garnish.

In Bulgaria a bottle of wine vinegar is always placed on the table when this soup is served. Each person adds his own vinegar, salt and pepper.

Kartofi sus Sirene
Baked potatoes and cheese

Ingredients that are always to hand in the larder combine in this very old Bulgarian recipe – a favourite evening dish all over the Balkans. The *sirene* cheese can be replaced by grated Cheddar. It makes a delicious and healthy supper dish.

serves 4–6

2 lb/900 g large potatoes, peeled and sliced thinly
12 oz/350 g/¾ lb *sirene* (*feta*) cheese, crumbled
4 oz/110 g/½ cup butter, softened
pepper
3 eggs
10 fl oz/300 ml/1¼ cups plain yoghurt

Arrange about a third of the potatoes over the bottom of a deep buttered baking dish. Beat the cheese and butter together until smooth and spread half the mixture over the potatoes. Sprinkle with pepper, then repeat these layers and arrange the remaining potatoes on top; dot with butter.

Bake in a pre-heated oven at 350° F/180° C/gas mark 4 for about 30 minutes or until the potatoes are softening.

Beat the eggs and yoghurt together to make a smooth mixture and pour it over the potatoes. Bake for a further 30 minutes to set the egg mixture and brown the top lightly.

Serve as a main dish with a green salad.

Türlü Güveç
Mixed vegetable casserole

This famous dish is common to all Balkan countries. Its names in the different countries are variants of the Turkish *güveç*, the earthenware casserole in which the vegetables are baked. The Turkish *türlü* means 'of all sorts' and refers to the mixture of ingredients. In the vine-growing regions of the Balkans the cook might add a handful of unripened green grapes for extra zest. In Bulgaria they add 2–3 chilli peppers and in Greece they may put in a few cloves of garlic. This recipe gives the classic proportions and ingredients.

serves 4–6

- 1 medium aubergine (eggplant), unpeeled and cut into cubes
- 4 oz/110 g okra, with stalks removed but pods unpierced (optional)
- 4–5 tomatoes, sliced into rounds
- 4 medium courgettes, unpeeled, sliced into rounds
- 11 oz/300 g/2 cups young dwarf green beans, fresh or frozen, trimmed and chopped into 2–3 pieces
- 11 oz/300 g/¾ cup shelled fresh peas, blanched, or frozen peas
- 2 medium onions, finely chopped
- 1 lb/450 g potatoes, peeled and cut into medium chunks
- 1½ lb/700 g peeled fresh or canned tomatoes
- 1 large green pepper, seeded and sliced
- 1 large bunch flat-leaved parsley, finely chopped
- 4–5 teaspoons salt
- 2 teaspoons paprika
- 5–6 tablespoons oil

Put the aubergine cubes in a colander, sprinkle lightly with salt and leave for 1 hour for the bitter juices to drain off.

If you cannot obtain any okra, the dish will still be full of flavour. If you can obtain it, remove the stalks with a short-bladed knife; run it round the leaf-rosette cap to remove the cap and stalk and leave a dome-shaped end. Do not slice open or pierce the pods as this will let the sticky juices seep out into the sauce.

Keep the sliced tomatoes on one side, then put all the other vegetables and the parsley in a large earthenware casserole or terrine. Season with the salt and paprika and pour over 4 tablespoons of the oil. Mix all the ingredients thoroughly; many cooks prefer to do this with their hands. Arrange the tomato rounds on top. Sprinkle with the remaining oil and smooth the surface with the back of the spoon.

Bake in a pre-heated oven at 375° F/190° C/gas mark 5 for 1–1¼ hours, until the tomatoes on top have browned. There should be only a very little sauce left in the casserole. Serve in the cooking dish either hot or cold, with fresh soft bread, such as *pogača*†.

Tyropitta
Layered pastry with cheese

This great dish is part of the national cuisine of all Balkan countries – *tyropitta* to the Greeks, *tepsi böreği* to the Turks, *banica* or *gibanica sa sirom* to the Yugoslavs, *banitza sus sirene* to the Bulgarians, *pita sa sirom* to the Macedonians. The paper-thin pastry sheets are widely available in pastry shops and bakeries in the Balkans; they are also available in Britain as *phyllo* (strudel) pastry. *Phyllo* is Greek for leaf.

serves 6

1½ oz/40 g/3 tablespoons unsalted butter
2 tablespoons oil
12 oz/300 g/¾ lb *phyllo* pastry

for the filling:
3 eggs, separated
3 tablespoons plain yoghurt
7 oz/200 g/1 packed cup *feta* cheese, crumbled with a fork

Melt the butter in a bowl over hot water, stir in the oil and keep the mixture warm. Use it to brush the inside of a roasting tin about 8 × 11 in/20 × 28 cm. Set the oven at 425° F/220° C/gas mark 7.

To prepare the filling, whisk the egg yolks with the yoghurt, then stir in the cheese and fold in the stiffly whisked egg whites.

Place a sheet of pastry in the tin, easing it into light folds before you trim off any excess. If the sheet is not big enough, patch it with a piece from another sheet. Sprinkle this layer with a brush dipped in the warm fat. Arrange a second layer of pastry on top, again gathering it into light folds; this introduces height and air into the dish, and allows for the expansion of the eggs during cooking. Sprinkle again with the warm fat, then scatter on 1–2 tablespoons of the filling.

Continue placing layer after layer of pastry in the tin, sprinkling each layer with warm fat and every second layer with filling – all this is much easier done than said. Place the best-looking sheet of pastry on top, gathering it only slightly. Brush it with the fat. Heat any remaining fat and pour it over the top.

Place the tin on a high shelf in the pre-heated oven and immediately lower the temperature to 350° F/180° C/ gas mark 4. Bake for 45 minutes, or until well browned, then remove from the oven, lift one edge of the pastry with a palette knife and look underneath. If it is lightly browned from the edge right to the centre, it is done; if not, cook for a further few minutes.

Cover with a tray or foil for 5–10 minutes, no more, to allow the pastry to soften slightly. Cut into 12 pieces and serve warm as a light supper with tea.

Alternatively, you can slice the *tyropitta* into small fingers to serve as *meze* (snacks) with salted roast walnuts or almonds and drinks.

Yumurta Çılbır
Poached eggs with yoghurt

When only eggs and yoghurt are left in the larder, this is the natural dish to prepare. Use this Turkish recipe to make a light supper dish and serve it with bread.

serves 6

2 pints/1.1 litres/5 cups plain yoghurt
2 cloves garlic, peeled and finely chopped
salt
1 tablespoon white wine vinegar
6 eggs
½ oz/15 g/1 tablespoon butter
paprika

Beat the yoghurt, garlic, salt and vinegar together and pour into a deep serving dish or into individual dishes.

Poach the eggs, drain them and trim the edges, then drop very gently into the yoghurt. Melt the butter in a small pan, sprinkling in just enough paprika to give it a good colour. Spoon over the yoghurt.

Serve the eggs hot or cold.

Riba s Kiselo Zele
Fish with sauerkraut

Every autumn when white cabbages are heaped on the market stalls, Bulgarians make a barrel of sauerkraut to keep in the cellar for use throughout the winter. They add it to many dishes including this one. Use any fresh fish; herrings and mackerel are very good as well as any firm-fleshed white fish.

serves 4

4 fl oz/125 ml/½ cup oil
2 lb/900 g sauerkraut†
6 tablespoons fine dry breadcrumbs
2 lb/900 g fish, cleaned
paprika

Rub a baking dish with oil, spread the well-rinsed sauerkraut over the bottom and sprinkle on the breadcrumbs. Lay on the fish and pour the remaining oil over it. Sprinkle generously with paprika, cover and bake in a pre-heated oven at 350° F/180° C/gas mark 4 until the fish is cooked through. The cooking time depends on which fish you use. Serve with bread.

Mousaka s Patladzhani
Aubergine (eggplant) moussaka

This traditional recipe from Bulgaria is prepared in a similar way throughout the Balkans. The name of the dish sounds the same in the various Balkan languages – with the stress on the last syllable – though the spelling varies. The Greek moussaka often has garlic added to the meat mixture. If you like, you can cook all the ingredients in advance, refrigerate them until the following day and then quickly assemble them for baking.

serves 6

2 aubergines (eggplants), unpeeled, cut lengthways into ½ in/1.25 cm slices
salt
18 oz/500 g courgettes (zucchini), unpeeled, sliced across into ½ in/1.25 cm rounds
4 onions, finely chopped
1½ lb/700 g potatoes, peeled and cut into ¼ in/5 mm slices
oil for frying
7 oz/200 g/1½ cups tomato paste
2¼ lb/1 kg lean lamb or veal, minced (ground)
2 teaspoons paprika
2 bunches flat-leaved parsley
1 teaspoon black peppercorns, crushed
2–3 eggs, lightly beaten
6 tablespoons plain yoghurt

Sprinkle the aubergine slices lightly with salt and arrange tilted in a colander to stand for 1 hour while the bitter juices drain off. Pat dry.

Fry the aubergines, courgettes, onions and potatoes separately in the oil. If you are not baking the dish straight away, cool the fried vegetables, cover and refrigerate until needed. Heat a little more oil and stir in the tomato paste for a few seconds until it turns a dark red. Add the meat, season generously with salt, add the paprika, and stir-fry for about 5 minutes, until the meat changes colour. If not for immediate use, cool, cover and refrigerate.

Start assembling the dish about 1 hour before serving time. Cut away the stalks of the parsley bunches and chop the rest finely. Add to the meat together with the peppercorns and onions and stir until the ingredients are combined.

In a large baking dish, arrange alternating layers of vegetables and meat, starting and finishing with a layer of potatoes and using the smaller rounds of courgette to fill any odd corners. Sprinkle each layer with salt. Press down the top layer of potatoes with the back of a spoon. There should be enough juice in the meat and vegetables to appear on the surface and colour the top potato layer; if there is not, add a little warm water or the moussaka will be dry.

Bake in a pre-heated oven at 375° F/190° C/gas mark 5 for 30 minutes. Then pour the eggs over the moussaka and return to the oven for a further 15 minutes, or until golden brown on top.

Slice with a knife into portions and serve on well-heated plates, with a tablespoon of yoghurt at the edge of each plate.

Köfte
Fried burgers

The Turkish term *köfte*, Persian in origin, means a food that has been finely chopped. The name appears in all the Balkan countries (*keftes* in Greece, *kyufte* in Bulgaria, *ćufte* in Yugoslavia) – and indeed in the *kofta kebab* of the Middle East. The basic recipe is the same in all the countries but the herbs and spices added may vary according to country, or to season. The Greeks add a crushed clove of garlic or a tablespoon of wine; the Bulgarians add dried crumbled summer savory when fresh parsley is out of season.

serves 4

- 1 thick slice of bread, crusts removed
- 1 egg
- 2 oz/50 g/1 tablespoon onion, finely chopped or grated
- 1–1½ teaspoons salt
- ½ teaspoon freshly ground black pepper
- 2 tablespoons finely chopped fresh flat-leaved parsley, or ½ teaspoon dried crumbled thyme, mint or summer savory
- 18 oz/500 g/2 packed cups lean lamb or veal, finely chopped
- flour for coating
- oil for frying

Soak the bread for a few seconds in a little water, squeeze it lightly and put into a bowl. Mash it with a fork, then drop in the egg and the onion and season with the salt and pepper. Stir in the parsley (or dried herb), then beat the mixture with the fork. Add the meat and mix in thoroughly with your hands. Pat down to level the surface, cover and put in the refrigerator for at least 1 hour.

Now divide the mixture into 8 pieces. Wet the palms of your hands with water and shape each piece into a flattened ball. Dip both sides of the burgers into the flour.

Pour oil into a large frying pan to a depth of ½ in/1.25 cm and set over a medium heat until very hot. Slip in the burgers and fry for about 2 minutes on each side to brown and seal the surfaces. If the oil is not hot enough they may stick or take too long to brown. Lower the heat and fry for about 5 more minutes on each side until cooked through.

Serve hot with beans (flavoured with a little fat left from frying) or boiled potatoes, or both. Sometimes *köfte* are garnished with buttered noodles and pickled peppers or pickled chilli peppers.

You can use the same meat mixture, seasoned more heavily with salt, to shape into miniature meatballs, the size of hazelnuts. Roll them in flour and fry in the same way. They are served throughout the Balkans as *meze* (snacks) with drinks.

Punjeni Paprike i Paradajz
Stuffed peppers and tomatoes

This dish is popular not only in the Balkans but in the Mediterranean area and throughout the Middle East – wherever peppers and tomatoes abound. This Macedonian version, and the Bulgarian version, are the only ones to enrich the cooking liquid with eggs and yoghurt. It makes the dish especially delicious.

serves 4

4 green peppers, weighing about 4 oz/110 g each
4 large, firm tomatoes, weighing about 5 oz/150 g each
2–3 teaspoons flour
1 oz/25 g/2 tablespoons butter
2 teaspoons tomato paste
½ teaspoon paprika
4–5 tablespoons water
salt

for the stuffing:
1–2 tablespoons oil
5 oz/150 g/3 tablespoons finely chopped onion
9 oz/250 g/1 cup lean lamb or beef, minced (ground)
1 oz/25 g/2 tablespoons short grain rice
1 teaspoon salt
1 teaspoon paprika
3–4 tablespoons stock or water
2 tablespoons chopped parsley
1 tablespoon chopped mint leaves
½ teaspoon black peppercorns, cracked or ground

for the sauce:
4 fl oz/125 ml/½ cup plain yoghurt
2 egg yolks, or 1 whole egg
1 rounded tablespoon flour
4 tablespoons water
salt and freshly ground pepper

Cut round the stalks of the peppers with a thin, sharp knife, remove them and carefully take out the cores with the seeds and the inner ribs. Cover the peppers with boiling salted water and keep them immersed for about 15 minutes. Rinse well, sprinkle inside with a little salt and leave to drain.

Wash the tomatoes, slice off the stem ends and scoop out the pulp with the seeds and the ribs. Do not salt the tomato shells; just invert them to drain in a colander. Chop the tomato pulp with the seeds and set aside.

To prepare the stuffing, heat the oil in a saucepan and brown the onion in it lightly. Put in the meat and fry until it changes colour. Add the rice, the reserved tomato pulp, the salt, paprika and stock. Stir well, then simmer, covered, for 10 minutes, or until the rice is partially cooked and most of the liquid has been absorbed. Remove from the heat and stir in the parsley, mint and pepper.

Oil an ovenproof serving dish just large enough to hold the vegetables. Spoon the stuffing loosely into the peppers and tomatoes, leaving room for it to expand as the rice swells. Arrange the vegetables in the dish, standing upright and just touching one another. If there is any stuffing left, spoon it into the gaps. Top the vegetables with a dusting of flour and dot with butter. Some cooks like to replace the cut-off stem ends as lids, but the vegetables taste much better and are nicely browned on top when baked without lids.

Blend the tomato paste and paprika with the water, season lightly with salt and pour round the vegetables. Bake in a pre-heated oven at 350° F/180° C/gas mark 4 for 50 minutes, or until the tops are browned. There should be a fair amount of cooking liquid in the dish, released by the tomatoes.

When the dish has been in the oven for 30 minutes, start preparing the sauce. Beat the yoghurt in a small saucepan with a wooden spoon until creamy. Drop in the egg yolks and beat until well blended. Sprinkle the flour over the whole surface of the mixture (it will not go lumpy) and beat again. Add the water, stir briskly, then season with salt and pepper. Place the pan over a very low heat and cook gently, stirring all the time, until the mixture is just thick enough to coat the spoon. Do not allow the sauce to become too thick.

Pour the sauce over and round the vegetables and shake the dish a few times to blend the sauce and cooking liquid; do not stir or you might split open the vegetables. Return the dish to the oven for another 10–15 minutes, or until the sauce is heated through and begins to bubble.

You can cook this dish on top of the stove, but its flavour will not be as good as when it is baked in the oven.

Serve the stuffed vegetables not too hot, with either hot herb or garlic bread, or a bowl of plain boiled rice. If any of the vegetables are left, take them out of the sauce; store the vegetables and sauce separately in the refrigerator until the following day.

Yahniya ot Spanak
Lamb with spinach

This Bulgarian recipe is typical of a very light stew eaten throughout the Balkans in spring when spinach and lamb come into season at the same time. During the cooking each releases its juices, often with enough liquid to braise the dish, but add a little water if necessary.

serves 4–6

- 2 lb/900 g stewing lamb
- salt and pepper
- 3 tablespoons oil
- 1 bunch spring onions or scallions, or more to taste, trimmed
- 2 lb/900 g spinach, picked over and washed
- 4–5 fl oz/125–150 ml/½–⅔ cup plain yoghurt

Wash the meat but do not dry it. Sprinkle it lightly with salt and cut it into cubes. Heat the oil in a flameproof casserole and add the meat and onions. Do not let them fry but cover at once and simmer gently for about 1 hour. Break the spinach leaves into small pieces and add to the casserole for the last 15 minutes of cooking. Taste and season as necessary with salt and pepper.

Serve with a tablespoon of yoghurt on each plate.

Şiş Kebap (Shish Kebab)
Skewered lamb grilled over charcoal

Grilling meat in the open on a wooden or metal spit over embers or in front of a fire is one of the most ancient cooking methods, and one used by all nomadic peoples. Grilling on skewers, which is spit-roasting in miniature, came many years later.

Cubes of spring lamb, skewered and grilled over charcoal, are served throughout the Balkans under a variety of names. The meat is served on the skewer and garnished with chopped raw onion, which need not be eaten but imparts an authentic flavour to the meat.

serves 4

- 2¼ lb/1 kg lamb from the leg or loin, cut into 1 in/2.5 cm cubes
- 2 tablespoons oil
- 1 teaspoon black peppercorns, coarsely crushed
- salt
- 1 large onion, finely chopped, or a bunch of spring onions or scallions, chopped
- 1 tablespoon finely chopped parsley

Sprinkle the meat cubes with oil and pepper and leave to stand at room temperature while the charcoal grill heats.

Thread the meat on to 4 large, or 8 small, flat-bladed skewers, arranging the pieces so that they are touching each other. Place the skewers on a greased, pre-heated rack close to the embers and cook for about 5 minutes, turning frequently. When the meat is seared on all sides, reduce the heat by raising the rack and cook for another 5–10 minutes. Season with salt to taste and serve, still on the skewers, on heated plates or wooden platters. Mix the onion with the parsley, and just before serving, sprinkle on some salt. Use the mixture to garnish the skewers. A good accompaniment to this dish is a crisp green salad.

To vary the dish, you can make *shashlik* (often, mistakenly, also called shish kebab) by alternating the lamb cubes with pieces of pepper, tomato, onion, mushroom or courgette (zucchini). The meat is less succulent as the vegetables have a drying effect; but the grilled vegetables are delicious and this is a centuries old method of making the meat go further.

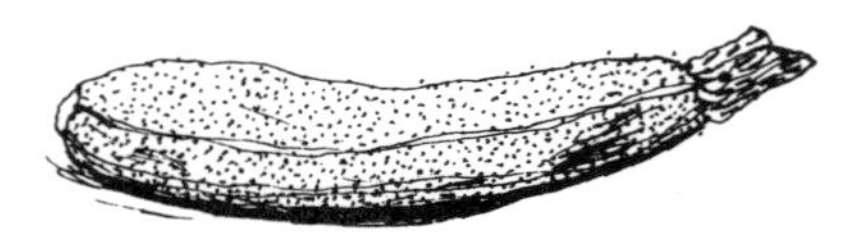

Bosanski Lonac
Bosnian stew

In Yugoslavian villages this aromatic peasant stew usually includes a mixture of different meats. The proportions of all the ingredients depend on what is available. A deep terracotta pot or *lonac*, with the meat and vegetables arranged in layers, is the traditional vessel for it, but any large, tightly lidded, flameproof pot will do. The stew goes straight to the table in its cooking pot.

serves 8–10

2 lb/900 g mixed beef, lamb, pork or veal, for stewing
4 oz/110 g speck or very fat bacon, in one piece
2 lb/900 g potatoes
carrots to taste
parsnips to taste
2–3 large onions
4–5 garlic cloves, peeled but whole
mixed green herbs to taste, coarsely chopped (such as parsley, thyme and chives)
salt and pepper
1 pint/575 ml/2½ cups dry white wine

Wipe the meat and cut into large cubes. Put the speck or bacon into the casserole and cook over a moderate heat until the fat runs. Fry the meat until brown. Add the potatoes, peeled and quartered, or left whole if small. Peel and slice the carrots, parsnips and onions and add to the pot with the garlic and herbs. Season with salt and pepper and pour on the wine. Cover and cook very slowly over a low heat for about 2–3 hours or until the meat is tender and the stew has an appetizing aroma.

Bosanska Kalja od Kapusa
White cabbage casserole

A common everyday lunch in the Balkans is a filling meat and cabbage stew. In this Yugoslavian recipe you can use either mutton or pork, but you need one of the heavy white cabbages to provide the cooking juices, and a well-fitting lid to keep them in.

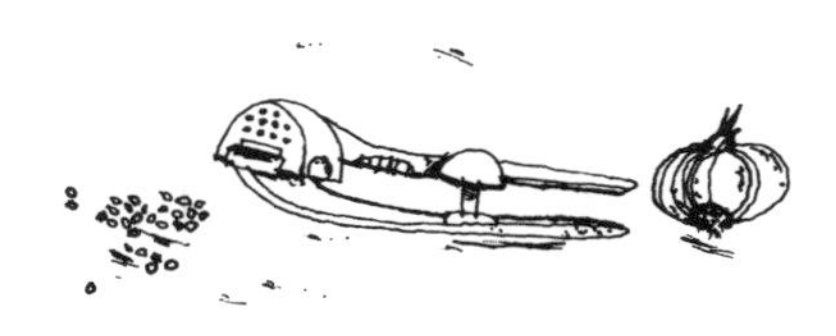

serves 6–8

3 oz/75 g/6 tablespoons fat or oil
2 lb/900 g stewing mutton or pork, cut into cubes
1 large onion, finely chopped
1 medium white cabbage, trimmed and cut into chunks
salt and pepper
paprika
3–5 cloves garlic, peeled and finely chopped
3–5 tomatoes, peeled and sliced

Heat the fat in a heavy flameproof casserole and put the meat in to brown over a high heat, stirring all the time and adding the onion when the meat begins to brown. When both are well coloured, lift out and set aside. Put a layer of cabbage in the dish, sprinkle with salt, pepper, paprika and garlic, and then add a layer of the meat and onion.

Repeat these layers until the ingredients are used up. Lay the tomatoes over the top, sprinkle lightly with salt, pepper and paprika, then cover tightly and cook over a very low heat for 2–3 hours, or until the meat is tender. Do not disturb the stew while it is cooking but shake the dish gently now and again to make sure there is still enough liquid. Water should not be needed but add just a little if the stew seems to be sticking.

Serve with bread and follow with a light dessert.

Kotopoulo Kapama
Greek chicken and tomato casserole

Throughout the Balkans, everybody has their own chicken and tomato dish. The success of this dish depends on using the rich, fleshy tomatoes that grow there and in Mediterranean countries. Canned Italian tomatoes make a good substitute.

serves 4–6

juice of 1 lemon
pinch of ground cloves
½ teaspoon ground cinnamon
salt and pepper
1 large chicken, jointed (cut up)
4 fl oz/125 ml/½ cup olive oil
6 tomatoes, peeled and chopped
2 tablespoons tomato paste
1 pint/575 ml/2½ cups hot water

Mix together the lemon juice, cloves, cinnamon, salt and pepper and rub well into the chicken pieces. Heat the oil in a large saucepan and fry the chicken in it until golden brown.

Lift out and keep hot while you stir the tomatoes and tomato paste into the oil; gradually stir in the hot water and cook over a gentle heat until the tomatoes are mushy and the sauce thick.

Return the chicken pieces to the pan, turn each piece over and over until coated with the sauce and then cover the pan. Cook over a very low heat for about 45 minutes, or until the flesh begins to fall off the bones. Serve with plain boiled rice.

Pui Gatit cu Vin si Masline
Chicken with wine and olive sauce

The Rumanian word *pui* denotes a very tender young chicken, but the wine and yoghurt ensure that any bird cooked in this way will be tender. You can use chicken pieces instead of jointing a whole chicken. Vary the herbs to suit your own taste.

serves 4–6

1 clove garlic, halved
6 tablespoons olive oil
1 roasting chicken, jointed
1 oz/25 g/1 tablespoon flour
chopped chives, fennel, parsley to taste
15 fl oz/450 ml/2 cups dry white wine
4 fl oz/125 ml/½ cup plain yoghurt
12–18 black olives, stoned
salt and pepper

Rub a deep frying pan with the garlic, then heat 4 tablespoons of the oil in it and add the chicken. Fry until just brown, then lift out and keep hot.

Pour the remaining oil into the pan and heat it. Stir in the flour and cook, still stirring, for 2–3 minutes. Add the chives, fennel and parsley and fry until they soften. Gradually stir in the wine. After 5 minutes add the yoghurt and olives, stir again and return the chicken to the pan. Season with salt and pepper to taste and continue cooking gently for about 45 minutes, or until the chicken is tender. Serve with rice.

Ratza cu Varza Acra
Duck with sauerkraut

Duck is a good choice when you are celebrating a special occasion or having a party of friends to dinner. This typical Rumanian dish combines it with cabbage – often sauerkraut, rather than fresh cabbage – to counteract the fattiness of the duck. Chicken pieces, pork chops or lamb cutlets can also be cooked in this way. The flavour improves with keeping, so try to make the dish a day in advance and reheat thoroughly to serve.

serves 3–4

2 oz/50 g/4 tablespoons butter
1 large duck, cut into pieces
salt and pepper
cayenne pepper
paprika
about 10 fl oz/300 ml/1¼ cups warm water
1½ lb/700 g sauerkraut
2 tablespoons tomato paste
3 medium onions, sliced
4 large tomatoes, sliced

Heat half the butter in a deep frying pan, add the duck pieces and fry until brown. Shake the pan from time to time to prevent burning. Season with salt and pepper and add cayenne pepper and paprika to taste. Stir gently, then add the water to prevent burning. Continue cooking over a gentle heat.

Put the sauerkraut in a colander or sieve and rinse thoroughly under cold running water to remove the salt. Drain it and squeeze well to remove all the liquid. Heat the remaining butter in another pan, add the sauerkraut and fry it carefully for 10–15 minutes, stirring frequently to turn it over. Thin the tomato paste with a little water and stir it into the sauerkraut.

Spread the sauerkraut over the bottom of a large casserole and cover with the duck and its juices. Put the onions on top and season with salt and pepper, then spread with the sliced tomatoes. Cover and cook in a pre-heated oven at 350° F/180° C/gas mark 4 for about 1 hour, or until the duck is quite tender; the exact time will depend on the age of the duck, but you can hardly overcook this dish.

Serve with boiled potatoes, rice or dumplings.

Prepelice s Pirinčem
Quail with rice

Yugoslavs have the benefit of wild quail for this moist rice dish, but you will probably be using specially reared quail. It is a matter of appetite how many quail you use; two per person is about right.

serves 4

- 3 oz/75 g/6 tablespoons butter
- 4–8 quail
- 1 small onion, finely chopped
- 2 green peppers, deseeded and diced
- 8 oz/225 g/1 cup short grain rice
- 2 medium tomatoes, peeled and chopped
- parsley to taste, coarsely chopped
- salt
- 1 pint/575 ml/2½ cups water

Heat the butter in a large saucepan and fry the quail in it until browned all over, then lift out and keep warm. Add the onion to the pan and cook until it begins to colour, then add the peppers and fry for a few minutes. Put in the rice and stir well while it fries for about 5 minutes. Add the tomatoes, put back the quail and sprinkle on the parsley. Season with salt and let the dish simmer for about 5 minutes before pouring in the water. Cover and simmer very gently until the rice is tender.

You can make the dish in a flameproof casserole instead of a pan, and, when the water is added, cover the casserole and finish cooking in a pre-heated oven at 325° F/170° C/gas mark 3 for 25 minutes. Serve with a green salad.

Yoghurt

Yoghurt, which is simply milk thickened by bacteria, is easy to make at home. This Bulgarian recipe makes a particularly good yoghurt; it uses only a small amount of starter and this produces little acidity or sour taste. An electric yoghurt-maker and a kitchen thermometer help, but you can manage just as well without them. Make sure that all your pots and utensils are spotlessly clean and rinsed with boiling water to prevent the introduction of undesirable bacteria.

serves 4

2½ pints/1.4 litres/6¼ cups milk
½–1 teaspoon plain live yoghurt, preferably home-made

Pour the milk into a wide, shallow enamelled or fireproof glass pan; do not use a metal pan. Bring the milk almost to the boil, then simmer gently over the lowest possible heat for 15–30 minutes, or until the milk is reduced by a third in volume. During this simmering the temperature of the milk should be 194–203° F/ 90–95° C; the milk will be barely moving, with only occasional bubbles rising to the surface.

Take the milk off the heat and leave it to cool to 115° F/46° C. At this temperature you can place your hands round the pan and count slowly to 20 without it feeling too hot; the pan should also feel pleasantly hot to your lips.

Mix the yoghurt until smooth, then gradually add a few tablespoons of the milk, stirring to blend. Pour back into the milk and stir or whisk to distribute the starter evenly. Cover with the lid, then wrap the pan in a sheet of plastic and a thick cloth and put in a warm place overnight.

Next day cool the yoghurt quickly without shaking it; you can cool it in a large container of iced water. Serve it after 4 hours or within 2–3 days; after that it will become progressively sourer.

Mamaliga Felii Prajita
Fried polenta slices

serves 4

4 slices *mamaliga*† (polenta)
1 egg, beaten
2–3 oz/50–75 g/¾ cup grated cheese
butter for frying
5 fl oz/150 ml/⅔ cup plain yoghurt or sour cream

In Rumania, where they eat *mamaliga* as often as the Scots eat porridge, a host of different ways of serving it have been devised. This is a way of turning left-over *mamaliga* into a simple and nourishing hot dish. You can use a full-flavoured hard cheese such as Parmesan or Pecorino, which is a piquant ewe's milk cheese, similar to the one used in Rumania.

Dip the slices of *mamaliga* in the egg, then coat generously on both sides with the cheese, patting it on well. Heat the butter and fry the slices on both sides until browned.

Serve very hot with the yoghurt or sour cream spooned over the slices.

Bulgur Pilâvı
Cracked wheat pilaf

serves 2–3

- 1 large onion, finely chopped
- 2 tablespoons oil
- 7 oz/200 g/¾ cup *bulgur* (cracked wheat)
- about 12 fl oz/350 ml/1½ cups hot lamb or chicken stock
- salt
- 2 oz/50 g/¼ cup pine nuts or blanched almonds, chopped
- 1 tablespoon sultanas (golden raisins) (optional)

The Balkan peoples, especially in the small towns and villages, eat a considerable amount of barley, oats or wheat that has been hulled and then either left whole or pounded to varying degrees of fineness. *Bulgur* is wheat treated in this way. Nowadays *bulgur* is produced commercially by machines where formerly it was made by hand. It is sold in specialist shops in Britain and America, often in Greek shops, where it may be called *pourgouri*.

This classic Turkish recipe goes well with grilled or fried meat, as an alternative to rice or noodles.

Brown the onion in the oil. Stir in the *bulgur* and fry for a few seconds. Add the stock and a little salt, cover with a lid and bring to the boil. Simmer gently for about 20 minutes, adding a little more stock, or hot water, if necessary. Check the seasoning and stir in the nuts and sultanas. Leave covered for 10–15 minutes, until all the stock has been absorbed. Serve in individual heated bowls.

If you want to make it into a main course, add pieces of boiled boned lamb or chicken to the stock.

Trahana
Shredded pasta

serves 4 (or 8–10 in soup)

- 9 oz/250 g/2 cups strong bread flour
- ½ teaspoon salt
- 1 egg, lightly beaten (optional)

Trahana is the simple and easily prepared Balkan version of pasta. This stiff flour-and-water dough, chopped, rubbed or shredded and originally dried in the sun, has been known in Mongolia, Persia and the Caucasus since time immemorial. It was brought to the Balkans by migrating tribes and became part of the staple diet.

This recipe is the version used in many towns and villages of Bulgaria – and also in Transylvania, where it is called *tarhonya*. You can use all white flour or a wholewheat and white flour mix. It is easy to make and as versatile as any other pasta.

Put the flour into a large bowl. Make a well in the centre, add the salt and the beaten egg, if used, and stir in enough water to bind the mixture to a very firm dough. Knead it thoroughly, then set aside for 10–15 minutes to dry a little. Grate the dough either coarsely or medium finely, over a pastry board, moving the grater so that the strands of dough are well spread out over the board. Separate the strands with two forks. Leave them as they are, or chop them lightly into smaller pieces.

The *trahana* was traditionally dried in the sun for 2–3 days but you can dry it in a very low oven. Before storing, test to see that it is completely dried out by placing in a roasting tin, covering with a sheet of glass or plastic and leaving in a warm room for a few hours. There should be no moisture droplets on the underside of the sheet.

Shake the *trahana* gently in a sieve to rid it of any tiny grains. Store as any other pasta in an air-tight jar in a cool, dry place. It will keep for at least 6 months.

To cook the *trahana*, drop it into boiling salted water and boil uncovered for 8–10 minutes, until soft except for a slightly firm core. Alternatively, fry in a little butter or onion-flavoured oil, then allow to swell in hot stock, milk or water.

It is traditionally served mixed with crumbled white cheese and topped with melted butter lightly coloured with paprika. But you can also serve it, like any pasta, in a variety of ways as a side dish or main meal: with vegetables, black olives, shrimps, grated cheese, pieces of meat or scrambled eggs.

Dyo-M' Ena Pilafi
Two-in-one pilaf

This savoury dish of rice is often used as the base for *souvlakia* (shish kebab).

serves 4

2 cups water or light stock
1 teaspoon salt
1 cup long grain rice
butter to taste

Bring the water or stock to the boil, add the salt, and then stir in the rice. Cook over a high heat for 2 minutes before lowering the heat to maintain a simmer. Wrap the pan lid in a cloth to absorb some of the moisture and put it on the pan. Continue simmering for 15–20 minutes, when the rice will have absorbed the liquid and the grains will have separated.

Heat the butter until it foams, then pour it over the rice and stir lightly with a fork to mix it in. Serve at once.

Instead of adding butter to the pan of rice, you can put the rice into a heated serving dish and place a large knob of butter on top.

Salata Fasolakia
Green bean salad

This summer dish is typical of the whole of the Balkans. Serve with ham or cold meats and potato salad for lunch or a light supper.

serves 4

1 lb/450 g/3 cups French (snap) beans
3 tablespoons olive oil
1 tablespoon lemon juice
salt and black pepper
garlic to taste, crushed

Boil the beans in salted water until just tender, then drain and put into a salad bowl. Add the oil mixed with the crushed garlic and stir well before adding the lemon juice and seasoning lightly with salt and pepper. Serve with grilled meatballs†.

You can vary the salad by including a little peeled and chopped tomato or finely chopped spring onion or scallions, or both.

Lahana Salata
Cabbage salad

This traditional Greek combination of beans with cabbage provides iron in a readily digestible form.

serves 8

1½ lb/700 g white cabbage, shredded
8 oz/225 g/1 cup haricot beans, cooked or canned
4 tablespoons olive oil
3 tablespoons lemon juice or mild wine vinegar
salt and pepper
8 black olives

Put the cabbage and beans into a deep bowl and mix well together. Combine the oil and lemon juice with salt and pepper to taste, blend well and pour over the vegetables. Turn the salad over and over so that it is well coated with the dressing. Garnish with the olives.

Zelena Salata s Kiselim Mlekom
Lettuce salad with yoghurt

This spring salad, popular in Yugoslavia, is cool and refreshing served with a main course for lunch, or with grilled meat in the evening.

serves 4–6

1–2 heads Cos (romaine) lettuce
salt and pepper
pinch sugar
2–3 tablespoons olive oil
10 fl oz/300 ml/1¼ cups plain yoghurt

Pull the lettuce apart and wash thoroughly, discarding any bruised or broken leaves. Dry the leaves well, put them into a salad bowl and sprinkle with salt. Combine the pepper, sugar and oil with the yoghurt, mix well, then pour this dressing over the lettuce. Gently toss the leaves over and over until well coated with the dressing.

Salata od Praziluka
Leek salad

All over the Balkans leeks are kept through the winter. People buy them in the markets and bury them in soil in the garden up to their green tops. The soil will freeze on the surface but beneath it the leeks are protected and kept fresh. This Yugoslavian recipe, identical to the Greek version, gives no exact quantities – all depends on personal taste, but two leeks per person would be plenty. Serve with cold meats, potato salad and green bean salad for lunch or a light supper.

serves 4

leeks
salt and pepper
olive oil
wine vinegar
black olives as a garnish

Clean and trim the leeks, keeping as much of the green as possible. Cut into long strips and cook gently in simmering salted water until just tender but not soft. Drain thoroughly and put in a serving dish. Make a dressing with 3 parts oil to 1 part vinegar and pour over the leeks. Add a generous seasoning of pepper and garnish with the olives.

Savanyú Káposzta
Sauerkraut

One of the oldest methods of preserving vegetables for the winter is by fermenting them in a solution of salt. Sauerkraut, fermented cabbage, is made throughout Europe, and in North Balkan countries is part of the staple winter diet and one of the chief sources of vitamin C. What is *savanyú káposzta* in Hungary is *kiseo kupus* in Yugoslavia, *kiselo zele* in Bulgaria and *varza acra* in Rumania.

The commonest method of preparation is to ferment whole heads of cabbage in wooden barrels, but with a small amount the cabbage is usually shredded. Make the sauerkraut in a large glass sweet jar with a capacity of about 5 pints/2.8 litres/6 US pints. Have ready two well-scrubbed flat strips of wood to fit inside the neck of the jar, and a stone about the size of an apple, sterilized in boiling water for 15 minutes.

makes about 5 pints/2.8 litres/12½ cups

6½ lb/3 kg white cabbage
3 oz/75 g/½ cup rock salt (not sea salt)

Remove the central core from the cabbage and trim off any damaged outer leaves. Wash the cabbage well, reserve 1–2 whole leaves, then slice the remainder finely into long thin shreds. Place on a large tray, sprinkle with the salt and mix thoroughly. Leave to stand for 30 minutes.

Pack the cabbage firmly into the glass jar, pressing each added layer down well with a wooden mallet until juice appears on the surface. Fill the jar to the neck, then fit the reserved whole leaves on top and criss-cross the wooden strips over them to prevent any loose shreds of cabbage from rising to the surface. Lay the stone on the strips of wood to hold them down. Cover the jar loosely and leave in a warm place at a temperature of 64–68° F/18–20° C for 10 days. If any scum should rise, spoon it off. Then move the jar to a cool, dry place where the temperature is 50–54° F/10–12° C. The fermentation should be complete within 10 days.

The sauerkraut is ready to eat 40 days after you first pack it in the jar. Store it in a cold shed or cellar where the temperature is 39–42° F/4–6° C. If you prepare it in the late autumn, it will keep until the end of January.

Each country, even each household, has its own traditional additions to the basic recipe – sliced quinces, a few pieces of beetroot (beet), shredded red cabbage, quartered apples, sliced raw potatoes, lemon wedges, sour green grapes, hot chilli peppers, vine leaves, peppercorns, juniper berries, dill seeds, bay leaves or pieces of horseradish.

Rasol Čorba
Sauerkraut juice soup

serves 4–5

1¾ pints/1 litre/4½ cups sauerkraut juice
1 leek, the white part only, finely chopped
9 oz/250 g/1 cup sauerkraut
2 tablespoons olive oil
1 teaspoon paprika
4–5 dried chilli peppers, lightly grilled (broiled) (optional)

The juice that is produced while sauerkraut ferments is not for discarding. There are those who add a handful or two of crushed dried maize grain (corn kernels) to it to turn it into a pleasant bubbly drink which is thought to be beneficial in dispelling a hangover. A more everyday use for the juice is in a soup such as this one from Yugoslavia. The Bulgarians make it too and call it *armeya chorba*, while the Rumanians call it *ciorba de praz*.

Pour the sauerkraut juice into a soup tureen or large bowl. Slide in the leek and sauerkraut. Add the olive oil and stir. Sprinkle with the paprika. Serve cold or at room temperature with the chilli peppers on a side plate.

In Rumania this soup is served for supper and followed by fried *mamaliga* slices†. Fish is also a good dish to follow it.

Kabuni
Raisin pilaf

This pilaf is for accompanying boiled chicken or serving alone (in twice the quantity) as a main course. It is an Albanian national dish.

serves 4

2 oz/50 g/4 tablespoons butter
6 oz/175 g/¾ cup long grain rice
1 pint/575 ml/2½ cups chicken stock
4 oz/110 g/½ cup sultanas (golden raisins)
1 oz/25 g/2 tablespoons sugar
pinch ground cinnamon

Heat the butter in a large pan and fry the rice in it, stirring often, until it begins to look translucent. Gradually stir in the stock, then cook over medium heat for 10 minutes. Add the sultanas, stir quickly, put on a tightly fitting lid and simmer for 15 minutes more, or until all the liquid is absorbed and the rice is tender. Mix the sugar and cinnamon together well and stir into the rice just before you serve it.

Rizogalo
Thick rice pudding

The milk available in huge quantities is often used in this everyday Greek dish. At one time it was made with ewe's milk but now it is usually cow's. Never serve the pudding hot – room temperature is about right.

serves 6

2 pints/1.1 litre/5 cups milk
5 oz/150 g/⅔ cup short grain rice
2–3 strips lemon rind
2 teaspoons cornflour (cornstarch)
5 oz/150 g/⅔ cup sugar
ground cinnamon

Pour the milk into a heavy saucepan with the rice and lemon rind. Stir well and then cook over a gentle heat for about 30 minutes, or until the rice is soft. Mix the cornflour into the sugar, spreading it evenly to avoid lumps when cooking, and stir into the rice. Continue cooking gently for a further 20–30 minutes until the pudding is like very thick cream. Stir from time to time to prevent sticking. Cool slightly, discard the lemon rind and spoon the rice into shallow individual glass bowls. Set aside until cooled to room temperature and covered with a skin. Put the cinnamon in a salt shaker and sprinkle over the puddings to make a face or pattern on each.

Pechena Tikva
Baked pumpkin

Every autumn, quickly erected stalls mushroom in the tree-lined boulevards of Sofia and other main towns of Bulgaria. They are covered with large trays holding baked pumpkin halves the size of beach balls. Slices of pumpkin are wrapped in paper and eaten in the streets. The fruits are special cultivated sugar or honey pumpkins with firm, dark orange flesh containing up to 9 per cent natural sugars, which are concentrated by the baking to nectar sweetness. American pumpkins are similar, and British pumpkins can be used. This recipe yields about 13 lb/6 kg and is plenty for a group of 15–20 people.

serves 15–20

- 1 large whole pumpkin, weighing about 20 lb/9 kg
- clear honey or *petmez* (thick, condensed grape juice)
- 9 oz/250 g/2 cups crushed or ground walnuts
- 1 teaspoon finely grated lemon rind
- ½ teaspoon ground cinnamon

Scrub the pumpkin under running water with a stiff brush, removing all traces of earth from the rind. Wipe dry, trim off most of the stalk, then cut in half lengthways to give two large basin-shaped shells. Scoop out the seeds but do not discard them. Scrape away a little of the fibrous matter from the centre of the pumpkin halves.

Place each half on a large baking tray and bake near the top of a pre-heated oven at 400° F/200° C/gas mark 6 for about 2 hours. It is ready when the cut surface looks burnt – this is the best-flavoured part of the baked pumpkin because the sugars have caramelized.

A sugar pumpkin will not produce juice in the hollow centre as it cooks, but if you bake an English pumpkin it will. Ladle out the juices as they collect and drink them as a hot tisane with a little honey stirred in. Do not use any juices that filter into the baking tray. English pumpkins need a longer cooking time, so allow 4 hours at 375° F/190° C/gas mark 5. The pumpkin is ready when it stops exuding juice. A large one will yield plenty for 10–12 people.

Cut the baked pumpkin into large chunks without removing the rind. Serve with lots of honey to spoon over it and the walnuts in a bowl, with the lemon rind and cinnamon mixed in, for sprinkling on top.

You can roast the pumpkin seeds (*semki*). Wash them thoroughly and remove all fibrous matter from them. Put them in a roasting tin, sprinkle with salt and bake at the same time as the pumpkin until just changing colour. Do not let them brown.

When they are cold, crack them between your front teeth and open the case. The kernel should fall into your mouth unbroken, and you can discard the case without spitting.

Prazheni Filii
The Sultan's slices

This economical Bulgarian dish gives you the pleasure of eating crisp fried food that is not too rich, because it has not absorbed much fat.

serves 4–6

6 fairly thick slices bread, crusts removed
2 eggs, beaten
clarified butter, or butter mixed with oil, for frying
6 tablespoons honey
ground cinnamon

Dip both sides of the bread into the egg. Heat the butter in a large frying pan and fry the slices until crisp and lightly browned. Lift them on to individual plates, put a spoonful of honey on each slice and spread it quickly over the surface. Dust lightly with cinnamon.

CHAPTER 3

THE MIDDLI

Although Israel is the most modern of the Middle Eastern states, the Arabs of the region suffer less from the diseases caused by a rich diet. Arabs living near and in the countries of the Fertile Crescent share a common approach to eating, influenced by traditions which go back to the eleventh and twelfth centuries, when Baghdad was the world's cultural centre.

These countries, Lebanon, Syria, Jordan and Iraq, may be politically separated today, but throughout history they have been bound geographically, and share similar agriculture providing the same basic ingredients. The area produces an enormously varied and healthy range of fresh vegetables, beans and grains and all kinds of fruit, from figs and dates to oranges, lemons and apricots, and nuts. Wheat is the staple crop and bread is the staple food: the most common is the delicious pitta, prepared in flat rounds. Meat is eaten, but only moderately. The quantity of animal fats and oil consumed is also comparatively small.

The work of Israeli doctors and scientists who have studied the diet of Jewish immigrants to Israel has confirmed the health of the Arab diet. Jews born in the United States or Europe are better off financially, but generally have poorer health in middle and old age. They are the most vulnerable to heart diseases and atherosclerosis, and diet-related cancers. The Jews of African and Asian origin have a better health record and Jews from the Yemen have a better record still. But Arabs living in Israel, who eat a diet similar to their neighbours in the Fertile Crescent, have the best record of all.

EAST

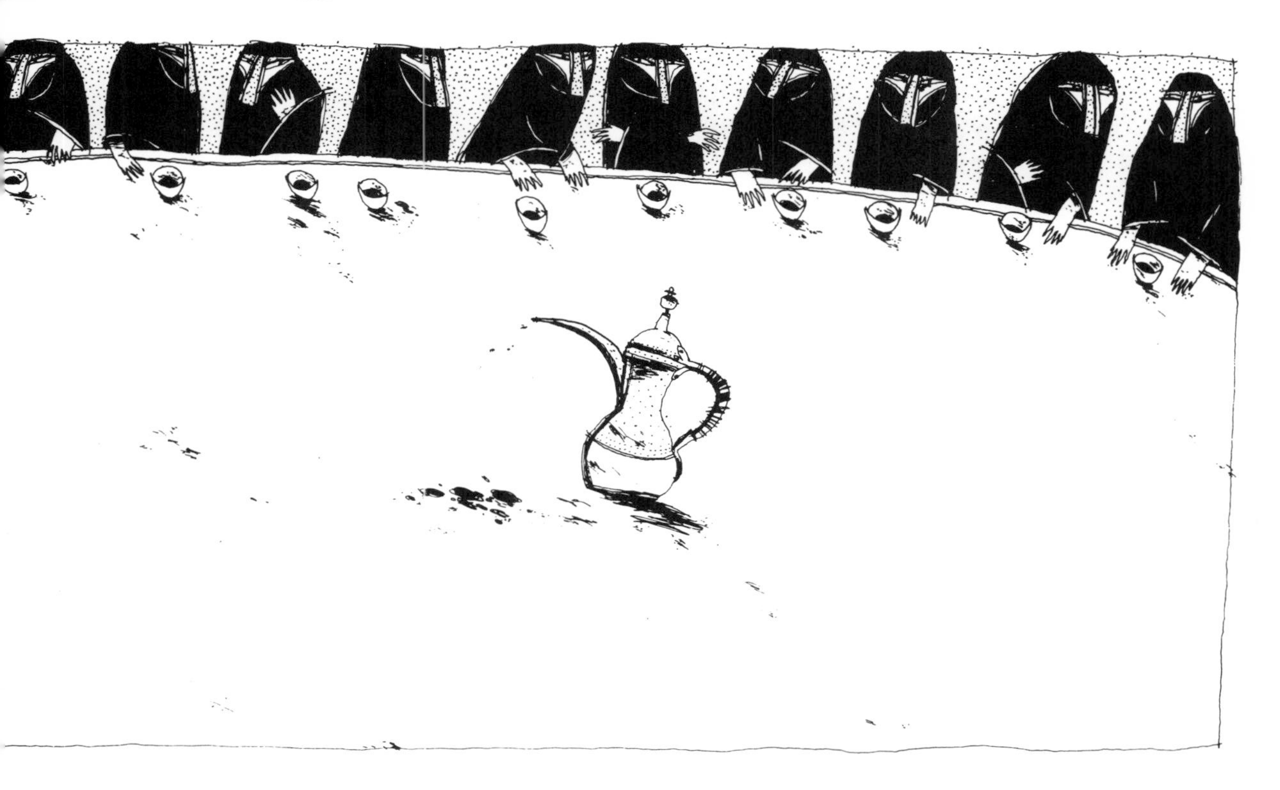

The main difference between these different groups is reflected in the consumption of bread and fats. The Arabs living in the Fertile Crescent use less than half the amount of fat consumed in the US and the UK and consume twice as much bread. Half of their fats are made up of olive and other seed oils, and not animal fats. This may surprise those who know of the Arab fondness for *samna*, a strong clarified butter, and their use of lamb fat (rendered down from sheep's tails).

The Arabs themselves would say that their healthy diet is not accidental. As far back as the eleventh century, Arab doctors were declaring which combinations of meat, vegetables, rice and beans were best for the functions of the body. Indeed, one of the earliest cookery books published in Europe was a Latin translation of a manual by a Baghdad doctor describing the principles of dietetics. Good healthy eating is an essential part of the Arab philosophy, which declares that there must be perfect concordance between the elements of the universe and the human body. Contemporary writers exalted cookery, and recipes were recorded by an aristocratic élite of poets, astrologers and even caliphs. The dishes they describe made use of dates and raisins, sesame seeds, dried apricots and prunes, pistachios and all kinds of nuts. The sweetness of honey was offset by the acidity of vinegar; foods were flavoured with combinations of herbs and spices, orange blossom, rose-water and sesame seeds. The sensual traditions of this court cuisine survive today in modern Arab cooking, where the refinements have mingled with the styles of Bedouin tribes and of the peasants, who have had to make the most of all potential ingredients in times of want.

The countries of the Fertile Crescent are still united in the special ways in which they make use of the varied produce available to them. Differences are regional rather than national, and depend on town or country, mountain, river, desert, marsh or coastland. They all share a diet that is as healthy as it is varied.

In this part of the Middle East, the differences between the foods eaten by the rich and the poor are the least pronounced. A basic recipe will remain the same, although a more wealthy family will elaborate on it with the addition of expensive ingredients such as nuts. For the rural and desert poor, meat is a luxury eaten only on special occasions, but even the more affluent cook would include only about half a pound (225 g) of meat in a bean stew or a stuffed vegetable dish expected to feed four people. It is not surprising, therefore, to learn that in Jordan, Iraq and Syria the consumption of meat and fish is a mere one-tenth of our own. Even in the Lebanon, the gateway to the Mediterranean, where the food, often referred to as the 'haute cuisine' of the Arab world, is the most sophisticated and influenced by European tastes, they eat only one-third the amount of meat and fish we do. Throughout the area lamb and goat make up more than 50 per cent of all meat products; there is also some beef and poultry and wild game, but the dietary laws forbid the consumption of any pork.

According to Arabic folk legend the forbidden tree which stood in the centre of Paradise was an enormous stalk of wheat, each grain the size of a man's head. When Adam disobeyed and was thrown out of the garden, the fruit that had been his undoing became his means of surviving in the world. Just as the maize (corn) plant is held sacred by the peoples of South America, so wheat, the staff of life, is treated with almost reverential respect by the peoples of the Arab world. Wheat is the staple cereal of the countryside and up to twice as much is consumed as in the US and the UK. It is prepared mainly in the form of pitta bread, or in the coarser wholewheat unleavened bread known as *shami*. It is bought fresh and warm from local bakeries, or it is made at home. A meal served without bread would be unthinkable, and indeed some people cannot enjoy eating anything without it. Bread simply dipped in a little crude salt is a popular snack and at street stalls you can buy a special spice mixture called *zahtar* which is used as a dip with warm bread. *Burghul*, or cracked wheat, is an essential ingredient in many soups and stews and it is also prepared as a side dish to be eaten with yoghurt, and as a simple breakfast 'porridge' which has been left to cook overnight in a pot on the stove or in the ashes of a fire. It is used for *kibbeh*, the national dish of Syria and Lebanon, and for *tabbouleh*, the much loved lemon-flavoured parsley and mint salad.

Barley is also used in many vegetable stew dishes, and in the towns rice is part of the staple diet. Maize (corn), millet and sorghum are only eaten in small quantities. The other main bulk food comes from beans of all types. Chick peas and lentils are the most popular and they have been a basic part of the diet since time immemorial; the rather unappetizingly named 'mess of pottage' which Jacob offered to his ageing father was a lentil stew, and when Daniel was in the court of King Nebuchadnezzar he asked to be given a diet of only beans and water – an experiment which left him looking 'fairer and fatter in flesh' than all the king's servants who were accustomed to eating quantities of meat.

The relative shortage of pasture land makes these countries unsuitable for beef or cattle rearing, so very few milk products are included in the diet. These are mostly eaten in the form of sheep or goat cheeses, and in yoghurt which accompanies most meals and mixed with water makes the perfect drink for a hot afternoon.

Another of our dietary indulgences, which is conspicuous if not by its absence then at least by its moderate appearance, is sugar, for consumption is only about half of ours. Dried or fresh fruit is served as a dessert, and the traditional sweet pastries stuffed with nuts and dates and the cream puddings are only for festivals or to be offered to special visitors. Very sweet and very black Turkish coffee is popular, and is drunk several times a day. So, too, is a strong aromatic tea which is served without milk, and with a lot of sugar. It is not that the people do not have a sweet tooth – in fact they enjoy sweet syrups, sherbets and cakes which we might find too cloying – but sugar is not a basic ingredient in nearly as many foodstuffs as those of the Western world.

A wide variety of marvellous fruit and vegetables is available throughout the year: figs, melons, grapes, bananas, mangoes, peaches, guavas, apricots, tomatoes, aubergines (eggplants), radishes, onions, cucumbers, courgettes (zucchini), cauliflowers, lettuces and peppers – and many more as well. Fruit is eaten dried and fresh. Vegetables are eaten raw in a variety of salads, and they are cooked in stews or stuffed. Perhaps the best loved vegetable is the aubergine and there are a hundred ways that it can be cooked. Since the area was the spice route to Europe from the time of the Middle Ages, all the usual and the more rare spices have been tried and many of them adopted into recipes, but usually with more moderation than in Far Eastern dishes. Cumin, coriander and cardamom, saffron, turmeric and cinnamon, nutmeg, cloves and a variety of different peppers all lend their subleties to the Arabic cuisine. Everyone favours the use of garlic, while fresh mint, flat-leaved parsley, celery and green coriander, and the juice of lemons and limes give zest to many delicious salads and cooked dishes.

The Yemen

Of all the people of the Middle East the Yemenis are most renowned for good health and long life. They are small eaters, accustomed to a hard and simple life. They like meat but cannot often afford it. Their simple diet has hardly changed for thousands of years. They do not have the rich agricultural advantages of their neighbours to the north but they make the most of what they do have in a very sound way.

The Yemeni diet is based on soup made from meat and vegetables and especially on bread. There are many types of bread made with coarse home-ground wheat, maize (corn) and sorghum (a type of millet) flour, with or without yeast. It is baked on hot stones, on metal sheets, in a frying pan or stuck on the sides of the oven. It is sometimes coated with *samna*, the aromatic clarified butter made by boiling ½ lb (225 g or 1 cup) of butter with 2 tablespoons of fenugreek seeds, and sprinkled with black cumin. People like to dip their bread in very strong, hot relishes called *zhug* and *hilbeh*.

A favourite breakfast is eggs and liver, or brown beans (*ful medames*) or *falafel*, chick pea rissoles which were adopted from Egypt.

The usual lunch is a one-dish meal. It may be a soup or stew with beans, lentils or chick peas and the vegetables in season – potatoes, tomatoes, cabbage, onion, beans, peas, marrow (squash) and peppers – or a thick wheat porridge. Tails, feet and bones are used in the stew when there is no meat or chicken.

In the villages a popular way of cooking

meat is on hot stones in a hole in the ground, wrapped in banana leaves. By the sea, fish is grilled straight on the fire, whole or skewered in pieces, or it is cooked with rice. An unusual, but ready, source of protein is the desert locust, baked in the oven. Milk from goats and ewes is used to make a smoked, hard, dry cheese.

Sunflower and sesame seeds, olives, almonds and nuts and dry, baked chick peas are everyday side dishes, with dried dates and raisins. Popcorn, too, is there to nibble at. It is not made by frying in oil, but by being heated in a heavy-lidded pot on the fire until it pops.

Cooking is done with hardly any fat, which would be either clarified butter or olive oil. The food is flavoured with onion and garlic, lemon juice, mint, parsley and coriander leaves. Spices include cumin, coriander, cardamom, caraway seed and fenugreek, and a variety of very hot peppers which are distinctive to this cuisine.

Almost the only way that sugar comes into the diet is lightly sprinkled on plain bread as an alternative to honey. Dates provide sweetness and with other fruit, grapes and bananas especially, are the usual dessert.

In the evening the meal is lighter and may be composed of cheese, vegetables and bread.

Curiously, for a country that provides the best coffee beans in the world, it is the hulls alone which are boiled for a drink which is flavoured with a mixture of spices. *Kat* is a narcotic leaf which is chewed or brewed like tea. Coffee trees are gradually being replaced by *kat* trees.

Eating habits in the Fertile Crescent

As far as the daily eating pattern is concerned there is only one main meal of the day, and that is lunch. For those who go out to work in the fields, or on Friday, the Muslim day of rest, a heavier breakfast, including a dish of beans or cracked wheat, might be eaten. The more usual breakfast is lighter – though never really light; it might be sweet strong tea, cheese and olives, home-made jam or honey, all eaten with pitta bread. The Bedouins favour a hard goat cheese, eaten with bread and dried dates and strong black coffee. In Iraq pieces of cheese, celery leaves and spring onions, or hard-boiled eggs and chutney, are eaten wrapped up in pitta. A popular breakfast snack which can be made at home or bought from a street vendor's stall is turnips cooked in date juice.

Lunch is eaten between 12 and 1 p.m. Appetizers, or *mezze* as they are called, play an important part in Arab life, not least because they are meant to be enjoyed in an unhurried way, sometimes accompanied by *arak*, a strong distilled grape spirit; but although a wide variety of side dishes will be offered in a restaurant or on a grand family occasion, an ordinary family lunch is often only a one-dish affair. This might be a rich vegetable stew with a little meat, accompanied by rice in the towns, or cracked wheat in the marshlands and villages where it grows. The Bedouins would choose to eat lamb, boiled or roasted, with rice. In the watery marshlands there are birds to be caught and fish to be speared or netted, and these are then simply grilled over a charcoal fire and eaten with bread and vegetables. The Assyrian and Chaldean peasants of the plains make wonderful dishes from the many vegetables which grow in that fertile region, and they will often have stuffed peppers, aubergines or tomatoes.

In the evening people tend to eat early and light, because they have a sensible dislike of going to bed on a full stomach. Even the wealthier would not expect or wish for a second meat meal in the day, and the evening meal is like an extended hors d'oeuvre with a variety of cheeses, yoghurt, olives, pickles, eggs and salads and, of course, bread.

The Middle East loves to sell on the streets, and foods of all kinds are always available from little stalls. In Iraq there are stands which display boiled broad beans and chick peas, and varieties of vegetable pickles, the favourites being turnips and a giant variety of garlic. There are also magnificent multi-coloured arrays of wholesome foods such as people would prepare in their own homes: eggs, salads and a variety of fresh herbs which are cut up on the spot and rolled into the flat round *khubz* bread. Cheese can also be bought from stalls, to be eaten with onion and herbs rolled in bread.

Until recently all Middle Eastern women were expected to be entirely dedicated to home-life, and they would spend long hours pounding, hollowing, wrapping and decorating elaborate dishes for their menfolk. Social and political changes, and the pressures associated with urban life, have made time a valuable commodity for both men and women, and the simple, humble food of the peasants and labourers has gained popularity with the wealthier. People even admit to liking it more than anything else, and in the present political climate this is ideologically acceptable. What used to be considered simple family food, or something that could be prepared quickly and without much fuss for a single person, has now become the food for entertaining and special occasions. However, this is not to say that the Middle East no longer considers food to be one of the chief sensual pleasures of life. People still go to the market to handle, taste and smell the beautiful spoils of a fertile land. They still come home laden with the best that their money and their passionate barterings can buy, and even if the more modest dishes take less time to prepare they are still produced with just as much care and reverence.

Samna
Clarified butter

It is convenient to make a large quantity of *samna* because the process is rather fussy and causes a certain amount of volume to be lost. *Samna* keeps for months without refrigeration, gives a fine taste to food and does not burn in cooking.

Heat the butter slowly in a pan until melted and bubbling vigorously. Chill until firm. Transfer carefully to another pan, leaving behind the sediment at the bottom. Heat the butter again and when it froths, strain it through a fine cloth into a jar. Cover to store It may be spiced with cumin or fenugreek.

Butter is primarily used for cooking in the Middle East and seldom spread on bread. Use *samna* sparingly in cooking, bearing in mind that total fat consumption in these countries is half that of the US or UK. Olive, cottonseed and sesame oils are the commonly used cooking oils in the Middle East.

Ful Medames
Brown beans dressed in oil and lemon

serves 4

1 lb/450 g/2 cups *fava* beans
2 oz/50 g/4 tablespoons red lentils (optional)
salt and pepper
olive oil
2 lemons, quartered
1 teaspoon cumin
finely chopped parsley
2 cloves garlic, peeled and crushed (optional)
bunch of spring onions or scallions, trimmed and washed

The heavier breakfast eaten by those who work in the fields – and by all on a Friday, the day of rest – includes beans and wheat cooked to melting tenderness overnight in a pot left on the stove or in the ashes of an open fire.

In Iraq, large broad beans are used and the dish is called *badkila*. Elsewhere *fava*, small Egyptian beans, are usually used. Some of the canned varieties available are very good and just need warming.

Soak the beans overnight in cold water to cover, then drain. Bring to the boil in enough fresh unsalted water to cover them, adding the lentils if you like; they will thicken the sauce. Cover and simmer until tender; the exact time will depend on the quality of the beans, but it will be at least 2 hours. Add salt to taste when they are nearly tender.

Serve hot in large individual bowls. Set out the other ingredients and let everyone dress their own bowl of beans as they like. Serve with pitta bread. An Egyptian variation includes chopped hard-boiled eggs.

Fattet Hummus
Chick peas with yoghurt

This dish derives its name from the word *fatteh*, which means to break into small pieces. This is what happens to the bread, which is used as a bed to soak up the juices. It makes a delicious and sustaining breakfast.

serves 4

- 3–4 oz/75–125 g/½ cup chick peas
- salt and pepper
- 1 pint/575ml/2½ cups yoghurt, at room temperature
- 3 cloves garlic, peeled and crushed
- 2 pieces pitta bread
- 1 tablespoon butter or *samna*†
- 1–2 tablespoons crushed dried mint, or 2–4 tablespoons chopped fresh mint
- 3 tablespoons pine nuts or slivered almonds

Soak the chick peas overnight in cold water, then drain. Cover with fresh water and simmer until very tender; the length of time varies depending on the quality of the chick peas, but it is usually well over an hour. Add salt to taste when they are nearly done.

Drain the yoghurt, in a muslin cloth (cheesecloth) placed in a sieve, until it is the thickness of mayonnaise; this usually takes about 45 minutes. Pour into a bowl, beat in the garlic and add pepper to taste.

Tear open the pitta bread and toast lightly. Quickly fry the pine nuts or almonds in the butter until they are light brown.

Break up the pitta bread into the bottom of a deep serving dish. Pour on most of the chick peas and enough of their water to soak the bread thoroughly. Keep back a few chick peas. Pour on the yoghurt mixture and scatter the mint over the top. Sprinkle on the nuts and reserved chick peas.

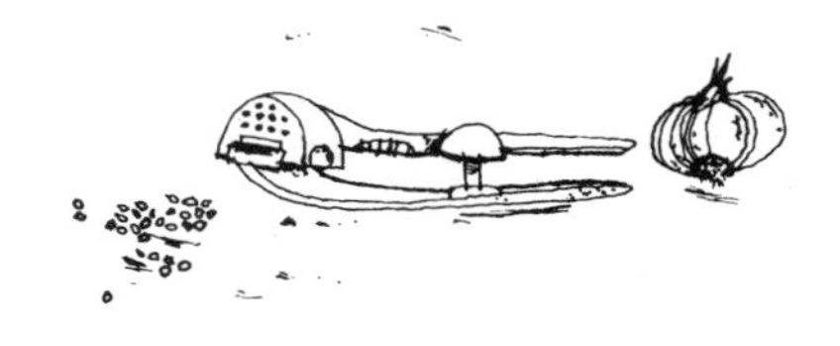

Serve at once with the chick peas hot and the rest lukewarm. Whole spring onions or scallions and green peppers cut into strips often accompany the dish. Some people like to sprinkle it with hot red chilli pepper or cayenne pepper. Strong, sweet tea is the drink to serve with it.

A Damascus version called *tasseia* has the cooked chick peas crushed in a mortar and mixed with 4–5 tablespoons of *tahina* paste (sesame meal), the juice of half a lemon and a crushed clove of garlic. If you wish, you can use a blender to reduce the chick peas, with a little of the cooking liquid, to a cream. Squeeze a little lemon juice in the chick pea water before sprinkling over the bread, spread the creamed chick peas over the top and cover with yoghurt, then garnish as before.

Mamounia
Semolina pudding

This is a sweet breakfast favourite of Damascus. People sweeten it to their own taste and some like it thicker than others. Some use only water and some only milk; a mixture of both is good. Semolina is a fine form of milled wheat, so this simple dish has the nutritional virtue of bread served in an attractive and quite different way.

serves 4

4 oz/110 g/½ cup butter
5 oz/150 g/1¼ cups semolina
12 fl oz/350 ml/1½ cups milk
9 fl oz/250 ml/1 cup water
about 6 oz/175 g/¾ cup sugar
ground cinnamon for sprinkling

Melt the butter in a large saucepan and fry the semolina in it for 5 minutes over a very low heat, stirring constantly with a wooden spoon. Pour the milk and water into another saucepan, add the sugar and bring to the boil, stirring until the sugar has dissolved. Add the liquid to the semolina, stirring all the time. Continue to stir over a low heat until the mixture has thickened to a cream. Remove from the heat and leave to stand for 15 minutes.

Serve in small bowls, sprinkled with cinnamon. Chopped almonds can be added as a garnish.

Harissa
Meat and wheat stew

In the region north of Baghdad, Iraqis are going back to this ancient soup of the mountain Kurds for breakfast on a cold day. Those who cannot afford meat make it with wheat alone. The name of the dish means well cooked.

In Syria and Lebanon, the stew is traditionally served on *Id es Saidi* (Assumption Day) or made in large quantities when a sheep is slaughtered and there is plenty of bone broth. Although lamb is usually used it is sometimes made with chicken.

serves 4

12 oz/350 g/1½ cups wholewheat grain
8 oz–1 lb/225–450 g stewing lamb (or chicken)
bones (optional)
about 2 pints/1.1 litres/5 cups water
salt and pepper
½–1 teaspoon ground cinnamon, according to taste
2 tablespoons melted butter or oil (optional)

Overnight soak the wheat in cold water to cover, then drain and rinse. Put the meat, and bones, if used, in a large saucepan with the water to cover. Bring to the boil and remove the scum. Add the wheat, salt and pepper and cinnamon. Simmer gently for at least 2 hours, stirring occasionally and adding more water if the pan becomes too dry. When the wheat is very soft, remove the bones and crush the meat with a fork. Some people put the stew through a blender so that you cannot distinguish the meat.

Serve hot in deep bowls, sprinkled, if you like, with sizzling hot butter or oil. In Iraq, they also sprinkle on sugar and cinnamon.

In Lebanese variations, a pinch each of cumin and ground cloves is sprinkled on, and chopped onion and peeled, chopped tomato may be added during the cooking.

Falafel
Fried chick pea rissoles

These fried chick pea rissoles are the national food of Israel. They are nourishing, cheap and tasty. Stuffed in a pouch of pitta bread with a chopped salad and *tahina*, they make a street snack at all times of the day. They originated in Egypt where they are made with large white beans (not chick peas) and where they are believed to be as old as the pharaohs. The Israeli Arabs make them with white beans like the Egyptians. It is the Yemenite Jews who arrived in the Holy Land before 1948 who began to make them with chick peas and they spiced them with peppers.

Most of the *falafel* sold anywhere nowadays are likely to be made with dehydrated powder which is far less good than the real thing.

serves 4

- 1 lb/450 g/2 cups chick peas (soaked in water for 24 hours)
- 1 onion, grated
- 6 spring onions or scallions, finely chopped
- 2 cloves of garlic, crushed
- 1–2 teaspoons ground cumin
- 1–2 teaspoons ground coriander
- salt and pepper
- a good bunch of fresh coriander leaves or a bunch of flat-leaved parsley, finely chopped
- a good pinch of Cayenne or chilli pepper (optional)
- oil for frying

The chick peas should have soaked enough to be tender right through when you bite into them. Drain them. Pound them to a smooth paste, or use a blender. Add the rest of the ingredients and work well into the paste with your hands. Let it rest for 30 minutes.

Take small walnut-sized lumps and shape into little round flat rissoles about 1 in/2.5 cm in diameter. Make them all before you start frying the first batch – it will give them time to rest again. Fry in hot oil, turning over once, until brown.

Serve hot, accompanied by a salad of chopped tomatoes, cucumber and Cos (romaine) lettuce and a bowl of *tahina* paste. Or pop everything into a pocket of pitta bread.

Shorbat el Adas
Lentil soup with rice

This sustaining Middle Eastern favourite is especially welcome in the winter months and is made almost every day during Ramadan for the breaking of the Muslim fast. The split red lentils are best because they disintegrate very quickly.

serves 4

8 oz/225 g/1 cup red lentils
2 tablespoons oil
1 large onion, chopped
1 clove garlic, peeled and crushed
1¾ pints/950 ml/4 cups chicken (or other) stock
salt and pepper
½ teaspoon ground coriander
½ teaspoon cumin
juice of ½ lemon
3 tablespoons rice

Pick over the lentils to remove any grit and wash if necessary. Heat the oil in a large saucepan and fry the onion in it until lightly coloured. Add the garlic and stir until golden. Stir in the lentils and pour on the stock. Season with salt and pepper and add the coriander, cumin and lemon juice.

Bring to the boil and simmer gently until the lentils have disintegrated, usually after about 40 minutes; the time varies according to their quality. Add the rice, and some water if the consistency is too thick. Simmer until the rice is tender. Instead of rice, 2 oz/50 g/¼ cup of vermicelli is often used.

Serve the soup piping hot with plenty of bread.

Shorba
Yemeni soup

The usual everyday meal in the Yemen is a rich soup of meat or chicken with the vegetables in season. Potatoes or beans and lentils give it extra substance. Those who cannot afford meat use marrow bones instead.

serves 4

6 oz/175 g/⅔ cup beans or brown lentils or both, soaked overnight
1 lb/ 450 g meat
meat bone (optional)
1 onion, chopped
3 tablespoons oil
2–3 cloves garlic, peeled and crushed
2 tomatoes, peeled and chopped
1 small squash or marrow, chopped
1 spring onion or scallion, sliced
small bunch fresh coriander leaves, chopped
salt and pepper

Drain the beans and put them to boil in fresh water with the meat and bone. Remove any scum as soon as it appears, then simmer for abouı 2 hours until the beans and meat are tender; add more water as necessary.

In another pan, fry the onion in the oil until golden. Stir in the garlic, cooking until it colours, add the tomatoes, marrow, spring onion and coriander. Cook for a minute, then add to the meat and beans. Season with salt and pepper and continue to cook until everything is soft and the flavours have blended.

Yemenis serve this with bread and sometimes flavour it from their pot of a peppery spice mixture called *hawayij*. To make this, grind together 2 tablespoons black peppercorns, 1 tablespoon caraway seeds, 1 teaspoon cardamom and 2 teaspoons turmeric.

Hummus bi Tahina
Chick pea and sesame meal spread

This thick, creamy paste carries the characteristic flavour of the Arab kitchen. It is the kind of food which is made by tasting constantly and adding gradually whatever seems to be missing. It is served as an appetizer with bread to dip into it and also as a side dish for kebabs and all types of grilled meat and fish.

serves 4

6 oz/175 g/¾ cup chick peas
salt and pepper
5 fl oz/150 ml/⅔ cup *tahina* paste (sesame meal)
juice of 2 lemons
2 cloves garlic, peeled and crushed
finely chopped parsley for garnish
Cayenne pepper or paprika for garnish
a few black olives (optional)

Soak the chick peas in cold water to cover for 4–5 hours, or overnight if more convenient. Drain and then boil them in fresh water for about 2 hours or until they are soft. Add salt when they are tender.

Drain off and reserve the cooking liquid and keep a few chick peas for decoration. Put the rest through a food mill or blender with as much of the cooking liquid as is needed to make a thick cream. Add the *tahina* paste, lemon juice, garlic and salt and pepper to taste, and beat to a smooth consistency.

Serve on shallow, individual plates garnished with the parsley, Cayenne pepper or paprika and the reserved chick peas. Add a few black olives if you like.

Betingan Meshwi
Aubergine (eggplant) purée

This purée, made out of one of the most popular vegetables in the area, is rated so highly that it is affectionately called the 'poor man's caviare'. Serve as a starter with bread to dip or as a side dish with grilled meats or fish.

serves 4

2 medium aubergines (eggplants)
4 tablespoons olive oil
1–2 cloves garlic, peeled and crushed
juice of 1 lemon, or more to taste
salt and black pepper
2 tablespoons finely chopped parsley

Cook the aubergines under a hot grill (broiler) or over the glowing embers of a charcoal fire, turning them slowly until their skins are charred and blistered all over. Split open and scoop out the flesh. Mash it with a wooden spoon or put through a food mill or blender. Add the oil, garlic and lemon juice and beat well. Season to taste with salt and pepper. Scoop on to a shallow plate and garnish with the parsley.

A popular variation, called *baba ghanouj*, has 2 tablespoons of *tahina* paste (sesame meal) beaten into it. For another variation, stir in 5 fl oz/150 ml/⅔ cup of yoghurt.

Laban Salateen
Cucumber and yoghurt salad

This light salad, scented and flavoured with mint, makes a refreshing first course at lunch.

serves 4

1 large cucumber or 2 small ones, peeled and diced
salt and white pepper
2–3 cloves garlic, or more to taste
1 pint/575 ml/2½ cups yoghurt
1 tablespoon crushed dried mint, or 2 tablespoons finely chopped fresh mint
dried mint for garnish

Sprinkle the cucumber lightly with salt and leave in a colander to drain for 30 minutes. Peel the garlic and crush with a little salt. Mix a few tablespoons of the yoghurt with the garlic, then add the mixture to the rest of the yoghurt and mix well. Add more salt and pepper to taste. Finally add the mint, whose aroma and flavour make the salad deliciously refreshing.

Drain the cucumber and mix with the yoghurt dressing. Pour into the serving dish and decorate with more mint.

Tabbouleh
Cracked wheat salad

One of the national dishes of Syria and Lebanon, this salad of humble peasant origins is sometimes called parsley salad because so much of that herb is used in it. Like everything else, it is made by judging the colour, and tasting after frequent additions of salt and pepper. In mountain villages, freshly picked sharp young vine leaves are used to scoop up the salad; in towns the pale, crisp leaves from the heart of a Cos lettuce are provided.

serves 4

3 oz/75 g/⅔ cup medium *burghul* (cracked wheat)
5 oz/150 g/3 tablespoons spring onions (scallions) or mild Spanish onions, finely chopped
3 tomatoes, chopped
3 oz/75 g/1 cup parsley, finely chopped
handful of fresh mint, finely chopped, or 2 tablespoons dried mint
salt and pepper
5–6 tablespoons olive oil
juice of 1½ lemons, or more to taste
vine leaves, lightly poached, or fresh Cos lettuce leaves

Soak the *burghul* (called *bulgur* by Turks and Cypriots) for 10 minutes in enough cold water to cover it. Drain well and put in a large bowl. Mix in the onions, tomatoes, parsley and mint and season to taste with salt and pepper. Stir in the oil and lemon juice and leave to stand for at least 1 hour before serving to allow the wheat to absorb the dressing and become plump and tender.

Serve in individual bowls lined with the vine leaves or lettuce leaves and provide a dish of firm young lettuce leaves for scooping up the salad. For a variation, pile the salad in a pyramid and garnish with halved and stoned (pitted) black olives. It makes a pleasantly simple first course for lunch.

Salata Filfil bi Outa
Tomato and pepper salad

Leave the peppers raw in this salad if you wish, but many people find them more digestible when grilled (broiled) in this way – and they are certainly deliciously soft and mellow.

serves 4

- 2 peppers
- 4 firm tomatoes, sliced
- ½ Spanish onion, finely chopped, or 6 spring onions (scallions), finely chopped
- small bunch of fresh coriander leaves, chopped, or small bunch of parsley, finely chopped
- salt and pepper
- 4 tablespoons olive oil
- 1–2 tablespoons wine vinegar

Spear the peppers with a fork and turn them over a flame, or turn them under a grill (broiler), until they are soft and the skin has blistered all over. Peel off the skin and remove any charred parts under a running tap. Remove the stalks and seeds and cut the flesh into ribbons.

Put in a serving bowl with the tomatoes, onions and coriander. Season with salt and pepper, pour on the oil and vinegar and toss well. Increase the amounts of oil and vinegar, in the given proportions, if you wish.

Serve as a first course at lunch, with bread to mop up the juices.

Sabaneh bi Loubia
Spinach with black-eyed beans (peas)

Olive oil gives the best taste to this salad, but you can use a light vegetable oil instead when the dish is a hot accompaniment to the main course. Swiss chard leaves (*silq*) often take the place of the spinach.

serves 4

- 5 oz/150 g/⅔ cup black-eyed beans (peas)
- salt and pepper
- 1 lb/450 g/4½ cups shredded fresh spinach, or 8 oz/225 g/1 packed cup frozen leaf spinach, completely thawed
- 1 large onion, finely chopped
- 5 tablespoons oil

Cover the black-eyed beans with water in a saucepan (they do not need soaking) and bring to the boil. Simmer until tender, generally after about 20 minutes; do not overcook or they will become mushy. Add salt to taste towards the end of the cooking time.

Meanwhile, wash the fresh spinach, the thick stems having been removed prior to shredding, and drain well. If using frozen spinach, squeeze all the water out of it.

Fry the onion in the oil until soft and transparent. Add the spinach and fry, stirring constantly, until well cooked. Season with salt and pepper, then stir in the drained beans and warm through together. Allow the dish to cool and serve as a first course at lunch, or hot as a side dish with the main meal.

Samak Meshwi
Grilled fish (with *Taratoor bi tahina sauce*)

Along the banks of the Tigris and Euphrates the fish is excellent. In Iraq, the country of two rivers, they have a special way of cooking it, called *masgoof*; at night people walking along the river banks are assailed by the magnificent aroma of the day's catch, split open and speared on stakes set upright like masts round the fire. When the inside is cooked by the fire, the fish is laid on a wire rack and put over the fire to cook the skin side and the sauce is spread on all over it.

Every type of fish can be grilled over the embers of a fire. If you have a firm fish (cod, tuna or mackerel), cube it, marinate it in olive oil and lemon juice with salt and pepper, then skewer the cubes alternately with pieces of bay leaf and cook on a wire rack over a fire, brushing frequently with oil. Less firm fish are best suited to grilling whole.

serves 4, depending on size of fish – a 2-lb fish serves 3–4

any whole fish, cleaned and gutted, with the head left on
2 cloves garlic, peeled and crushed
small bunch of fresh coriander leaves
salt

for the sauce:
5 fl oz/150 ml/⅔ cup *tahina* paste (sesame meal)
juice of 1–2 lemons
1 clove garlic, or more to taste, peeled and crushed
salt and pepper

If the fish is large, slash the skin diagonally in several places so that the heat can penetrate evenly. Leave on the scales to protect the flesh and keep it moist; they will practically melt away. Put the garlic and coriander inside the fish and sprinkle it with salt. Lay the fish on an oiled rack over a gentle heat and cook until the flesh flakes easily, turning over once; the cooking time depends on the size of the fish.

If you want a crisp, brown skin, first scale the fish; brush it often with olive oil during the cooking.

To prepare the sauce beat all the ingredients together, then beat in enough water to give a light-textured cream.

Serve the fish with the sauce poured over. If you prefer, serve without the sauce and instead garnish with parsley, black olives, gherkins and quartered lemons. Either way it makes a succulent lunch dish. Serve with pitta bread†.

Kibbeh nayyeh
Paste of raw lamb

In this lamb and wheat paste, which is said above all others to be the national dish of Syria and Lebanon, the proportions are varied according to personal taste.

Great satisfaction is derived from the laborious traditional process of pounding in a mortar and then kneading by hand. However, you will find that a blender or food processor achieves perfect results in minutes. Some people like to add a little allspice or cumin to the mixture, but purists prefer it with only onion as flavouring.

serves 4

- 4 oz/110 g/½ cup fine *burghul* (cracked wheat)
- 1 lb/450 g lean, cubed, tender lamb – leg is best, but shoulder trimmed of fat can be substituted
- 1 medium onion, chopped
- salt and pepper
- 3–5 tablespoons olive oil
- sprig of mint leaves to garnish
- 2 spring onions or scallions, chopped, to garnish

Rinse the *burghul* in cold water and leave it in water to soak and become plump while you trim the lamb of fat and cut it into cubes.

Put the onion in the blender and mash it well. Add the meat cubes, season with salt and pepper, and blend to a paste. Then drain the *burghul* and squeeze out the excess water. Add the grain to the paste with 2–3 tablespoons of the oil and blend to a soft purée. Spread on a dish and decorate by pressing little cuts all round the edges. Garnish with the mint leaves and spring onions. Sprinkle with 1–2 tablespoons of oil.

Serve with a basket of pitta bread or a bowl of crisp lettuce leaves; these are used instead of forks or spoons to scoop up the paste and eaten with it.

The following dish is a good accompaniment:

- 2 onions, finely chopped
- 2 tablespoons oil
- 1 lb/450 g/2 packed cups lean veal, minced (ground)
- 2 oz/50 g/½ cup pine nuts
- salt and black pepper
- juice of 1 lemon

Fry the onion in the oil until golden. Add the veal and continue to fry until the meat changes colour. Add the pine-nuts, season with salt and pepper and add enough water to cover. Bring the boil, then simmer gently until the meat is tender and the sauce well reduced. Some people prefer to fry the pine nuts lightly and add them just before serving. Sprinkle with lemon juice, leave until cold and serve in a separate bowl.

Lahma bi-ajeen
Arab pizza with a meat filling

To vary the everyday Arab bread there are several coverings or toppings, which are spread on the dough before cooking. This one is a paste of minced meat, tomato and onions.

serves 8–10

for the dough:

- ½ oz/15 g fresh yeast or ¼ oz/7g/½ tablespoon dried yeast
- scant ½ pint/300 ml/1¼ cups lukewarm water
- pinch of sugar
- 1 lb/450 g/4 cups plain white flour
- 1 teaspoon salt
- 2 tablespoons oil

Dissolve the yeast with a pinch of sugar in about ½ cup of lukewarm water. Leave aside in a warm place for about 10 minutes, or until the mixture begins to bubble.

In the meantime, sift the flour and salt into a large warmed mixing bowl. Make a well in the centre and add the oil and the yeast mixture. Work the dough vigorously, adding the remaining lukewarm water gradually to make a soft dough. Knead vigorously for about 15 minutes until the dough is pliable and elastic, and comes away from the sides of the bowl. Cover with a damp cloth and set aside in a warm, draught-free place for 2–3 hours, or until doubled in bulk. To prevent a dry crust forming on the surface, put a very little oil in the bottom of the bowl and roll the ball of dough in it to coat the entire surface before leaving it to rise.

for the filling:
1 lb/450 g onions, finely chopped
oil
1½ lb/700 g lean lamb or beef, minced
1 lb/450 g fresh tomatoes, skinned and chopped, or a 14 oz/450 g can of skinned tomatoes
5 tablespoons tomato paste
1 teaspoon sugar
¾ teaspoon ground allspice
1–2 tablespoons lemon juice
salt and black pepper
3 tablespoons finely chopped parsley (optional)
pinch of Cayenne pepper (optional)

Soften the onions in a little oil, until they are transparent and have lost their water, taking care not to let them colour. Mix the meat, tomatoes and tomato paste in a large bowl. If you are using fresh tomatoes, discard as much of their juice and seeds as possible and crush them to a pulp. If you are using a can of tomatoes, drain them well, as too much liquid will make the dough soggy. Add the sugar, allspice and lemon juice, and season to taste with salt and pepper. Drain the onions of oil and add them to the meat mixture. Knead well by hand. Some people like to add chopped parsley and a little cayenne pepper as well. The filling is sometimes varied by omitting the tomatoes altogether, and adding 2 oz/50g/¼ cup pine nuts and 2–3 tablespoons of tamarind instead.

Knead the dough, which will have risen by now, a few times and divide it into walnut-sized balls. Allow to rest for a few minutes, then roll each piece on a lightly floured board with a lightly floured rolling pin into a round flat shape 5–6 in/12–15 cm in diameter. Alternatively, oil your hands lightly, take smaller lumps of dough, and flatten each piece as much as possible with the palm of your hand on an oiled plate.

Spread the prepared filling very generously over each piece, covering the entire surface (otherwise the filling will look meagre when they are baked). Transfer each round to a lightly oiled baking sheet as you prepare it.

Bake in a pre-heated oven 450–475° F/230–240° C/gas mark 8–9 for 8–10 minutes only. The pastries should be well done but still white, and soft enough to roll up or fold in the hand to be eaten.

Lahma bi-ajeen can be reheated by putting them in a warm oven for a few minutes. They can also be warmed up in the top of a double saucepan. Serve with various salads, such as cucumber and yoghurt, or any other Arab salad.

Yakni
Stew

The most popular Arab way of feeding a large family is a ribwarming stew with one, two or three vegetables in season, very little meat and a dish of rice.

Lamb is the usual meat and favourite vegetables are marrow (squash) or courgettes (zucchini), aubergines (eggplants), tomatoes, onions, green beans, okra, cabbage, spinach and artichoke hearts. Sautéed potatoes and all types of beans, chick peas, lentils and split peas, soaked and boiled, are added for extra nourishment. Sometimes marble-sized meatballs are dropped into the stew instead of pieces of meat.

serves 4

1 lb/450 g assorted vegetables, as available
1 large onion, chopped
2 tablespoons oil or butter
½–1 lb/225–450 g stewing lamb or beef, cut into small pieces
2–3 tablespoons tomato paste
small bunch of parsley or fresh coriander leaves, chopped
½ teaspoon ground allspice, cumin or coriander (optional)
salt and pepper
8 oz/225 g/1½ cups potatoes, cut in small pieces and sautéed, or 4 oz/110 g/1 cup beans, soaked, then cooked until tender (both optional)

Wash and trim the vegetables and cut into pieces. If using tomatoes, peel them; cut off the hard stems of okra; sprinkle aubergine pieces with salt and leave to drain in a colander for 1 hour.

Fry the onion in the oil until lightly browned, then put in the meat and fry until it changes colour. Add the vegetables and stir for a minute or so; some people like to brown them. Cover with water. Stir in the tomato paste, parsley and spice if used, and season with salt and pepper. Simmer gently for about 1½ hours, until the meat is very tender and the sauce rich and much reduced; add water if the stew becomes too thick. Near the end of the cooking time, add the potatoes or beans if you wish.

Your stew will have an aroma reminiscent of millions of kitchens in the Middle East if you include okra or spinach and fry 4 cloves of peeled and crushed garlic and ½ teaspoon ground coriander with the onions for 2 minutes before putting in the meat and vegetables.

Serve as a main course for lunch with fluffy rice.

Salata
Mixed salad

At the start of a meal, a plate of several raw vegetables is put on the table. In restaurants there may be as many as forty items to choose from, but at home people are content with far fewer. Traditionally, the right hand, with sleeve rolled up to the elbow, is the 'clean' hand used to pick up the food. Serve mixed salad with drinks before the start of a meal. This salad can be dropped into a pitta or served with kebabs or *falafel*.

serves 4

cucumber, cut in sticks
tomatoes, quartered
lettuce leaves (or cabbage in the winter)
spring onions (scallions) or mild Spanish onions, sliced
salt and pepper
olive oil
lemon juice
chopped flat-leaved parsley

Simply arrange the vegetables chopped and sprinkled with salt and pepper and dressed with plenty of oil and lemon juice. Scatter the parsley on generously.

You can also add chopped mint or coriander leaves. Serve with young leaves of Cos (romaine) lettuce (or bread to tear into pieces) to scoop up morsels of the salad.

A peasant way of turning this salad into a more substantial lunch is to put pieces of broken-up toasted bread, usually pitta bread, at the bottom of a bowl and soften it slightly with a sprinkling of water. Lay the vegetables on top and add the seasonings and dressings. The bread absorbs the other flavours.

Kousa Mahshi
Stuffed courgettes (zucchini)

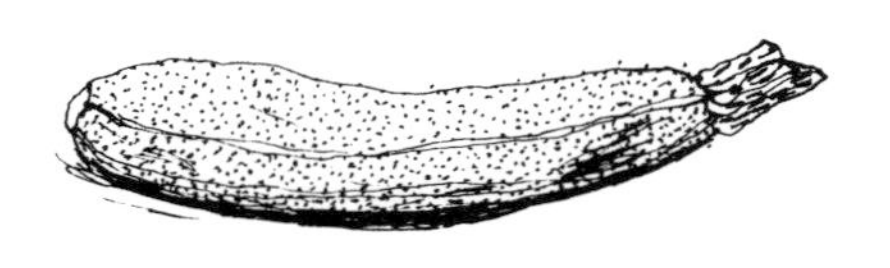

In the past, it was usual to fry the stuffed courgettes in butter before stewing them. The tendency today is for lighter food and many people omit this preliminary frying.

serves 4

12 medium courgettes (small zucchini)
1–2 tomatoes, sliced thinly
2 tablespoons tomato paste
10 fl oz/300 ml/1¼ cups water
juice of 1½ lemons
2–4 cloves garlic, peeled
salt
1 teaspoon dried crushed mint or 2 teaspoons chopped fresh mint

for the filling:
½ lb/225 g/1 cup lean stewing lamb or beef, minced (ground)
3 oz/75 g/⅔ cup rice, washed and drained
1 tomato, peeled and chopped (optional)
2 tablespoons finely chopped parsley (optional)
salt and black pepper
½ teaspoon ground cinnamon, or ¼ teaspoon ground allspice

Wash the courgettes and cut off the stems. Using an apple corer, make a hole at the stem end of each courgette and scoop out the pulp, taking care not to break the skin. The other end must remain closed. Keep the pulp for a stew or salad.

To prepare the filling, put all the ingredients together in a bowl and knead well by hand until thoroughly blended. Put the filling into the courgettes. Do not pack tightly and only half fill, so the rice has plenty of room to swell. There is no need to block the openings.

Cover the bottom of a large, deep saucepan with a layer of tomato slices. Lay the courgettes side by side, in more than one layer if necessary. In a small saucepan, mix the tomato paste with the water and about two-thirds of the lemon juice. Bring to the boil and simmer for a few minutes, then pour over the courgettes. Cover the pan and simmer very gently for about 1 hour, until the courgettes are tender and the filling cooked, adding a little more water if necessary.

Crush the garlic with a little salt and mix with the mint and remaining lemon juice. Sprinkle over the courgettes and continue simmering for a few minutes longer.

Serve hot as a main dish at lunch with plenty of bread.

Lahm Meshwi (Shish Kebab)
Skewered lamb

The distinctive flavour of *meshwi* (grilled meats) cooked over charcoal or wood embers belongs to the Middle East. The method is cheap on fuel and time, it is fun, and a brazier can easily be improvised from an old metal box or tray pierced with little holes and set on four bricks to let air through the bottom. The secret lies in waiting for the fire to die down to embers, and in keeping the food moist with fat. Of course, you can use an ordinary grill (broiler), but the taste will not be the same.

When served with salad, hummus and bread, also warmed over embers, this makes a healthy outdoor meal – recommended as an alternative to barbecued steaks and sausages.

serves 4

1½ lb/700 g lean lamb from the leg or shoulder
salt and pepper
fat from the lamb, cut into small pieces

Cut the meat into ¾ in/2 cm cubes. Sprinkle with salt and pepper and thread on to skewers, preferably with flat, twisted blades so that the meat does not slip off. Alternate the meat cubes with pieces of fat, to lubricate the meat as it cooks. Turn the skewers over the embers for 7–10 minutes until well browned outside but still pink and juicy inside.

Slip from the skewers into rounds of pitta bread† warmed over the fire and partly opened to make a pouch.

Kofta Kebab
Minced (ground) meat on skewers

This is often cooked with *lahm meshwi* but on separate skewers as it needs less time over the fire. These kebabs are tender and well flavoured with spices, but you must be careful not to dry them out; fat meat is best for them because it stays moist and juicy. The secret is to work the meat to a soft paste so that it holds on to the skewer. Have it minced twice by the butcher or use a blender to grind it to a paste.

serves 4

1½ lb/700 g fat lamb or beef, minced twice or reduced to a paste
1 large onion, grated, or a small bunch of parsley, finely chopped
2 teaspoons ground cinnamon, or 1 teaspoon ground cinnamon and 1 teaspoon ground allspice, or 1 teaspoon cumin and 1 teaspoon ground coriander
salt and pepper
pinch of Cayenne pepper (optional)

Mix the meat with the onion, spice, salt and pepper and Cayenne pepper if used. Work with your hands to a soft, smooth paste. Take small lumps of the mixture and press firmly round skewers (with flat, wide blades) to form sausage shapes that hold well together. Turn them over the embers for a few minutes until they are browned all over but still soft and juicy inside. Serve as for *lahm meshwi*.

Kibbeh bil Sanieh
Cracked wheat and minced (ground) meat baked in a tray

This is one version of a whole family of dishes that epitomize the cuisine of Lebanon and Syria. It is a very ancient dish mentioned in Assyrian and Sumerian writings. Iraq boasts dozens of similar *koubba* – the most popular a speciality of Mossul.

Many of the versions use time and skill to shape and stuff the shells of paste formed into oblongs, little balls or large flat cakes. The following layered *kibbeh* is the easiest to make.

serves 4

6 oz/175 g/¾ cup fine *burghul* (cracked wheat)
¾ lb/350 g finely minced (ground) lean lamb
2 medium onions, grated or minced
1 teaspoon ground allspice
salt and pepper
2 tablespoons butter, melted

for the filling:
1 medium onion, chopped
2 tablespoons oil
¾ lb/350 g lamb or beef, minced (ground)
½ teaspoon ground allspice, or 1 teaspoon ground cinnamon
3 tablespoons pine nuts or chopped walnuts
2 tablespoons raisins

Rinse the *burghul* well in cold water and drain it. Reduce the meat and onions to a paste, either using a pestle and mortar or, with a little cold water, in a blender. Add the allspice and season with salt and pepper. Add the *burghul* and continue to pound or blend until the mixture has become a smooth paste.

To make the filling, fry the onion in the oil until it is soft. Add the meat, crush with a wooden spoon and stir until it changes colour. Stir in the allspice, pine nuts and raisins.

Grease a shallow baking tray or ovenproof dish. Spread half the meat and wheat mixture on the bottom, cover with the filling and top with the rest of the meat and wheat paste. Mark into diamond shapes with a knife and run the knife round the sides of the dish. Pour the melted butter over the top and bake in a pre-heated oven at 400° F/200° C/gas mark 6 for 30–40 minutes, until the top is well browned.

Serve with a salad – cucumber and yoghurt salad† goes well – and *hummus bi tahina*†.

Burghul bi Dfeen
Cracked wheat and chick pea stew

Each family adjusts the proportions of ingredients in this stew to suit their own taste. Those who cannot afford meat use peeled tomatoes instead. Usually a large quantity of stew is made, so that there is some left for another meal.

Fry the onion in the butter until browned, then add the meat and fry until it changes colour. Add the bone and the drained chick peas, cover with water and bring to the boil. Remove the scum, season with pepper and ½ teaspoon of the cinnamon. Simmer gently for at least 1 hour, until the chick peas and meat are tender. Remove the bone, season with salt and add the *burghul*. Cook gently, stirring for about 15 minutes until tender and the stew is thick; add more water if necessary.

Serve on a shallow dish with the melted *samna* poured over if you wish. Sprinkle with the remaining cinnamon. Serve as a main dish at lunch. Yoghurt, drained through a piece of muslin (cheesecloth) until thickened a little, makes a good accompaniment.

serves 4

1 large onion, chopped, or 6 button onions
2 oz/50 g/4 tablespoons butter or *samna*†
1 lb/450 g lean stewing lamb or beef, cubed
bone (optional)
4 oz/110 g/½ cup chick peas, soaked overnight
salt and pepper
about 1 teaspoon ground cinnamon
8 oz/225 g/1 cup coarse *burghul* (cracked wheat)
2 oz/50 g/4 tablespoons melted *samna* (optional)

Mahshi Silq
Stuffed chard leaves

Everyone knows the stuffed vine leaves of the Middle East. When vine leaves are out of season, Swiss chard leaves are used instead. They look rather like spinach, but have their own distinctive taste.

Remove the stalks from the chard. Soften the leaves by plunging them in boiling water for 1 minute; drain well.

To prepare the filling, wash the rice and mix with the tomatoes, onion, parsley, mint, cinnamon, allspice and salt and pepper. Put a teaspoon of this mixture near the bottom of each leaf, fold the bottom over the mixture, then the sides towards the centre, and roll up like a cigar.

Line a large saucepan with any left-over or torn leaves, or with the sliced tomatoes. Pack in the rolls tightly, slipping the cloves of garlic between them if you wish.

Mix the olive oil with the water, sugar and lemon juice and pour over the rolls. Put a small plate on top of the rolls to prevent them from unravelling. Cover the pan and simmer very gently for at least 2 hours, until the rolls are thoroughly cooked; add a little water occasionally as the liquid in the pan is absorbed. Cool in the pan before lifting out carefully. Serve cold as a main course at lunch with plenty of bread.

An alternative filling replaces half the rice with 2 oz/50 g/¼ cup chick peas. Soak them overnight in cold water, then drain and grind in a blender before combining with the filling.

serves 4

1 lb/450 g fresh chard leaves
2 tomatoes, sliced (optional)
3–4 cloves garlic, peeled (optional)
5 fl oz/150 ml/⅔ cup olive oil
5 fl oz/150 ml/⅔ cup water
1 teaspoon sugar
juice of 1 lemon, or more to taste

for the filling:
8 oz/225 g/1 cup long grain rice
2–3 tomatoes, peeled and chopped
1 large onion, finely chopped, or 4 tablespoons finely chopped spring onions or scallions
2 tablespoons finely chopped parsley
2 tablespoons dried crushed mint or 4 tablespoons chopped fresh mint
pinch ground cinnamon
pinch ground allspice
salt and black pepper

Djaj Meshwi
Grilled chicken

One of the best ways of eating chicken is grilled, but frequent brushing with oil is needed to keep it moist. The people of the marshlands in Southern Iraq also use this method for cooking duck, quails, pheasants or pigeons that they find between the reeds.

serves 4

1 chicken, skinned
4–5 tablespoons olive oil
juice of 1 lemon
salt and pepper
1 clove garlic, or more to taste, peeled and crushed

Cut the chicken into pieces of convenient size and remove the bones. Mix the oil, lemon juice and black pepper together with the garlic. Lay the chicken pieces in this marinade and leave for about 1 hour. Sprinkle with salt when you are ready to cook and lay the pieces on a well-oiled wire rack over a charcoal grill. Brush with the marinade and turn over a few times during the cooking. Grill until crisp and brown outside but still moist inside.

Serve as the main course at lunch, with salads and pitta bread†.

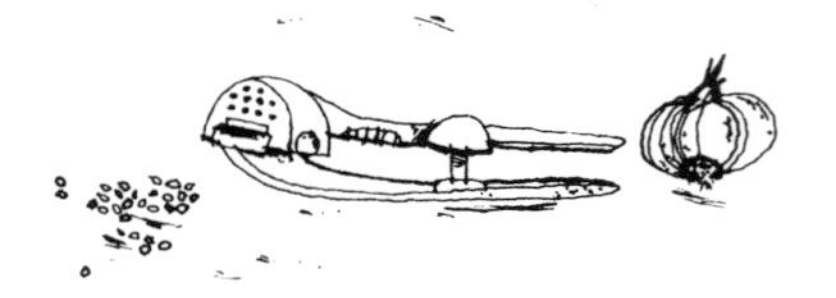

Laban
Yoghurt

The health-giving virtues of yoghurt have for centuries been part of Arab lore and many attribute the longevity of peasants to it. In some households yoghurt is served as a side dish at almost every meal.

It is simple to make and needs no elaborate equipment. Once you have found the right spot and the right blanket to wrap it in, you will find it hard to fail. Use any live yoghurt as a starter; commercial yoghurt will do. Make sure it is not sterilized.

serves 4

1 pint/575 ml/2½ cups milk
1 tablespoon plain yoghurt

Bring the milk to the boil and simmer for about 2 minutes to kill any unwanted bacteria. Draw off the heat and leave to cool until you can just bear to hold your finger in it and count up to 10. On a thermometer, the temperature should be 106–109° F/41–43° C. If it is outside this range, the yoghurt might fail. Remove the skin from the top of the milk.

Beat the starter in a large bowl, add a few tablespoons of the hot milk, then gradually add the rest of the milk, beating all the time. Cover the bowl with a large plate, and wrap it in a woollen blanket or shawl. Put it in a warm, draught-free place and leave it undisturbed for at least 8 hours, or overnight if more convenient.

The yoghurt will now have set like a thick cream. Remove it from the warm place or it will gradually go sour. Store it in the refrigerator. Use it for making fresh cheese†, in salads, and in *fattet hummus*†.

Labna
Fresh cheese

This is simply made from your home-made yoghurt†. It is a good soft cheese to serve with a salad and bread for a light evening meal.

serves 4

1 pint/575– ml/2½ cups yoghurt
salt and pepper
crushed garlic to taste
crushed dried mint, or chopped fresh mint, to taste
olive oil for sprinkling

Line a colander with a thin piece of muslin (cheesecloth) and pour in the yoghurt. Leave it for several hours for the whey to drain off; the longer you leave it, the firmer the cheese will be.

Season with salt and pepper and mix in the garlic and mint. Sprinkle the olive oil over the top. Cover and keep in a refrigerator if you are not going to eat it right away.

You can also serve the cheese with honey as a dessert.

Gebna Meshwi
Grilled (broiled) cheese

While a hard, dry goat cheese is the best to use for this simple snack or light supper dish, the Greek *halumi* will do very well for it. You could also use a hard Cheddar cheese that has been left to dry out.

serves 4

about 8 oz/225 g/2 cups firm, dry cheese, or more to taste

Cut the cheese into slices or cubes and lay on an oiled grill. Put over the glowing embers of a fire, or under a hot domestic grill. When the cheese blisters and becomes spotted with brown, turn the pieces over and grill the other side.

Eat with bread and a salad.

Eggah bi Korrat
Leek omelette

Egg dishes belong to the evening, when people take a light, early meal. Firm, flat omelettes filled with various vegetables are eaten either hot or cold.

serves 4

1 lb/450 g leeks
butter for frying
½ teaspoon sugar
squeeze of lemon juice
salt and black pepper
4 eggs

Wash the leeks, trimming off the roots and removing the outer leaves. Cut off the tough tops of the leaves and wash the leeks again thoroughly. Slice fairly thinly and fry lightly in a little butter. Season with the sugar, lemon juice and salt and pepper. Leave them to cook over a gentle heat in the juices until soft and lightly coloured.

Alternatively, you can boil the prepared whole leeks in salted water until just soft, then drain and chop.

Beat the eggs lightly in a large bowl. Add the leek mixture, mix again and season with salt and pepper. Pour into 2 tablespoons of sizzling hot butter in a heavy-based frying pan. Turn the heat very low and cook very gently for 10–15 minutes, until the eggs are set. Dry and brown the top lightly under a grill (broiler).

An omelette with spinach (*eggah bi sabaneh*) is as popular as the leek omelette. Use instead of the leeks 1 lb/450 g/4½ cups prepared fresh spinach, well washed, or ½ lb/225 g frozen leaf spinach, completely thawed and drained. Stew gently in its own juice until tender, then drain and chop before mixing with the eggs and salt and pepper. Cook as the leek omelette.

Serve the omelette hot or cold with a salad, yoghurt and bread.

Zhug
Yemeni relish

The Yemeni people sometimes coat bread with clarified butter flavoured with fenugreek and cumin. They also like to dip their bread in this strong, hot relish.

serves 4

4 small chilli peppers
1 whole head of garlic, peeled
large bunch of fresh coriander leaves
3–4 cardamom pods
1 tablespoon caraway seeds
salt and pepper

Put all the ingredients in a blender and blend until smooth. Store in a covered jar. Use very sparingly; just a spot will set your mouth aflame.

Hilbeh is a slightly milder variation: blend ½ teaspoon *zhug* with 1 large peeled tomato and 2 tablespoons fenugreek seeds.

Roz
Rice

Wheat is the staple of the rural Arab world, but rice is the everyday food of cities and of the marshlands where it grows. Rice with a thin grain, long or short, is used for this side dish which accompanies many foods. It is often the essential base for a sauce or stew.

- 8 oz/225 g/1 cup long grain rice
- 9 fl oz/250 ml/1 cup water
- salt
- 2 oz/50 g/4 tablespoons butter

Soften the rice by pouring boiling water over it in a bowl. Stir, then leave to stand for 15 minutes. Drain in a fine colander or sieve and rinse with cold water.

Bring the water to the boil in a saucepan and add salt to taste and the butter. When the butter has melted, put in the rice. Let it come to a vigorous boil, then turn down the heat and simmer very gently undisturbed, covered with a well-fitting lid, for 20 minutes. It should be tender and separate, with little holes all over the mass in the pan. Draw off the heat and leave to stand for about 10 minutes before serving.

Smothered lavishly with yoghurt†, this makes a light meal by itself.

Mujaddarah
Lentils and rice

In this cheap and nourishing dish the lentils and rice complement each other in providing protein. The proportions vary in every family. Olive oil gives a distinctive flavour to the dish, but a lighter vegetable oil will do.

serves 4

- 8 oz/225 g/1 cup large brown lentils, carefully cleaned and soaked for 1–2 hours
- 1 onion, finely chopped
- 7–8 tablespoons oil
- salt and black pepper
- 4 oz/110 g/½ cup long grain rice,
- 2 onions, sliced into half-moon shapes

Drain the lentils, then cover with fresh water and boil for 20–30 minutes, or until tender. Fry the chopped onion in 2–3 tablespoons of the oil until soft and golden. Add it to the lentils and season with salt and pepper. Mix well and add the rice, together with enough water to make the liquid in the pan about equal to the volume of rice. Season again and simmer gently, covered, for about 20 minutes, until the rice is tender; add a little more water during the cooking if it is absorbed too quickly. Fry the sliced onions briskly in the remaining oil until dark brown, sweet and almost caramelized.

Serve the lentils and rice in a large shallow dish garnished with the fried onion slices. Either hot or cold, it is a delicious light supper dish to have dressed with yoghurt.

Roz ou Ful
Rice with broad (*fava*) beans

serves 4

1 onion, chopped
2 tablespoons oil
1–2 cloves garlic, peeled and chopped
½ teaspoon ground coriander
8 oz/225 g/1 cup shelled broad (*fava*) beans
10 fl oz/300 ml/1¼ cups water
salt and pepper
8 oz/225 g/1 cup rice

Broad beans with their strong flavour make an excellent combination with the bland taste of rice. If fresh broad beans are not available, you can use frozen beans; they need only 7–8 minutes' cooking, about half as long as fresh beans.

Fry the onion in the oil in a saucepan. When it begins to brown, add the garlic and coriander and stir. When the garlic colours, add the beans and water, season with salt and pepper and simmer until the beans are tender.

Meanwhile, wash the rice with boiling water and rinse with cold water. When the beans are cooked, add the rice, stir and cook, covered, for about 20 minutes or until the rice is done; add a little water during this time if necessary.

Serve as a side dish at a main meal.

Roz bel Shaghria
Rice with vermicelli

serves 4

12 oz/350 g/1½ cups long grain rice
2 oz/50 g/4 tablespoons butter
a drop of oil
4 oz/110 g/½ cup vermicelli
2 teaspoons salt, or to taste

Rice and pasta together combine the virtues of two of the world's staple grains. Another way to vary rice is by adding cooked chick peas instead of the vermicelli or by adding raisins or sultanas (golden raisins).

Measure the volume of rice in a measuring jug, then measure out an equal volume of water. Wash the rice in boiling water, then rinse with cold water and drain well.

Melt the butter in a saucepan, adding the oil to prevent it from burning. Crush the vermicelli in your hands and add to the pan. Fry, stirring constantly, until it is golden. Add the rice and stir thoroughly so that it is completely coated with butter. Pour in the measured water, season with salt and stir well.

Bring to the boil, then turn the heat as low as possible and simmer gently, covered, for about 20 minutes, until the rice is tender but not mushy. Add a little water during the cooking if it is all absorbed before the rice is cooked.

Serve as a side dish at a main meal.

Burghul Pilaf
Cracked wheat

Burghul, called *bulgur* in Greek shops, is the most usual and enjoyable way of eating wheat in the Middle East. *Burghul* is parboiled wheat which is dried and cracked. In the villages this is still done with a stone hand-mill.

Grinding can produce various degrees of coarseness: the finest is required for *kibbeh*, a medium one for *tabbouleh*, and a coarse one for adding to stews or for making pilaf.

The traditional, and most convenient, way of measuring is with a cup.

serves 4

1 onion, chopped
2 oz/50 g/4 tablespoons butter or *samna*†
1 teacup coarse *burghul*
2 teacups stock (or water)
salt and pepper

Cook the onion in the butter in a heavy-based saucepan until softened. Add the *burghul* and stir for a minute or two. Add the stock, season with salt and pepper and continue to cook gently, stirring frequently, until all the liquid has been absorbed and the wheat is tender and fluffy. This will take about 20 minutes.

Serve hot as a side dish to a main meal, or eat it simply with yoghurt poured over it.

An attractive variation adds 2 tablespoons each of sultanas (golden raisins), slivered almonds and pine nuts to the *burghul*.

Betingan
Aubergines (eggplants)

There are 100 ways of cooking aubergines, but none better nor more popular than simply frying them.

serves 4

2 medium aubergines (eggplants)
salt
oil for frying
2 tablespoons chopped parsley, or to taste
1 tablespoon wine vinegar (optional)

Slice the aubergines into a colander, sprinkle with salt and leave for 1 hour for their bitter juices to drain away. This also makes them absorb less oil.

Rinse to remove excess salt and squeeze the slices to rid them of all their juices. Fry in hot oil, turning over once, until tender and lightly coloured on both sides. Drain on absorbent paper.

Serve as a side dish, with the parsley scattered over and, if you like, the vinegar sprinkled on top.

Khoshaf
Dried fruit salad

serves 4

1 lb/450 g dried apricots
8 oz/225 g prunes, preferably stoned, or 8 oz/225 g/1½ cups seedless raisins or sultanas
4 oz/110 g/⅓ cup almonds, blanched and halved
2 oz/50 g/¼ cup pistachios or pine nuts, halved
6 oz/175 g/¾ cup sugar, or to taste
2 tablespoons rose-water or orange blossom water

Salads of local sun-dried fruit are prepared in large quantities during the month of Ramadan for the Muslim faithful to break their daily fast. Purists use only apricots and raisins with some nuts, but many others prefer to balance the sharpness of apricots with the sweetness of prunes, and some put in all the dried fruit and nuts of the area. Prepare the salad a day or, better still, two days in advance – and make a large quantity to eat over a few days; it gets better each day.

Wash the fruit if necessary and put in a large bowl with all the other ingredients. Add enough water to cover, stir, cover and put in the refrigerator for 1–2 days.

Serve chilled as a succulent dessert.

Belila
Wheat in syrup

serves 4

1 lb/450 g/2 cups wholewheat grain
8 oz/225 g/1 cup sugar
5 fl oz/150 ml/⅔ cup water
squeeze of lemon juice
2 tablespoons rose-water or orange blossom water
slivered almonds, pistachios and pine nuts (optional)

This fragrant dessert is traditionally given to nursing mothers to enrich their milk; the wholewheat supplies additional vitamins. It is also served to commemorate happy occasions such as a baby's first tooth, and at such times is garnished with slivers of pistachio, almond and pine nut.

Boil the wheat in plenty of water until it is tender and the skins begin to open; this usually takes 1 hour or more, depending on the grain. Drain well and turn into a bowl.

Put the sugar, water and lemon juice in a pan over a steady heat, stir until the sugar has dissolved, then simmer for about 10 minutes to form a syrup thick enough to coat a spoon. Add the rose- or orange-blossom water and pour over the wheat. Leave to cool and then garnish with the nuts, if you like.

You can make the dish with barley instead of wheat.

Kahwa
Turkish coffee

The drink was discovered by Muslim pilgrims in Mecca at the end of the fifteenth century. Throughout the Middle East people drink coffee several times a day but in very small cups. Though its flavour is strong, the coffee is less potent than that made in other ways because some of the caffeine is lost in the boiling. Because of this, people find that it does not keep them awake as other types of coffee often do.

The authentic vessel for making it is an *ibrik*, but you can make it in a saucepan. Use coffee ground almost to a powder.

serves 4

4 teaspoons sugar, heaped according to taste
4 small coffee cups water, filled to the brim
4 very heaped teaspoons pulverized or Turkish coffee
1 cardamom pod, cracked

Bring the sugar and water to the boil, stirring, then add the coffee and cardamom. Stir well and return to the heat. When the coffee froths up to the rim, draw off the heat. Repeat the frothing twice more. Let the grounds settle, remove the cardamom and serve very hot. Make sure that each cup is given a little topping of the froth.

Ayran
Yoghurt drink

This is the most popular drink on a hot day; it is sold in the streets.

serves 4

15 fl oz/450 ml/1⅞ cups yoghurt
15 fl oz/450 ml/1⅞ cups cold water
salt
1–3 tablespoons dried crushed mint, or a handful of chopped fresh mint (optional)

Beat the yoghurt well in a large bowl. Gradually add the water, continuing to beat vigorously until thoroughly blended. You can use an electric blender for this. Season to taste with salt and add the mint if you like.

Serve chilled, with a lump of ice for each person.

CHAPTER 4

JAPAN AND SOUTH-EAST

A certain style of Japanese food is becoming familiar to Westerners, particularly in chic restaurants in New York and London. The style of presentation is pleasing to the eye, and the unique flavourings and sauces freshen the palate. But underneath the glamour, the cuisine is built on sound dietary principles. For one thing, Japan has been influenced by centuries of Buddhism, which preaches vegetarianism; for another, animal fats are not much eaten, either as meat or dairy products. But fish is readily available, both fresh (eaten braised or finely sliced and raw with soy sauce and horseradish) and dried (tough planks of horn-hard bonito, grated to make the basis of a daily breakfast soup, or small fish or little squid, reconstituted in water before cooking). It is a rice-based diet, providing plenty of carbohydrate, which again contributes to good health. Extra protein in the diet is provided by the soya bean, which appears in many forms, from almost tasteless white bean curd, set like a stiff custard, to fermented beans with the rich odour of an over-ripe cheese, to soy sauce – again fermented – which is eaten with almost everything.

The health record of the Japanese has been very well documented. There have

ASIA

been extensive comparative studies of Japanese people living in Japan, Hawaii and California which show that the good health of the native Japanese is not a racially inherited characteristic, but the result of their traditional diet. Coronary heart disease occurs four or five times less commonly among Japanese men than among Britons and Americans, and two or three times less among Japanese women. The cancers associated with a high-fat diet are also less common among the Japanese. But those Japanese who migrated to Hawaii and California and have taken to Western food are beginning to suffer from the American pattern of disease. We would expect Japan's good health rate to falter in the coming decade as they, too, swing towards the Western pattern of eating more meat and less rice. The Japanese only compare badly with Western countries in their higher rate of stomach cancer, and evidence points strongly to the use of nitrate and nitrite salts used in pickling vegetables and curing meat and fish. The Japanese traditionally eat large amounts of pickled vegetables, although this has now decreased with the spread of freezing and refrigeration (accordingly, this is reflected by a fall in stomach cancer). We have avoided choosing recipes which call for large quantities of pickled food. In small quantities they are quite acceptable because they carry no more risk than the equivalent quantities of Western pickled foods – bacon, corned beef and preserved sausage.

In the Far East, Japan does not have the monopoly of the good health which goes with a rice-based diet. The people of Malaysia, Indonesia, the Philippines, and Taiwan all have similar eating patterns associated with low risk of heart disease and certain cancers.

As long ago as 1916 a Dutch physician, C. D. De Langen, who had practised for some years in the Dutch colonies (which now form Indonesia), noted that the native Indonesians had low levels of cholesterol in their blood, and were free of disorders thought to be related to a cholesterol intake. They seldom suffered from coronary heart disease and atherosclerosis (a blocking of the blood vessels which leads to heart attacks). At the time these differences were usually dismissed as racial peculiarities. But De Langen then discovered that Indonesian stewards on Dutch passenger ships, who ate European food, had cholesterol levels as high as the Dutch. He had already noticed that heart disease was common among Dutch patients and the rich Chinese who saw him privately. Yet working in a large hospital in Jakarta he only ever saw one Indonesian patient suffering from heart disease, and only six Chinese, over a period of five years. The Dutch and the rich Chinese ate a European type of diet; the patients in the hospital ate traditional Indonesian food.

In Japanese literature the poor man's bean curd soup or his bowl of plain-boiled rice is often used as a symbol of hardship and poverty. But it also stands for the virtues of a simple life. Such dishes are austere, ungarnished and unseasoned. But with the addition of a few carefully chosen ingredients, they are transformed into nourishing meals, which are also appetizing.

In all aspects of Japanese cuisine the aesthetic qualities of the food are important. Even the simplest dish of rice is served in such a way as to please the eye as well as the palate. A good cook is judged by the clearness of her soup; even the plainest *dashi*, a golden soup made with dried bonito flakes and little pieces of dried seaweed, must have a delicate translucence which makes it typically Japanese. Much about Japanese food is unfamiliar to the Westerner – who may only know it from the smart restaurants of New York and London, which are delightful but do not serve typical everyday dishes. The home cook will attempt to separate the individual flavours and textures, rather than let them blend as we do in the West.

A typical day might begin with pickled red plums, *umeboshi*, surprisingly sour and salty, but said to clear the palate, to aid digestion and cleanse the system.

Breakfast is often a simple fish stock soup, thickened with soya bean paste, *miso shiru*. The same soup may be gently reheated for the evening. Breakfast can be a bowl of rice served with flaked dried seaweed, *nori*, the same laver seaweed enjoyed by the Welsh with their breakfast egg and bacon; or plain-boiled sticky rice may be mixed with a beaten raw egg flavoured with a dash of soy sauce.

A more substantial first meal will include a fish or egg dish, such as an omelette; or one of the many kinds of dried fish, such as *hoshi zakana*, which are quickly and easily grilled.

The midday meal is taken between midday and 1 p.m. This is a snack. Lunch at home will probably be the leftovers from yesterday's supper. Someone at work might buy a bowl of spiced noodles from one of the *soba* stalls. There are bars which specialize in *sushi*, which are sticky rice balls which carry slices of raw fish or pieces of omelette. Many cafés sell *onigiri*, rice balls filled with fish, vegetables or pickles. It used to be common for men and schoolchildren to take a packed lunchbox, one side containing rice, the other an assortment of pickles and cold morsels left over from the day before.

The evening meal is eaten between 6 and 7 p.m. A clear fish soup or a thickened soup might be followed by a main dish of meat or fish with vegetables, or a dish of spicy mixed vegetables; and, of course, rice or noodles.

Desserts are not usual. There might be fresh fruit, or rice served with a selection of pickles. These pickles, *tsukemono*, are a crucial part of the day's menu, and years ago a poorer family would often have had a main meal of rice and pickles alone.

According to Japanese mythology, the benevolent gods gave rice to mankind, and they also gave him *miso*, the fermented bean curd which appears in most meals in one guise or another, sweetened as a cake, fried, or mixed into a soup.

Miso paste is derived from the versatile soya bean, the 'meat of the earth', as the Japanese sometimes call it. It provides Japan with its cheapest and most commonly available source of protein. It has a much stronger taste than *tofu* because it is made from the fermented bean curds. It keeps indefinitely and as flavour improves with age each household will probably have several varieties and vintages. It is rich in protein and vitamins. Combined with rice it provides essential amino-acids and is therefore particularly important in frugal and vegetarian diets. The Japanese have always maintained that *miso* is an indispensable element in a healthy diet, and recent evidence has indeed shown that it is the extensive use of soya beans as well as the high cereal intake (mainly rice) and low consumption of fats and meat which have contributed to the Japanese health record. Special soya bean diets are used today by doctors in the West as an effective way of lowering the cholesterol level in the blood.

Salty, strong-flavoured soy sauce, dark or light, is a basic ingredient in all Japanese cookery. *Tofu*, which is of Chinese origin, is made from white bean curd. As a source of protein, it is used like cheese in the West. But, unlike cheese and other dairy products, it contains no fat. It is reputed also to aid the digestion of other foods. *Tofu* is added to soups, salads and other dishes and it can be fried or grilled. Although it can be made at home there are so many *tofu* shops and stalls that people usually buy it ready-made.

The Japanese also eat large quantities of vegetables, either fresh in mixed salads, or lightly cooked. The climate and soil encourage some extraordinary specimens – ringed beans, deeply ridged or giant cucumbers, firm Chinese cabbages, enormous Mediterranean-style tomatoes and aubergines (eggplants), as well as small aubergines, bean sprouts, okra, pumpkin, and sweet potato; lotus root (*renkon*), giant radish (*daikon*), bamboo shoots and the tender leaves of chrysanthemum. Most of the more exotic vegetables can be bought in the UK and USA dried or canned.

The strict code of Buddhism demands a vegetarian diet – although it does not exclude fish – and this explains why the Japanese have evolved a mastery of vegetable cookery. A certain amount of poultry and pork is consumed nowadays although it is still only small compared with American and British intake. Beef is popular, but the high prices of recent times make it a luxury.

The Japanese, however, eat vast quantities of fish by comparison with Britons or Americans. Everything is considered potentially edible, from whale steaks to the smallest crustacea. In the inland areas there is plenty of freshwater fish; some varieties, like carp, are farmed. Even the poorest people would expect to eat fish whenever there was a festival or other celebration.

The Japanese lead the world in their consumption of seaweed. *Kombu*, a kind of kelp, is an essential ingredient in the basic fish soup stock, *dashi*; *nori*, dried sheets of laver, is used for many purposes; *wakame* is good in soups and salads; and *hijiki* is often cooked with soy sauce and served as a side dish.

Japanese seasonings are unique and there is a wide range, combining sweet, salt, bitter and sour flavours. There is *gomashio*, sesame seed which has been toasted and crushed, and sometimes mixed with salt. *Gomashio* is especially good with spinach. *Mirin* is a sweet fortified wine used for sweetening savoury dishes and glazing; *shoga* is root ginger, cooked whole in some dishes, or grated raw or pickled. *Wasabi*, Japanese horseradish, is sold in powder form in small cans. It makes a hot and pungent sauce, perfect with raw fish, *sushi*; *shichimi-togarashi*, seven-flavours spice, is a hot peppery mixture which is good with noodle and rice dishes; *konasansho* is a powdered pepper. For seafood flavouring, *katsuobushi,* dried, smoked bonito fillet resembling a very hard stick of wood, is shaved off thinly as required. It can also be bought in ready-prepared packets or in powder form for mixing into soups. Many Japanese cooks use a seasoning based on monosodium glutamate, *aji-no-moto*, but although it does serve to bring out the taste of the ingredients used, it is not an essential, and really it is much more rewarding to work without using it at all. It is not recommended by doctors who are concerned to keep sodium at a low level in the diet to counter high blood pressure. It can also cause severe headaches. All these spices and preparations can be bought in Japanese shops in major towns and cities.

JAPAN

Dashi
Basic soup stock

This pale, clear stock with a delicate taste of the sea is the foundation of almost all Japanese soups. It is also very healthy since seaweeds are a useful source of minerals, particularly iodine. You can buy packets of dried *kombu* (kelp) in Oriental grocery shops and some health-food shops. Today some Japanese even buy packs of dried *dashi*, much as we buy stock cubes. But, as with all stocks, it is best to prepare it yourself.

serves 4

2 pints/1.1 litres/5 cups water
1 piece dried *kombu* (kelp) about 4 in/10 cm square, wiped
½ oz/15 g/3 teaspoons *katsuobushi* (dried bonito) shavings

Pour the water into a pan, add the *kombu* and bring to the boil. When it is boiling vigorously, remove the *kombu* and put in the *katsuobushi* shavings. When the water comes back to the boil, remove the pan from the heat. Leave to stand until the shavings have sunk to the bottom, then strain the clear liquid into a bowl and discard the shavings.

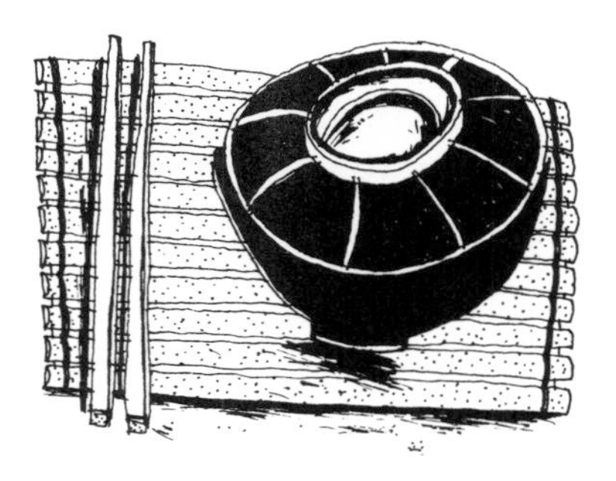

Kakitama-Jiru
Scrambled egg soup

This makes a very light soup, with pale threads of egg and dark flakes of laver floating in a delicate, clear consommé.

serves 4

2 pints/1.1 litres/5 cups *dashi*†
2 teaspoons *shoyu* (Japanese soy sauce)
2 teaspoons salt
2 teaspoons cornflour (cornstarch)
2 eggs, lightly beaten
1 piece *nori* (laver), crumbled

Pour the *dashi* into a saucepan and put on to boil. Mix the *shoyu* with the salt and cornflour and stir into the *dashi* as it heats. As soon as it comes to the boil, spread the egg over the surface as quickly as possible, letting it trickle through a perforated spoon into the stock to form slender threads. As soon as all the egg is in, remove from the heat and add the *nori*.

Serve immediately, piping hot.

Miso Shiru
Soya bean paste soup

Miso is a fermented paste of soya beans with rice. It is rich in protein and vitamins, and is regarded by the Japanese as vital to a healthy diet. Combined with rice, it provides a well-balanced source of amino-acids, and is therefore particularly valuable in vegetarian diets. It keeps indefinitely, and indeed improves its flavour with age. A Japanese cook will not usually use it until it is two years old, and will have several ages of paste in the larder. Soya bean paste soup is one of the most common dishes of Japan, and a popular breakfast dish.

serves 4

- piece of *kombu* (kelp) about 2 in/5 cm square, wiped with a wet cloth
- 2 pints/1.1 litres/5 cups water
- 1/8 oz/3–4 g/1/2 teaspoon *wakame* (a lobe-leafed seaweed)
- 1/3 oz/9 g/2 teaspoons *katsuobushi* (dried bonito) shavings
- 2 tablespoons *aka miso* (red soya bean paste), or 2 1/2–3 tablespoons milder *shiro miso* (white soya bean paste)
- 4–6 oz/110–175 g *tofu* (Japanese bean curd), cut into cubes

Put the *kombu* in a bowl with the water and leave to stand for 2–3 hours (or overnight if you are going to have the soup for breakfast).

Shortly before you are going to have the soup, put the *wakame* to soften in a little water for not more than 10 minutes, then cut it into small pieces.

Put the *kombu* and its water in a pan over a medium heat; just before the water comes to the boil, remove and discard the *kombu*. Add the bonito shavings, bring back to the boil, simmer 2–3 minutes and remove the pan from the heat. Leave to stand for 4–5 minutes, until the bonito shavings have sunk to the bottom. Pour off the clear liquid and add a few tablespoons of it to the soya bean paste. Stir until smooth, then stir back into the soup and bring to the boil. Add the *wakame* and *tofu*, heat through and serve immediately.

Instead of *wakame* and *tofu*, you can use well-washed bean sprouts or diced pumpkin or aubergine.

Yu-Dofu
Simmered bean curd

Tofu, which is of Chinese origin, is a white soya bean curd with the consistency of a custard – set but not firm. It is a high-protein food, contains no fat and is said to aid the digestion of other foods. There are *tofu* shops and *tofu* barrows everywhere in Japan selling this versatile foodstuff. You can cut it into cubes to add to soups, salads and other dishes; or slice it thinly, pat it dry and deep-fry it to make a crisp, puffy snack (*aburage*); or you can put cubes of it in cold water, bring to the boil until it floats, remove and serve garnished with chopped spring onion, grated fresh ginger and dried bonito shavings, and sprinkled with soy sauce. The following recipe from Kyoto makes a simple, nourishing dish.

serves 4

piece of *kombu* (kelp) about 4 in/10 cm square, wiped
2 lb/900 g *tofu* (Japanese bean curd), cut into 1 in/2.5 cm cubes
8 tablespoons *shoyu* (Japanese soy sauce)
4 tablespoons *sake* (rice wine)
1 tablespoon sugar
1 tablespoon *katsuobushi* (dried bonito) shavings
5 fl oz/150 ml/⅔ cup water
4 tablespoons chopped spring onions or scallions
2 tablespoons grated fresh ginger
2 lemons, halved

Put the *kombu* in a shallow, flameproof earthenware casserole. Add the *tofu* and pour on boiling water to cover. Leave over a medium heat until the water starts to bubble, then take off the heat and place the casserole on the table.

In a small saucepan, heat the soy sauce, *sake*, sugar and dried bonito with the water until simmering. Simmer for 3 minutes, then remove from the heat.

Give each diner a small dish with some of the sauce in it, a small saucer with some of the onion and ginger, and another saucer with half a lemon. The diners squeeze lemon juice into their sauce; then they remove *tofu* cubes from the casserole, dip them first into the sauce, and then into the spring onion or ginger before eating them.

Zaru Soba
Buckwheat noodles on bamboo plates

Buckwheat noodles have a good flavour, so they are especially suitable for eating cold. Serve this dish on a hot day – the very spicy sauce is surprisingly refreshing. The noodles are traditionally served on bamboo plates.

serves 4

3 tablespoons *mirin* (sweet rice wine for cooking)
10 fl oz/300 ml/1¼ cups water
5 tablespoons *shoyu* (Japanese soy sauce)
1 tablespoon sugar
½ oz/15 g/3 teaspoons *katsuobushi* (dried bonito) shavings
piece of *kombu* (kelp) 4 in/10 cm square, wiped
10 oz/275 g *soba* (buckwheat noodles)
1 tablespoon *wasabi* (green horseradish powder)
2 sheets *nori* (laver), lightly toasted, then crumbled
1 spring onion or scallion, trimmed, both white and green parts finely chopped

Bring the wine to the boil and add the water, soy sauce, sugar, bonito shavings and the kelp, cut into a fringe. Cook gently, uncovered, and as the mixture comes to the boil, remove and discard the kelp. Simmer for 5 minutes more and then strain through a sieve lined with a double layer of muslin (cheesecloth) into a very shallow bowl. Cool as quickly as you can, then pour into 4 soup bowls and put in the refrigerator to chill slightly.

Cook the noodles in plenty of boiling water until just tender, then drain, rinse with plenty of cold water and leave in cold water until chilled. Drain thoroughly and serve on 4 plates. Mix the horseradish powder to a thick paste with 1 tablespoon water and heap a small spoonful beside each serving of noodles. See *wasabi* in the glossary.

To serve, give each diner a plate of noodles with *nori* sprinkled over, a bowl of sauce and a tiny dish of chopped onion. The diners mix horseradish and onion into the sauce to suit their own taste, then dip the noodles in it before eating them.

Tsukimi Udon
Noodles with poached eggs

The Japanese name of this soup literally means 'looking-like-the-moon noodles' – a reference to the poached egg floating like a moon among the noodles in the soup bowl. It is traditionally served in bowls with lids; this keeps the soup very hot while the raw eggs poach lightly. You can use saucers as lids.

serves 4

1¾ pints/1 litre/4 cups water
piece of *kombu* (kelp) about 4 in/10 cm square, wiped and cut into a fringe
½ oz/15 g/3 teaspoons *katsuobushi* (dried bonito) shavings
4 fl oz/125 ml/½ cup *usukuchi shoyu* (light soy sauce)
2 tablespoons *mirin* (sweet rice wine for cooking)
5 oz/150 g/1½ cups prepared fresh spinach, well washed
10 oz/275 g/1¼ cups dried, thick wheat-flour noodles
4 eggs
piece of *nori* (laver) about 4 in/10 cm square, cut into 4 and lightly toasted
shichimi-togarashi (seven-flavour spice) for sprinkling

Pour the water into a large saucepan, add the *kombu* and bring to the boil, uncovered. Just before it boils, remove and discard the *kombu*. Add the bonito shavings and simmer for 2–3 minutes. Add the soy sauce and wine, bring back to the boil, then remove from the heat. Strain through a sieve lined with a double layer of muslin (cheesecloth), and keep warm.

Drop the spinach into a large saucepan of boiling salted water and simmer for 2–3 minutes. Drain, rinse 3 times in cold water and drain well again. Squeeze to remove excess moisture and form into a roll. Cut into 4 slices and set aside.

Cook the noodles in a large pan of boiling water until just tender, then drain well and divide among 4 large warmed bowls with lids. Bring the soup back to the boil, pour it over the noodles and put a slice of spinach in each bowl.

Break an egg carefully into each bowl, cover with the lid and let the egg poach lightly.

Serve very hot, garnished with a piece of toasted *nori* and *shichimi-togarashi* to sprinkle over the top.

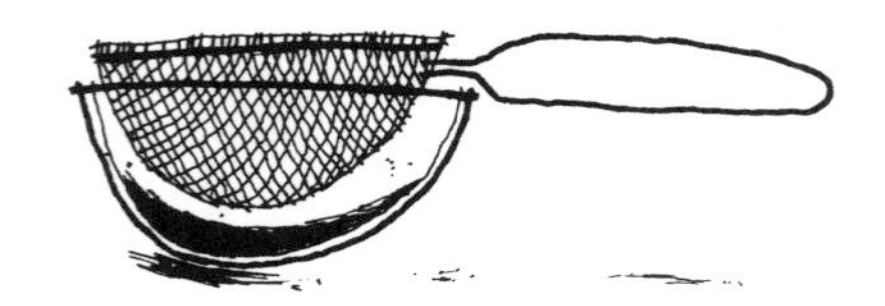

Miso Udon
Noodles with bean paste

A chicken and noodle broth thickened and flavoured with soya bean paste makes a warming winter dish in Japan, where it is usually served in *donburi* (earthenware) bowls.

Wipe the fresh mushrooms, trim the stems and cut into quarters; or soak the dried mushrooms with the sugar in warm water for 30 minutes, then drain, remove the stems and cut the caps into quarters.

Cook the noodles in plenty of boiling water until just tender. Drain, rinse with cold water, drain again and set aside.

Chop the chicken, still on the bone, into roughly 1 in/2.5 cm chunks. Put into a large saucepan with the water, cover and bring to the boil. Skim, then reduce the heat and simmer for about 15 minutes, or until the chicken is tender.

Mix the bean paste to a thin, smooth cream with a little of the chicken stock and add to the rest of the stock in the pan. Stir well, then add the noodles, mushrooms and onions and simmer very gently for about 3 minutes. Serve very hot.

serves 4

- 4 fresh mushrooms, or 4 *shiitake* (dried Japanese mushrooms) with a pinch of sugar
- 10 oz/275 g/2½ cups dried, thick wheat-flour noodles
- 1 lb/450 g chicken pieces on the bone
- 2 pints/1.1 litres/5 cups water
- 8 tablespoons *miso* (bean paste)
- 2 spring onions or scallions, trimmed, both white and green parts cut into ¼ in/5 mm lengths

Chawan Mushi
Savoury custard

The Japanese eat *chawan mushi* like a soup and use spoons for it – practically the only dish they eat with a spoon. It is a substantial hot dish, but it is also sometimes eaten cold on a summer's day.

Cut into the inner curve of the prawns, without cutting right through, and open them out flat, butterfly-fashion. Sprinkle them with the wine and a little salt and leave for 30 minutes.

Put the mushrooms to soak in plenty of boiling water for 30 minutes, then rinse well and drain. Trim away any tough stem and slice.

Sprinkle the soy sauce over the chicken, stir well to mix and leave to stand for 20–30 minutes.

Stir the eggs continuously while you pour the hot *dashi* on to them in a thin stream. Season well with salt.

Take 4 individual bowls and arrange in each a portion of the chicken, prawns, *kamaboko*, mushrooms, celery leaves and lemon rind. Carefully pour on the egg mixture, dividing it equally between the bowls. Put the bowls in a large roasting tin and pour boiling water into the tin to come about halfway up the sides of the bowls. Bake in a pre-heated oven at 325° F/170° C/gas mark 3 for about 20 minutes, until just set but not browned.

Lift the bowls on to heated plates and serve the custards at once.

serves 4

- 4 large prawns or shrimps, cleaned and shelled
- 1 tablespoon *mirin* (sweet rice wine for cooking)
- salt
- 4 dried mushrooms
- 3 teaspoons *shoyu* (Japanese soy sauce)
- 4 oz/110 g/1 cup chicken meat, cut into slivers
- 8 fl oz/225 ml/1 cup beaten egg
- 1½ pints/850 ml/3¾ cups *dashi*† or other stock, hot
- 4 slices *kamaboko*† (Japanese fish cake), or 6 oz/175 g/1½ cups packed cooked pork, cubed
- 4 small sprigs celery leaves, chopped, or 4 young spinach leaves, chopped
- 4 small strips lemon rind

Tamagoyaki
Japanese omelette

Skilful rolling of several layers of very thin omelette makes this unusual but simple light egg dish. Each layer is cooked in a few seconds and does not have time to toughen. Traditionally the omelette is made in a small square frying pan, but a small round one will do just as well. Japanese cooks use a special mop-like brush for oiling the pan very lightly, as they make each layer of the omelette.

serves 4

4 eggs
pinch salt
few drops *shoyu* (Japanese soy sauce)
pinch sugar
oil for brushing pan
shoyu (Japanese soy sauce) for dipping
grated fresh ginger

Break the eggs into a bowl, season with the salt, soy sauce and sugar, and beat lightly.

Heat the omelette pan and brush it sparingly with oil. Pour in just enough egg to make a very thin omelette – and as soon as it is set, use chopsticks or a spatula to make it into a small, tight roll at one edge of the pan. Pour in more egg to make another thin omelette, and as soon as it is set roll the first omelette back over it, then roll the two up together. Leave the roll on the opposite edge of the pan. Make another thin omelette and roll it up with the others as before — and continue in this way until all the egg is used up.

Turn the omelette on to a plate, slice it slightly diagonally into 1½ in/4 cm pieces and serve hot or warm. Provide a little bowl of soy sauce with the grated fresh ginger stirred in; the diners take pieces of omelette with their chopsticks and dip them in the sauce before eating them.

Ochazuke
Rice with green tea

In a country where rice is eaten as often as in Japan, ways of giving it a different flavour – or of using up any that is left from a meal – are welcome. This is a quick, everyday snack served at home with whatever garnishes are to hand. Green tea is a refreshing drink to serve, without milk or sugar, towards the end of a meal.

serves 4

about 12 oz/350 g/6 cups cooked rice
2 heaped teaspoons green tea
about 7 fl oz/200 ml/⅞ cup boiling water

for garnishing:
crumbled toasted *nori* (laver)
pickled *daikon* (Oriental radish)
pickled cabbage strips
roasted chestnuts
katsuobushi (dried bonito) shavings

Put the rice in individual bowls. Spoon the green tea into a very small teapot and pour on the boiling water. Pour all the tea over the rice immediately; do not leave any in the pot because the delicate flavour of the tea is spoiled if the leaves are left to stew.

Sprinkle the rice with the chosen garnish, or lay out a selection of garnishes to choose from.

You can make two more infusions with the same green tea before starting with fresh leaves. Two heaped teaspoons of green tea will make 4 bowls of tea in all.

Nigiri Zushi
Rice-balls

This recipe needs sticky (glutinous) rice to make balls that will hold together properly. As you shape them, moisten your hands with rice vinegar to prevent the balls from sticking to your skin. The rice-balls can accompany a wide variety of dishes. They are served in *sushi* bars topped with *sashimi*†, but you can use any savoury topping you like.

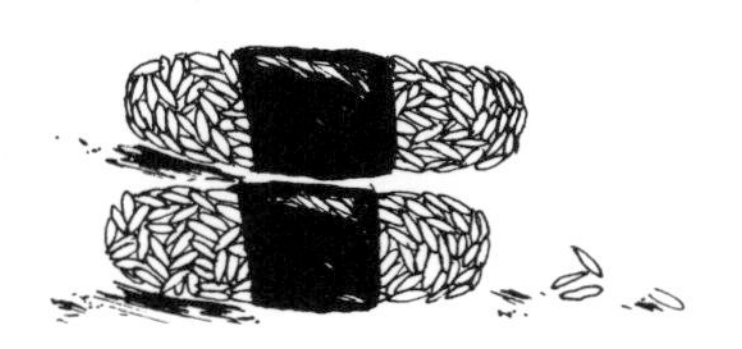

serves 4

11 oz/300 g/2 cups Japanese sticky (glutinous) rice†
14 fl oz/400 ml/1¾ cups water
1 tablespoon rice vinegar
1 tablespoon *wasabi* (green horseradish) paste
watercress to garnish

for the dressing:
4 tablespoons rice vinegar
2 tablespoons sugar
2 teaspoons salt

Wash the rice well and then put it in a heavy-based pan with the water. Cover with a well-fitting lid, bring to the boil, and simmer for 15 minutes. Remove from the heat and leave to stand, covered, for 10 minutes. Then, while it is still hot, put the rice in a bowl and pour on the dressing, well blended. Toss the rice until the dressing is completely mixed in.

Moisten your hands with the vinegar and take about 1 tablespoon of the rice in your left hand. Curl your fingers over it and roll in the palm to make a sausage shape; from time to time press the roll with the two first fingers of your right hand to compress the rice firmly. When the ball is firmly shaped, lay it on a serving dish. Continue until the rice is used up.

To make the *wasabi* paste, mix 1 level tablespoon of green horseradish powder with 1 tablespoon of water until smooth. Put a dab of the paste on each rice-ball. Cover each rice-ball with *sashimi* sliced to fit exactly, or with rectangles of omelette cut to fit exactly, or with Pacific prawns or large shrimps sprinkled with vinegar, or with another topping of your choice. Garnish the dish with watercress.

A very similar dish is *Onigiri*, made with cooked rice (not sticky rice) dressed simply with salt water and then formed into little sausage shapes containing a morsel of fruit, vegetable, meat or fish – tuna, chicken, a plum, a rolled piece of *nori* (laver), a stick of cucumber or a piece of pickled radish, for example.

Kiritampo
Rice-cakes with chicken and mushrooms

serves 4

- 1 lb/450 g/8 cups moist cooked rice
- 8 fl oz/225 ml/1 cup *dashi*†
- 6 tablespoons *shoyu* (Japanese soy sauce)
- 4 tablespoons *sake* (rice wine)
- 2 tablespoons sugar
- 2 chicken breasts, cut into thin slices
- 4 spring onions or scallions, cut into 1½ in/4 cm lengths
- 4 oz/110 g/1½ cups mushrooms, sliced
- 4 oz/110 g/1½ cups *gobo* (burdock root, available in cans), peeled and sliced

This dish is from Akita in Northern Japan, where the cakes are speared lengthways on thin wooden skewers and cooked over an open fire. When they are ready they are taken to the table where the rest of the dish is cooked. Burdock root has a fine flavour similar to that of Jerusalem artichokes; take care not to expose it to the air, or it will discolour.

Put the cooked rice in a large wooden bowl and chop it well; a multi-bladed chopper does this quickly and thoroughly. Knead and mould into sausage shapes about 1 in/2.5 cm thick and 4 in/10 cm long. Lay them on a lightly oiled baking sheet and grill (broil), turning several times, until crisp and browned all over. Leave to cool, then cut into ½ in/1.25 cm slices.

Mix the *dashi*, soy sauce, *sake* and sugar in a pan, bring to the boil, then simmer for a few minutes. Add the chicken, onions, mushrooms and burdock root. Simmer for about 8 minutes, or until the chicken is tender. Add the rice-cakes and continue to simmer until they are heated through. Serve in small individual bowls.

Nasu No Shigiyaki
Aubergine (eggplant) with sesame

serves 4

- 2 aubergines (eggplants), cut into small cubes
- salt
- 2 tablespoons sesame seeds
- 4 tablespoons sesame oil, or other vegetable oil and sesame oil mixed
- a little chopped fresh chilli pepper (optional)
- 2 tablespoons *miso* (soya bean paste)

The flavour and fragrance of toasted sesame seeds and hot sesame oil permeate the absorbent flesh of the aubergines.

Sprinkle the aubergines with salt and leave in a colander for 1 hour for the bitter juices to run out. Drain thoroughly.

Toast the sesame seeds in a hot, dry frying pan until they are light brown. Heat the oil and fry the aubergine until brown. Add the chilli pepper, if you are using it. Dilute the *miso* with a little water and stir into the aubergine until well coated. Sprinkle on the sesame seeds and serve as a vegetable dish to accompany grilled fish or *tempura*.

Horenso No Hitashi
Spinach dressed with sesame seeds

A salad to serve as a side dish with meat or fish. Sesame seeds are a frequent seasoning in Japanese food. They are usually toasted and crushed, then sometimes mixed with salt to make *gomashio* – an alternative seasoning. This is a delicious way to eat spinach, which is an excellent source of vitamins.

serves 4

1 lb/450 g fresh spinach
2 tablespoons *goma* (sesame seeds), black or white
2 tablespoons *shoyu* (Japanese soy sauce)

Cut the spinach leaves across into 1 in/2.5 cm strips. Wash well to get rid of any grit, then put in a pan with a little boiling, unsalted water. Cook for 3 minutes, then drain thoroughly.

Roast the sesame seeds for a few minutes in a dry frying pan over a good heat, tossing them frequently to make sure they do not burn. Pound them in a mortar, add a little of the soy sauce and pound again.

Mix the spinach with the sesame seed dressing and the remaining soy sauce. Serve cold, in small saucers or bowls.

Wakame To Kyuri No Sunomo
Seaweed and cucumber salad

The Japanese make more use of seaweed in their cuisine than any other nation. It provides iodine in their diet. This cool, astringent salad is dressed without any oil. Be sure to use Japanese rice vinegar to enjoy the authentic flavour of the dish.

serves 4

piece of dried *wakame* (a lobe-leaved seaweed) about 3 in/8 cm square
½ cucumber
3 tablespoons rice vinegar
2 teaspoons sugar, or more to taste
1 tablespoon *shoyu* (Japanese soy sauce)
pinch salt

Wash the *wakame* and put it in cold water to soak for 30 minutes. Then drain it well, cut it into ½ in/1.25 cm squares and squeeze out any remaining moisture.

Slice the cucumber into the thinnest possible slices and then mix the cucumber and *wakame* together in a small bowl. Blend the vinegar, sugar, soy sauce and salt together and pour over the salad.

Sashimi
Raw fish or other seafood

The Japanese apply very high standards to the freshness of fish – partly because a Japanese food speciality is *sashimi*, raw fish. They eat *sashimi* at least once a week, but usually buy it at a *sushi* bar rather than preparing it at home. It is most often served with rice-balls†. Although raw fish seems very strange to Western tastes, it has a silky texture and delicate flavour; furthermore, no vitamins or minerals are lost in the cooking process.

serves 4

- 1 lb/450 g cleaned, very fresh fish (for example, sea-bream, salmon, lemon sole, tuna)
- 1 handful greenery, such as parsley, watercress, lettuce, cooked laver or sliced raw vegetables
- 1½ teaspoons *wasabi* (green horseradish) paste, or grated fresh ginger
- 4 tablespoons *shoyu* (Japanese soy sauce)

Scale the fish, wash it carefully and let it soak in clean water for an hour. After this, remove the skin and cut the flesh free of the bone. Chill the fish to make it easier to slice neatly, and use an extremely sharp knife when slicing.

Cut thin, neat, diagonal slices or, with close-textured fish such as tuna, cut ½–1 in/1.25–2.5 cm cubes. Arrange a little greenery round an oval or rectangular serving plate. Lay the slices of fish overlapping one another like roof tiles, in the middle of the greenery. You can curl some slices to represent breaking waves, or wrap them around paper-thin slices of lemon.

To prepare *wasabi* paste (see glossary), mix a level teaspoon of green horseradish powder with a teaspoon of water. Stir the paste, or the grated ginger, into the soy sauce; or, since the *wasabi* is very hot, serve the paste and the soy sauce separately for the diners to mix a sauce to their own taste. Dip each piece of fish in the sauce before eating it.

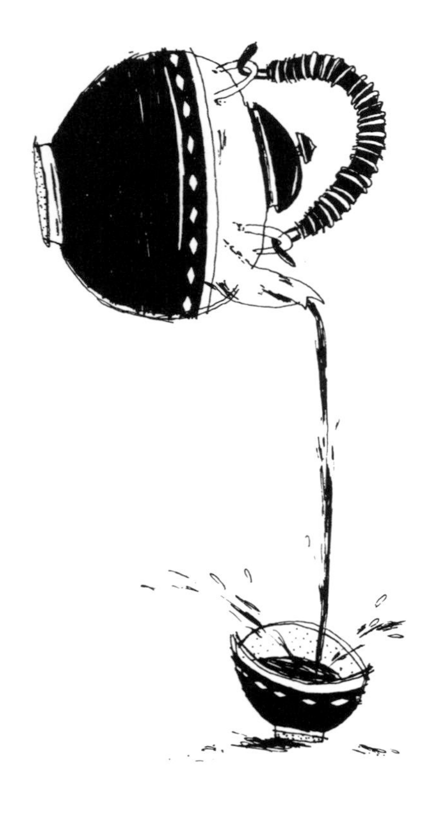

Kamaboko
Japanese fish cakes (or sausage)

Fish cakes with a sweet delicate flavour and firm texture are very popular in Japan. They are usually bought ready-made, but you can easily make them at home. Either shape the mixture into small cakes or make one large cake and steam it as described below.

Put the *kombu* and water in a small pan, bring to the boil and boil for 2 minutes. Remove from the heat and leave to stand for 5 minutes. Lift out the *kombu* (and keep for use in another dish) and mix 3 tablespoons of the liquid with the rice flour to make a smooth paste.

Make sure that the fish is free of all skin and bone, chop finely, then reduce to a paste in a blender. Combine with the rice flour paste. Add the honey, salt, *sake* and egg whites, and beat the mixture until very smooth.

Oil a baking tin 4 × 8 in/10 × 20 cm and put the mixture into it, levelling the surface. Cover with foil and stand on a trivet in a large saucepan with boiling water beneath it. Put the lid on the pan and steam the fish mixture for 30 minutes or until firm. Add more boiling water to the pan during steaming if necessary. Lift out the baking tin and leave to stand for 10 minutes.

Mix together the ingredients for the glaze and brush it over the top of the fish cake. Brown under the grill (broiler). Chill, then cut into squares, cubes or strips.

Serve as an appetizer, or add to soups, stews or savoury custards.

serves 4

piece of *kombu* (kelp) about 3 in/8 cm square, wiped
2¾ fl oz/80 ml/⅓ cup water
1¼ oz/30 g/2 tablespoons brown rice flour
14 oz/400 g/1¾ cups fish fillets (cod, or any salt-water fish of firm texture)
1 teaspoon honey
1 teaspoon salt
3 tablespoons *sake* (rice wine)
2 egg whites, lightly beaten

for glazing:
1 egg yolk, well beaten
1 teaspoon honey
1 teaspoon *sake*

Shio Yaki
Salt-grilled (broiled) fish

The Japanese make this dish in the autumn and winter, when the mackerel are at their best – nice and plump. The salt-grilling means that no extra fat or flavouring is added and you can enjoy the true taste of the fish.

Bone the fish and lift off the fillets but do not skin. If the fish is a thick, meaty one, make diagonal cuts in the flesh at 1 in/2.5 cm intervals. Sprinkle both sides with salt and leave it to soak in for 30 minutes.

Pre-heat the grill (broiler) and put the fillets under it, skin side uppermost, not too close to the heat or the skin will burn. Grill until the skin is crisp, then turn to grill the other side. When the flesh flakes easily, the fish is done.

Divide each fillet into 4 pieces and place on a dish on the table. Each diner takes a piece of fish with chopsticks and dips it into a little bowl of soy sauce before eating it.

serves 4

1 mackerel, or 2 small lemon sole
salt
shoyu (Japanese soy sauce) for dipping

Aji Nitsuke
Braised horse mackerel

serves 4

- 4 small horse mackerel, cleaned and with heads cut off
- ½ in/1.25 cm piece fresh ginger, peeled and sliced
- 3 tablespoons *shoyu* (Japanese soy sauce)
- 1 tablespoon *sake* (rice wine), or *mirin* (sweet rice wine for cooking), or sherry
- 3 tablespoons water
- 1 tablespoon sugar
- ½ teaspoon salt

The horse mackerel used in this Japanese dish is a well-flavoured fish, but it is not often eaten in Europe because of its numerous bones. If you prefer not to tackle removing so many bones, use lemon sole, sea-bream (porgy) or halibut cut into 3 in/8 cm pieces.

Scrape the horny scales off the fish and make 2 diagonal cuts in each side. Wash well in salted water, drain, sprinkle lightly with salt and leave for a few minutes.

Put the ginger in a shallow saucepan or small casserole with the soy sauce, *sake*, water, sugar and salt. Bring to the boil, put in the fish and turn down the heat so that the liquid simmers gently. Cook, uncovered, for 15–20 minutes or until the fish is tender, turning over carefully halfway through.

Serve with rice and *tempura*† for a simple meal.

Yasaino Nimono
Braised vegetables with fish sausage

serves 4

- 4 small *tsatsu mage* (fish sausages) each 2 in/5 cm long
- 3 fl oz/90 ml/⅓ cup *dashi*†
- 1 tablespoon sugar
- 2 tablespoons *shoyu* (Japanese soy sauce)
- 1 tablespoon *sake* or dry sherry
- pinch salt
- 2 medium turnips, cut into 1 in/2.5 cm cubes
- 6 oz/175 g pumpkin, cut into 1 in/2.5 cm cubes (optional)
- 1 leek, cleaned and cut into 1 in/2.5 cm lengths

The fish sausage can be made at home, but it is also sold ready-made in some Japanese shops. As it provides a certain amount of flavour in the cooking liquid, you can use water instead of the *dashi* if you are in a hurry.

Cut each fish sausage into 4 slices. Put the *dashi*, sugar, soy sauce, *sake* and salt in a shallow saucepan or casserole and bring to the boil. Then put in the turnips and pumpkin and cook gently for 10 minutes. Add the leek and fish sausage and continue to cook for 5–10 minutes, until the vegetables are tender.

Serve at a simple family meal with dishes such as grilled (broiled) mackerel and aubergines (eggplants) with sesame seeds†.

Tempura
Fritters

Deep-frying has become a well-known Japanese speciality, but it is said that the Portuguese first introduced it to Japan. The Japanese use a very light batter to coat vegetables, fish or shrimps. Make the batter quickly at the last minute and dip in the items to be fried without coating them completely – their colours and textures will show through here and there. Fry the fritters in a light vegetable oil such as safflower or corn oil, perhaps with a little dark sesame oil added for flavour. You can simply sprinkle the fritters with lemon juice or dip in soy sauce as an alternative to the sauce given here.

serves 4

1¼ lb/575 g/2½ packed cups of any of the following: shelled prawns or shrimps, tiny squid, strips of white fish, thin rounds of courgette (zucchini) or aubergine (eggplant), thin slices of pumpkin, sprigs of cauliflower or broccoli, button mushrooms, thin rings of onion, green pepper cut into 4–6 pieces, small bundles of carrot strips, or other vegetables cut in small pieces
oil for deep-frying

for the batter:
1 egg
12 tablespoons water
4 oz/110 g/1 cup sifted plain flour

for the dipping sauce:
1 pint/575 ml/2½ cups *dashi*†
2 tablespoons *shoyu* (Japanese soy sauce)
pinch salt
½ teaspoon sugar
1 tablespoon finely chopped spring onion or scallion
6 tablespoons grated *daikon* (Oriental radish)

First prepare the dipping sauce. Heat the *dashi*, soy sauce, salt and sugar together, stirring well to blend, then leave to cool before adding the onion and radish.

Pour oil into a large frying pan to a depth of about 1 in/2.5 cm and put to heat. It is at the right temperature when a single drop of batter dropped into the oil sinks to the bottom and immediately returns to the surface. If the batter does not rise at once, the oil is not hot enough; if the batter does not sink but sizzles on the surface, the oil is too hot.

Prepare the batter at the last minute. Beat the egg lightly in a bowl, then add the water and beat again for a few seconds. Add the flour and mix it in roughly without beating, leaving small lumps of dry flour here and there.

When the oil is at the right temperature, quickly dip the pieces for frying into the batter without coating them completely. Fry a few pieces at a time; too many in the pan at once will make the temperature of the oil drop and the batter will not be crisp.

Fry for about 2 minutes, turning to cook evenly, and when the batter is pale golden, lift out and put on paper towels to drain. Skim off any loose bits of batter as they rise. As soon as one batch is fried, put in another until everything is cooked.

Serve the *tempura* very hot and as soon as possible after they come out of the pan; serve them on a wicker basket or plate, and offer the sauce in little bowls. Everybody around the table enjoys the excitement of the *tempura* arriving in relays, like pancakes, but the cook has to keep cooking and does not get a chance to sit down.

Torinabe
Chicken roasted in the sukiyaki style

The sukiyaki manner refers to cooking meat at the table in a special heavy pan. Eating meat is not a strong Japanese tradition, but it has gained approval in recent times. Fine quality beef is usually cooked in the sukiyaki pan, but it is not traditional, since beef was virtually unknown in Japan before World War II. This recipe uses the sukiyaki technique for roasting chicken – a less expensive and more traditional food in Japan.

serves 4

- 1½ lb/700 g chicken pieces, skinned
- 4 oz/110 g/½ cup *harusame* (Japanese vermicelli)
- oil for frying
- 6 fl oz/175 ml/¾ cup *shoyu* (Japanese soy sauce)
- 8 tablespoons white sugar
- 8 fl oz/225 ml/1 cup *dashi*†
- 4 teaspoons *sake* (rice wine)
- 8 oz/225 g leeks, trimmed, washed and sliced
- 3–4 medium onions, sliced
- ¼–½ lb/110–225 g mushrooms, trimmed and sliced
- 1 lb/450 g/2 cups *tofu* (Japanese bean curd), cut into slices
- 4 eggs

Cut the chicken meat into thin strips, trimming off any pieces of tendon or gristle. Soak the *harusame* for 3 minutes in hot water, then drain and cut into 2 in/5 cm lengths.

Heat a large, heavy frying pan and pour in enough oil to cover the base. When the oil is very hot, add the soy sauce and then the sugar. Stir over a low heat, then add the *dashi* and *sake*. Next add the leeks, onions, mushrooms, *harusame* and bean curd and cook for a few minutes. Then add the chicken.

Simmer for 15 minutes. Meanwhile, put a beaten, raw egg in a small dish for each person. Make sure the chicken does not burn; turn the pieces so that they brown all over.

When the chicken is cooked, leave a very low heat under the pan while the diners help themselves to the meat and vegetables and dip them in the beaten egg before eating them. You may need to add a little *dashi* to the pan to keep the dish moist.

Serve *torinabe* with some rice after a clear soup. Warmed *sake* or cold beer is the usual drink to serve with it.

Hoo Wan T'heng
Fishball soup

Numerous fish soup stalls in Penang, West Malaysia, sell this soup. The fishballs can be of any shape and are not only served in soups but stuffed into fresh red chilli peppers or rings of cucumber; they are sometimes hugged by walls of bean curd; or they contain bright strips of chilli pepper and herbs to give attractive glimpses of colour on the surface. Prawns, shrimps and crab meat make more luxurious fishballs but any white fish will do well. As an accompaniment serve a small bowl of thin soy sauce with slivers of fresh red chilli peppers in it.

serves 4

1½ lb/700 g/3 packed cups white fish on the bone, such as cod or haddock
½ lb/225 g/1 packed cup fish trimmings (bones, heads)
1½ pints/850 ml/3¾ cups water, lightly salted
2 oz/50 g/¼ cup thick rice noodles
4 spring onions or scallions, finely chopped
oil for frying

Remove the skin and bones from the fish and flake the flesh into a bowl of heavily salted water; leave to stand for about 20–30 minutes. Put the skin, bones and trimmings to simmer gently in the lightly salted water for about 20 minutes, then strain off the clear broth.

Drain the fish and pound it to a paste using a pestle and mortar or an electric blender. Mould half the paste into small balls about ½ in/1.25 cm in diameter. Shape the rest of the paste into a flat rectangular cake about 2 in/5 cm across.

Slice the cake thinly and deep-fry the slices until crisp and golden. Poach the fishballs very gently in the broth for 5–6 minutes, and at the same time boil the noodles until just tender, in another pan of boiling water, then strain.

To serve the soup put a portion of the noodles in each individual bowl with some fishballs on top. Pour on the hot broth and float the fried fish slices on top. Sprinkle on the onion.

Tofu
Soya bean curd

Its smooth, soft texture and mild flavour make this vegetable protein increasingly popular as it becomes more widely known. It is traditional Chinese food and is available in Oriental food shops, but you can easily make it at home. It keeps well and is very versatile; eat it cold in salads, dice it to add to soups, or serve it with pickles. Perhaps best of all is bean curd that has dried for a few days, then been sliced and fried in oil until crisp and puffy. It is known as *doufu* in Chinese shops.

1 lb/450 g/2 cups soya beans
3 pints/1.7 litres/7 cups cold water
1 rounded tablespoon Epsom salts
3 tablespoons warm water

Wash the beans, cover them with cold water and leave to soak overnight.

Next day, rinse the beans well and put them into a blender. Add twice their volume of cold water. Blend until completely smooth and free of any gritty bits. Stir the pulp into the remaining cold water.

Pour the mixture into a fine cloth, such as a piece of muslin (cheesecloth), over a saucepan. Squeeze through into the pan as much of the liquid (bean milk) as possible. Bring the bean milk to the boil, boil for 3 minutes, then remove from the heat.

Dissolve the Epsom salts in the warm water and stir it briefly into the bean milk. Leave for 5–10 minutes; the milk will then have thickened into a mass of curds. Lift it carefully on to a clean cloth and rinse well with cold water. Wrap the cloth round the curd, place a saucer and weight on top, and leave to drain on a dish for 2–3 hours. For a neater curd, you can drain and press it in a small wooden frame such as honeycombs are made in.

Store the drained curd in an uncovered bowl of water in the refrigerator. It will keep there for up to a week if you change the water every other day.

Liangmian Huang
Two sides yellow (Fried bean curd)

Fried bean curd has a mild fresh taste and soft texture which make it popular in the Chinese diet. In this Taiwanese recipe the bean curd is first left to dry for a few days.

serves 4

4 spring onions or scallions, trimmed of roots
2 cakes *doufu* (Chinese bean curd), left to dry for a few days
5–6 tablespoons peanut or other oil
3 cloves garlic, peeled and coarsely chopped
½ teaspoon *lajiao jiang* (hot pepper paste) or *ladouban jiang* (hot bean paste)
¼ green pepper, deseeded and cut into thin strips
pinch salt
1 teaspoon sugar
6 teaspoons light soy sauce

Crush the heads of the onions, then cut both white and green parts into 2 in/5 cm lengths. Rinse the *doufu*, then cut each cake horizontally into 3 slices and divide each slice into 4 strips.

Heat a large frying pan over a high heat for 15 seconds, then put in 3–4 tablespoons of the oil to cover the base. When a haze begins to rise, put in a layer of *doufu* slices and fry for about 6 minutes, turning gently once or twice, until both sides are golden. Lift out and set aside while you fry another batch, and continue until all are done.

Heat a *wok*, or the cleaned frying pan, over a high heat and put in 2 tablespoons of oil. When it is hot, put in the garlic and stir-fry for 30 seconds. Add the *lajiao jiang* and the green pepper and stir-fry for another 30 seconds; then the spring onions and stir-fry for 15 seconds; then the slices of *doufu* and stir-fry for another 15 seconds. Finally add the salt, sugar and soy sauce and stir-fry for 2 minutes before serving.

SOUTH-EAST ASIA

Pansit Molo
Pork-stuffed noodles in shrimp and chicken soup

Although the Filipinos eat rice as their staple food, they consume wheat on quite a large scale too. It is almost all imported grain, but it is milled locally. They use it for bread and particularly for noodles (*pansit*). In this dish, originally a Malay Chinese recipe, the noodle dough is stuffed with meat, like ravioli.

serves 4

for the noodle dough:
4 oz/110 g/1 cup flour
pinch salt
1 egg yolk
about 1½ : oz/35 ml/ 3 tablespoons water

for the filling:
3 oz/85 g/⅓ cup pork, very finely minced (ground)
1 tablespoon chopped leek
1 egg yolk
2 tablespoons soy sauce
pinch pepper

for the soup:
oil for frying
3 large cloves garlic, finely chopped
1 medium onion, chopped
1 lb/450 g/2 cups prawns, peeled and sliced
8 oz/225 g/1 cup dried, cooked chicken, if available
8 tablespoons soy sauce
2 pints/1.1 litres/5 cups prepared prawn stock (see below)
1 pint/575 ml/2½ cups prepared chicken soup or stock
4 tablespoons chopped leek
1 teaspoon salt, to taste

To prepare the noodle dough, sift the flour and salt into a bowl, drop in the egg yolk and mix together using your fingers. Add the water gradually and continue working the dough until it is very smooth. Then roll it out on a floured board into a paper-thin sheet. Cut into triangular pieces with sides no more than 2 in/5 cm long.

To prepare the filling, put all the ingredients together in a bowl and mix until thoroughly blended. Spoon small amounts of the mixture on to half the triangles of dough. Dampen the edges, top with the remaining triangles and pinch the edges together to seal firmly.

To make the soup, heat the oil and fry the garlic and onion until they just start to colour. Add the shrimps and fry for 1–2 minutes, with boiled chicken pieces, shredded, if using freshly made chicken stock. Stir in the soy sauce and continue cooking for 3 minutes more. Pour in the prawn stock (see below) and the chicken soup or stock. Add the leeks, and salt if necessary, and then cover and simmer over a low heat for 1 hour.

Finally, drop the stuffed noodles into the simmering soup, bring to a gentle boil and cook for 5 minutes. Serve immediately.

To make prawn stock, pound the shells of the prawns with a pestle. Put them in a saucepan and bring to the boil with 2 pints/1.1 litres/5 cups water, and simmer for 20 minutes. Do not add salt – the shells are already very salty. Strain and press out as much fluid as possible.

Chaomian
Fried noodles

A simple, classic Chinese dish, essentially made with stir-fried noodles and whatever meat, seafood and green vegetables there are available. Elaborate modern versions of the dish, called chop suey, may marinate the fish and meat, extend the list of vegetables and add a sticky sauce, but in this authentic Taiwanese recipe the crisp noodles are mixed with Chinese cabbage, shrimps and pork, and given a smoky flavour by the dried mushrooms. The soft flakes of tree ears (an edible fungus that grows on trees, also known as wood ears or black fungus) add variety to the texture rather than extra flavour.

serves 4 (or more)

- 6 dried black mushrooms
- 1 handful dried tree ears (optional)
- 8 oz/225 g/1 packed cup peeled shrimps
- 3½ teaspoons salt
- 6 oz/175 g/¾ cup dried Chinese noodles
- 1½ lb/700 g/6 cups Chinese cabbage, trimmed of outer leaves
- 2 pork chops, boned and trimmed of fat
- 3 spring onions or scallions, cut across into 2 in/5 cm lengths, then lengthways into fine shreds
- 2 tablespoons soy sauce
- 1 tablespoon sesame oil
- 1 tablespoon Chinese rice wine or dry sherry
- 1 tablespoon cornflour (cornstarch)
- 9 tablespoons peanut or other vegetable oil
- 1 in/2.5 cm piece fresh ginger, peeled and cut into matchstick strips

Put the mushrooms and tree ears in a bowl, cover with plenty of boiling water and leave to soak for about 20 minutes. Drain and rinse well under running water. Pick over the tree ears to remove any fragments of wood or other impurities. Discard the mushroom stalks and cut the caps into slivers. If the shrimps are large, cut them into ½ in/1.25 cm pieces. Mix with 1 teaspoon of the salt.

The noodles have to be parboiled before they are fried. Bring a large pan of water to a rolling boil and put in the noodles, according to packet instructions. Cook until only just tender. Drain well and set aside.

Wash the cabbage leaves carefully and cut across into strips about 1 in/2.5 cm wide. Cut the pork into shreds about 2 in/5 cm long and ¼ in/5 mm wide. Add the onions to the meat and stir in the soy sauce and sesame oil. Mix well and set aside. Add the wine and cornflour to the shrimps and mix well.

Heat a *wok* or large, heavy-based pan for 15 seconds over a high heat and then pour in 6 tablespoons of oil. As soon as it begins to smoke, put in the ginger and mushrooms and stir-fry for 30 seconds. Add the meat mixture and stir-fry for 20 seconds. If using tree ears, add next and stir-fry for 30 seconds. Keep stirring over high heat while you add the shrimps a handful at a time; when they are all in, stir-fry for 15 seconds more. Take the mixture from the pan and set aside.

Clean and wipe the pan thoroughly with kitchen paper, then place it over a high heat for 15 seconds. Put in the remaining oil, and when it begins to smoke, put in the cabbage and stir-fry for 1 minute. Add the drained noodles and stir gently just to prevent sticking while they fry for 2½ minutes.

Return the meat and shrimp mixture to the pan, stir well to combine all the ingredients, then cook 5 minutes more, stirring from time to time to make sure everything is very hot, and nothing sticks to the pan. The noodles should be crisp in parts and soft in others.

Turn out on to a heated serving plate and serve at once. There will be substantial helpings for four people as a main course, or for many more people if the dish is one of a selection of main dishes at a Chinese meal.

Dan Dan Mian
Cold noodles with sesame sauce

In Taiwan this is bought and eaten in the streets. Each ingredient of the sauce is ladled separately over the cold, cooked noodles for the buyer to mix together himself.

serves 4

- 1 lb/450 g Chinese noodles
- 4 teaspoons *lajiao you* (hot pepper flakes in oil, see below)
- ½ teaspoon ground, roasted *huajiao* (Szechwan peppercorns)
- 12 cloves garlic, peeled and coarsely chopped
- 3 in/8 cm piece fresh ginger, peeled and very finely chopped
- 1 teaspoon salt
- 5 tablespoons water
- 4 tablespoons finely chopped spring onion or scallions, both white and green parts
- 4 tablespoons sesame paste
- 8 tablespoons light soy sauce
- 2 teaspoons sugar

Cook the noodles in plenty of fast-boiling water for about 5 minutes, until they are just tender but not too soft. Drain, rinse well in cold water and drain again.

To make *lajiao you*, heat 2 fl oz/50 ml/3 tablespoons of peanut or other oil until it is smoking hot, then remove from the heat. Leave to cool for 5 seconds, then add 2 oz/50 g/¾ cup dried chilli pepper flakes (bought or made by coarsely chopping dried red chilli peppers). The oil will foam up. When it subsides, add ½ teaspoon of salt, stir well and store in a sealed jar. Stir well each time before use.

To prepare the ground roasted *huajiao*, put 1 level teaspoon of the dark brown Szechwan peppercorns in a hot, dry pan and shake over a low heat for 2–3 minutes until they give out a strong aroma. Do not let them burn. Let them cool, then crush or grind to a powder.

Pound the garlic, ginger and salt together in a mortar to make a coarse paste, then add the water and mix well.

Serve out the noodles on to 4 plates. Arrange a portion of the *lajiao you*, roasted pepper, garlic and ginger mixture, onion, sesame paste, soy sauce and sugar around the noodles. Each diner should mix the sauce ingredients and noodles together very thoroughly before eating the dish.

Chiaotse
Crescent-shaped ravioli

This Taiwanese recipe is a good example of the fine art of making a little go a long way and turning humble ingredients into an interesting spicy dish.

serves 4

for the dough:
9 oz/250 g/2¼ cups plain flour
5 fl oz/150 ml/⅔ cup water
about 4 tablespoons peanut or other oil for frying

for the filling:
12 oz/350 g Chinese cabbage, cut into fine strips
10 oz/275 g/1¼ cups pork shoulder, minced (ground)
2 spring onions or scallions, chopped finely
¼ in/5 mm piece fresh ginger, peeled and chopped very finely
1 teaspoon salt
2 tablespoons light soy sauce
½ teaspoon sugar

To make the dough, put the flour into a bowl, make a well in the middle and pour in the water. Mix to work up a dough, then knead on a floured board for 10 minutes until even textured and very firm. Shape into a ball, cut into quarters and shape each quarter into a roll about 6 in/15 cm long. Leave to rest for at least 10 minutes covered with a damp cloth.

Cut each roll into 7 slices, dust with a little flour and roll out into paper-thin circles about 3 in/8 cm across.

To prepare the filling, blanch the cabbage strips in boiling water for 2 minutes, drain, rinse with cold water and drain again. Mix with the pork, onions, ginger, salt, soy sauce and sugar until well blended.

Take a circle of dough in one hand and put a well-heaped teaspoon of filling in the centre. Using the fingers of the other hand, make 6–7 pleats round half the edge of the dough. Bring up the pleated and unpleated edges to meet over the filling and pinch together firmly to seal. The dough will be formed into a small curved pasty with a ridge running along the top. Space out the filled crescents on a floured board; you can leave them in a cool place for some time before use.

To fry the ravioli, use two 10 in/25.5 cm frying pans. Heat about 2 tablespoons of the oil in each pan and when it is very hot, lay half the ravioli in each pan, arranging them in circles. Immediately reduce the heat and fry for 3 minutes, until the crescents are lightly browned underneath. Carefully pour 5 fl oz/150 ml/⅔ cup water into each pan and bring to the boil, then cover and leave to simmer for 10 minutes. Remove the lids and continue cooking for another 5 minutes, or until the liquid has evaporated.

To serve, invert the pans on to heated plates and turn out the ravioli so that they lie in circles with the browned side uppermost. Serve with soy sauce and rice vinegar to sprinkle on.

Another way of cooking the ravioli is simply to drop them into a very large pan of boiling water and boil for 10 minutes.

Empanadas de Mais
Sweet-corn patties

This simple recipe from the Philippines makes crisp fritters that combine the saltiness of prawns with sweet, crunchy kernels of sweet-corn. Use fresh corn whenever you can to enjoy the patties at their best.

serves 4

- 8 small cobs of corn, or 8 oz/225 g/2 cups drained canned sweet-corn or frozen sweet-corn, thawed
- 8 oz/225 g/1 cup cooked prawns or shrimps, shelled and finely chopped
- 4 cloves garlic, peeled and finely sliced
- 1 medium onion, finely chopped
- green parts of 3 spring onions or scallions, finely chopped
- pinch salt
- pinch freshly ground black pepper
- ½ teaspoon sugar
- 3 tablespoons cornflour (cornstarch)
- 2 tablespoons water
- 1 egg, lightly beaten
- oil for deep frying

If you are using cobs of corn, scrape off the kernels. Combine the corn with the prawns, garlic, onion, spring onion, salt, and pepper and sugar. Mix the cornflour to a smooth paste with the water, then combine it with the egg. Stir into the corn mixture.

Pour oil into a frying pan to a depth of ¼ in/5 mm and heat it until a haze rises. Put in spoonfuls of the mixture, a few at a time, and fry until light golden brown on both sides, turning over once. Lift out and drain on paper towels. Continue until all the mixture is used. Serve crisp and hot.

Nasi Goreng
Fried rice

This is a traditional and elaborate method from Malaya of using up any left-over boiled rice. You can vary the ingredients to use whatever fish or meat is available, including cooked fish or meat left from a previous meal. The Chinese make it with pork and decorate it elaborately with slivers of omelette, chopped spring onion, fried onion, red chilli peppers and parsley; it is served with chilli sauce.

serves 4

- 5 oz/150 g/⅔ cup rice or 2 cups cooked rice
- oil for frying
- 1 large onion, chopped
- 1 clove garlic, peeled and finely sliced
- 1 tablespoon soy sauce
- 5 oz/150 g/⅔ cup chopped cooked chicken, pork, beef, or baked fish, or a combination of these
- 5 oz/150 g/¾ packed cup peeled prawns

for garnish use any of the following:

- 1 medium onion, sliced and fried
- 2 fresh red chilli peppers, deseeded and cut into slivers
- 3 spring onions or scallions, finely chopped
- a 1-egg omelette, rolled and cut into strips, or a fried egg

Heat the oil in a frying pan and fry the onions and garlic until brown. Stir in the rice and soy sauce, the cooked meat or fish and the prawns. Continue to fry gently until the rice is thoroughly heated and evenly browned.

Turn on to a hot serving dish and decorate with the chosen garnishes.

Taiwan Nuo Mi Fan
Taiwan rice with shrimp and pork

serves 4

9 oz/250 g/4½ cups sticky (glutinous) rice†
4 oz/110 g/⅔ packed cup prawns or shrimps, shelled
4 tablespoons peanut or other oil
4 tablespoons sesame oil
½ onion, chopped finely
3 oz/75 g lean pork, cut into matchstick strips
2 small dried mushrooms, soaked in a few tablespoons of water for 20 minutes, then sliced finely
1 tablespoon light soy sauce
1 tablespoon Chinese rice wine or dry sherry
½ teaspoon salt

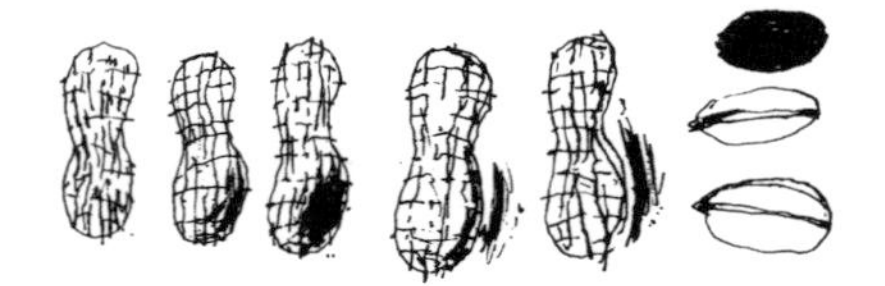

The delicate flavours of pork and shrimp combine with the pungent mushrooms, sesame oil and peanut oil to give character to this simple Taiwanese rice dish. The sesame oil is also a valuable source of polyunsaturates. The mixture, formed into little balls, makes a convenient snack or picnic lunch.

Put the rice in enough warm water to cover it generously, stir well, then leave to stand for 30 minutes. Drain well, reserving 9 fl oz/250 ml/1 cup of the water. Cut into the prawns lengthways without cutting right through, and open them out butterfly-fashion.

Heat the oils together in a heavy-based pan until a haze rises, then stir-fry the onion for 30 seconds. Add the pork, prawns and mushrooms and continue to stir-fry for about 1 minute. Sprinkle in the soy sauce and wine, stir quickly and add the drained rice. Sprinkle in the salt, stir again and pour in the reserved rice water. Bring to the boil, then reduce the heat, cover and cook for about 20 minutes more, or until the rice is cooked and almost all the water is absorbed.

Serve the dish hot or cold, either as it is or formed into small balls.

Karedok
Mixed salad with peanut dressing

serves 4

4 oz/110 g sweet potato
salt
4 oz/110 g/¾ cup *kacang pajang* (yard-long beans) or young dwarf green beans, cut into ½ in/1.25 cm lengths
4 oz/110 g/¾ cup bean sprouts
4 oz/110 g/¾ cup white cabbage, finely shredded
4 small round aubergines (eggplants), or large radishes, quartered
½ cucumber, peeled and sliced
2 tablespoons chopped fresh mint

This recipe from West Java shows the Indonesian liking for raw vegetables combined with a rich sweet peanut dressing. You can buy prepared *sambal ulek* (see below), and either powdered or whole root *kencur*, in some specialist Oriental food stores. *Kencur* is a ground root with a mild camphorous flavour. There is no substitute for it, but it can be omitted if necessary.

Peel the sweet potato and cut it into tiny matchstick strips; immediately plunge into cold water with 1 teaspoon salt added until you are ready to dress the salad.

To prepare the dressing, put the peanuts in a dry, heavy-based pan and toss over a good heat for 4–5 minutes until well browned; or fry them in very little oil.

Grind them finely or pound them in a mortar, then put them into a saucepan. Fry the *terasi* in a little oil for about 30 seconds on each side (but shut the kitchen door while you do it as the smell is powerful). Pound the *terasi* with the garlic, *kencur*, *sambal ulek* and a little salt. Add to the peanuts. (If you are using root *kencur* and have difficulty pounding it up, simply put it in the pan whole, but remember to discard it before serving.) Pour on the boiling water and add the sugar and lime juice. Stir well, then cook over a medium heat for 2 minutes, stirring continuously. Leave to cool.

Drain the sweet potato and arrange with the beans, bean sprouts, cabbage, aubergines and cucumber in a shallow bowl or on a plate. Pour the peanut dressing over them and garnish with the mint.

Serve the *karedok* by itself or to accompany rice and meat.

for the dressing:
4 oz/110 g peanuts, shelled but still in their skins
oil for frying
slice of *terasi*/(firm shrimp paste also known as *blachen*) the size of a postage stamp
1 clove garlic, peeled
pinch powdered *kencur*, or thin slice root *kencur* about half the size of a postage stamp (optional)
1 teaspoon *sambal ulek* (crushed red chilli powder and salt)
salt
10 fl oz/300 ml/1¼ cups boiling water
1 teaspoon brown sugar
juice of ½ lime

Acar Campur
Cooked mixed vegetable salad

Indonesians are great vegetable eaters, for such food is plentiful on their islands. They can raise one or even two crops of many vegetables between gathering one rice crop and planting the next. Vegetables are seasoned generously with herbs and spices, which are said to have medicinal value as well as giving extra flavour.

serves 4

8 oz/225 g/1¼ cups dwarf green beans, topped and tailed
8 oz/225 g/1¼ cups carrots
1 cucumber, peeled
1 red or green chilli pepper, deseeded
2 tablespoons oil
3 *kemiri* (candle-nuts, Macadamia nuts)
1 shallot, chopped
2 cloves garlic, peeled
½ teaspoon turmeric
½ teaspoon ground ginger
10 pickling onions, peeled
4 tablespoons rice vinegar
salt
8 oz/225 g/1¼ cups cauliflower, trimmed and divided into sprigs
1 red pepper, deseeded and cut into strips (optional)
1 green pepper, deseeded and cut into strips (optional)
10 fl oz/300 ml/1¼ cups water
2 teaspoons brown sugar
1 teaspoon French mustard or mustard powder

Cut the beans into 2–3 pieces each and cut up the carrots and cucumber into pieces of about the same size as the cut beans. Cut the chilli pepper into 4.

Heat the oil in a *wok* or heavy-based deep saucepan. Crush the *kemiri*, shallot and garlic together to a paste and sauté in the oil for 1 minute. Add the turmeric, ginger, chilli pepper and onions. Stir everything together for a few seconds, then put in the vinegar and a little salt. Cover and cook for 3 minutes. Then put in the carrots, cauliflower, beans and peppers. Pour in the water, cover again and continue cooking for 8 minutes more.

Add the sugar, mustard and cucumber. Cover and cook for 2 minutes. Then take the lid off and stir continuously as the vegetables cook for another 3 minutes.

Serve *acar campur* either hot or cold with rice.

Bapsetek Ikan
Mackerel with potatoes in a hot red sauce

This recipe comes from Perlis in West Malaysia. The *kembong* used there are so closely related to the Atlantic mackerel that there is little difference between them from the cook's point of view. Mackerel is an oily fish full of polyunsaturated fats which are so good for the heart. It is also a cheap and delicious source of protein.

serves 4

8–10 tablespoons palm oil or ground-nut oil
8 small mackerel, cleaned
4 medium potatoes, sliced
2 medium onions, chopped
4 cloves garlic, peeled and chopped
2 teaspoons cornflour (cornstarch) or rice flour
5 fresh red chilli peppers, split lengthways
2 tablespoons tomato sauce
salt to taste

Heat the oil and fry the fish until it is well browned all over. Lift out and keep warm.

Fry the potatoes in the same oil until they are just tender and browned. Lift out and keep warm.

Next fry the onions and garlic until they are golden. Mix the flour with enough water to make a thin paste and add this to the onions and garlic. Let it simmer briefly before adding the chilli peppers, tomato sauce, and salt.

When the mixture is simmering again, put in the fish and potatoes. Let it all cook for a couple of minutes longer, adding a little water if the sauce is too thick. Taste and correct the seasoning and serve at once.

Chin Kou Yu Yu Ssu
Shredded squid and pork

This dish from Taiwan combines squid and pork, two of the favourite foods of the Chinese. They often buy small dried squid, which are very good value and available from most Chinese food shops. The flavours and textures complement each other exquisitely.

serves 4

5 oz/150 g/1 cup dried squid
2 fresh red chilli peppers, deseeded, or 2 dried red chilli peppers, previously soaked in water
1 bamboo shoot (canned)
1 large leek, trimmed of all green parts
6 tablespoons peanut or other oil
4 oz/110 g pork, trimmed of excess fat and cut into matchstick strips
2 tablespoons light soy sauce
2 teaspoons Chinese rice wine or dry sherry
2 teaspoons rice vinegar
1–2 teaspoons sesame oil

Roll up each squid, starting from the pointed end, then cut into thin strips. Put in a bowl, cover with boiling water and leave to stand for 20 minutes before draining. Cut the chilli peppers, bamboo shoot and leek into matchstick strips.

Heat half the oil in a *wok* or frying pan until very hot, add the squid and stir-fry for 5–10 seconds, until the strips curl up. Remove from the pan and set aside.

Put the rest of the oil in the pan and heat well. Stir-fry the pork for about 10 seconds, then add the chilli peppers and bamboo shoot. Stir-fry for a few seconds, then put back the squid. Add the soy sauce, wine and vinegar. Stir until the mixture is hot again, then add the leek and immediately turn off the heat. Stir, splash on the sesame oil and turn out on to a heated serving dish. Serve at once with rice.

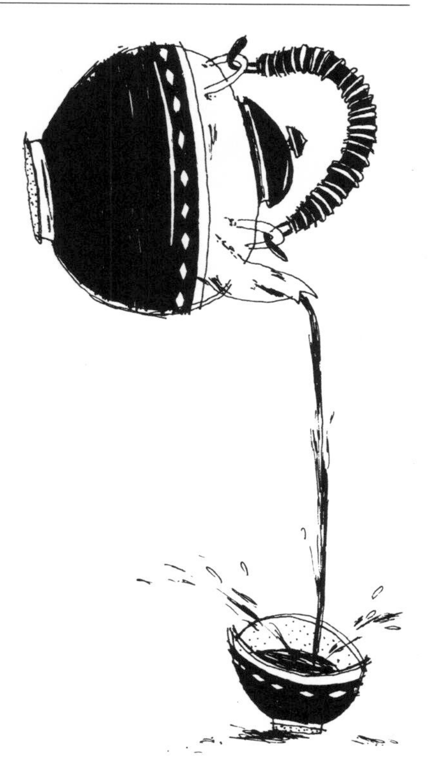

Udang Bakar
Grilled (broiled) prawns

Since Indonesia consists of islands stretching across an area larger than Europe, it is scarcely surprising that fish appears frequently in the diet – and not only seafood but freshwater fish that breed in the flooded rice-fields. Fresh, large, green prawns would be used for *udang bakar*, but large Mediterranean or Pacific prawns make an excellent substitute.

serves 4

12–16 large Mediterranean or Pacific prawns or large shrimps
2 tablespoons lime juice
1 tablespoon olive oil or melted butter
3 cloves garlic, peeled and crushed
very small slice *terasi* (firm shrimp paste – *blachen*), grilled (broiled) and crushed (optional)
pinch chilli powder
1 teaspoon brown sugar

Clean the prawns and discard the heads. Leave on the tails and the shell over the back but remove the shell from the underside. Cut lengthways into the flesh so that you can open the prawns out flat.

Combine the lime juice with the oil and mix in the garlic, *terasi*, chilli powder and sugar. Put the prepared prawns into this marinade for at least 30 minutes, turning them from time to time.

Cook the prawns under a hot grill for 6–8 minutes, turning and brushing with the marinade several times. Serve hot with rice as a main course; occasionally they are served alone as a first course.

Tau Yu Bak
Pork with soy sauce

This is a popular dish among Straits Chinese – the descendants of the Chinese who settled in Malaysia, mainly in Malacca, Penang and Singapore. Their distinctive Nonya cookery demands heavy spicing, and uses some Chinese ingredients, such as pork, which the Malays do not use. Sugar, which is seldom used in Malaysian cooking, is added to this dish because of the large quantity of soy.

serves 4

2½ tablespoons light soy sauce
2½ tablespoons dark soy sauce
1 tablespoon Chinese five spices (see glossary)
12 oz/350 g pork leg or shoulder, cut into 1 in/2.5 cm cubes
vegetable oil for frying
2–3 cloves garlic, crushed but not peeled
6 peppercorns, crushed
1 stick cinnamon
6 cloves
1 piece star anise (or 1 stick fennel)
10 fl oz/300 ml/1¼ cups water
½ teaspoon sugar or more to taste
4 oz/110 g/½ cup *tau hoo* (white bean curd), diced
4 hard-boiled eggs, whole or halved

Mix together 2 teaspoons of the light soy sauce with an equal quantity of the dark and stir in the Chinese Five Spices. Turn the pork in this marinade until the cubes are coated, then leave to stand for 1 hour.

Heat enough oil in a large saucepan to stir-fry the garlic, peppercorns, cinnamon, cloves and anise. Stir-fry over medium heat until they give off a good fragrance. Turn up the heat, add the pork and fry quickly on all sides, again until a good aroma comes from it.

Stir in the remaining light and dark soy sauce, the water and the sugar. Bring to the boil, lower the heat and leave to simmer for about 25 minutes, or until the meat is tender. The dish should not have much liquid left – just enough to moisten the meat and give a little gravy.

Add the *tau hoo* and eggs and cook for a further 5 minutes. Lift out the cinnamon and anise (or fennel). Serve with plain boiled rice.

Sinigang
Beef and pork stew

A *sinigang* is a chowder or thick stew of vegetables with meat or fish, sharpened with fruit purée and thickened with rice water or a starchy root such as taro. Eaten with rice, it makes one of the Philippines' many single-dish meals. The distinctive sour taste of tamarind is characteristic of Filipino cooking.

serves 4

8 oz/225 g pork, sliced, or 4 oz/110 g pork, sliced, and 4 oz/110 g chuck steak, cut in small pieces.
8 oz/225 g beef bone
1 large tomato, sliced
1 medium onion, sliced
2 oz/50 g/¼ cup tamarind pulp (seeds removed), mashed with a little water
4 taro tubers, peeled and cubed
6 oz/175 g/1 cup *daikon* (Oriental radish), sliced into fairly thick rounds
1 handful greens (spring greens, turnip tops or Brussels sprout tops), roughly sliced
1 green pepper, cut in half, deseeded and sliced
1 handful dwarf green beans, trimmed
2 tablespoons *patis* (commercial fish sauce) or anchovy sauce, or salt and pepper to taste

Put the meat into a large saucepan with the bone. Just cover with boiling water, bring to simmering point, cover and cook for 10 minutes. Add the tomato, onion and tamarind pulp. Continue to simmer gently with the lid on for about 45 minutes, then add the greens, taro cubes and after 15 minutes further simmering add the *daikon*, green pepper and beans. Cook for another 5 minutes, and season either with the *patis* or with salt and pepper.

Discard the bone, and serve hot with boiled rice.

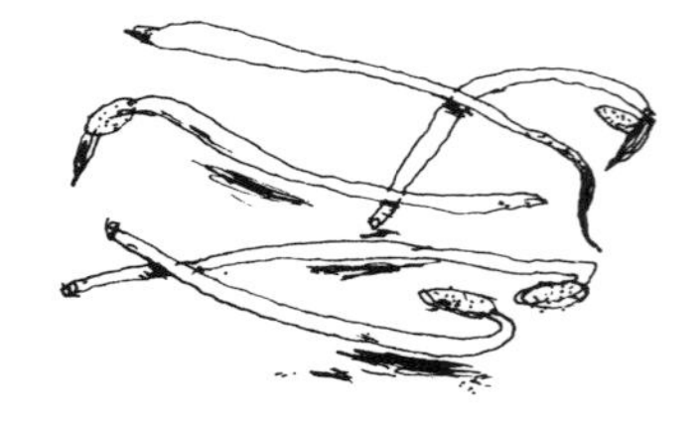

Ts'ui P'i Fei Chi
Crisp-fried chicken

This Cantonese dish is a favourite in Taiwan. The chicken, basted with a vinegar and honey sauce and deep-fried, is divided into small pieces and then carefully put together again and presented at the table apparently whole. Cantonese cooks keep ready a pot of the pepper-flavoured salt, which is a popular seasoning in their cookery. Start this dish a day ahead.

serves 4

- 4 pints/2.2 litres/10 cups boiling water
- 2 pieces star anise
- 1 in/2.5 cm cinnamon stick
- 1 teaspoon black peppercorns
- 1 chicken, weighing about 2 lb/900 g cleaned, but with head attached if possible
- 2 teaspoons cornflour (cornstarch)
- 1½ teaspoons salt
- 2 tablespoons rice vinegar
- 2 tablespoons honey
- 4 teaspoons pepper-flavoured salt (see below)
- about 2 pints/1.1 litres/5 cups peanut or other oil for deep-frying
- 1 small lemon, sliced

Pour the water into a deep saucepan and add the anise, cinnamon and peppercorns. Boil for 5 minutes, then put in the chicken. Bring back to the boil and continue boiling, uncovered, for 10 minutes. Lift out the chicken, let it cool and then pat dry.

Mix the cornflour to a paste with a tablespoon of cold water. Stir it into 10 fl oz/300 ml/1¼ cups boiling water in a small saucepan. Add the salt, vinegar and honey and continue boiling for about 5 minutes, until slightly reduced. Tie a string round the neck of the chicken and suspend it over a bowl. Baste it over and over again with the vinegar and honey sauce, until you have used up as much of it as possible. Then hang the chicken in a cool, draughty place to dry for 6–8 hours, or overnight if more convenient.

To make the pepper-flavoured salt, put 3 teaspoons of salt and 1 teaspoon of black peppercorns into a dry pan over a good heat and stir for 1 minute. Remove from the heat, leave to cool and grind finely.

Heat the oil for deep-frying in a *wok* or deep saucepan until very hot, then put in the chicken. Reduce to a medium heat and keep it there, or the honey will blacken. Fry the chicken, turning it several times and basting with the hot oil to cook it evenly. When it is cooked and well browned all over, lift out and drain well.

Using a cleaver, or poultry shears, cut the chicken quickly but carefully into pieces about 1½ × 1 in/4 × 2.5 cm. Put the pieces together again on a serving plate to re-form the whole chicken if you are going to serve it in the authentic way. Otherwise, arrange the pieces as you wish on the plate. Serve at once, giving each person 1 teaspoon of the pepper-flavoured salt to dip the chicken in and a few slices of lemon to squeeze over it. Offer plain boiled rice as an accompaniment.

Saté Ayam
Skewered grilled chicken

serves 4

2¼ lb/1 kg chicken, boned
3 shallots, peeled and crushed
2 cloves garlic, peeled and crushed
1 teaspoon ground ginger
pinch chilli powder or freshly ground black pepper
½ teaspoon salt
2 tablespoons dark soy sauce
1 tablespoon lime juice or lemon juice

Bumbu Kecap (chilli-flavoured sauce):
2 green chilli peppers, deseeded and chopped
1 clove garlic, peeled and crushed
2 tablespoons dark soy sauce
2 teaspoons lime juice or lemon juice
1 tablespoon boiling water

Bumbu Kacang (peanut sauce):
4 oz/110 g/½ cup shelled peanuts, unskinned
oil for frying
2 shallots, sliced finely
2 cloves garlic, peeled and chopped
1 tiny slice *terasi* (firm shrimp paste – *blachen*)
½ teaspoon ground ginger
½ teaspoon ground coriander
½ teaspoon chilli powder
salt
15 fl oz/450 ml/1¾ cups water
1 teaspoon brown sugar
juice of ½ lemon

In Indonesia, where pasture-land is scarce, meat is expensive, but chickens range freely round the village gardens and roadsides. They are full of flavour but rather tough – overcome in this recipe by tenderizing the chicken pieces in a marinade. The finished dish is delicate and subtle. Serve the chicken pieces with either of the following sauces. You can buy the peanut sauce in powder form (satay powder) from Oriental grocers.

Cut the chicken into small cubes. Mix the shallots and garlic in a large bowl with the ginger, chilli powder and salt and stir in the soy sauce and lime juice. Put in the chicken and mix well until the cubes are coated with the mixture. Cover the bowl and leave for at least 1 hour.

To make *Bumbu Kecap*, put the chilli peppers and garlic in a small bowl, add the soy sauce, lime juice and water and mix well. Leave for at least 1 hour.

To make the *Bumbu Kacang*, fry the peanuts in very little oil for 4–5 minutes, until browned, then leave to cool before grinding to a powder. Pound the shallots, garlic and *terasi* in a mortar until they become a smooth paste. Stir in the ginger, coriander and chilli powder and season with salt. Heat 1 tablespoon of oil in a saucepan and sauté the shallot paste in it for a few seconds. Add the water and when it is boiling put in the ground peanuts and sugar. Stir, taste and add more salt if necessary. Go on boiling and stirring until the sauce is quite thick. Add the lemon juice just before serving time.

When the chicken is well marinated, thread on to bamboo (or metal) skewers, putting 6–7 pieces on each. Put on a rack and grill (broil) over charcoal, or cook under a hot grill, for 6–8 minutes, turning frequently.

Serve at once, still on the skewers, with rice and the chosen sauce. Serve it without rice as a first course.

Rices of the world, reading from 12 o'clock
Medium grain: 1. Louisiana or Carolina brown (polished) 2. Yellow, Halian Cristallo for risottos (polished) 3. White Halian Avorio for risottos (polished)
Narrow, long grain: 4. Brown unpolished Patna type 5. White Basmati 6. White Patna (Uncle Ben type)
Sticky or glutinous: 7. Short brown unpolished, China 8. Short white polished, China 9. Long black unpolished, Japan 10. Medium white polished, Japan
Short, round grain 'pudding' rice: 11. Brown unpolished, Italy 12. White polished, Italy

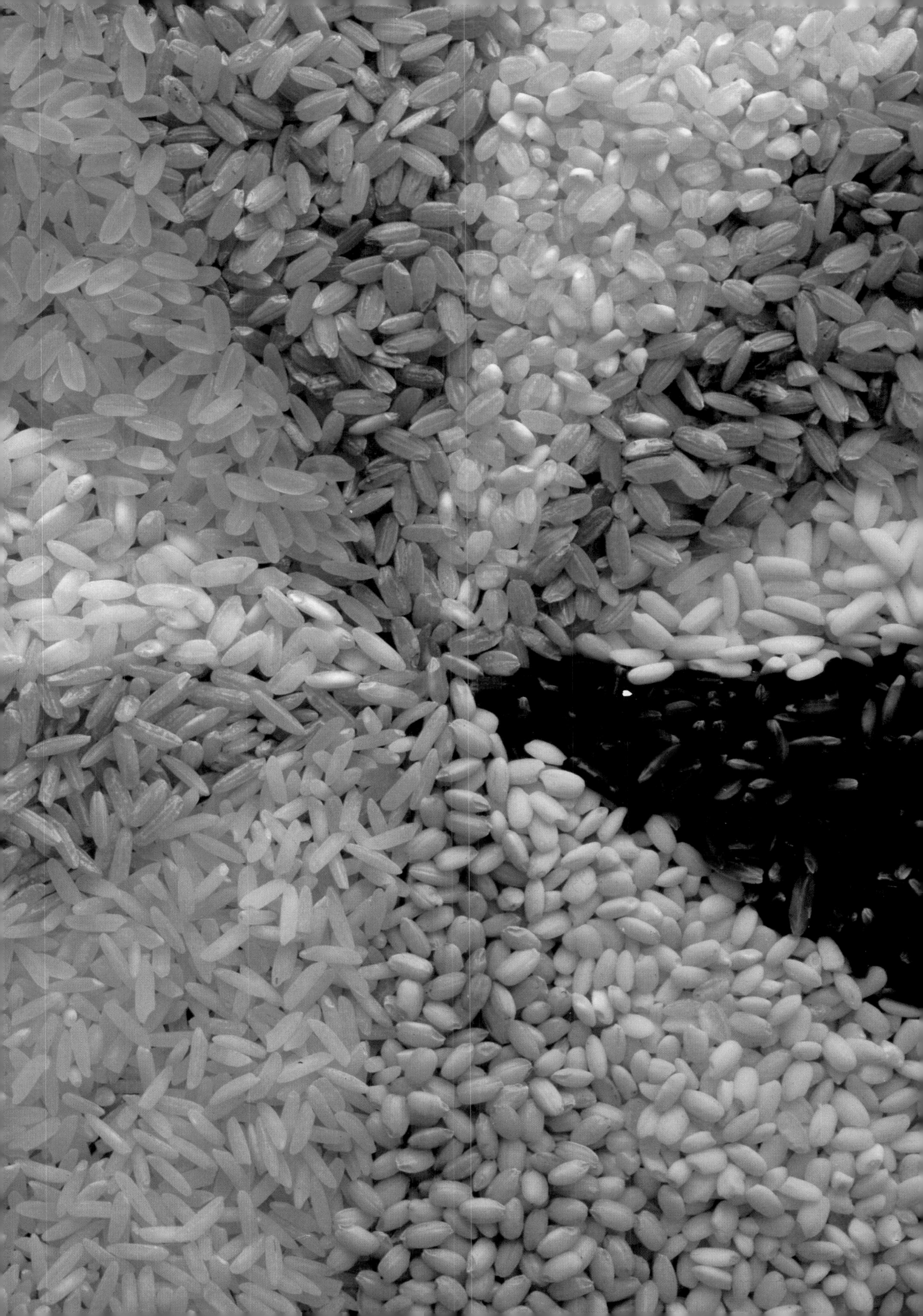

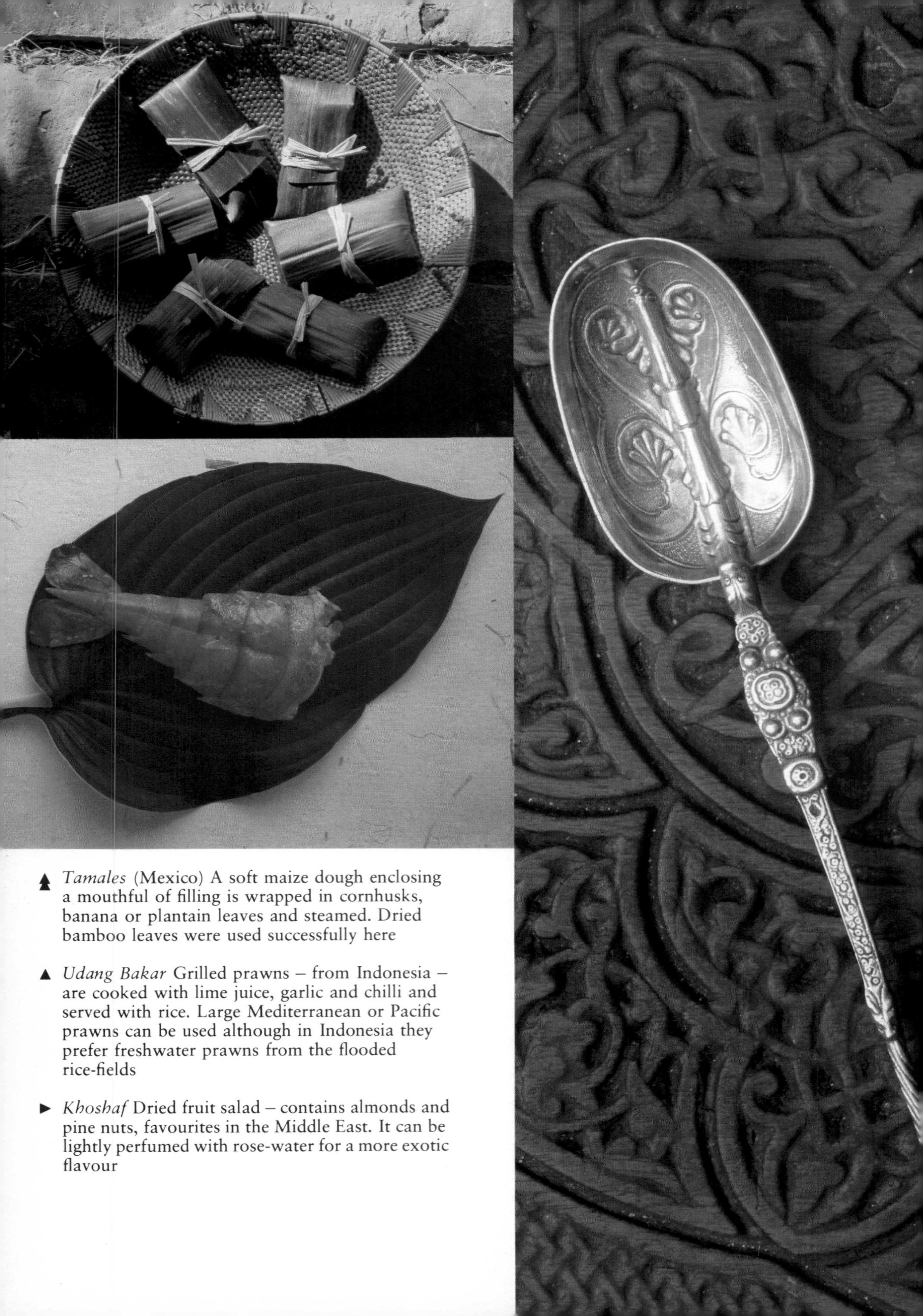

▲ *Tamales* (Mexico) A soft maize dough enclosing a mouthful of filling is wrapped in cornhusks, banana or plantain leaves and steamed. Dried bamboo leaves were used successfully here

▲ *Udang Bakar* Grilled prawns – from Indonesia – are cooked with lime juice, garlic and chilli and served with rice. Large Mediterranean or Pacific prawns can be used although in Indonesia they prefer freshwater prawns from the flooded rice-fields

► *Khoshaf* Dried fruit salad – contains almonds and pine nuts, favourites in the Middle East. It can be lightly perfumed with rose-water for a more exotic flavour

Ingredients for the world's best food

1 Bacalao (dried salt cod)
2 Seaweed (wakame)
3 Sliced sausage – salami
4 Salchichón
5 Morcilla
6 Lemon grass
7 Tocino
8 Okra (gumbo, ladies fingers)
9 Phyllo pastry
10 Coriander leaves (fresh)
11 Feta cheese
12 Seaweed (nori)
13 Buckwheat pasta (soba)
14 Bamboo shoots (tinned)
15 Jamon serrano (ham)
16 Dried apricot paste (kamardine)
17 Seaweed (kombu)
18 Sweet potato
19 Chorizo (sausage)
20 Yam
21 Sake
22 Mirin (sweet rice wine)
23 Rice vinegar
24 Mozarella (cheese)
25 Tofu or doufu (bean curd)
26 Haloumi (cheese)
27 Haloumi
28 Katsuobishi
29 Chilli peppers
30 Mulato (dried peppers)
31 Pascillo (dried pepper)
32 Ancho (dried pepper)
33 Daikon or moli
34 Yellow peppers
35 Pecorino sardo (hard cheese)
36 Swiss chard (biette)
37 Limes
38 Miso (fermented bean curd)
39 Fennel (fresh)
40 Rose-water
41 Vine leaves (fresh)
42 Green papaya
43 Ricotta cheese
44 Orange flower water
45 Chayote
46 Tahina paste
47 Masa harina
48 Shittake (dried mushrooms)
49 Burghul (pourgouri)
50 Tree (wood) ears
51 Katsuobishi
52 Corn chips
53 Tamarind
54 Macadami nuts (kamiri, canole nuts)
55 Pine nuts (pignoli)
56 Funghi porcini (dried ceps)
57 Soya sauce
58 Harusame (transparent Chinese vermicelli)
59 Pancetta
60 Annatto seed
61 Paprika
62 Chinese spice powder
63 Carob powder

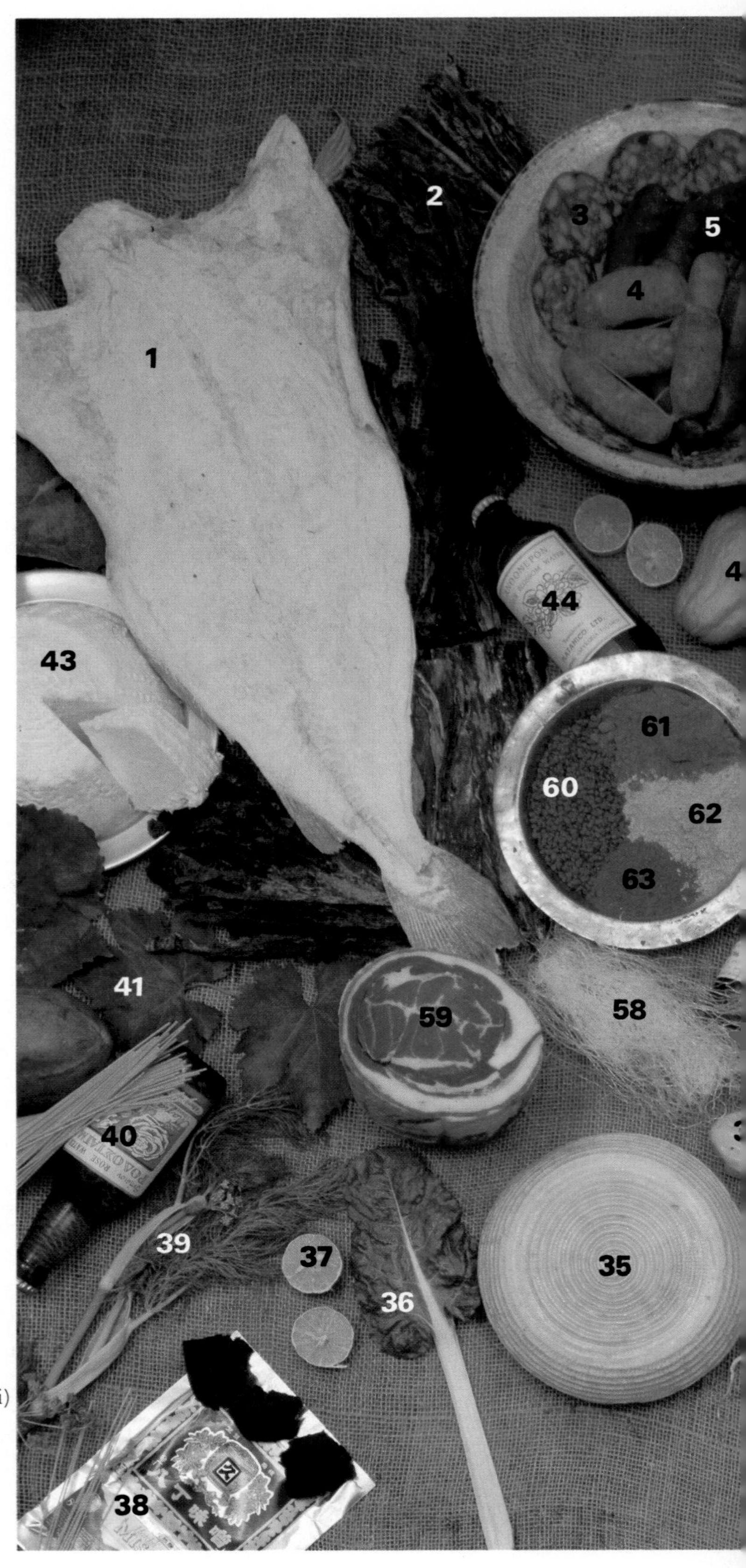

6
10
11
14
7
8
9
15
DRIED APRICOT PASTE
16
46
47
48
17
18
52
49
20
51
50
19
21
12
22
53
23
54
33
56
24
27
55
13
25
29
28
DRIED SHAVED FISH
26
32
30
31

RIVAL

◀ *Tyropitta* Paper-thin phyllo pastry layered with cheese is a universal Balkan dish. Use either salty feta cheese or more homely Cheshire, Lancashire or white Stilton

▲ *Frijoles* Beans are a staple food in South America, served with almost every meal. Here they are stewed and eaten with tortillas, ripe avocados and corn-bread

▲ *'Wings of Life' Salad* A vegetarian bowl of fresh vegetables, like broccoli, spinach and green beans, are jumbled with tofu – fresh bean curd – and grated Parmesan cheese. The wholewheat pasta that accompanies it has a green sauce of fragrant herbs

Breads of the World

1 Horiatika: Greece
2 Pita or pitta bread: Middle East
3 San Francisco sourdough
4 Caraway bread: Yugoslavia
5 Sweet twisted bread: South America
6 Flat bread: Italy
7 Pain de campagne, French country bread
8 Pan de leche: South America
9 Home-made wholemeal: Britain
10 White cob: Britain
11 Multi-grain sourdough: USA
12 Greek bread with sesame seeds: Balkans
13 Pan de fiesta: Mexico
14 Wholemeal bloomer: Britain
15 White bloomer: Britain
16 Pan de agua: Mexico
17 Potato bread with caraway: Balkans
18 Franzola: Spain
19 Pain de seigle, rye bread: France
20 Caraway bread: Balkans
21 Pane Casareccio: Italy
22 Poppy seed loaf: Vegetarian
23 Bun loaf: Britain
24 Wholemeal bloomer: Britain
25 Wholemeal cob: Britain
26 Pane Cafone: Naples, South-West Europe
27 Baguette: France
28 Cob: Britain
29 Spiedino, flat bread with salt crystals
30 Cocoles: Mexico
31 Granary loaf: Britain
32 Milk loaf: Britain
33 Brown loaf, home-made: Britain
34 Poppy seed plait: Britain
35 Pogaca: Yugoslavia
36 Pig-shaped rolls: Latin America
38 Italian household loaf: Abruzzi
37 and 39 Bollilos rolls: Mexico
40 Vegetarian buckwheat loaf
41 Pain: France, South-West Europe
42 Grant loaf: Britain
43 Cob, white: Britain
44 Proja: Balkans
45 Vanilla flavoured bread: Latin America
46 Harvo, malt bread: Britain
47 Panchon: Spain
48 Lepinja: Balkans
49 Pita or pitta bread, home-made: Middle East
50 Rosetta rolls: Italy
51 Cocole de leche roll: South America
52 Croissants: France

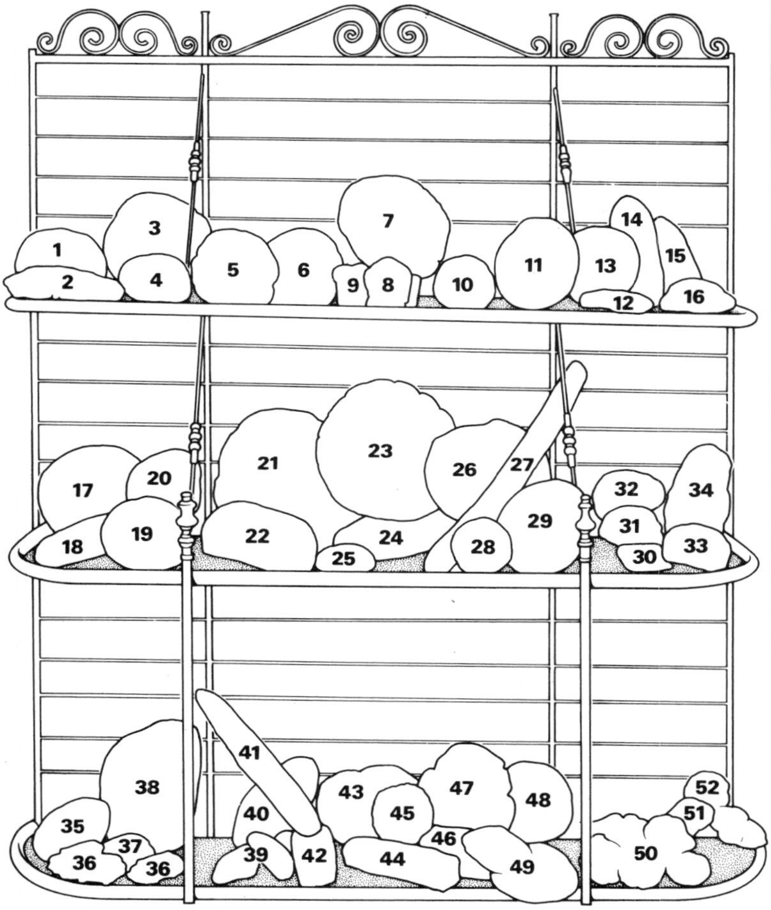

Tinola
Chicken and papaya

serves 4

- corn oil for frying
- 1 piece fresh ginger, crushed
- 1 tablespoon crushed garlic
- 1 medium onion, sliced thinly
- 1 small chicken, cut into pieces
- 10–15 fl oz/300–450 ml/1¼–1¾ cups rice water
- 6 oz/175 g chopped green papaya or common gourd or squash
- 3–4 tablespoons *patis* (commercial fish sauce) or anchovy sauce
- 4 peppercorns, crushed

Tinola is another of the Filipinos' most popular complete meals in one dish. This version uses rice water, which not only contains vitamins but is starchy and therefore acts as a thickener. To prepare the rice water cover 12 oz/350 g/2¼ cups long grain rice with warm water. Stir well for a minute or two, then strain off the water to use. Boil the rice later to serve with the dish.

Heat the oil in a heavy-based pan and sauté the ginger, garlic and onion in it until the onion just begins to colour. Add the chicken pieces and fry until lightly browned.

Pour in just enough rice water to cover the chicken. Put a lid on the pan and simmer for 20–30 minutes, until the chicken is tender. Add the papaya and continue simmering for 10–15 minutes, or until it is just tender. Season with the fish sauce and crushed peppercorns.

Jemput-jemput
Fried banana cakes

A large reddish-skinned banana known as *pisang rajah* is used in Malaysia for this dish, but ordinary bananas are also suitable. Eat the cakes hot or cold, as an accompaniment to tea or as a snack.

serves 4

- 4 large bananas, ripe enough to mash
- 2 teaspoons sugar, or to taste
- 2 tablespoons flour
- ½ teaspoon salt
- oil for deep-frying

Peel and mash the bananas in a bowl until completely pulped, then add the sugar. Stir the flour and salt together and add little by little to the bananas, stirring well with a wooden spoon. The mixture should just drop from the spoon. Add water, or more flour, to obtain this consistency.

Pour oil into a frying pan to a depth of ½ in/1.25 cm. Heat until a haze rises, then drop in the mixture a spoonful at a time. Do not put too many in the pan at once. Let the cakes fry until just golden brown, then lift out and drain on paper towels. Serve hot or cold, sprinkled with sugar.

Bibingkat Malagkit
Sticky rice with coconut cream

For many Filipino families bread is now the staple breakfast food, but the traditional Filipino breakfast is a hearty meal. It may include rice and fish, with a drink of chocolate, coffee, or scented tea. The most traditional of all breakfast dishes is *bibingkat*, a rice cake, often eaten with cheese and salted eggs. This recipe is for a simple *bibingkat* made with *malagkit* (sticky rice) and flavoured with coconut. The Filipinos cook it in a pan lined with wilted banana leaves, to prevent burning, and with a flat lid to hold live coals so there is heat above as well as below the food. You can use a heavy-based saucepan or casserole.

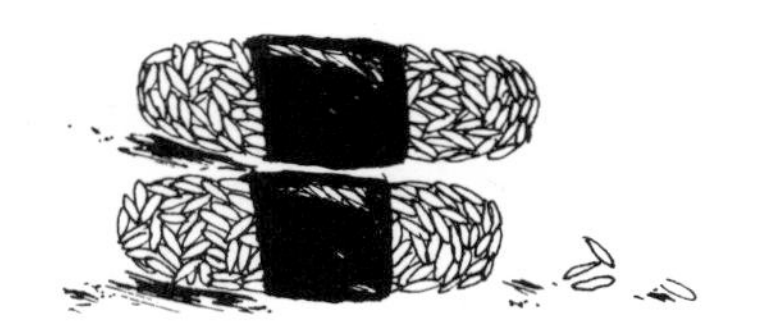

serves 4

1 coconut, grated, or 12 oz/350 g/3¼ cups desiccated (shredded) coconut
2½ pints/1.4 litres/6¼ cups water
12 oz/350 g/6 cups uncooked sticky (glutinous) rice†
1 teaspoon salt
8 oz/225 g/2 cups brown sugar
pinch powdered anise

Put the coconut in a saucepan with 5 fl oz/150 ml/⅔ cup of the water and heat until just bubbling. Leave to cool to blood heat, then press through a sieve to extract as much liquid (coconut cream) as you can. Use the coconut again in the same way, but with a clean bowl under the sieve, with all the remaining water to make a second, more diluted, extraction (coconut milk). Keep these two infusions separate.

Bring the coconut milk to the boil in a deep iron frying pan or a *wok*. Add the rice and salt and continue to boil, stirring constantly to prevent burning, until all the liquid has been absorbed.

Stir in half the sugar and turn out the rice into a large, greased baking dish. Pour the coconut cream on top. Sprinkle on the rest of the sugar and the anise and bake in a pre-heated oven at 350° F/180° C/gas mark 4 for 30 minutes. Brown the top under a hot grill before serving.

CHAPTER 5

LATIN AMER
CARIBBEAN

The peoples of Mexico, South America and certain islands of the Caribbean do not have all the economic advantages of the modern world, but they do enjoy a record of health that Britons and North Americans can envy. And this record, with its low incidence of heart disease, can be partly ascribed to their reliance on healthy staples in the diet: maize (corn), beans and rice are eaten in great quantity with plenty of fresh vegetables and only small amounts of meat and dairy produce. The bulk of their protein comes from these major crops.

Inevitably, cooking styles must vary widely in such a large area, which extends from populous Mexico and the scattered islands of the Caribbean, through the west coast of South America, Colombia, equatorial Ecuador (where some of the world's longest-living people are to be found) to Peru and Chile.

Although the area is vast and tremendously varied both geographically and climatically, there are strong similarities in the cooking which show themselves time and again. This is due partly to early Spanish influence, which has spread and imposed itself on country after country, and partly to the fact that none of these countries is suited to the rearing of beef.

CA AND THE

The large region on the eastern seaboard of South America, Argentina and Uruguay, where beef is produced in quantity, is not included in the chapter, since the health record of this area is poor and the incidence of heart disease is high.

The Latin American approach to eating is not entirely drawn from Spanish sources, however. Although Spain's ruthless adventurers conquered the continent, many of the South American Indians have ancient civilizations behind them: the Incas, the proud Mayas, the Aztecs and the Chibcha, the goldworkers of Colombia.

The merging of the Latin and Indian cultures and races produced not only a new civilization, but a new culinary tradition as good Spanish livestock (beef, pigs, lamb, chickens, goats) were adapted to Aztec cooking techniques. Along with a fantastic booty of gold, silver and emeralds, the Spaniards also took back to Europe hitherto unknown foods such as tomatoes, potatoes, maize (corn), green beans and lima beans, avocados, vanilla, chocolate and turkeys. They also imported fiercely piquant peppers, which range from the tiniest and hottest green chillies to the large sweet, shiny red peppers. In exchange, the Indians were introduced to onions and pigs, sheep, goats and chickens. Spain has had an enormous influence on Latin American cooking, but mostly in the way it embellished the traditional pre-conquest recipes. This is especially true for the cooking of the rural areas, and it is this country cuisine that we are interested in from the point of view of health.

The Spanish chroniclers who wrote about Mexican life when Cortés first came to the court of Montezuma described one grand feast where they were presented with a thousand dishes. Many of these are still recognizable as traditional and authentic recipes which you might be offered in Mexico and in much of Latin America today. There were *tortillas*, large and small, prettily shaped; *tamales* and red beans; turkey served with a sauce made with small chillies; tomatoes and ground squash seeds; white fish with yellow chilli; squash flowers; cactus fruits; and a selection of elaborately decorated chocolates (forerunners of the fattier, blander chocolates of today).

The writers also noted that the peasants of the day lived on a simple diet, basically beans, maize (corn) and chillies, with a supplement of fruit, vegetables and small quantities of meat when it was available. To extend their choice of meats in some countries they domesticated the cuy (guinea pig) and rabbit-like animals, the ñeque and paca (especially in Peru and Bolivia).

Apart from rice, introduced by the Spanish, the diet of the mass of the people is almost unchanged. The combination of unrefined carbohydrates, the low quantity of meat and very little fat ensures good health. Indeed, until the Spanish introduced dairy produce and pork, the local diet was almost free from oil or fat consumption, since they did not use seed oils. And as the meat was mostly game, it tended to be very lean.

The most important staple food of the South Americans is maize (corn). It has been so for thousands of years. And still today the seed of seeds, the daughter of life, plays a crucial role in the diet. *Tortillas*, made with ground maize (corn), are freshly made, or bought, every day. They are eaten, like bread, with every meal. When they are stale they are broken into soups or stews or deep-fried. They are also made into *enchiladas*, filled with spiced shredded pork or chicken breasts and fried, or *tacos*, the same kind of thing filled with meat. *Tamales*, the traditional fiesta dish of the Mexican Indians, are made with cornmeal dough which is steamed, and has a sweet or non-sweet filling. *Empadas*, *empanadas* and *empanaditas* – the use of the diminutive seems to be more to do with affection than description – are all meat pies usually made with wheat flour.

Corn *tortillas* are seldom made at home nowadays, except by peasants in remote districts, and affluent families with a big kitchen staff. The majority of *tortillas* are made by an automated process in small *tortilleriás* (*tortilla* shops) and bought fresh daily from itinerant street vendors who either occupy a pitch in the main shopping area of the market, or deliver them to the door. The frozen variety sold in supermarkets is still no match for a freshly made *tortilla* from a *tortillería*.

One Peruvian recipe uses ground maize (corn) kernels combined with fierce *ají* chilli as a soup mixture, to which fish or meat may be added. Maize is also used in many soups and stews, while Indians in Mexico and Guatemala enjoy *atole*, a drink which is made from maize, and flavoured with sugar, crushed fruit, chocolate or even chilli. (It is not usually to Western taste.) Maize has its own mythology, and Peruvians will tell you when you should and shouldn't plant it in order to enjoy good fortune.

During the Industrial Revolution in the nineteenth century, maize was introduced to Europe for the masses. The poor of Southern Europe had to depend on it as a main food source. Because their diet was not supplemented by sufficient niacin (nicotinic acid) and other vitamins, pellagra, the 'disease of the mealies', appeared and cornmeal got a bad name.

Europeans do not, therefore, accept the versatility of maize and generally grow it for feeding animals in winter – the maize used in Europe for cornbread and *polenta* is a coarser type than South American maize. Their maize flour, *harina de maiz*, is made from kernels that have been soaked in lime-water before grinding and this makes a refined meal and also frees the niacin, one of the B vitamins, so that it can be absorbed by the body. For this reason pellagra is in fact unknown in Latin American countries.

Another staple food in Latin America is beans: in Mexico and Central America they eat six times the amount of beans eaten in the UK; in South America at least twice as many. Red kidney beans, black beans and pinto beans are the most popular. Beans are seldom cooked with a meat dish. They are usually boiled until soft, and served with every meal, usually after the main course. They are also eaten as snacks and appetizers, and in Mexico mashed and fried beans make *refritos*, a popular breakfast dish served with hot chocolate or milky sweet coffee.

The third important staple is the potato, particularly in the high Andes of Peru. There are many varieties including red-skinned ones and black-skinned ones. The most prized variety, confined exclusively to the region, has bright yellow flesh, and is perfect for making the delicious Peruvian dish of *papas a la huancaina* with milk, cheese and *ají*, the Peruvian hot chilli. Potatoes are baked, boiled and mashed. The Incas were the first to invent freeze-drying – they left potatoes exposed to cold mountain air during the night and hot sun in the day until the potatoes dried out and could be stored through the winter.

The range of crops is enormous: bananas and plantains, manioc (also known as cassava and yuca) and coconut. In Caribbean cookery many dishes are cooked in coconut milk. In Central America they have avocados, papayas, pumpkins or squashes, called *calabacita* when young and tender and *calabaza* when mature and hard, pineapples, mangoes and oranges. Lime juice is important in many recipes such as *ceviche*. Mexicans eat quantities of onions, garlic, pumpkins, green beans and peas. They also have less familiar vegetables, such as *chayote* (vegetable pear, also known as christophene), *nopalitos* (baby cactus leaves) and green tomatoes (nothing like green tomatoes but a cousin of the Cape gooseberry), the last of which frequently appear in sauces and stews and are an important ingredient in the Mexican kitchen.

The preparation of food in Latin America is often elaborate and time-consuming. In Mexico the making of *tortillas*, for example, is a skilled craft; few Westerners, even if they can obtain the correct flour, find it easy to make the supple little pancakes that are eaten every day over a very wide area. The people of the region like hot and spicy flavours, so although their basic ingredients of maize, beans and rice are rather humble, the food is never dull, and can sometimes be quite overpowering. This is the world of the chilli and young men measure manliness by the ability to chew raw hot peppers without apparent pain. In fact, not all chillies of the vast number of varieties grown are hot. There are over 100 varieties in Mexico alone – yellow, green, black and purple as well as fiery red – many being mild and subtle. Much of the food cooked is not actually hot at all, but is served with chilli sauces and relishes, which are added at the table. Chillies do more than add piquancy, for they are a useful source of vitamin C.

Much less meat is eaten in Latin America than in the US and UK. In Central America they eat one-fifth; in South America one-third. Cattle are normally fed on corn and grass, but their flesh is very lean. It is usually tough and best suited to slow cooking in stews – prepared in large earthenware pots. For many farming families meat is often little more than a flavouring for stews.

Fish is naturally popular in South American coastal regions. The Peruvians eat more fish than Britons, whereas in Chile they eat about the same and even the poorest families expect to eat clams, giant sea urchins and abalone, as well as the more conventional fish. The delicious *ceviche*, raw fish marinated in the juice of limes, is a dish especially prized in Peru, but it is popular throughout Latin America. Fish deteriorates quickly, but is often preserved by drying. In Mexico dried shrimp is especially popular in soups and stews.

Sweets are plentiful in Latin America. The Spanish brought sugar cane from the Old World and the manufacture of all sorts of *dulces* began. Candied fruits and fruit pastes are plentiful and cheap in the markets. In Mexico they love brightly coloured jellies, custards and pastries which are sold on carts. The ubiquitous *flan* (caramel custard) is a favourite dessert. In Peru they will eat with relish *manjar blanco*, made from slowly reduced sweetened milk. (Similar sweets are *cajeta* in Mexico, *arequipe* in Colombia.) Yet, in spite of a delight in all things sweet, they still consume less sugar than the UK and US.

The common drinks in Latin America are hot chocolate and coffee. In Chile, where coffee is not grown, an accepted stimulant is *yerbe mate*, a tea made from the dried leaves of a shrub belonging to the holly family. Otherwise they drink *refrescos* made with fresh fruits; and the local alcoholic beverages, such as *pisco*, the brandy of Chile and Peru, *chica de jora* (also Peruvian and made from maize (corn), *tequila*, from the agave, *pulque*, a beer-like drink from the maguey plant, or *aguardiente*, a fierce spirit distilled from sugar cane. For the digestion the country people drink lemon grass and camomile tea.

The people who live on the basic simple peasant diets of the regions of Latin America are remarkably untroubled by Western dietary diseases. But the most impressive advertisement for the benefits of this menu of maize, beans and chillies is a little village called Vilcabamba, in the Ecuadorian foothills of the Andes. A study made in 1974 showed that the population of 819 inhabitants included a good number of centenarians. Nine people were over 100 years old. Three were over 120. The ancient vellum pages of the village register of births testified to the evidence. These people ate the ordinary Latin American diet. Their good health and longevity speak for themselves.

The typical day's eating habits vary from north to south. In southernmost Chile, for example, breakfast might be omelettes or boiled, fried or baked eggs, or a kind of porridge made from toasted wheat grains and hot milk, *harina tostada*. There is a coffee made from toasted wheat grain. Similar toasted cereal drinks are obtainable at health-food shops.

The main meal of the day is lunch: a hot meal of beans, lentils, pumpkin and other vegetables. Fish is freely available, and abalone and other shellfish are popular.

There is always fruit for dessert – grapes, peaches, plums. A curd cheese, *quesillo*, may also be eaten with bread. Wine is often drunk with the meal.

Dinner is a lighter meal, often the remains of lunch with a small amount of meat, such as chicken, lamb or seafood, added. There may be a rice pudding to follow, or occasionally dried fruit. Wine is drunk and sometimes a cider, *chicha de manzana*.

Besides salt, pepper, garlic and vinegar, condiments include green chillies. *Pebre*, a sharp and highly seasoned sauce, accompanies many meat dishes. 'Color' is the brand name of an orange-red mixture used to add colour and flavour to many dishes: it is a blend of garlic and paprika heated in cooked oil. It keeps indefinitely.

Further north in Colombia, breakfast (*desayuno*) may be a more substantial meal as workers often have to travel long distances to their work-places. It might be *buñuelos*, golden balls of maize, flour and cheese or banana and potatoes and or a filling soup made from maize (corn), potatoes and heavily seasoned chicken stock; and with it, a cup of strong black Colombian coffee – never tea.

Almuerzo (or second breakfast) may be light or not taken at all: probably a maize-based soup with vegetables and rice, with fruit juice to drink. Dinner would normally include soup, *tamales* (corn dough wrapped round meats and vegetables and wrapped in banana leaves before stewing or steaming). Bread, made from yuca flour with cottage cheese, is liked. Beer is drunk and a fermented cane juice called *guarapo*, also the fiery cane sugar spirit called *aguardiente*.

Further north still, eating habits are more like those of Mexico. A hearty breakfast, early in the day, with *huevos rancheros*: fried eggs smothered in a very hot tomato sauce, perhaps served with slices of avocado, or *tortillas*. They may even be followed by a bowl of kidney beans and chillies. A cup of hot chocolate accompanies the meal.

The main meal of the day is taken around 2 p.m. It will include beans again, and *tortillas* in many guises: *enchiladas* filled with spiced meat and chicken or *tacos*, the same thing, but deep fried. There is often a supper, *merienda*, in the early evening, with coffee, chocolate, or the rich maize drink, *atole*, or on special occasions around 9 p.m., or later, dinner or *cena* will be a light meal, but it is certain to include beans and *tortillas* again.

Central America is similar in style. In Nicaragua, for example, maize is the staple, and is used to make drinks as well as *tortillas*. The *tortilla* is eaten for breakfast and supper, often with fillings of fried beans, tart white goat cheese, avocados, *chorizo* sausage, minced meat, or sweet fillings such as chocolate. The most common main dish is rice and beans, which may be eaten twice a day, probably with a soup such as *sopa de pescado*, or a salad. Fruit is abundant and, fresh or stewed, it accompanies most main meals. The poorer people drink black coffee for breakfast and maize drinks with main meals, the better-off have coffee with milk for breakfast, and chocolate with milk (*chinaque*) at lunch and dinner.

The cooking of the Caribbean, based on abundant tropical fruit and vegetables and large catches of fish and shellfish, is an interesting mixture of the exotic and the mundane. On the one hand, mysterious fruits and vegetables, citrus groves, huge crayfish, flying fish and tuna, and on the other hand pig's feet and tripe and boiled beans with rice. The rich variety of foodstuffs contributes to the good health of the West Indians, which is most evident in the former Spanish islands. These islands cannot support large herds, although nowadays a certain amount of beef is imported and there is a lot of lamb and goat available. Pork is plentiful – pig's heads, tails and feet, often pickled and dyed bright crimson, are all eaten, sometimes with a fresh lime and chilli sauce. The pickling or sousing originated from the need to preserve the pork which would have deteriorated alarmingly fast in the tropical climate before the days of refrigeration. However, the taste for salted food is probably the cause of a high incidence of stroke on some islands and we do not recommend salt food as a regular item in the diet. Fresh pork is popular; roast pork, or even better, stuffed roast suckling pig is served on special occasions accompanied by boiled or roasted yams and sweet potatoes. Pumpkin is another favourite, and is eaten both as a vegetable – often in soup – and sweetened as a dessert.

The range of vegetables is enormous, and includes root vegetables such as taros, malangas and dasheen (whose leaves are sold separately as calaloo, the chief ingredient in the well-known calaloo soup). The earliest crops grown by the Arawak Indians were the cassava root, yams and sweet potatoes. They grew maize (corn) as well as peppers, pineapples, guavas and avocados, together with some of the foods from the Old World – rice, wheat, barley, oats, olives and olive oil.

The African slaves who settled in the West Indies brought okra and black-eyed beans, or peas as they are often called, while the Indian workers brought curries and chutneys.

Naturally, there was always plenty of fish and shellfish around these islands with their miles and miles of coastline. Fish is still eaten everywhere and the fishermen bring in marvellous crayfish, prawns and crabs, and huge turtles as well as flying fish, grouper, red snapper, tuna and king-fish. Good mackerel is another valuable source of food – as cheap and plentiful there as it is all over the world.

Becoming more familiar in the West are some of the West Indian fruits, the soursops, mangoes, fresh coconuts and plantains – eaten unripe as vegetables and ripe as fruits, while the huge leaves are used as wrappings for steamed foods. As airfreight gets easier and the demand increases, the fruit and vegetables of the tropics are finding their way into Western markets.

Sugar cane is grown in many islands and sugar is cheap throughout the Caribbean. In some parts the taste for sugar is excessive and the incidence of diabetes is very high. We have chosen the best of the West Indian diet and omitted dishes which we thought to be excessively sweet.

Meals are often simply made – soups and stews, for example, that contain plenty of vegetables cooked and served in one pot. They have adopted some English recipes, some Dutch and Javanese recipes, some Indian curries and some American-style cocktails. Favourite drinks are ginger beer, a sweet milky liquid made from the juice of soursops, and, when celebrating, rum. They drink fresh fruit juices and a thin liquid flavoured with pineapple skins or melon-rinds which is said to be very healthy. They also like sweet coffee and weak tea.

The Caribbean cuisine in fact is a mixture of so many styles that it is hard to define it, but the peoples of the Caribbean know it is unique, and we know it is healthy.

Tortillas

Fresh hot *tortillas* are delicious simply sprinkled with a little salt and rolled up, for a good *tortilla* can be rolled up into a tight tube without cracking. You may not make the perfect *tortilla* without quite a lot of practice, but you will certainly enjoy even imperfect ones. Always serve them hot – just with salt, or filled with spicy *picadillo*†.

to make up to six dozen ***tortillas***

1 lb 2 oz/500 g/4 cups Quaker *masa harina* (or cornmeal flour if *masa harina* is not available)
3½ oz/90 g/⅞ cup white flour
enough water to form a soft, pliable dough (8 fl oz/225 ml/ 1 cup or more)
several 6 in/15 cm squares of cooking parchment or foil
hot griddle or heavy iron frying pan, lightly oiled
tortilla press (optional), or small flat board such as a chopping board

Put the *masa harina* and flour in a bowl and gradually stir in enough water to make a damp and pliable dough that leaves the sides of the bowl clean. Work the dough with your hands for a few minutes until it is really malleable – you can use an electric mixer for this. At this point, test a tiny ball in a tumbler of cold water. If it soon disintegrates, you need to work it a little longer. If the ball drops to the bottom of the glass and stays whole, it is ready.

Leave the dough to rest, wrapped in a damp cloth, until you are ready to cook the *tortillas* and keep it wrapped while you break bits off. Take a small knob of the mixture and mould it in the middle of your palms, kneading it for ½ minute and then forming it into a little ball. Now flatten it slightly, and if you are making it by hand place the flattened ball between two sheets of paper or foil and then flatten it into a thin round, ⅛ in/ 3 mm thick, with the heel of your hand, or roll it out with a rolling pin, or flatten it with a chopping board.

If you are using a *tortilla* press, put a piece of cooking parchment or foil on the press, place the ball of dough off-centre, slightly towards the hinge, stamp it down gently with the palm of your hand, put another piece of paper or foil on top, lower the lid of the press and stamp gently with the lever until you have flattened the *tortilla* to ⅛ in/3 mm thick.

To cook, peel off one layer of paper, and place the *tortilla* on a heated oiled griddle or heavy frying pan, paper side uppermost. As the *tortilla* starts to cook, peel off the paper or foil. The *tortilla* should cook for about a minute, until the edges begin to curl up. Turn over and cook on the other side. *Tortillas* should not brown, or cook till dry; they will be pliable and springy and a little thicker than when they went into the pan.

Make and cook a succession of *tortillas* in the same way. Stack one on top of another and cover with a clean cloth, or wrap in foil.

To reheat, wrap securely in an aluminium foil parcel, and place in a steamer for about 30 minutes. *Tortillas* must always be eaten when they are warm and pliable; if you try to bend a cold *tortilla* it breaks. You can keep *tortillas* indefinitely wrapped in foil, in a freezer; reheat in a steamer as above.

If you are putting *tortillas* into casseroles and stews, they must be shallow fried for a few seconds on each side; they can be kept like this in a plastic bag in the refrigerator for about four days.

A simple way of serving *tortillas* is to place two ripe avocados on the table, with a stack of hot *tortillas*. Each person takes a quarter of an avocado and spreads it on a *tortilla* with a fork, instead of butter. It is then sprinkled with salt, rolled and eaten, and is perfectly delicious.

Tacos

Tacos are the most common snack in Mexico. A warm *tortilla*† is filled with meat, fish, fried beans or cheese, moistened with sauce, rolled up and eaten by hand. *Tacos* are sometimes lightly fried in oil or lard.

Shredded chicken with a little shredded lettuce or a slice of avocado, and freshly grilled meat chopped while it is still hot, make good *taco* fillings, and most leftovers can be heated up and used. To accompany a main meal, serve them with avocadas, as described for *tortillas* above. The *tortillas* should be fresh and served hot, and *tacos* are always accompanied by *salsa verde*† or *salsa cruda*† or both.

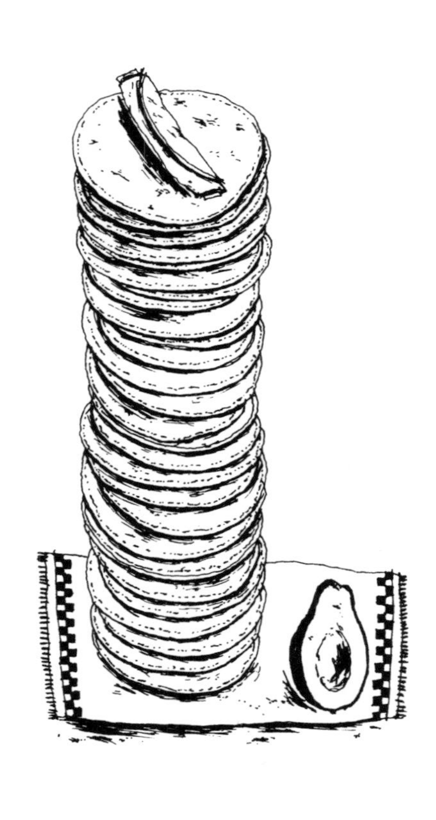

To make *tacos* with leftover *tortillas*, first reheat them by steaming, then roll them around the filling or fold them in half over it. Fry the *tacos* in very little oil, and serve on a bed of shredded lettuce.

Tacos make excellent barbecue food. Cook thinly cut steaks or lamb and pork chops or a selection of all three over a charcoal grill. Immediately before serving chop the meat into pieces about 1 in/2.5 cm square on a wooden board. Heat *tortillas* over the charcoal and place about four overlapping on each plate with the meat on top of them.

Serve immediately with a large bowl of *guacamole*†, a mild *salsa cruda* and a very hot *salsa verde* to enable people to choose the sauce they like to season their *tacos*.

Tamales
Steamed pancakes with spicy fillings

Tamales are eaten in various forms all over Latin America. In Peru they are known as *humitas*; in Colombia as *hallacas*. They are spongy and light with tasty fillings. They are eaten as snacks, accompanied by a cup of *atole*†, and always served at fiestas.

serves 4

for the tamales:
12 corn husks (outer leaves), banana leaves or sheets of greaseproof (wax) paper 4 × 9 in/10 × 23 cm
2 oz/50 g/¼ cup lard
6 oz/175 g/1¼ cups Quaker *masa harina* (or cornmeal flour)
¾ teaspoon baking powder
1 teaspoon salt
about ½ pint/300 ml/1¼ cups water

for the filling:
any of the following – strips of Munster cheese with a teaspoon of chopped fresh chilli pepper; chopped turkey; chicken or pork in *mole poblano* sauce†; *picadillo*† (see *chiles rellenos*†). Ingredients must be chopped small, and, if using leftovers, moistened with their sauce. Fruits such as pineapple or cherries cooked with sugar and cinnamon are used for sweet *tamales*

To make the *tamales* cover the corn husks with hot water and leave them to soak while you prepare the dough.

Cream the lard with an electric beater or wooden spoon until fluffy. Mix the *masa harina*, baking powder and salt together in a separate bowl. Gradually beat into the lard, alternating with the water, until you have a smooth, moist batter.

Pat the corn husks dry. Spread a tablespoon of dough on each husk to form a rectangle about 3 × 3½ in/8 × 9 cm. Put a tablespoon of filling in the centre and fold the sides of the husk together. Turn up the ends to cover the centre seam, overlapping at the top. The aim is to create moisture-proof packets. If necessary you can tie the husks with string.

Place the *tamales* in a steamer, with the flat sides of the husks underneath. Cover with a thick cloth and tightly fitting lid, and steam for about an hour. They are done when the batter comes away from the husks.

Tamales keep well in a refrigerator for about a week. They can also be frozen. To reheat, wrap in foil and bake in an oven pre-heated to 350° F/180° C/gas mark 4 for 30 minutes.

Serve a variety of fillings, and keep the *tamales* warm by wrapping in a cloth and placing in a bread basket. Eat them either in the hand or with a fork.

Chilaquiles
Fried *tortillas*

This popular Guatemalan snack differs completely from the Mexican dish of the same name. The *tortillas* are filled with a cheese mixture and fried in batter. *Salsa verde*† or *salsa cruda*† add spice to the dish.

serves 4

4 oz/110 g mozzarella or Munster cheese, grated
1 medium onion, finely chopped
1 tomato, skinned and chopped
8 hot *tortillas*†

for the batter:
2 eggs, separated
1 tablespoon flour
salt to taste
about 3 tablespoons vegetable oil

Mix the cheese, onion and tomato together. Place the mixture on the *tortillas* and fold them in half. To make the batter beat the egg whites until stiff. Add the yolks, flour and salt.

Dip the *tortillas* in the batter and fry in the vegetable oil until lightly browned.

Tortillas de Trigo
Wheat *tortillas*

In the north of Mexico and other parts of Central America, *tortillas* are made with wheat flour. Most people find these easier to make than *masa harina* (or ordinary cornmeal flour) *tortillas*†, but they lack the distinctive corn flavour.

serves 4

4 oz/110 g/½ cup lard
1 lb/450 g/4 cups flour, sifted
2 teaspoons salt
8 fl oz/225 ml/1 cup water

Rub the fat into the flour with your fingers. Dissolve the salt in the water and add to the flour and fat mixture. Mix thoroughly, knead the dough for 5 minutes and set aside covered with a damp cloth for 2 hours.

Knead the dough again briefly. Roll a piece out into a ball about 1½ in/4 cm across. Place on a floured surface and press with a rolling pin until you have a circle about 7 in/18 cm across.

Cook over a high heat on a lightly greased frying pan or griddle for about 20 seconds on each side. The surface should be speckled with dark brown.

Serve immediately, or store in a plastic bag and reheat before serving.

Arepas
Tortilla pancakes

This is the Colombian and Venezuelan equivalent of Mexican *tortillas*. It is made from a starchy local corn flour. The nearest available equivalent is *masa harina* (or ordinary maize flour).

Arepas are not flat like *tortillas*, but more like Greek pitta bread – crisp outside, and a little under-cooked and doughy inside.

makes 8–10 "arepas"

1 lb/450 g/3½ cups *masa harina* (or cornmeal flour)
1 teaspoon salt
¾–1 pint/450–600 ml/1¾–2½ cups water

Pre-heat the oven to 350° F/180° C/gas mark 4. Combine the flour and salt. Stir in enough water to make a stiff dough. Allow the dough to stand for 5 minutes. Form into slightly flattened balls about 3 in/8 cm wide and ½ in/1.25 cm thick.

Cook on a lightly greased griddle for 5 minutes on each side, then place on a baking dish in the pre-heated oven for 20–30 minutes, turning occasionally.

Empanadas
Meat turnovers

This spicy meat pastry is a favourite Chilean dish. It is portable, makes a small quantity of meat go a long way, and makes a good snack or supper dish.

serves 4

for the filling:
1 tablespoon olive oil
6 oz/175 g/¾ cup minced (ground) beef
1 small onion, chopped
1 clove garlic, peeled and chopped
1 dried red chilli pepper, finely crumbled
pinch ground cumin
salt and pepper
2 hard-boiled eggs, cut into thin wedges
12 black olives, stoned

for the pastry:
8 oz/225 g/2 cups flour
pinch salt
2 tablespoons softened lard
4 fl oz/125 ml/½ cup milk
vegetable oil for deep frying

To make the filling heat the oil in a frying pan and brown the meat. Add all the remaining ingredients except for the hard-boiled eggs and the black olives and cook over medium heat, stirring, for 5 minutes. Cool.

To make the pastry sift the flour and salt into a large bowl. Gradually add the lard and the milk. Stir well.

Knead the ingredients until they hold together. Break the dough into 2 or 3 pieces and roll them out as thinly as possible without breaking them. Cut into rounds 3–4 in/8–10 cm across.

Spoon a tablespoon of meat mixture, a piece of hard-boiled egg and an olive in the centre of each circle of dough.

Fold the pastry over to make a turnover, moistening the edges with a little water. Curve the turnover slightly to make a crescent shape. Press the outside edge with the prongs of a fork.

Pour vegetable oil into a deep, heavy frying pan until it is 2 in/5 cm deep. Heat until very hot but not smoking. Fry the *empanadas* 3 or 4 at a time, until golden brown. Remove with a slotted spoon and drain on kitchen paper. Serve hot.

Huevos Rancheros
Ranch-style eggs

These eggs, popular for breakfast all over Mexico, are one of the many ways of using up yesterday's *tortillas*†.

serves 4

4 *tortillas*†
4 eggs

for the sauce:
2 tomatoes, skinned and chopped
2 *serrano* chillies, peeled, seeded and chopped
½ clove garlic, peeled
1 small onion, chopped
3 tablespoons vegetable oil
1 tablespoon chopped fresh coriander
coarse salt
freshly ground pepper

Mix the tomatoes, chillies and garlic in a blender until smooth. Heat one tablespoon of oil in a heavy saucepan. Add the onion and cook until soft. Add the puréed tomato mixture and cook over a medium heat stirring occasionally for 5–10 minutes until thickened. Add the coriander and salt and pepper to taste, and keep warm.

Heat the remaining oil in a frying pan. Fry the *tortillas* for 1–2 minutes on each side. Do not let them get crisp. Drain on paper towels and keep warm.

Fry the eggs. Place an egg on top of each *tortilla* and coat with the sauce. *Huevos rancheros* are often served accompanied by slices of avocado and a small portion of *frijoles refritos*†.

Guacamole
Avocado sauce with tomatoes and coriander

This delicate green purée, hot and cool, is normally eaten with *tortillas*† at the beginning of a meal. It is also used as a sauce with *tacos*†, or you can serve it as a dip with pitta bread.

serves 4

¼ onion, finely chopped
1 tomato, skinned, seeded and chopped
1–2 *serrano* chilli peppers, seeded and chopped
4 sprigs fresh coriander, chopped
coarse salt to taste
juice of ½ lime
2 ripe avocados

Combine the onion, tomato, chilli peppers and coriander. Scoop out the flesh from the avocado and mash with the onion-tomato mixture. Season to taste. Squeeze on the lime juice to stop the *guacamole* from turning brown. Serve immediately.

The avocado stones are sometimes left in the serving bowl for decoration. (They are supposed also to prevent the purée from turning brown.)

Ají Molido con Aceite
Red chilli paste

This paste can be used as a substitute for fresh chilli peppers. It will keep for 2–3 weeks in the refrigerator.

Open the chillies and remove the seeds. Cover with boiling water and leave to soak for 2 hours. Drain. Combine in a blender with oil, garlic, salt and stock, or pound using a pestle and mortar. The paste should be a smooth purée.

- 8 dried red chilli peppers
- boiling water to cover
- 3 tablespoons olive oil
- 2 cloves garlic
- coarse salt
- ½ pint/300 ml/1¼ cups boiling stock or water

Pebre
Chilli sauce

This is served with beans and fish dishes in Chilean homes. It varies in spiciness, and in some homes can be very hot indeed. For a hotter relish, see *salsa de aji*†.

Combine all the ingredients in a bowl and let them stand for 2–3 hours before serving so that the flavours will be developed.

- 1 fresh green or 1 dried red chilli, seeded and chopped (chilli paste may be used instead)
- 1 clove garlic, peeled and chopped
- 1 medium onion, chopped
- 4 tablespoons chopped fresh coriander
- 1 tablespoon red or white wine vinegar
- 2 tablespoons olive oil
- 3 tablespoons water
- salt

Salsa de Ají
Very hot chilli sauce

This typical freshly made table relish is served with most meals in Colombia. It is extremely hot – for a milder sauce halve the quantity of chillies.

Combine all the ingredients and put them through a food mill or blender. Serve in a small bowl with meat, fish or chicken dishes.

- 1 medium onion, finely chopped
- 6 oz/175 g/1½ cups seeded and finely chopped fresh green chillies
- 1 teaspoon salt

Salsa Verde
Green tomato sauce

Salsa verde† and *salsa cruda*† appear at almost every Mexican meal. The strength of *salsa verde* can vary enormously from mild to searingly hot according to the amount of chillies used. Serve as a relish with meat, or spread it on your *tortillas*† during the meal.

Pound the chilli peppers, onion, garlic and coriander using a mortar and pestle. Then add the tomatoes, sugar and salt, and mix into a smooth sauce. If you are using a blender, combine all the ingredients and purée until smooth.

makes about ½ pint/300 ml/1¼ cups

- 2 *serrano* chilli peppers (use more for a very hot sauce)
- ½ medium onion, chopped
- 1 small clove garlic, peeled
- 6 sprigs fresh coriander, chopped
- ½ lb/225 g/1 cup canned Mexican green tomatoes, drained
- pinch sugar
- pinch salt

Salsa Cruda
Fresh Mexican tomato sauce

makes about ½ pint/300 ml/1¼ cups

2 tomatoes, skinned and chopped
½ medium onion, chopped
8 sprigs fresh coriander, chopped
3 *serrano* chilli peppers, seeded and chopped
coarse salt to taste
4 tablespoons water

There are many regional variations of this spicy but fresh Mexican sauce. As with *salsa verde*† its hotness varies according to the number of chilli peppers used, which is as much a question of personal preference as regional custom.

Combine all the ingredients in a bowl. Mix well and serve as an accompaniment to meat, chicken and egg dishes. Or eat with *tortillas*† throughout the meal.

Cream of Pumpkin Soup

A delicately flavoured, golden soup from Jamaica to start a leisurely family dinner. You can make it with any variety of pumpkin or squash.

serves 4

1½ oz/40 g/3 tablespoons butter
3 onions, finely chopped
about 1½ lb/700 g/3 cups pumpkin flesh, cut into 1 in/2.5 cm cubes
1¼ pints/725 ml/3 cups chicken stock
5 fl oz/150 ml/⅔ cup cream
salt and freshly ground pepper
dash of hot pepper sauce or Tabasco
freshly grated nutmeg (optional)

Heat the butter in a large, heavy-based saucepan and sauté the onions until tender but not browned. Add the pumpkin and chicken stock and bring to the boil. Reduce the heat, cover and simmer for about 45 minutes, until the pumpkin is disintegrating.

Cool slightly and put through a sieve or food mill. You can quickly reduce it in an electric blender, but do not overblend as the texture is better if not completely smooth. Return to the pan, stir in the cream and season to taste with salt, pepper and hot pepper sauce. Reheat gently without boiling, then pour into a warmed soup tureen.

Serve very hot, sprinkled with a little nutmeg.

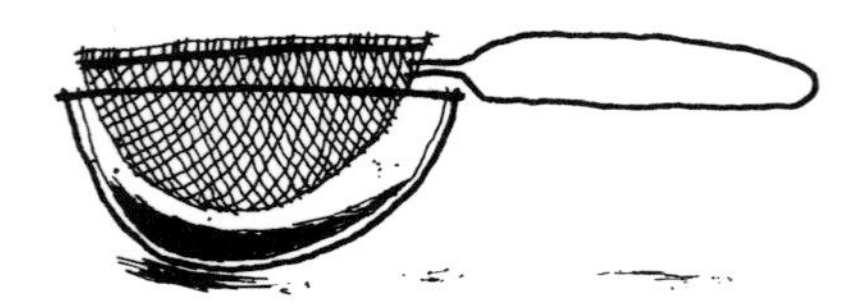

Chupe de Camarones
Shrimp soup

This soup originates in the Peruvian coastal region. It is very rich and thick, and is normally served as a midday meal.

serves 4

2 tablespoons olive oil
1 small onion, chopped
1 clove garlic, peeled and chopped
2 tomatoes, skinned and chopped
2 green peppers
1 fresh red or green chilli pepper, seeded and chopped
pinch marjoram or oregano
salt and pepper
4 oz/110 g/⅓ cup shelled peas (about ½ lb/225 g peas in the pod)
8 oz/225 g potatoes, peeled and cubed
1¼ pints/725 ml/3 cups water
½ pint/300 ml/1¼ cups milk
2 oz/50 g/⅓ cup uncooked rice
1 lb/450 g/2 packed cups bass fillets, cut into 1 in/2.5 cm pieces
12 oz/350 g shelled, deveined shrimps or large prawns
2 eggs, lightly beaten

Heat the oil in a large, heavy saucepan. Gently fry the onion with the garlic until soft but not browned. Add the tomatoes, green peppers, chilli peppers, marjoram, salt and pepper. Cook, stirring all the time, for 3 minutes.

Add the peas, potatoes and half the water. Cover and cook until the potatoes are tender. Add the remaining water, the milk and the rice. Cover and simmer for about 15 minutes, or until the rice is cooked. Add the fish and cook for 10 minutes. Add the shrimps and cook for 3 minutes. Stir in the eggs and cook until they thicken into threads. Correct the seasoning and serve.

Chupe de Pescado
Fish stew

Chupe is the general term for a stew or hotpot in Chile. With such a long coastline, fish is both cheap and plentiful, and the following fish stew is a typical everyday midday meal. Use any firm white fish such as sea-bass, eel, cod or haddock. For a hotter version add a chopped, deseeded red chilli.

serves 4

4 medium potatoes, boiled and halved
1 onion, chopped
2 tablespoons vegetable oil
1 tablespoon sweet paprika
4 oz/110 g/1 cup fresh white breadcrumbs
½ pint/300 ml/1¼ cups milk
½ pint/300 ml/1¼ cups fish stock made with fish bones, heads and other trimmings
1½ lb/700 g fish fillets, cut in 1 in/2.5 cm pieces
salt and pepper
½ teaspoon oregano
2 eggs, hard-boiled and chopped

Heat the oil in a heavy casserole and fry the onion with the paprika until soft. Add the breadcrumbs, milk, stock, fish, salt, pepper, oregano and potatoes. Cook for about 5 minutes, or until the fish is done.

Sprinkle hard-boiled egg over the top of the stew just before serving.

Daube de Poisson
Fish stew

Marinated fish steaks in an onion and tomato sauce sharpened with lime juice are a favourite in Martinique and Guadeloupe. This dish is successful with any firm-fleshed white fish that can be cut into steaks.

serves 4

4 medium steaks of white fish (such as halibut, hake or cod)
4 tablespoons olive oil
flour for coating
1 onion, finely chopped
3 spring onions or scallions, trimmed, both white and green parts chopped together
2 tomatoes, skinned and chopped
salt and freshly ground pepper
bay leaf
½ teaspoon chopped fresh thyme, or pinch dried thyme
4–5 tablespoons water
1 clove garlic, peeled and crushed
2 tablespoons fresh lime juice or lemon juice

for the marinade:
3 tablespoons fresh lime juice or lemon juice
1 fresh chilli pepper, preferably red, deseeded and crushed
1 clove garlic, peeled and crushed
2 teaspoons salt
about ½ pint/300 ml/ 1¼ cups water

First prepare the marinade by mixing together all the ingredients in a wide shallow dish. Add the fish and, if necessary, add a little water to make sure it is covered. Leave to stand for 1 hour, then lift out the fish and pat dry with paper towels. Discard the marinade.

Heat 3 tablespoons of the oil in a heavy frying pan. Dust the fish with flour, then sauté lightly until golden on both sides. Lift out and keep warm.

In the same pan sauté the onion and spring onions. When the onion is tender but not browned, add the tomatoes, salt, pepper, bay leaf and thyme. Cook for 5 minutes, stirring occasionally.

Add the fish and the water, cover and cook gently for 10–15 minutes, or until the fish is tender. Discard the bay leaf. Just before serving, beat together the remaining oil, the garlic and the lime juice and pour over the fish.

Serve piping hot with *coo-coo*† or rice, and with fried plantains†.

Ceviche
Marinated fish

Variations on *ceviche* – raw fish marinated in lime juice and spices – are served throughout Latin America.

serves 4

1 lb/450 g striped bass fillets

for the marinade:
juice of 2 lemons
juice of 2 limes
2 dried red chilli peppers, ground
1 mild purple or Spanish onion, thinly sliced
½ clove garlic, peeled and chopped

for the garnish:
2 large sweet potatoes
2 fresh corn on the cob
lettuce leaves
strips of red chilli pepper

Cut the fillets into 1 in/2.5 cm cubes. To make the marinade, combine the ingredients in a bowl and mix well. Toss the fish in the marinade and leave for about 3 hours, or until the fish has turned opaque.

Meanwhile, boil the sweet potatoes and corn until tender. Place portions of the fish on lettuce leaves on individual plates and garnish with slices of sweet potato and halved cobs of corn. Arrange strips of red chilli pepper on top.

Arroz a la Costa Rica
Costa Rican style rice

This is a Costa Rican example of the way in which good basic rice appears all over the world, dressed up in different ways, to vary it and make it appetizing. This beautiful red-gold rice is served all over Central America.

serves 2–4

6 oz/175 g/1 cup long grain rice
2 tablespoons vegetable oil
1 tablespoon achiote oil or
  1 tablespoon olive oil mixed with paprika
1 small onion, chopped
1 tomato, chopped
1 teaspoon paprika
salt

Fry the rice with the onion in the vegetable and achiote oil until the rice turns pale gold. Add the tomato, paprika and salt. Pour in enough water to rise 1 in/2.5 cm above the rice. Bring to the boil, turn down the heat, cover and simmer gently until all the liquid is absorbed (about 20 minutes). To vary the dish add a handful of freshly cooked peas towards the end of the cooking time and garnish with slices of hard-boiled egg.

Arroz Guatemalteco
Rice with vegetables

Rice and fresh vegetables – the simplest sort of food you can have – makes a complete meal by itself or it can be served with a meat dish, such as *carne en jocón*†. You can add any fresh vegetables in season to the rice, creating your own combinations.

serves 4

9 oz/250 g/1½ cups long grain rice
2 tablespoons peanut oil
1 small onion, chopped
1 tomato, skinned and chopped
1 clove garlic, peeled and chopped
1 cup chopped mixed vegetables (such as carrots, peas, green peppers, celery)
salt and pepper
1 pint/575 ml/2½ cups water
salt
2 tablespoons fresh coriander, chopped, as a garnish

Wash the rice thoroughly. In a heavy casserole heat the oil, add the rice and fry, stirring constantly until golden. Add the remaining ingredients except the coriander, bring to the boil, cover and simmer over low heat without stirring until all the liquid has been absorbed and the rice is tender (about 20 minutes). Add more water if necessary. Garnish with coriander.

Arroz con Coco y Pasas
Rice with coconut and raisins

This is a typical dish from the Colombian coast where coconut milk is often used in cooking, particularly with rice and fish.

Coconuts often do not travel well, so it may be better to use canned, unsweetened coconut milk which is sold in specialist shops.

serves 4

1¼ pints/725 ml/3 cups coconut milk (see below)
4 oz/110 g/¾ cup raisins
6 oz/175 g/1 cup long grain rice
1 teaspoon sugar
salt

If you can get fresh coconuts for the coconut milk choose the heaviest ones and shake to see how much liquid there is inside. Do not buy coconuts with soft or wet 'eyes'. A 1½ lb/700 g coconut should yield about 1¼–1½ pints/725–850 ml milk. (Fresh coconut milk keeps in the refrigerator for up to a week.)

To open a coconut, puncture the eyes and pour the milk into a bowl. Pre-heat the oven to 400° F/200° C/gas mark 6 and bake the coconut for 15 minutes. Remove it, put it on a hard surface and split with a hammer. The flesh should then come off easily. Peel the skin and grate the flesh. Alternatively, it can be ground in a blender with water and the water discarded.

To make the coconut milk put equal amounts of grated coconut and hot water into a blender. Blend until you have a thick liquid. Sieve the liquid through a cheesecloth. Press down with a wooden spoon to squeeze out the remaining liquid, adding water or making a second fusion from the coconut if necessary. Discard the pulp.

To make this rice dish put the coconut milk, raisins, rice, sugar and salt in a saucepan. Bring to the boil, stir and cover. Reduce the heat to very low and cook for 20–25 minutes until the rice is done.

Serve as a side dish with a main course. It is especially good with any spicy fish dish.

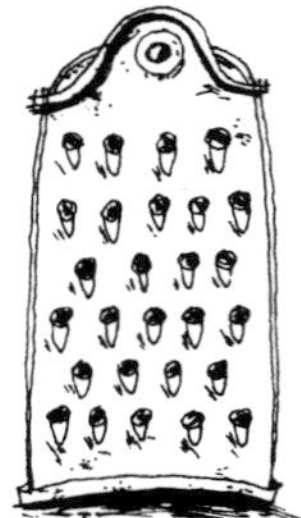

Coo-coo
Okra vegetable dish

This is traditionally regarded as a dish from Barbados, but very similar dishes are eaten in a great many of the Caribbean islands; some include saltfish and many omit the okra. These green pods, which are also called gumbo and ladies' fingers, are used frequently for thickening soups and stews because of the sticky juices they give out when cut.

serves 4

12 small, young okra
2½ pints/1.4 litres/6¼ cups water
salt
8 oz/225 g/1½ cups yellow cornmeal
1½ oz/40 g/3 tablespoons butter

Wash the okra, trim off the stems and cut across into ¼ in/5 mm slices. Bring the water to the boil, season well with salt and put in the okra. Cover and boil for 10 minutes. Slowly pour the cornmeal into the pan in a steady stream, stirring all the time with a wooden spoon. Cook over a medium heat, stirring constantly, for about 5 minutes, or until the mixture is thick and smooth.

Turn the mixture into a greased bowl to mould it neatly, then turn out on to a warmed serving plate and spread the butter on top; or you can turn it directly on to a warmed plate without moulding. Serve hot as a vegetable dish to accompany fish or meat.

Any *coo-coo* that is left makes a good breakfast dish when sliced and fried. You can serve it with bacon, grilled (broiled) tomatoes, or a fried egg.

Platanos Fritos
Fried ripe plantains

The plantain is a member of the banana family. It is eaten both green and ripe (when the skin is quite black), but in either case it must be cooked before it is eaten. It is served in all the Caribbean islands as an appetizer, in soups, as a starchy vegetable and as a dessert. Fried, as in this recipe, it goes well with any meat or fish dish. A similar dish is cooked in Mexico and other Central American countries, where it is served with rice as a first course at the midday meal. It can also be served with beans and *tortillas*† to accompany any main dish.

serves 4

2 large ripe plantains
butter or oil for frying

Cut off both ends of the plantains and peel them. Ripe plantains will usually peel as easily as ripe bananas. If there is any difficulty, cut through the skins lengthways on the ridges with a small, sharp knife, then peel off the skin in sections. Cut the plantains in half lengthways and crossways, giving 4 pieces from each.

Heat a thin layer of butter in a large, heavy frying pan. Sauté the pieces until browned on both sides, and then drain on kitchen paper. (You can cook bananas in this way as well; use ripe but firm ones with the skins still yellow.) Serve immediately while hot.

Ensalada Mixta
Mixed salad

serves 4

8 oz/225 g/2 cups chopped cabbage or lettuce
2 tomatoes, chopped
1 onion, sliced
1 avocado, sliced
1 carrot, grated
2 hard-boiled eggs, chopped

for the dressing:
2 tablespoons vinegar (banana, wine or cider vinegar)
6–8 tablespoons vegetable oil
salt and pepper

This salad varies, though the usual ingredients are lettuce, cabbage, carrots, tomatoes, onions, avocados and hard-boiled eggs. In Costa Rica the dressing is made from banana vinegar – but you can use white wine vinegar or cider vinegar instead.

Combine all the salad ingredients in a large bowl. Mix the oil and vinegar in a different receptacle, season, taste the dressing, adding more oil or vinegar as necessary, and pour on to the salad. Toss and serve.

La Salade de Leyritz
Leyritz salad

serves 4

4 green (unripe) bananas
salt
1 large tomato, skinned, deseeded and coarsely chopped
1 medium cucumber, peeled and coarsely chopped
6 sticks celery, sliced
2 medium carrots, scraped and shredded
1 ripe avocado, peeled, stoned and sliced
lettuce leaves, washed and shaken dry

for the vinaigrette dressing:
2 teaspoons mustard, preferably Dijon
1 clove garlic, peeled and crushed (optional)
salt and freshly ground pepper
1½ tablespoons white wine vinegar
5 tablespoons olive oil or vegetable oil

This a recipe from northern Martinique produces a pleasing combination of colours and textures. Use a ripe avocado or it will be hard and tasteless. It is ripe when it yields to gentle pressure at the stem end; keep it in a brown paper bag to speed the ripening.

Peel the bananas by cutting lengthways through the skin in 2 or 3 places, then lifting it off in sections. Put the peeled, whole bananas in a saucepan with enough cold, salted water to cover. Put on the lid, bring to the boil, then simmer for 10–15 minutes, or until tender. Drain and leave to cool, then cut across into ½ in/1.25 cm slices.

To prepare the vinaigrette dressing, combine all the ingredients in a bowl and beat together with a fork.

Put the banana, tomato, cucumber, celery, carrot and avocado in a bowl, pour on the dressing and mix lightly but thoroughly to coat everything. Line a salad bowl with the lettuce leaves and fill with the banana mixture.

Serve the salad as a first course at either lunch or dinner; or have it as a side dish to accompany your main course.

Frijoles
Red kidney beans

These are eaten in Nicaragua by rich and poor alike, daily for breakfast, dinner and supper. They can be mixed with rice; on top of *tortillas*; with *chorizo*; in soups; as a snack; and as the main meal. They are cooked in large quantities and reheated by frying in oil when required. To acquire the best taste from the *frijoles* it is important to cook them the day before they are to be eaten.

2 lb/900 g/4 cups red kidney beans
head of garlic
1 tablespoon salt

Soak the beans in plenty of water overnight. Rinse well, and boil them in plenty of water until they are tender – about two hours in an ordinary pan or 30 minutes in a pressure cooker. When the beans are just tender, add a whole head of garlic, each clove peeled and crushed, and the salt. Do not add the salt earlier or the beans will become hard. Simmer gently for 30 minutes more.

Frijoles de Olla
Beans in the pot

Beans form an important part of the diet in Mexico and Central America and are usually eaten daily for lunch after the main meat and vegetable course.

Every household has its own favourite way of cooking beans. This recipe is a classic countryside dish, owing much of its distinctiveness to the herb *epazote* – the nearest equivalent is a bay leaf. Most families cook enough beans for several days, bringing them back to the boil each day before serving. You can make double quantities to have a batch left over for frying – see *frijoles refritos*†.

serves 4

8 oz/225 g/1 cup dried beans (black, red, pinto or kidney)
1 onion, chopped
2 cloves garlic, peeled and chopped
sprig of *epazote* (or bay leaf)
2 *serrano* chilli peppers, seeded and chopped
about 2 pints/1.1 litres/5 cups water
1 oz/25 g/2 tablespoons lard
salt to taste – about 1 teaspoon

Soak the beans for 3–4 hours or overnight. Rinse the beans thoroughly and discard any broken or shrivelled ones. Place in a narrow-necked earthenware pot or heavy casserole. Add the onion, garlic, *epazote*, chilli peppers, lard and enough water to cover. Simmer gently for 1½–2 hours or until the beans are tender, adding more boiling water to keep the beans covered. If you are using a casserole keep the pan partially covered to allow for some evaporation. Add the salt at the end of the cooking. For a thicker sauce mash a tablespoon of beans and return them to the pot.

Serve the beans steaming hot in individual bowls after the main course. For a special occasion place a bowl of slightly salted cream on the table as an accompaniment.

Frijoles Refritos
Refried beans

As an alternative to beans in the pot†, the beans are fried almost dry and served at lunch after the main course and as an accompaniment to breakfast and supper dishes. The amount of lard used varies according to taste, and no other seasoning is added.

serves 4

about 1½ oz/40 g/3 tablespoons of lard or dripping(s)
about 8 tablespoons cooked beans (see *frijoles de olla*†)

Heat about 1 tablespoon of lard in a heavy frying pan. Add 2 tablespoons of beans and mash well over a high heat. Add more lard and more beans and continue mashing. Continue until you have finished the supply of beans and lard, and have a coarse purée.

When the beans are hot and sizzling and have become crisp underneath turn them out on to a dish and serve immediately.

Crisply fried strips of *tortilla*† are often stuck into the top of the beans as a decoration before serving. *Salsa cruda*† can be served as an accompaniment.

Gallo Pinto
Beans with rice and onions

Beans and rice boost each other nutritionally: this is a Nicaraguan version of a traditional recipe.

serves 4

1½–2 cups cooked rice
3 cups cooked *frijoles*†
oil for frying
1 onion, sliced in rings
salt and pepper to taste

Heat the oil in a frying pan. Fry the onion until it is soft and transparent. Add the *frijoles* and fry gently on a low heat for about 30 minutes, stirring them from time to time so that a skin does not form and so that they do not stick. Add the rice and stir for a few minutes more until the rice is warmed through. Season to taste with salt and pepper.

The Spanish red sausage, *chorizo*, is delicious with this, though it is not used often. Simply fry the *chorizo* chopped in pieces with the onion and a little less oil (as *chorizo* contains enough oil itself) and then follow the same procedure.

Porotos Granados
Cranberry beans with sweet-corn and pumpkin

The pumpkin and fresh sweet-corn in this Chilean recipe make a plain dish of beans more exciting. If you cannot obtain fresh cranberry beans, use small white beans such as Italian *cannellini* or navy beans (*saluggia*).

If using fresh beans, cover them with water, bring to the boil and simmer for 45 minutes. If using dried beans, rinse under cold water, cover with water and simmer for about 2 hours, or until tender.

Heat the oil in a deep, heavy frying pan and add the paprika. Mix well, add the onion and garlic and cook until the onion is soft but not browned. Add the tomatoes, oregano, salt and pepper and simmer for 5 minutes.

Drain the beans, reserving the liquid, return to the saucepan and add the tomato mixture. Add a little of the bean liquid if necessary. Add the pumpkin and simmer for 15 minutes. Stir in the corn and cook a further 10 minutes. Adjust the seasoning.

Serve in individual bowls as a side vegetable to accompany meat and fish main courses. A spoonful of *pebre*† (hot table sauce) in each bowl or a dash of bottled chilli sauce brings the dish alive.

serves 4

1 lb/450 g/3 cups fresh cranberry beans or 8 oz/225 g/1 cup dried white or navy beans
3 tablespoons olive oil
2 tablespoons sweet paprika
1 large onion, chopped
1 clove garlic, peeled and chopped
1 lb/450 g tomatoes, skinned and chopped
½ teaspoon oregano
salt and pepper
1 lb/450 g/2 cups chopped pumpkin (or vegetable marrow or winter squash), cut in 1 in/2.5 cm cubes
kernels from 2 large fresh corn on the cob

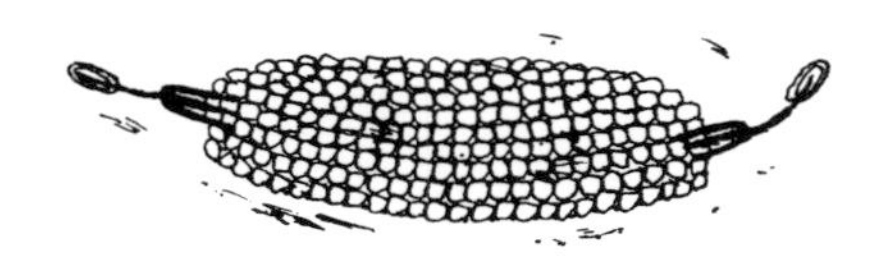

Papas a la Huancaina
Potatoes with cheese sauce

By adding a richly flavoured and coloured sauce to your potatoes and serving them with marinated onion rings, black olives and hard-boiled eggs, they are transformed into a decorative and nourishing meal.

Combine the lemon juice, dried chillies, salt and pepper in a bowl. Add the onion and leave to marinate while you boil the potatoes until cooked. To make the sauce combine the ingredients in a blender until smooth.

Heat the olive oil in a frying pan. Add the sauce and cook over a low heat, stirring constantly for 5 minutes or until the sauce thickens.

Arrange the potatoes in a heated serving dish and pour the sauce over them. Drain the onion rings from the marinade, and arrange them over the potatoes with the fresh chilli strips.

This dish is often served garnished with halved hard-boiled eggs, black olives and lettuce leaves.

serves 4

juice of ½ lemon
3 dried hot red chillies, seeded and crumbled
salt and pepper
1 large onion, sliced into thin rings
8 medium potatoes, peeled
3 tablespoons olive oil
1 fresh green or red chilli, cut in ⅛ in/3 mm strips

for the sauce:
6 oz/175 g/¾ cup coarsely grated mozzarella or Munster cheese
8 fl oz/225 ml/1 cup double (heavy) cream
1 teaspoon turmeric
1 fresh green or red chilli, finely chopped

Chileis Rellenos
Stuffed chilli peppers

This is a popular dish all over Mexico with numerous regional variations ranging from humble domestic versions, using leftovers or fried beans for the stuffing, to the luxurious dish smothered in cream and topped with walnuts served in the Puebla district on special occasions. This everyday version makes an attractive dish, the pink tomato sauce contrasting with the green peppers when they are cut open.

serves 4

4 *poblano* chillies (or 4 green peppers, whole, and 2 *serrano* chillies, chopped)
lard for frying

for the filling (picadillo):
2 tablespoons lard or olive oil
1 lb/450 g/2 cups minced (ground) pork or beef
1 small onion, chopped
2 cloves garlic, chopped
2 tablespoons raisins
1 apple or pear, peeled and chopped (optional)
3 medium tomatoes, peeled, seeded and chopped
1 oz/25 g/1 tablespoon blanched, slivered almonds
small pinch cinnamon
small pinch ground cloves
salt to taste
1–1½ tablespoons flour for coating peppers

for the sauce:
1 lb/450 g tomatoes, skinned, seeded and chopped
½ medium onion
1 clove garlic, peeled
2 tablespoons lard or olive oil
8 fl oz/225 ml/1 cup meat or chicken stock
salt and pepper

for the batter:
2 eggs, separated
½ teaspoon coarse salt

Char the peppers over an open flame or electric burner, turning them with a fork. Wrap in a damp cloth or place them in a covered saucepan and set aside while you make the filling; this makes them easy to peel.

To make the filling heat the lard in a frying pan and brown the meat. Add the onion and garlic and *serrano* chillies (if using green peppers). Cook for 5 minutes. Add the raisins, apple, tomatoes, almonds, cinnamon, cloves and salt to taste. Simmer uncovered for 20 minutes.

To make the sauce, combine the tomatoes, onion and garlic in a blender until smooth. Heat the lard in a frying pan, and add the tomato mixture, stock, and salt and pepper to taste. Simmer gently for 15 minutes.

Scrape the skin off the peppers. Make a slit in the side of each one with a knife and remove the seeds and veins.

To make the batter beat the egg yolks until thick. Beat the whites until stiff. Add the salt and gently fold the yolks into the whites.

Stuff the peppers with the meat and coat them in flour. Dip into the egg mixture. Heat the lard in a deep frying pan to a depth of ¾ in/2 cm. Fry the peppers until golden on all sides, remove and drain on paper towels. Heat the tomato sauce, add the peppers and cook for 2–3 minutes.

Serve with plenty of hot *tortillas*† to mop up the sauce, and follow with a bowl of *frijoles*†.

Beef Stew with Beans, Peas and Rice

A hearty one-dish meal blending a variety of tastes and colours. This recipe, from Trinidad, uses dried beans (or peas) to add vegetable protein to the meats, and the rice absorbs all the flavours.

serves 4

- 6 oz/175 g/1 cup dried red kidney beans or dried pigeon peas
- small smoked ham hock (shank)
- 1 lb/450 g stewing beef, cut into 1 in/2.5 cm cubes
- 1 teaspoon salt
- 1 teaspoon crushed garlic
- ½ teaspoon ground cloves
- 2 tablespoons oil
- about 1 pint/575 ml/2½ cups chicken or beef stock
- 2 tomatoes, skinned, deseeded and chopped
- 1 green pepper, deseeded and chopped
- 1 fresh green chilli pepper, deseeded and chopped
- 2 onions, coarsely chopped
- 9 oz/250 g/1½ cups long grain rice

Soak the beans overnight in cold water to cover. Put the ham to soak overnight in enough cold water to cover.

Next day, drain the ham, cut off the meat and divide it into 1 in/2.5 cm pieces. Mix with the beef, and sprinkle on the salt, garlic and cloves.

Heat the oil in a heavy, flameproof casserole and sauté the meats until browned all over. Drain the beans and add to the casserole. Pour on enough hot water to cover, then put on the lid and simmer until tender; this will take 1½–2½ hours depending on the type of beef used. Add a little hot water from time to time if necessary.

Pour off the liquid, measure it and make it up to 1¼ pints/725 ml/3 cups with the stock. Pour it back into the casserole and add the tomatoes, green pepper, chilli pepper, onions and rice. Bring to the boil, then reduce the heat, cover and cook very slowly until the rice is tender and all the liquid absorbed.

Serve very hot with mango chutney to make a satisfying lunch.

Picadillo
Meat with raisins and almonds

This is eaten in varying forms all over Latin America at the midday meal. It is also used as a filling for *empanadas*†, *tamales*† and *tacos*†. You can use it to stuff green peppers and other vegetables and as an appetizing filling for pancakes (crêpes).

serves 4

- 2 tablespoons olive oil or lard
- 1½ lb/700 g lean minced (ground) beef
- 1 medium onion, chopped
- 1 clove garlic, peeled and chopped
- 1 lb/450 g tomatoes, skinned and chopped
- 2 oz/50 g raisins
- salt and pepper
- 2 oz/50 g/⅓ cup chopped almonds or walnuts

Heat the oil in a frying pan and brown the meat. Add the onion and garlic and cook until soft. Add the tomatoes, raisins, salt and pepper. Simmer for 20 minutes, stirring occasionally. Stir in the nuts.

Serve as a main course with plain white rice, followed by a mixed salad and rounded off by a bowl of *frijoles*†.

Carne en Jocón
Beef stew

serves 4

3 tablespoons peanut or other oil
1 onion, chopped
2 cloves garlic, peeled and chopped
1 *serrano* chilli, seeded and chopped
2 green peppers, seeded and chopped
8 oz/225 g can of Mexican green tomatoes (or fresh *miltomates*)
2 lb/900 g stewing beef cut in 1 in/2.5 cm cubes
1 bay leaf
2 cloves
½ teaspoon oregano
¼ pint/150 ml/⅔ cup beef stock or water
1 stale *tortilla*† (or 1 tablespoon *masa harina* or cornmeal flour)
coarse salt

This is served at the midday meal with *arroz guatemalteco*†. Stew is a universal dish – this one from Guatemala is spiced with chillies, garlic and oregano. If you cannot get green tomatoes, leave them out.

Heat the oil in a heavy casserole and gently fry the onion, garlic, chilli and green peppers until the onion is soft.

Crumble the *tortilla* and soak briefly in water, or mix the flour to a smooth paste with a little of the beef stock. Add this with the remaining ingredients to the casserole and simmer very gently for about 2 hours.

Sobrebarriga
Casseroled steak

serves 4

2 tablespoons olive oil or lard
2 lb/900 g flank steak, rolled and tied with string
1 onion, chopped
1 clove garlic, chopped
2 stalks celery, chopped
1 teaspoon ground cumin
1 teaspoon salt
pepper to taste
water
1 oz/25 g/2 tablespoons butter, melted
2 oz/50 g/1 cup breadcrumbs

After long simmering with the vegetables and spices in this Colombian recipe, flank of beef tastes excellent. The appearance of the dish is improved by sprinkling the meat with breadcrumbs and butter.

Heat the oil in a heavy casserole and cook the meat until it is browned. Remove the meat, add the onion and garlic to the casserole and cook for 5 minutes. Return the meat to the casserole with the celery, cumin, salt and pepper. Cover with water and simmer for 2 hours, or until the meat is tender.

Remove the meat from the broth, pat dry and untie. Place on a grill (broiler) rack, coat with butter and breadcrumbs and brown under a hot grill (broiler). Slice and serve.

Bistec
Beefsteak

This is a thinly cut steak eaten at the midday meal with rice, beans, vegetables and salad. The meat is served very well done.

serves 4

4 minute steaks
oil for frying the steaks
2 onions, thinly sliced
Tabasco sauce
salt to taste

Brown the steaks in an oiled frying pan. Add the onions and cook until they are soft. Season with Tabasco and salt and serve.

Anticuchos
Ox (beef) heart cubes

These tender cubes of ox heart with their fiery sauce are sold by street-vendors in Peru. They are also sometimes served as a first course. For a milder version, you can halve the amount of chillies.

serves 8 as a first course

1 ox (beef) heart (about 4 lb/1.8 kg)

for the marinade:
1 pint/575 ml/2½ cups red wine vinegar
8 cloves garlic, peeled and chopped
2 fresh chillies, seeded and chopped
1 tablespoon ground cumin seed
salt and pepper

for the sauce:
1 tablespoon ground *achiote* (*annatto*) seeds or paprika
2 oz/50 g/⅓ cup dried chillies (or less according to taste)
1 tablespoon olive oil
coarse salt to taste

Trim off the gristle from the heart and cut into 1 in/2.5 cm cubes. Combine the ingredients for the marinade in a large bowl and toss the pieces of heart in the mixture. Marinate overnight.

To make the sauce, place the chillies in a bowl, cover with hot water and soak for 30 minutes. Drain, and combine the chillies in a blender with the *achiote* seeds, ¼ pint/150 ml/⅔ cup of the marinade, oil and salt. Blend until smooth.

Brush the heart cubes with some of the sauce, thread them on skewers and cook under a grill (broiler) or over hot coals for about 3–4 minutes. Serve with the remaining sauce on the side.

Mole Poblano de Guajolote
Turkey in hot chilli sauce

serves 8

8 lb/3.6 kg turkey, diced
2 oz/50 g/¼ cup lard

for the sauce:
6 *mulato* chillies, seeded and veined
6 *ancho* chillies, seeded and veined
4 *pasilla* chillies, seeded and veined
1 medium onion, chopped
2 cloves garlic, chopped
1 lb/450 g tomatoes, skinned, seeded and chopped
1 stale *tortilla*† (or 1–2 slices stale bread)
pinch ground cinnamon
small pinch ground coriander seed
small pinch ground aniseed
3 oz/85 g/⅓ cup sesame seed
4 oz/110 g/½ cup blanched almonds
1 oz/25 g/2 tablespoons raisins
coarse salt
freshly ground pepper
2 oz/50 g/¼ cup lard
1 oz/25 g/5 tablespoons grated plain chocolate

This Mexican dish is served throughout the country on Sundays and festive occasions. Every village or family has its own version, varying the richness, thickness and spiciness of the sauce. The same sauce is often poured over chicken. It is worth hunting for these chillies which are flavoursome rather than hot. For a milder dish use half the specified quantities of chilli peppers.

Prepare the chillies the night before by frying them in 1 oz/25 g/⅛ cup lard for about 6 minutes, or until their skins pucker. Place them in a bowl and cover with water.

Cover the turkey pieces with water and boil for one hour. Drain, and keep the broth. Dry the turkey pieces, heat 2 oz/50 g/¼ cup lard in a frying pan and brown them. Transfer the turkey to a large casserole.

In a blender combine the chillies with their liquid, the onion, garlic, tomatoes, *tortilla* or bread, cinnamon, coriander, aniseed, 1 oz/25 g/2 tablespoons of sesame seeds, raisins, almonds, salt and pepper, adding turkey broth if needed to make it into a smooth purée.

Heat the remaining lard in the same frying pan used to brown the turkey. Add the purée and cook over a high heat for 5 minutes. Add ¾ pint/450 ml/nearly 2 cups of the turkey broth and the chocolate and season to taste. Simmer for 30 minutes. Pour the sauce over the turkey and simmer for 10 minutes.

Garnish with the remaining sesame seeds. Serve with *tortillas*†, boiled rice, *frijoles*† and *guacamole*† for a veritable feast.

Coco Quemado
Coconut pudding

This rich, sweet pudding from Cuba is made with care for special occasions. It uses the sugar and coconut produced so abundantly in the area.

serves 4

12 oz/350 g/1½ cups sugar
5 fl oz/150 ml/⅔ cup water
12 oz/350 g/4½ cups grated coconut, preferably fresh
3 egg yolks, lightly beaten
¾ teaspoon ground cinnamon
4 tablespoons dry sherry

Stir the sugar and water together in a saucepan over a low heat until the sugar has dissolved completely, then boil hard until it reaches a temperature of 220–225° F/104–107° C on a sugar thermometer. To test without a thermometer, take some of the syrup on a spoon and, wearing a rubber glove, pinch up a little between thumb and forefinger and then pull apart; a fine thread should form between them.

Add the coconut to the syrup, then stir in egg yolks, cinnamon and sherry. Cook over a low heat, stirring all the time with a wooden spoon, until thick.

Pour into a flameproof serving dish and put under a hot grill (broiler) to brown the top. Serve with cream.

Flan
Caramel custard

This is one of the most popular desserts in Mexico and is related to the Spanish version†. This Mexican recipe is made in one generous dish instead of several small ones and includes ground almonds for their texture.

serves 4

6 oz/175 g/¾ cup sugar
1½ pints/850 ml/3¾ cups milk
6 egg yolks
2 whole eggs
1 oz/25 g/2 tablespoons ground almonds
pinch salt
1 vanilla pod (bean) or 1 teaspoon vanilla extract

To make the caramel, place half the sugar in a saucepan over medium heat. Stir with a wooden spoon until it is a deep brown, but do not let it burn. Warm a 2½ pt/1.4 litres/3¾ cup mould by standing it in hot water, then pour the caramel into it, tipping the mould so that the caramel coats the bottom and halfway up the sides.

Pre-heat the oven to 325° F/170° C/gas mark 3. Scald the milk with the vanilla and cool. Beat the eggs and egg yolks together with the rest of the sugar until thick and sticky. Gradually add the milk, the almonds and the salt. Mix thoroughly. Pour the mixture into the mould. Place the mould in a roasting tin containing hot water.

Bake for 15–20 minutes, then turn down the heat to 250° F/130° C/gas mark ½ and cook for a further 40 minutes or until the blade of a knife inserted in the *flan* comes out clean.

Cool and turn the *flan* out carefully on to a plate. Serve at room temperature.

Picarones
Fritters

These pumpkin or vegetable marrow fritters from Guatemala are served at the end of the midday meal. They are doughnut-shaped and crisp on the outside with a soft, light centre. Serve hot with a bowl of sugar syrup.

serves 4

4 oz/110 g/½ cup sliced pumpkin or vegetable marrow or winter squash
1 medium-sized sweet potato, peeled and sliced
7 oz/200 g/1¾ cups flour
½ teaspoon salt
¼ oz/7.5 g fresh or 1 level teaspoon dried yeast
a little warm water
oil for deep frying

for the sugar syrup:
8 oz/225 g/1 cup dark brown sugar
8 fl oz/225 ml/1 cup water
lemon peel

Boil the pumpkin and potato in a little water until tender. Drain thoroughly and mash through a sieve.

Sift the flour with the salt. Soften the yeast in a little warm water and mix with the flour. Add the pumpkin and potato purée and mix thoroughly, adding more water if necessary. Knead to make a smooth dough. Place the dough in a bowl, cover with a cloth and leave to rise for 2 hours or until it has doubled in bulk.

Take a tablespoon of the dough at a time and shape into rings on a floured surface. Deep-fry the rings in hot oil until browned. Drain on paper towels.

To make the syrup simmer the sugar with the water and lemon peel until it thickens.

Empanadas de Platanos
Deep-fried plantain pasties

This is a popular Guatemalan dessert, usually served at the midday meal, and sometimes as a snack before bedtime. It has a sweet, creamy banana taste.

serves 4

2 plantains (or 2 large bananas)
½ teaspoon salt
2–3 tablespoons flour (enough to make a thick paste)
3–4 oz/85–110 g/⅓–½ cup cream cheese
oil for deep frying
sugar

Cut the plantains into 2 in/5 cm pieces and boil them with the skins on for about 6 minutes or until tender. Skin and mash in a bowl with salt and enough flour to make a thick paste.

To make an *empanada* put 1 tablespoon of the mixture on a floured surface, flatten it to a thickness of about ¼ in/5 mm and put about ¾ oz/20 g/1½ tablespoons of cream cheese in the centre. Fold over and press the edges together. Continue until the mixture is used up.

Heat the oil and deep-fry the *empanadas* for about 6 minutes until they turn a deep golden brown. Sprinkle with sugar and serve hot.

Manjar Blanco
Paste of condensed milk

Although there is a longer and more complicated way of making this accompaniment to sweet dishes, using fresh ingredients, people throughout Chile, and indeed most of Latin America, use the following recipe. It is perhaps the most popular dessert and is used as a topping for ice cream or *flan*†, as a filling for cakes, to spread on bread, and with fruit, especially bananas. It is very popular with children, but it is less sweet then one might expect.

To make *manjar blanco* simmer an unopened tin of sweetened condensed milk in water for 4 hours. Be sure to allow the tin to cool completely before opening. The result will be a caramel-coloured paste which can be eaten by itself, or according to the suggestions above.

Atole
Maize (corn) gruel

This is a very popular beverage all over Mexico, but the rather musty flavour and thick gluey consistency given by the *masa harina* make it difficult for most foreigners to like at first taste.

However, it is very much appreciated in the cold mountain air at early morning markets, and as a warming bedtime drink. It is usually a feature of village fiestas, when it is flavoured with crushed fruit or chocolate. In some regions it is flavoured with chilli. *Atole* is the traditional drink to serve with *tamales*†.

serves 4

2 oz/50 g/½ cup *masa harina* or cornmeal flour
½ pint/300 ml/1¼ cups water
1 vanilla pod (bean)
1 pint/575 ml/2½ cups milk
sugar to taste

Mix the *masa harina* with 8 fl oz/225 ml/1 cup of the water. Bring the remaining water to the boil. Add the flour mixture and, vanilla pod and cook, stirring constantly until thick. Add the milk and sugar and bring back to simmering point; remove the vanilla pod. Serve very hot in earthenware mugs.

Melón Fresco

makes about 1 pint/575 ml/2½ cups

¼ melon
3 tablespoons sugar or to taste
pinch salt
squeeze of lemon juice
water
lots of ice

This refreshing and delicious drink is very popular in Nicaragua. It is made by simply grating or squeezing fruit, mixing with salt, sugar and water and chilling. Frescos can also be made with grated apples and orange juice, grapefruit or lemon.

Cut the melon into small pieces and grate into a large jug. Add the sugar, salt and lemon juice. Pour on water, add ice and chill. The quantity of water added depends entirely on taste, but it should be roughly 1 pint/575 ml/2½ cups for each ¼ melon. Serve in glasses full of ice.

Mangoade

serves 4–6

2 oz/50 g/¼ cup sugar, or to taste
15 fl oz/450 ml/1¾ cups water
1 teaspoon grated orange rind
1 lb/450 g/2 cups coarsely chopped ripe mangoes
15 fl oz/450 ml/1¾ cups orange juice
5 fl oz/150 ml/⅔ cup fresh lime juice or lemon juice

A long, cool drink served on long, hot Jamaican days. Make it with ripe mangoes, not the hard green ones used for chutney. The skin of a ripe mango may vary from green to rose-red, but you can tell if it is ripe by pressing it gently to see if the flesh yields.

Combine the sugar, water and orange rind in a saucepan and heat, stirring, until the sugar has dissolved. Rub the mango through a sieve and add to the syrup. Add the orange juice and lime juice and stir, then put in the refrigerator to chill.

Serve as a drink with ice. For a celebration, you can add 3–4 tablespoons of rum to each glass.

Bacon and Bananas

serves 2–4

4 medium bananas, unpeeled
8 slices bacon

The tradition of a robust bacon-and-egg breakfast is strong in the English-speaking Caribbean islands. But bacon combines equally well with a local partner – bananas – and it's a healthier dish.

Grill (broil) the bananas for about 8 minutes, turning several times until the skins are black all over. At the same time, grill or fry the bacon. Peel the bananas and serve with the bacon and toast, bread or rolls.

Alternatively, if you are frying the bacon, you can peel the bananas, slice them across and along their length and fry them in the fat from the bacon.

CHAPTER 6

THE VEGETA

Vegetarians may choose their lifestyle for religious reasons, or because they do not like to see animals killed; more recently they have decide that meat eating is bad for them, and economically bad for the planet too. Some, more selfishly, decide that vegetarian food simply tastes better. However, it is only in recent years that scientific evidence has emerged supporting the benefits of a vegetarian diet.

The effect has been to bring vegetarians into a Golden Age. Although vegetarianism has been advocated by philosophers and religious enthusiasts since ancient times, it is only in the last decade that the cult has become joyful. Networks of stores across the country sell whole grain, nuts and fresh vegetables. Vegetarian restaurants open with adventurous dishes from across the world – even smart restaurants take some pride in offering vegetarian alternatives to meat dishes.

Vegetarianism has needed a new image for a long time. By inventing dishes which obviously lacked the main ingredient, they seemed to be denying some of life's chief pleasures: nut cutlets in gravy, bean rissoles masquerading as hamburgers. The best of modern vegetarianism has shrugged off these shackles. Today the vegetarian re-examines the skills and insights which have evolved in the peasant cooking of the world. The modern vegetarian is international, and will cook an aubergine dish from the Balkans, a hummus made of chick peas from the Middle East, a hot spiced bean dish from Mexico, deep-fried shredded carrots or mushrooms in tempura batter from Japan.

Although the other sections of this book

RIANS

include recipes which are purely vegetarian, their peoples are not, and so they may include meat and fish to their liking and the food's availability. In this section meat and fish are naturally excluded, and it is important that the dietary relevancy of all vegetarian foods is properly understood.

Zen macrobiotic diets and similar fad diets usually turn out to be insufficiently varied, and in the long run can be damaging to the health. Over-indulgence in dairy products too, may be as detrimental to health as over-indulgence in meat. A good nutritional balance needs to contain more than the average quantity of unrefined starches and grains, seed oils in preference to animal fats, and plenty of leafy vegetables. Most vegetarians do eat eggs and dairy products, but it is possible to eat no animal protein at all and still be perfectly healthy.

If no animal produce is included in the diet it is then advisable to be sure to eat green vegetables and to take yeast extract as a supplementary source of vitamin B12 which otherwise may be deficient in such a diet. This type of diet has been recommended for people who have suffered warning heart attacks or other symptoms suggestive of blood vessel disease. However, any specialized diet should not be undertaken without seeking medical advice.

The following recipes are often labour intensive and even sometimes highly inconvenient, but are much the better for it. They include fresh herbs in quantity, enlivening spices such as chillies, and ingredients new to the West, like *tofu* – fresh bean curd. They take *trouble* to make the food fresh, lively and interesting, but the effort is rewarded.

Muesli

Cereal, nuts, fruit and milk combine to give a nourishing and filling start to the day – and one that stays with you longer than the more usual coffee and toast breakfast. When Dr Bircher-Benner devised this recipe early in the century for patients at his sanatorium in Switzerland ordinary milk was not always wholesome, so he used sweet condensed milk. Now, of course, you can safely use fresh milk and sweeten it with honey.

serves 4

4 tablespoons oat flakes or oatmeal
6 fl oz/175 ml/¾ cup water
4 tablespoons lemon juice
4 tablespoons sweet condensed milk diluted, or 1 pint/575 ml/2¼ cups fresh milk mixed with 4 tablespoons honey
4 large dessert apples
4 tablespoons grated nuts, raw or toasted

Put the oat flakes or oatmeal to soak overnight in the water. Next morning stir the lemon juice into the condensed milk (or fresh milk and honey) and pour over the oats. Grate the apples into the mixture, stirring in frequently so that the pieces do not go brown. Sprinkle the nuts on top and serve at once.

Muesli is infinitely versatile. You can use rolled oats or porridge oats for speed, since they do not need soaking. You can add ingredients to suit your own taste and the season – raisins or sultanas (golden raisins), sunflower seeds, or sesame seeds, whole toasted cashews or almonds, chopped bananas or soft fruits such as raspberries and strawberries, a little wheat germ, and yoghurt or fresh orange juice instead of milk.

Split Pea Soup

A cold, foggy, drizzling day in New York is sometimes called an English day – and that's the kind of day to use this American recipe for a thick soup to warm you right through. It is easily made from ingredients readily available.

serves 6–8

1 lb/450 g/2 cups green split peas, soaked
3 oz/85 g/⅓ cup pearl barley
4 pints/2.3 litres/10 cups water
2½ teaspoons sea salt
2 bay leaves
2 tablespoons olive oil
1 medium onion, chopped finely
1 carrot, chopped finely
2 cloves garlic, peeled and crushed
2 teaspoons chopped fresh thyme, or 1 teaspoon dried thyme

Put the peas and barley in a large, heavy-based pan with the water, salt and bay leaves. Bring to the boil, then reduce the heat, cover and simmer for about 1 hour, stirring occasionally to prevent sticking.

Heat the oil in a frying pan and sauté the onion, carrot, garlic and thyme in it until the carrot is tender. Add to the peas and barley and simmer for at least 30 minutes more.

Remove the bay leaves, taste and add more salt if necessary. Serve piping hot with plenty of hot cornbread† to make a simple and sustaining lunch.

Tomato Bisque

This is a never-fail soup that is very quick to make. It is thick with tomatoes and vegetables, and smooth with sour cream.

serves 4

2 pints/1.1 litre/4 cups canned whole tomatoes with their juice
1 carrot, finely grated
3 sticks celery, finely chopped
4 spring onions or scallions, finely chopped
2 tablespoons olive oil
1 medium onion, finely chopped
1 green pepper, finely chopped
2 cloves garlic, peeled and crushed
1 tablespoon finely chopped fresh basil, or 1 teaspoon dried basil,
1 teaspoon chopped fresh marjoram, or ½ teaspoon dried marjoram
about ½ teaspoon freshly ground black pepper
1 medium courgette (zucchini), finely chopped, and
8 oz/225 g/½ lb fresh spinach, chopped
5 fl oz/150 ml/⅔ cup cultured sour cream
salt to taste

Boil the tomatoes and their juice hard in a large, heavy-based pan to remove bitterness, then add the carrot, celery and spring onions and leave to simmer.

Heat the oil in a frying pan and sauté the onion and green pepper until they soften. Add the garlic, basil, marjoram and black pepper and fry for about 1 minute. Add the courgette and spinach and cook until tender. Combine the fried vegetables with the tomatoes and simmer for 30 minutes.

Just before serving, ladle about ½ pint/300 ml/1¼ cups of the soup into a separate bowl. Mix the sour cream into it thoroughly, then stir back into the rest of the soup.

Taste and add salt as necessary. If the soup is too thick, thin it with a little tomato juice. Serve very hot with plenty of wholewheat bread†.

To vary the soup, you can add any extra vegetables you like; broccoli, cauliflower and aubergine are especially good. Add them at the same time as the courgette.

Lentil Spinach Soup

This rich green soup makes a satisfying lunch when served with thick slices of home-made wholewheat bread†. You can also make a good soup with Swiss chard or frozen spinach. If you are using brown or green (whole) lentils soak for 2–3 hours before cooking. Split lentils (red) do not need soaking.

serves 4

6 oz/175 g/¾ cup lentils
2 oz/50 g/¼ cup green split peas
1½ pints/850 ml/3¾ cups water
1 teaspoon sea salt
1 bay leaf
1 potato, scrubbed but not peeled, diced
1 tablespoon olive oil
1 medium onion, chopped finely
1 clove garlic, peeled and crushed
1 tablespoon finely chopped fresh dill, or 1 teaspoon dried dill
pinch freshly ground black pepper
8 oz/225 g fresh spinach, well washed, stems and leaves chopped together
1 tablespoon red wine vinegar, or 1 teaspoon malt vinegar

Put the lentils, peas and water into a large, heavy-based pan with the salt and bay leaf. Bring to the boil, then reduce the heat and simmer, covered, for about 1 hour. Stir occasionally to prevent sticking.

Boil the potato in a separate pan in enough water to cover, until just tender but still firm. Add the potato and its cooking liquid to the lentils and peas.

Heat the oil in a frying pan and sauté the onion in it for 1–2 minutes, then add the garlic, dill and pepper and sauté for 1 minute more. Add the spinach a handful at a time, waiting for one handful to wilt before adding the next. Cook for 2–3 minutes.

Add the spinach mixture to the lentils and peas. Then stir in the vinegar and simmer for at least 30 minutes more. Remove the bay leaf, then taste and add salt and pepper if necessary.

Serve piping hot with plenty of bread.

Cream of Butternut Squash Soup

This American recipe makes a good winter soup, slightly sweet with a hint of cinnamon. You can make it with other varieties of winter squash (such as Hubbard or Acorn) or with carrot or pumpkin. Serve it as a first course, or with plenty of buckwheat bread† for a light meal.

serves 4

1 potato, scrubbed but not peeled
1 oz/25 g/1 tablespoon butter
1 small onion, chopped
pinch ground cinnamon
pinch dried marjoram
nutmeg
pinch sea salt
about 1 lb/450 g/2 cups cubed butternut squash flesh, marrow or carrot
1 tablespoon cream sherry
1 pint/575 ml/2½ cups milk

Cook the potato in water to cover until soft. Set aside, peel and reserve the water. Heat the butter in a heavy-based pan and cook the onion in it until soft and golden. Add the cinnamon, marjoram, a light grating of nutmeg and the salt. Fry for 1 minute more.

Put in the squash and cook, covered, until it is very tender. Stir occasionally to prevent sticking; add a little of the potato water if the pan becomes too dry. When the squash is soft, add the potato with its cooking water and boil for 20 minutes.

Put the mixture in a blender with the sherry and milk and blend until smooth and velvety; or mash the mixture very thoroughly and add the sherry and milk gradually. Taste, adjust the seasoning and keep hot over a low heat until serving time. Serve hot with bread, perhaps with a quiche and salad afterwards.

To vary the soup, use 1½ lb/700 g scrubbed, unpeeled carrots in place of the squash. Cut them into 1 in/2.5 cm pieces and cook as the squash, but add 2 extra tablespoons sherry and a little more salt at the end.

Scrambled Tofu

Tofu is especially popular with vegetarians who do not eat eggs, because it has that same tender, succulent texture. This American dish makes an excellent light meal.

Fry the *tofu* briskly in a frying pan or skillet in 2 tablespoons of the oil. Turn the cubes occasionally until they are crisp on all sides and lightly browned. Sprinkle on half the lemon juice, ½ teaspoon of the salt, and the pepper. Remove from the pan and set aside; leave any fragments of *tofu* that stick to the pan.

Put the beans in the pan with enough boiling water to cover them and ½ teaspoon of salt. Boil for about 8 minutes, until just tender. Drain off the liquid (you can use it in a soup) and set aside the beans.

Heat the remaining oil in the same pan and fry the onion in it for about 5 minutes. Add the thyme, caraway seeds and the remaining salt and fry for 1 minute. Put the *tofu* and beans back in the pan and cook until heated through. Stir in the remaining lemon juice.

Taste and add more seasoning if necessary. Serve hot with toast.

serves 6

- 2 lb/900 g hard *tofu*†, cut into ½ in/1.25 cm cubes
- 3 tablespoons corn oil, or other light vegetable oil
- juice of 1 lemon
- 1½ teaspoons salt
- freshly ground black pepper
- 1 lb/450 g dwarf green beans, snapped or cut into 1 in/2.5 cm lengths
- 2 medium onions, cut in slices and halved to make crescents
- 2 teaspoons chopped fresh thyme, or 1 teaspoon dried thyme
- 1 tablespoon caraway seeds

'Wings of Life' Salad

Since salads are often a whole meal for vegetarians, they must be nourishing and filling. American vegetarians make great use of *tofu* (soya bean curd), a vegetable protein from the Far East, available in Oriental food shops, or you can make it yourself. Here it is mixed with fresh salad greens and lightly cooked broccoli to make a meal that appeals to the eye and the palate.

serves 4

for the salad:

- 1 tablespoon corn oil or olive oil
- 8 oz/225 g hard *tofu* (bean curd) cut into ½ in/1.25 cm cubes
- salt and freshly ground black pepper
- juice of ½ lemon
- about 8 oz/225 g cups broccoli, cauliflower or green beans, cut into 1 in/2.5 cm pieces
- salad greens, or Swiss chard or young spinach to taste
- 1 Spanish onion, finely sliced
- 3–4 tablespoons freshly grated Parmesan cheese
- 1 tablespoon chopped fresh dill, if available

for the dressing:

- about 3 tablespoons olive oil
- 2 teaspoons fresh lemon or lime juice
- 2 cloves garlic, peeled and crushed
- sea salt and freshly ground black pepper to taste

To prepare the salad, heat the oil in a small frying pan and fry the *tofu*, turning frequently until the cubes are crisp and brown all over. Sprinkle with salt and pepper and the lemon juice. Leave to cool.

Put the broccoli or other vegetable in a wide pan, pour boiling water over it, stand it over a good heat for 5 minutes, then drain, saving the liquid for a soup. The broccoli will be lightly cooked and still crisp. Leave it to cool.

Put your chosen salad greens in a big salad bowl with the onion, *tofu*, broccoli, cheese and dill. To dress it, spoon on just enough olive oil to coat everything lightly when it is tossed. Just before serving, mix the lemon juice in a small bowl with the garlic and season with salt and pepper. Pour over the salad and toss well.

Serve the salad with plenty of home-made bread.

Yoghurt-Tahina Salad

serves 4

salad greens and chopped raw vegetables to taste
2–3 carrots, sliced very thinly
2–3 tablespoons cashew nuts, toasted
1 oz/25 g/1 tablespoon grated Cheddar cheese
4 tablespoons alfalfa sprouts

for the dressing:
15 fl oz/450 ml/1¾ cups plain yoghurt
5 fl oz/150 ml/⅔ cup *tahina* paste (sesame meal)
2 cloves garlic, peeled and crushed
juice of ½ lemon
½ teaspoon sea salt
1 oz/25 g/1 tablespoon fresh parsley, stems and leaves both finely chopped

The flavour of the Middle East is in the American dressing for this salad – yoghurt and *tahina*, a paste made from sesame seeds, are favourites in that region. You can also use the dressing as a sweet-sharp dip for strips of raw vegetables.

Put your chosen salad greens and raw vegetables into individual bowls and scatter on the carrot.

To make the dressing, whisk together all the ingredients until smooth. Spoon the dressing over the salads, then sprinkle on the nuts and cheese. Top each bowl with a mound of alfalfa sprouts.

To make the salad even more substantial you can include rice in it. Spread cooked rice on a baking dish, cover it with grated Cheddar cheese and heat in the oven until the cheese bubbles. Prepare the bowls of salad greens and vegetables as before and spoon on the dressing. Then put a portion of the baked rice on the dressing and sprinkle with the nuts and plenty of alfalfa sprouts.

Hummus Sandwich

Almost all the vegetarian restaurants in the United States serve a hummus sandwich – hot, buttered bread thickly spread with hummus, made of chick peas and sesame seed, and garnished with tomato, cucumber and alfalfa sprouts. Wholefood bakeries, too, sell slices of fresh bread with hummus. It makes a nourishing snack; prepare the spread at home and store it in the refrigerator.

makes 1 pint/575 ml/2½ cups hummus

7 oz/200 g/1 cup chick peas, soaked
2 pints/1.1 litres/5 cups water
7 fl oz/200 ml/⅞ cup *tahina* paste (sesame meal)
2 cloves garlic, peeled and crushed
1 teaspoon sea salt
juice of 1 lemon
1 oz/25 g/1 tablespoon finely chopped fresh parsley, stem and leaves together

Simmer the chick peas in the water for 3–3½ hours, until they are very soft. Drain, reserving the cooking liquid. Grind or mash the chick peas until smooth, adding a little of the liquid if necessary to give a soft, even texture.

In a separate bowl, beat together the *tahina*, garlic and salt, using a wooden spoon. Add the lemon juice little by little, beating all the time. Then add cooking liquid from the chick peas little by little, still beating continuously, until the mixture is light and creamy with a texture similar to mayonnaise. You will not need much of the cooking liquid.

Stir the ground chick peas into the *tahina* mixture until thoroughly combined, and add a little more of the cooking liquid if the paste becomes too stiff. Stir in the parsley, taste and add more salt or lemon if necessary.

Use the paste as a spread on home-made bread and garnish it with salad or raw vegetables.

To vary the paste, you can add some finely chopped spring onions, scallions or celery. For a hot snack using hummus, spread it thickly on buttered bread, cover with grated Cheddar cheese, and grill (broil) until the cheese bubbles and browns a little.

Wholewheat Piecrust

Wholewheat flour makes pastry full of flavour and beautifully crunchy. Use it for fruit pies and tarts as well as for quiches and meat pies. Be sure to use a fine-ground flour for a crisp, tender crust. Wholewheat pastry flour is sold at health-food shops.

serves 4 – makes a 9 in/23 cm pastry case

4½ oz/125 g/1 cup wholewheat pastry flour or fine-ground wholewheat flour
pinch sea salt
3 oz/85 g/⅓ cup butter
about 3 tablespoons cold water

Mix the flour and salt together in a mixing bowl and put in the butter. Using 2 forks, cut in the butter until it is in small pieces the size of peanuts. Add the water a little at a time, working it in with a fork and adding only enough to make the pastry stick together when you press it lightly with your hand. The amount of water needed varies with the flour.

Gather the pastry into a ball and knead it a little on a floured working surface, until it just holds together. Form it into a neat, flattened ball and roll it out on a floured surface with a floured rolling pin. Roll from the centre outwards, giving the pastry frequent quarter-turns sideways.

Continue rolling out the pastry until about 1 in/2.5 cm of it shows all round a 9 in/23 cm pie-dish. Rub the dish lightly with butter, then fold the pastry in half and lift it into the dish. Unfold it and fit it neatly into the dish, making sure that there are no air bubbles trapped beneath it. Trim off or fold under any pastry overhanging the dish, then decorate the edge with a fork.

For a sweet filling you can mix the pastry with apple juice or milk instead of water, roll it out on shredded coconut instead of flour, and sprinkle it with ground cinnamon before filling. For other dishes, try adding a little finely chopped dill or grated Parmesan cheese to the flour, and mix with plain yoghurt or white wine instead of water.

Sesame-Cauliflower Quiche

Sesame seeds give an unusual, slightly sweet flavour to vegetable tarts, and combine particularly well with cauliflower – as this American recipe will show. The savoury cheese and spring onion balance the sweetness.

serves 4

4½ oz/125 g/1 cup wholewheat pastry†
2 tablespoons sesame seeds
1 tablespoon corn oil
12 oz/350 g/3 cups cauliflower florets, in 1 in/2.5 cm pieces
1 teaspoon sea salt
1/- teaspoon pepper
1 [illegible] spoon dried thyme
4 sp[illegible]ing onions or scallions, trimmed, both white and green parts cut in ½ in/1.25 cm pieces
4 oz/110 g/1 cup grated Cheddar cheese
3 eggs
10 fl oz/300 ml/1¼ cup milk

Roll out the pastry to line a lightly oiled 9 in/23 cm flan or quiche tin.

Put the sesame seeds in a hot, dry frying pan or skillet and cook them over a brisk heat until lightly browned. Remove from the pan and set aside.

Heat the oil in the same pan and cook the cauliflower until tender; add small amounts of water from time to time to prevent sticking. When the cauliflower begins to soften, add half the salt, the pepper and the thyme; when the cauliflower is tender, put back the sesame seeds and add the onions. Stir well and remove from the heat.

Sprinkle half the cheese into the pastry case and spread the cauliflower mixture over it evenly, but without packing it down; the quiche will be lighter with egg custard appearing between the pieces of vegetable. Sprinkle the remaining cheese on top.

Beat the eggs in a bowl with the remaining salt, then stir in the milk. Pour over the cheese and cauliflower, taking care not to let it overflow the pastry case.

Bake in a pre-heated oven at 350° F/180° C/gas mark 4 for 30–45 minutes. The pastry should be crisp and the custard set and lightly browned.

Serve the quiche hot with a salad. A cold piece of quiche that has been left over can be reheated in a warm oven and will taste just as good.

For a variation, replace the cauliflower and sesame seeds with broccoli and toasted almonds tossed in a little soy sauce.

Carrot, Cashew and Ginger Quiche

This American quiche sounds extraordinary but tastes wonderful. The carrot and cheese filling is soft, while the nuts and ginger add both kinds of bite.

serves 4

4½ oz/125 g/1 cup wholewheat pastry†
½ oz/15 g/1 tablespoon butter for frying
4 oz/110 g/½ cup cashew nuts
1½–2 in/4–5 cm piece fresh ginger, very finely chopped
4 cloves garlic, peeled and chopped
3 medium carrots, cut in thin slices
1½ tablespoons sherry
salt
4 oz/110 g/1 cup grated Gruyère, Emmenthal or Jarlsberg cheese
3 eggs
10 fl oz/300 ml/1¼ cups milk
½ teaspoon grated nutmeg

Roll out the pastry to line a 9 in/23 cm flan or quiche tin.

Heat a knob of butter in a small frying pan or skillet and toast the cashew nuts in it until they are light brown. Stir frequently while they are cooking to prevent burning. Remove from the pan and set aside.

Heat the remaining butter in the same pan. Put in the ginger and garlic and cook for 1 minute, stirring constantly. Add the carrots and cook until tender. When the carrots begin to stick to the pan, pour in 1 tablespoon of the sherry and season lightly with salt.

When the carrots are tender, return the cashew nuts to the pan and cook for 2–3 minutes. Pour in the remaining sherry and stir well, scraping all the brown crust from the pan into the juices. Take the pan off the heat.

Sprinkle half the cheese over the pastry in the flan tin. Spread the carrot mixture over it, then sprinkle on the rest of the cheese.

Beat the eggs in a bowl together with the milk, nutmeg and a good seasoning of salt. Pour the mixture over the cheese and carrots. Bake in a pre-heated oven at 350° F/180° C/gas mark 4 for about 45 minutes, or until the filling is set and lightly browned and the pastry is crisp and well cooked.

Serve the quiche hot with a light salad.

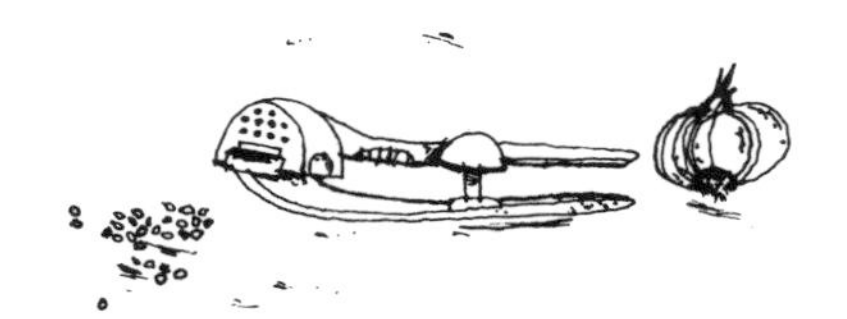

Blue Cheese Salad

serves 4

salad greens
4 oz/110 g button mushrooms, wiped, trimmed and thinly sliced
4 tablespoons cooked chick peas
½ small cucumber, sliced
2 tomatoes, sliced
1 medium courgette (zucchini), grated

for the dressing:
15 fl oz/450 ml/1¾ cups sour cream
4 oz/110 g/1 cup crumbled blue cheese, such as Gorgonzola
pinch salt
½ teaspoon black pepper
juice of ½ lemon
3 spring onions or scallions, finely chopped, or 1½ tablespoons finely chopped fresh chives

Blue cheese dressing always makes something special of a salad, and this American version – with lemon and spring onion for extra bite – is especially good. For the best flavour, make the dressing the day before you are going to eat it, and if that is impossible let it stand for at least an hour after you make it so that the flavours can blend. The dressing also makes a good dip for strips of raw vegetables.

Put the chosen salad greens into 4 individual bowls and scatter the raw mushrooms on top. Sprinkle on the chick peas and arrange the cucumber and tomato on top.

Put all the ingredients for the dressing into a large bowl and mix well together until smooth. Spoon it over the salads and top with the courgette.

You can vary the salad to include any chopped raw vegetables you like. In winter when cucumbers, tomatoes and courgettes are expensive, leave them out and instead pile grated beetroot (beet), carrot and alfalfa sprouts on top of the dressing; use a little raw onion instead of the spring onions.

Cheese Fritters

These cheese fritters, made with semolina, are reminiscent of Italian semolina *gnocchi*, with a delicate and interesting taste.

serves 4

4 oz/110 g/½ cup semolina
1 pint/575 ml/2½ cups milk
1 small onion, studded with 1–2 cloves
1 bay leaf
4 oz/110 g Parmesan and/or Emmental cheese, grated
½ teaspoon Dijon mustard
salt and freshly ground pepper
1 egg beaten with 1 tablespoon cold water, for coating
dried breadcrumbs for coating
1 lemon, sliced
oil for frying

Mix the semolina to a smooth paste with a little of the milk and set aside. Bring the remaining milk to the boil in a saucepan with the onion and bay leaf. Remove from the heat, cover and leave to infuse for 10 minutes, then lift out the onion and bay leaf. Reheat the milk to boiling and pour over the semolina, stirring all the time. Return to the pan and stir over a gentle heat until thickened. Simmer for 10 minutes, stirring occasionally, then remove from the heat and stir in the cheese, mustard and a good seasoning of salt and pepper.

Spread the mixture ½ in/1.25 cm deep on a lightly oiled plate and leave until cold and firm. Cut into 8–12 pieces and dip each in the egg mixture, and then into the breadcrumbs. Shallow-fry in hot oil and drain well on paper towels.

Serve hot with the slices of lemon, fresh tomato sauce and a green vegetable or salad.

Vegetable Stir-fry

Using the Oriental technique of stir-frying, you can make delicious and nutritious meals very quickly. This American recipe uses broccoli, cauliflower, cabbage and carrots, but you can substitute whatever vegetables you like. Serve the stir-fry as a side dish with a quiche perhaps, or make it into a meal by serving it with a cooked grain such as brown rice, buckwheat or sorghum (millet).

serves 4

about 1 lb/450 g broccoli, cut into 1 in/2.5 cm lengths
about 8 oz/225 g cauliflower, divided into 1 in/2.5 cm pieces
2 tablespoons oil (corn, safflower, sesame or peanut)
2 medium onions, sliced and then halved to make crescents
2 green peppers, deseeded and cut into thin strips
2 medium carrots, cut into thin rounds
2 sticks celery, sliced diagonally
about ½ in/1.25 cm piece fresh ginger, finely chopped
3 cloves garlic, peeled and finely chopped
2 tablespoons soy sauce
2 tablespoons sherry
about 4 oz/110 g/1 cup coarsely chopped green cabbage
4 oz/110 g/1 cup mung bean sprouts (optional)
juice of ½ lemon
salt and pepper

Put the broccoli and cauliflower into a wide pan, pour on boiling water to cover, then boil for 5 minutes. Drain off the water (keep it to use in a soup) and set aside the vegetables.

Heat a large frying pan or *wok* and pour in the oil. When it is very hot, put in the onions, peppers and carrots. Stir constantly while you fry the vegetables over a high heat for 3 minutes. Add the celery, ginger, garlic, soy sauce and sherry. Stir-fry for 2 more minutes. Add the broccoli and cauliflower and fry to heat through, then add the cabbage and fry for 2 minutes. Finally, put in the mung bean sprouts, if using, and lemon juice and stir-fry for 2 minutes.

Taste and add salt and pepper as necessary. Serve immediately while crisp and hot.

For variety add any vegetables you like, remembering to boil hard ones such as potatoes, green beans or Brussels sprouts for 5 minutes, and stir-frying first those that need the longest cooking. You can add *tofu*† (soya bean curd) to the stir-fry, and toasted almonds and sesame seeds. Try adding cooked grain or pasta as well.

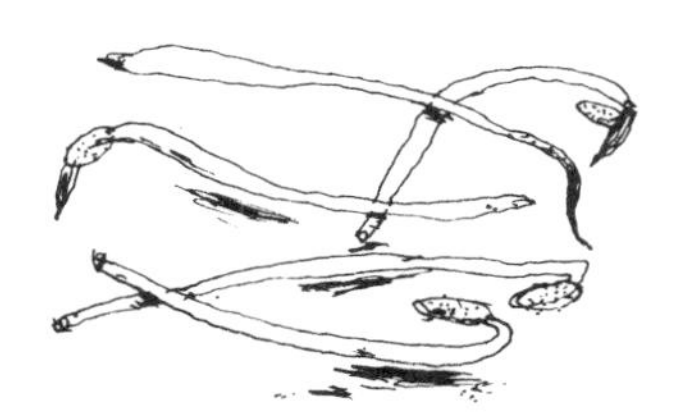

August Garden Stir-fry

A mixture of vegetables stir-fried with tomatoes makes a delicious dish and is easy to cook because the juice from the tomatoes prevents the vegetables from sticking. This recipe from America will give you a crisp lunch or dinner dish to serve with brown rice or wholewheat pasta.

serves 4

knob of butter for frying
½–1 lb/225–450 g mushrooms, wiped, trimmed and thickly sliced
sea salt and freshly ground black pepper
juice of ½ lemon
1 tablespoon olive oil
2 medium onions, cut in slices and halved to make crescents
2 green peppers, deseeded and cut into thin strips
3 cloves garlic, peeled and crushed
2 teaspoons fresh rosemary, or 1 teaspoon dried rosemary
1 tablespoon chopped fresh basil, or 1 teaspoon dried basil
1 teaspoon fresh marjoram, or ½ teaspoon dried marjoram or oregano
2 tablespoons red wine
3 medium courgettes (zucchini) cut in thin slices
3 medium tomatoes, cut into wedges

Heat the butter in a large frying pan or a *wok* until it sizzles. Put in the mushrooms and fry over a fierce heat, sprinkling with salt, pepper and lemon juice. When the mushrooms are browned and all the liquid has dried up, remove them and reserve.

Heat the oil in the same pan. Put in the onion, peppers and garlic and fry over a high heat, stirring constantly, for 5 minutes. Add the rosemary, basil and marjoram to the pan and season with salt and pepper. Stir in the wine, then put in the courgettes and tomatoes. Cover the pan and cook over a medium heat for about 10 minutes, until the tomatoes are juicy and the courgettes tender. Stir from time to time during the cooking to prevent sticking.

Remove the lid and return the mushrooms to the pan. Cook uncovered until the mushrooms are heated through. Taste and add more seasoning if necessary. Serve very hot with rice or noodles.

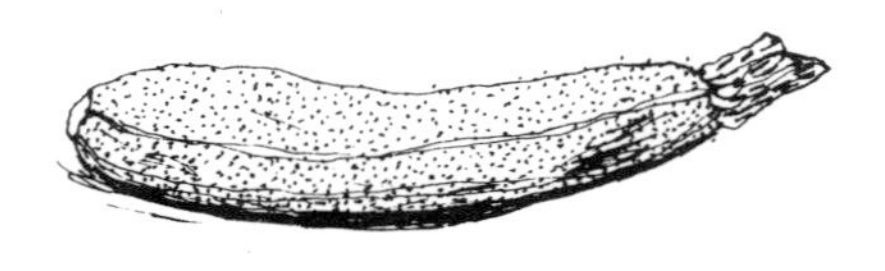

Curried Lentils and Vegetables

Curried lentils with their warm spicy flavour are excellent value nutritionally and very cheap and easy to make.

serves 4

2 tablespoons oil
2 medium onions, sliced into rings
1 large carrot, thinly sliced
2 cloves garlic, peeled and crushed
1 teaspoon ground ginger
1 teaspoon ground turmeric
2 teaspoons ground coriander
2 teaspoons ground cumin
6 oz/175 g/¾ cup split red lentils
1 lb/450 g potatoes, peeled and cut into 1 in/2.5 cm cubes
8 oz/225 g/1 cup canned tomatoes with their juice
1 pint/575 ml/2¼ cups vegetable stock or water
1 teaspoon salt
freshly ground black pepper
juice of ½ lemon
1 teaspoon coarsely chopped fresh coriander

Heat half the oil in a large saucepan and fry 1 onion and all the carrot gently for 10 minutes, until tender. Add the garlic, ginger, turmeric, half the cumin and half the coriander and stir-fry for 1–2 minutes. Add the lentils, potatoes, tomatoes, stock, salt and a generous amount of freshly ground pepper. Bring to the boil, cover, then reduce the heat and cook gently for about 30 minutes, until the lentils and vegetables are cooked and the liquid absorbed.

Heat the remaining oil in a small pan and fry the remaining onion without stirring until it is a deep cinnamon brown, then add the remaining cumin and coriander and fry for a further 2–3 minutes, stirring all the time. Scatter over the vegetables, together with the lemon juice and coriander. Add more salt and pepper if necessary. Serve very hot, with brown rice, mango chutney and poppadums.

Brown Rice

Brown rice still has its natural covering of bran. This not only retains the roughage and vitamins in the rice, but gives it a distinct flavour which is lost in white rice. Allow a longer cooking time as the brown grain is slower to absorb liquid.

serves 4

- 8 oz/225 g/1 cup long grain brown rice
- 1 pint/575 ml/2½ cups water
- 1 teaspoon salt

Wash the rice under cold water, drain well and put in a heavy-based saucepan with the water and salt. Bring to the boil, cover, then turn the heat right down and leave to cook very gently for 40 minutes.

Take the saucepan off the heat and leave, still covered, for a further 5–10 minutes for the rice to continue cooking in its own heat. Fluff up the rice gently with a fork.

Serve hot with a vegetable dish such as curried lentils and vegetables†, chilli† or August garden stir-fry†.

Pasta with Garlic and Fresh Herbs

You really need fresh herbs for this dish. In the summer use a mixture of fresh basil, dill, parsley and coriander, which gives a wonderful flavour. When fewer fresh herbs are available in the winter, use just parsley and a little raw onion; it is better not to make it with dried herbs because the flavour is nowhere near as good.

serves 4

- 1 lb/450 g wholewheat pasta (spaghetti, noodles or shells)
- 3 tablespoons olive oil
- 6 cloves garlic, peeled and cut in thin slices
- 2 knobs butter
- 6 oz/175 g/1½ cups mixed fresh herbs, finely chopped
- 1½ teaspoons sea salt
- freshly ground black pepper
- about 10 fl oz/300 ml/1¼ cups milk

Cook the pasta in plenty of boiling, lightly salted water until almost tender – they should be just firm in the middle. Drain well. Heat the oil in a frying pan and fry the garlic until lightly browned.

Return the pan of pasta to the heat and add the garlic and its oil. Using 2 forks toss the pasta to mix in the garlic; then add the butter and toss it in. Add the herbs, salt and pepper to taste and toss again.

Now add the milk slowly, cooking and tossing the pasta as you do so. At first the milk will be absorbed; you will know that enough of the milk has been added once it forms a little sauce round the pasta.

Taste and add more seasoning if necessary, and serve at once. A green salad or August garden stir-fry† makes a good accompaniment.

Chilli

serves 4

- 8 oz/225 g/1 cup dried pinto or kidney beans (or other dried beans) soaked overnight
- 2 bay leaves
- 1½ pints/850 ml/3¾ cups water
- 2 tablespoons corn oil
- 2 medium onions, chopped
- 4 cloves garlic, peeled and crushed
- 2 green peppers, deseeded and chopped
- 2 sticks celery, trimmed and chopped
- knob of butter
- 2 tablespoons ground cumin
- 1 tablespoon ground coriander
- pinch cayenne pepper
- ½ teaspoon dried oregano
- 1 teaspoon chopped fresh basil, or ½ teaspoon dried basil
- 1 teaspoon chopped fresh dill, or ½ teaspoon dried dill
- ½ teaspoon freshly ground black pepper
- 1 pint/575 ml/2½ cups tomatoes, skinned and crushed
- 2 teaspoons sea salt
- 2 teaspoons red wine vinegar, or 1 teaspoon malt vinegar

Chilli, a thick, spicy stew made from pinto or kidney beans, is an American speciality. It is inspired by Mexican cooking, but quite different from a Mexican chilli. This version is well seasoned and full of fresh vegetables.

Put the beans in a pan with the bay leaves and water, bring to the boil, then cover and simmer for 1¾–2 hours, until they are tender.

Heat the oil in a large, heavy-based saucepan. Sauté the onions and garlic for about 2 minutes. Add the peppers and celery and cook for about 5 minutes, until they are softening but still crisp. Add the butter to the pan, and when it has melted put in the cumin, coriander, cayenne pepper, oregano, basil, dill and black pepper. Fry for 2–3 minutes to enhance the flavour of the spices and herbs, but stir frequently to prevent burning.

Add the tomatoes to the pan and sprinkle on the salt. Simmer for 10 minutes. Add the beans and their cooking liquid and stir in the vinegar. Simmer for 30 minutes more to blend the flavours. Serve the chilli very hot with freshly baked cornbread†.

For variety, you can put some cooked brown rice† in individual ovenproof bowls, ladle on a good helping of chilli, then top with grated cheese and toasted cashew nuts and brown in the oven or under the grill (broiler).

Carob Brownies

makes 16 small squares

- 2 oz/50 g/¼ cup butter
- 3 oz/75 g/⅓ cup carob powder, sieved to remove any lumps
- 5 fl oz/150 ml/⅔ cup honey
- 1 egg
- ½ teaspoon pure vanilla extract
- ½ teaspoon salt
- 4 fl oz/110 ml/½ cup milk
- 2 teaspoons fresh lemon juice
- 3 oz/75 g/¼ cup shelled walnuts, chopped
- 3 oz/75 g/¾ cup wholewheat pastry flour or fine-ground wholewheat flour
- 1 teaspoon baking powder

The sweet, rich, chocolate flavour of carob powder makes it a popular ingredient in many wholefood desserts. The highly nutritious powder is made by grinding the roasted beans of the carob tree. In this recipe, carob powder is used in that American favourite, brownies – a soft, fudgy cake cut into small squares.

Melt the butter in a saucepan, then take it off the heat and mix in the carob powder thoroughly. Stir in the honey, then the egg, then the vanilla and the salt. Mix the milk and lemon juice together and stir them into the carob mixture to blend thoroughly. Add the nuts.

Mix together the flour and baking powder, add to the pan and blend in very thoroughly.

Pour the mixture into a lightly oiled cake tin 8 in/20 cm square and bake in a pre-heated oven at 350° F/180° C/gas mark 4 for about 30 minutes. The brownies are ready when a knife inserted in the centre comes out clean. Leave to cool before cutting.

Amy's Orange Buttercream Torte

In this American *torte* for a special occasion, the layers of light, delicate cake are alternated with layers of rich orange filling. Serve it at a birthday or dinner party, perhaps sprinkled with liqueur for extra flavour.

serves 4

5 oz/150 g/⅔ cup butter
5 fl oz/150 ml/⅔ cup honey
4 egg yolks
grated rind of 1 orange
3 fl oz/90 ml/⅓ cup milk
½ teaspoon pure vanilla or almond extract
8 oz/225 g/2 cups fine-ground wholewheat flour
1½ teaspoons baking powder
4 egg whites, beaten until stiff
cream whipped with a little vanilla and honey, for coating
chopped walnuts, for coating

for the filling:
2 oz/50 g/¼ cup butter
8 oz/225 g/¾ cup cream cheese
2 fl oz/50 ml/¼ cup honey
juice and grated rind of 1 orange
½ teaspoon pure vanilla or almond extract
2 teaspoons cornflour (corn starch) or arrowroot

Prepare the filling first. Put the cornflour in a bowl and mix it to a thin paste with some of the orange juice. Heat the rest of the orange juice with the honey and add it to the cornflour paste, stirring all the time. Heat this mixture until it thickens, then set aside.

Melt the butter in the top of a double-boiler over a low heat. Keep the pan on the heat while you beat in the cream cheese and vanilla with a fork. Pour this on to the orange and honey sauce and beat well. Chill in the refrigerator for 4 hours before using.

To make the cake, cream the butter in a mixing bowl with a wooden spoon until it is light and smooth. Add the honey and beat until creamy. Add the egg yolks one by one, beating each in well before adding the next. Stir in the orange rind.

Mix the milk and vanilla together. Mix 2 oz/50 g/½ cup of the flour with the baking powder and set aside. Add the remaining flour, a tablespoon at a time, to the creamed mixture, alternating with tablespoons of the milk. Beat well after each addition and continue until both are used up, then beat in the combined flour and baking powder. Fold in the egg whites gently but thoroughly.

Pour the mixture into a deep well-buttered 6–7½ in/15–19 cm cake tin and bake in a pre-heated oven at 350° F/180° C/gas mark 4 for 30–40 minutes. The cake is ready when a knife inserted in the middle comes out clean.

Leave the cake to cool in the tin for 10 minutes, then turn it out on to a wire rack and leave until completely cold.

Cut across the cake to make 3 layers. (For extra flavour you can sprinkle the layers with a little Cointreau or Kirsch before sandwiching them together.) Sandwich the layers together with the filling. Spread the whipped cream over the top and sides of the cake and sprinkle the walnuts lightly on to the cream.

Carrot Cake

This very moist, spicy cake is a favourite in the wholefood restaurants and bakeries of America. It is an easy cake to mix, with no creaming or rubbing. Be sure to bake it in a deep tin because it rises considerably during baking.

serves 4

10 fl oz/300 ml/1¼ cups honey
4 oz/110 g/½ cup finely grated carrot
4 oz/110 g/¾ cup raisins
3 oz/75 g/⅓ cup chopped dates
1 teaspoon ground cinnamon
1 teaspoon grated nutmeg
½ teaspoon ground cloves
4 oz/110 g/½ cup butter
8 fl oz/225 ml/1 cup water
8 oz/225 g/2 cups wholewheat pastry flour, or fine-ground wholewheat flour
pinch salt
2 teaspoons bicarbonate of soda
4 oz/110 g/½ cup shelled walnuts, chopped

Mix the honey, carrot, raisins, dates, cinnamon, nutmeg, cloves, butter and water together in a pan over a gentle heat, then bring to the boil and boil for 5 minutes. Remove the pan from the heat and leave the mixture to cool for about 30 minutes, or until lukewarm.

Stir the flour and salt together in a large mixing bowl, then mix in the bicarbonate of soda after first rubbing it in your palm to rid it of any lumps. Add the walnuts to these dry ingredients, then make a well in the middle and pour in the carrot mixture. Mix until they are thoroughly blended.

Pour into a well-buttered and lightly floured cake tin 9 in/23 cm square, or a round cake tin 10 in/25.5 cm across. Bake in a pre-heated oven at 350° F/180° C/gas mark 4 for 55–65 minutes. The cake is ready when it feels firm at the centre if you press it lightly and when a skewer inserted in the centre comes out clean.

Leave the cake to cool in the tin for 10 minutes before turning it out on to a cake rack. It is at its best if eaten while still warm. If you like you can top each serving with a little thick cream whipped with honey and vanilla for flavour.

Sunday Brunch Muffins

In the United States, brunch is a special Sunday treat – a leisurely late breakfast large enough to make any lunch unnecessary. There is time to read the newspapers, linger over cups of coffee and enjoy food that takes a little too long to prepare on working mornings. These hot, spicy muffins are a perfect brunch dish, but they would be equally good in the afternoon with tea.

Combine the flour, baking powder, salt, cinnamon, ginger, nutmeg and allspice in a large mixing bowl. Mix in the raisins, nuts and orange rind.

In a separate bowl, beat the eggs, honey, milk, vanilla extract and butter. Make a well in the centre of the flour mixture and pour in the egg mixture. Stir together gently until blended, but do not mix too long or the muffins will have too dense a texture.

Leave the batter to rest for 5 minutes for the baking powder to start working. Meanwhile, lightly oil the cups in a muffin tray (or bun tray). Spoon in the batter until each cup is three-quarters full.

Bake in a pre-heated oven at 350° F/180° C/gas mark 4 for 25–30 minutes, until lightly browned. Leave to cool in the tray for 3–5 minutes, then lift out. Serve hot with butter and jam or honey, or eat with a fruit salad and yoghurt.

You can vary the muffins by adding 1 chopped apple or 1 chopped banana to the batter.

makes 12–18 muffins

8 oz/225 g/2 cups wholewheat pastry flour or fine-ground wholewheat flour
1 tablespoon baking powder
pinch salt
2 teaspoons ground cinnamon
1 teaspoon ground ginger
½ teaspoon grated nutmeg
½ teaspoon ground allspice
4 oz/110 g/¾ cup raisins, or chopped dates or figs
4 oz/110 g/½ cup shelled walnuts or almonds, coarsely chopped
grated rind of 2 oranges
2 eggs
5 fl oz/150 ml/⅔ cup honey
10 fl oz/300 ml/1¼ cups milk
1 teaspoon pure vanilla or almond extract
4 oz/110 g/½ cup butter, melted

Two-crust Pumpkin Pie

One of the traditional American dishes for Thanksgiving in November is pumpkin pie. In this variation a two-crust wholewheat pastry is used which gives a wonderfully crunchy texture. Serve the pie warm from the oven with vanilla ice-cream.

Roll out the pastry to make a lining and a lid for a 9 in/23 cm pie-dish. Butter the dish lightly and fit in the pastry lining.

Mix the pumpkin with the honey, cinnamon and flour and fill the pie-dish with it. Dot with butter, then cover with the pastry lid. Press the edges together firmly to seal and flute them for decoration. Make a slit in the lid for the steam to escape.

Bake in a pre-heated oven at 350° F/180° C/gas mark 4 for about 1 hour, until the pumpkin is tender and the pastry crisp and browned.

You can use any hard-skinned variety of squash instead of pumpkin. You will need to mix only 3 tablespoons of flour with it instead of 5 since squashes are less watery than pumpkins.

serves 4

9 oz/250 g wholewheat pastry†
1½ lb/700 g/3 cups diced pumpkin flesh, cut into ¼ in/5 mm cubes
5 fl oz/150 ml/⅔ cup honey
1 teaspoon ground cinnamon
5 tablespoons wholewheat pastry flour or fine-ground wholewheat flour
a little butter

Date Slices

makes 20 slices

8 oz/225 g/1 cup dates
4 tablespoons water
4 oz/110 g/1 cup fine-ground wholewheat flour
4 oz/110 g/1½ cups rolled oats
pinch salt
4 oz/110 g/½ cup soft margarine
1–2 tablespoons Demerara or light brown sugar for sprinkling

These slices get their sweetness from the dates, while the sugar just adds a crisp top to bite into. They make a delicious cake to serve with tea or coffee, but you could also serve them hot as a dessert with a creamy sauce.

Chop the dates and put them in a saucepan with the water. Heat gently, stirring frequently, until they have softened to a thick purée. Beat well, remove from the heat and leave to cool a little.

Put the flour, oats and salt into a mixing bowl, then add the margarine. Using a fork, mix together to form a dough. Press half the mixture into a lightly oiled baking tin 7 in/18 cm square. Spread with the date purée, then cover with the remaining mixture. Sprinkle on the sugar and press down lightly with the back of a spoon.

Bake in a pre-heated oven at 350° F/180° C/gas mark 4 for 25–30 minutes. Mark into 20 pieces while still warm, then leave to cool in the tin. Cut and lift out when cold.

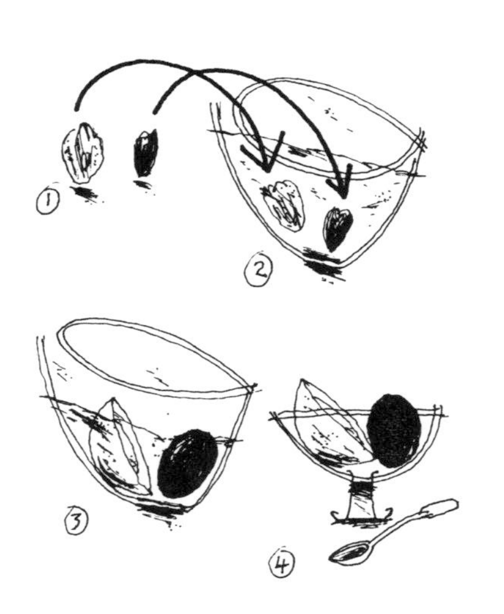

Dried Fruit Compôte with Ginger

serves 4

1 lb/450 g mixed dried apricots, peaches, pears, prunes and apple rings
2–3 thin strips lemon rind
1–2 pieces preserved stem ginger with 4 tablespoons of their syrup
lightly whipped cream (optional)

When fruits are dried, their flavour and sweetness is intensified. They make an excellent compôte with a rich, glossy syrup and pieces of fruit that are plump and tender but hold their shape. Ginger adds a hot note to the fruit in this recipe.

Just cover the fruit with cold water and leave to soak for several hours, or overnight if more convenient.

Put the fruit and water into a saucepan with the lemon rind. Bring to the boil, then reduce the heat, cover, and simmer gently for about 30 minutes. The fruit should be very tender and the liquid reduced to a syrup.

Remove the lemon rind. Chop the ginger finely and add it, and its syrup, to the fruit. Stir to blend.

Serve chilled, in a large dish or in individual glasses, and top with a little cream.

Wholewheat Fruit Cake

A standard fruit cake has an agreeably different texture and nutty flavour when you make it with wholewheat flour. Be sure to rinse the syrup off the cherries and pat them dry so that they will not sink to the bottom of the cake.

Cream the butter or margarine in a large mixing bowl with the sugar. When the mixture is light and fluffy, stir in the lemon rind. Add the egg a little at a time, beating well after each addition.

Mix the flour and baking powder together thoroughly and fold into the egg mixture, then gently fold in the mixed dried fruit and the cherries.

Oil a deep, round cake tin 8 in/20 cm in diameter and line it with a double layer of greaseproof paper or non-stick paper. Spoon the cake mixture into the tin and smooth the top. Arrange the almonds lightly on the cake.

Bake in a pre-heated oven at 325° F/170° C/gas mark 3 for 2–2½ hours, until a skewer inserted into the centre of the cake comes out clean. If the top is browned enough before the cake is cooked, lay a double sheet of paper, with a hole in the middle, lightly over the tin.

Leave the cake to cool for 10 minutes in the tin, then turn out and stand on a wire rack; remove the paper when the cake is cold.

serves 6–10

- 6 oz/175 g/¾ cup soft butter or margarine
- 6 oz/175 g/1 cup light brown sugar
- grated rind of 1 lemon
- 3 eggs, beaten
- 8 oz/225 g/2 cups wholewheat pastry flour or fine-ground wholewheat flour
- 1 teaspoon baking powder
- 1 lb/450 g/2 cups mixed dried fruit
- 2 oz/50 g/¼ cup glacé cherries, rinsed, dried and halved
- 1–2 oz/25–50 g/1–2 tablespoons blanched almonds for decoration

Apricot Fool

This dessert blends the concentrated flavour of dried apricots with the piquancy of yoghurt.

Cover the apricots with boiling water and leave to soak overnight. Next day put the apricots and water into a saucepan and simmer until tender. Purée the fruit in a blender or food mill, adding just enough of the cooking liquid to give a thick purée. Leave to cool.

Beat the eggs in a bowl with the sugar and stir in the milk. Strain into the top pan of a double-boiler and place it over the bottom pan of boiling water, making sure that the top pan does not touch the water. Put on a low heat and stir constantly with a wooden spoon until the mixture thickens enough to coat the spoon. Remove the top pan immediately and pour the custard into a wide, heatproof dish, stirring until it has cooled to lukewarm.

Mix together the apricot purée and custard and, when completely cold, fold in the yoghurt and half the orange rind. Taste and add sugar or honey as necessary.

Serve the fool chilled, in individual glasses, with the remaining orange rind sprinkled on top. For a change, you can replace the plain yoghurt with lightly whipped cream.

serves 4

- 8 oz/225 g/1 cup dried apricots
- 3 eggs
- 1 tablespoon sugar, light brown or white
- 10 fl oz/300 ml/1¼ cups milk
- 5 fl oz/150 ml/⅔ cup plain yoghurt
- grated rind of 1 orange
- sugar or honey to taste

THE FOOD OF THE SEVENTH DAY ADVENTISTS

Throughout history there have been times when people have refused to eat meat for religious or moral reasons. In Western countries the most forceful movements did not emerge until the nineteenth century. These cults are rather unfashionable now, but they created the climate in which today's vegetarianism could flourish; they also provide further proof of the health benefits of eating this kind of diet.

The most detailed evidence on Western vegetarianism comes from the studies made of an American religious group, the Seventh Day Adventists. In their early years in America they invented breakfast cereals, declaring them to be 'one of the Lord's own instruments'. The Kellogg's brothers were early Adventists, and the Kellogg's cornflakes on today's breakfast table have their origins in this movement.

At Loma Linda University, California, researchers compared the health records of the vegetarian and non-vegetarian members of the Seventh Day Adventists. Among the vegetarians the risk of heart disease among men under 65 was found to be three times less than for non-vegetarian Adventists. Although female Adventists did not show such marked differences, the female vegetarians were three times less likely to develop breast cancer. Both male and female vegetarians had three times less incidence of cancer of the colon than their meat-eating brothers. Strict Adventists do not smoke or drink alcohol, and this too showed in their better health record.

Seventh Day Adventists have developed their own style of vegetarian food based originally on Biblical inspiration but heavily influenced by industrial methods of preparing and marketing food. The recipes in the Middle Eastern section of this book are probably much closer to the diet of Palestine in Biblical times. However, the diet of the Seventh Day Adventists is interesting as an example of a healthy diet adapted to mass distribution of food and convenience living. Here are some typical Adventists dishes which are universally popular.

Raw Granola

- 1 lb/450 g/5 cups rolled oats or quick oatmeal
- 4 oz/110 g/½ cup sesame seeds, ground
- 4 oz/110 g/½ cup sunflower seeds, ground
- 4 oz/110 g/½ cup pumpkin seeds, ground
- 4 oz/110 g/½ cup desiccated (shredded) coconut
- 4 oz/110 g/½ cup date sugar or brown sugar
- 4 oz/110 g/½ cup chopped pecans, raisins or slivered almonds
- 1½ teaspoons sea salt
- 1½ teaspoons finely grated orange rind, or ½ teaspoon ground anise seed

This makes a very good breakfast cereal. Make it in large quantities and store it in glass jars or tightly closed plastic bags. Seventh Day Adventists, inventors of the first breakfast cereals, serve it just as it is – no cooking is needed – and provide a jug of nut milk (or ordinary milk) to pour on. Trickle a little thin honey over your bowl of granola if you like your cereal sweet.

Toast the oats for a few minutes in the oven to crisp and brown them lightly, or leave them untoasted if you prefer. Mix them with all the other ingredients, then store in glass jars or plastic bags. Serve with nut milk.

To add extra vitamins to the granola, you can include 4 oz/110 g/½ cup ground flax seed (linseed); this is also high in unsaturated fatty acids.

Nut Milk

Nut milk is an alternative to ordinary milk and can be used in any recipe as a substitute for milk. Try it instead of milk on all breakfast cereals, particularly granola†.

serves 4

1½ pints/850 ml/3¾ cups water
2 oz/50 g/1 level tablespoon shelled almonds
2 oz/50 g/1 tablespoon cashews or sesame seeds
pinch sea salt
2 tablespoons honey

To make nut milk, put all the ingredients together in an electric blender and reduce to a smooth purée. Strain this through a fine strainer to obtain the milk.

Fresh Nut Butter

Seventh Day Adventists enjoy the sweet flavour of nuts by making their own nut butter. Almonds, hazelnuts, walnuts, Brazil nuts or cashews are all equally good – and preferable to peanuts, as it has been suggested that a high intake of these causes atheroma. Spread the nut butter on wholemeal bread to give you a nourishing breakfast or a tea-time snack.

15 fl oz/450 ml/1¾ cups vegetable oil such as soya
4 oz/110 g/½ cup shelled fresh nuts
sea salt

Pour the oil in a blender, add the nuts and blend to a paste, stopping every few seconds to scrape down the sides of the container with a plastic or rubber spatula. Stop when the paste still has fragments of the nuts to give it a crunchy texture; or you can continue blending until it is completely smooth.

Season lightly with salt, stir well, then pack the butter in a screw-top glass jar for storing. Keep in the refrigerator.

Stir-Fried Sprouted Lentils

When seeds are sprouted, their starch reserves are mobilized to make sugar and this gives the sprout an attractively sweet flavour. As it sprouts, the seed also doubles its content of some vitamins and more than doubles others. You will enjoy sprouting your own lentils, or other vegetables. Their tender but crisp texture makes them good raw in salads and also stir-fried.

12 oz/350 g/1½ cups dried brown lentils, sprouted (see below)
3 tablespoons olive oil, or soya and olive oil mixed
4 sticks celery with their leaves, chopped
1 large onion, chopped
1 clove garlic, peeled and finely sliced
3–4 tablespoons soy sauce
½ teaspoon sea salt
olive oil for sprinkling

Put the lentils in a large glass jar and fill it with cold water. Cover the top with a piece of muslin (cheesecloth) held on with a rubber band. Leave the jar overnight with the water in, then next day pour off the water through the cloth. Put the jar in a cool dark place. Twice a day bring it out, fill it with fresh cold water to rinse the seeds, and then pour it off through the cloth. The sprouts are ready after a few days when they are ½–1 in/1.25–2.5 cm long.

To stir-fry the sprouts, heat the oil in a large, deep frying pan or *wok*. Put in the celery and onion and cook gently, stirring, until tender. Add the lentil sprouts, garlic and soy sauce and stir-fry briskly for 3–4 minutes. Sprinkle on the salt, turn down the heat, cover the pan and steam gently for 10–15 minutes until just tender.

Serve hot sprinkled with a little olive oil. Wholewheat bread and a fresh salad go well with the dish.

Summer Salad with Russian Dressing

serves 6

1 medium lettuce
8 oz/225 g spinach leaves
1 bunch watercress, washed and trimmed
4 oz/110 g courgettes (zucchini), thinly sliced
2 small cucumbers or 1 long cucumber, cut into small dice
1 small onion, thinly sliced
3 oz/75 g/1 cup raw button mushrooms, thinly sliced
3 inner sticks celery, thinly sliced

for the Russian dressing:
5 fl oz/150 ml/⅔ cup tomato juice
4 tablespoons oil
4 tablespoons fresh lemon juice
1 small spring onion or scallion, trimmed and roughly sliced
1 tablespoon honey
2 teaspoons sea salt
1 teaspoon paprika
1 clove garlic, peeled

Raw young spinach leaves and slivers of raw mushroom give an unusual flavour to a crisp salad. In this recipe, the slight bitterness is offset by the sweet tomato dressing. The salad goes well with vegetarian roasts and cutlets.

Wash and trim the lettuce and spinach leaves, dry carefully and put them in the refrigerator in a plastic box or closed plastic bag to crisp.

To prepare the dressing, put all the ingredients in a blender and blend until smooth.

To make the salad, tear the lettuce and spinach leaves into small pieces and put them in a bowl. Add the watercress, courgettes, cucumber, onion, mushrooms and celery. Pour on the dressing, toss well and serve while still crisp.

Instead of Russian dressing, use a vinaigrette dressing made with olive oil, lemon juice, garlic and sea salt.

Strawberry Pignolia

serves 4

8 oz/225 g/1½ cups fresh hulled strawberries
2 oz/50 g/¼ cup pine nuts
1 tablespoon raw honeycomb or thin honey
4 bananas

This is one of the best ways to enjoy summer's strawberries – and one that releases all their juices. The *pignoli* (pine nuts) add their special flavour as well as giving substance to the fruit purée.

Put the strawberries, pine nuts and honeycomb in a blender and reduce to a smooth, creamy purée. Chill in the refrigerator. Just before serving, pour over freshly sliced bananas.

This pignolia can be eaten with other fruits besides bananas, and also with cereals such as granola†.

OTHER VEGETARIAN RECIPES

There is an infinite variety of recipes for the vegetarian in the cuisines of countries represented in this book:

South-West Europe
Sopa de Ajo Garlic soup
Panzarella Cold tomato soup with bread
Pan Bagnato Egg salad with bread
Xató Curly endive salad in hot dressing
Ensalada de Tomate y Cebolla Tomato and onion salad
Insalata di Verdure Fresh vegetable salad from Sicily
Aubergines Farcies Stuffed aubergines (eggplants)
Caponata alla Siciliana Sweet-sour aubergines (eggplants)
Melanzane Sott'Olio Aubergines (eggplants) in oil
Melanzane al Funghetto Aubergines (eggplants) cooked like mushrooms
Orecchiette Little ears of pasta
Maccarones a la Catalana Catalonian macaroni
Torta di Vermicelli e Pomodori Vermicelli and tomato gratin
Petits Pois en Bouillabaisse Pea soup with eggs
Pipérade Scrambled eggs with sweet peppers
Tortilla Española Spanish omelette

The Balkans
Popara Hot milk breakfast dish
Patlıcan Salatas Aubergine (eggplant) purée
Biber Yoğurtlu Peppers with yoghurt
Patlican Tavasi Aubergine (eggplant) with yoghurt
Tarator Cucumber and yoghurt soup
Fasolado Bean soup
Kartofi sus Sirene Baked potatoes and cheese
Türlü Guveç Mixed vegetable casserole
Yumurta Çılbır Poached eggs with yoghurt
Tyropitta Layered pastry with cheese
Yoghurt
Mamaliga Felii Prajita Fried polenta slices
Trahana Shredded pasta
Salata Fasolakia Green bean salad
Lahana Salata Cabbage salad

Salata od Praziluka Leek salad
Zelena Salata s Kiselim Mlckom Lettuce salad with yoghurt
Savayú Káposzta Sauerkraut
Rasol Corba Sauerkraut juice soup

The Middle East
Ful Medames Brown beans dressed in oil and lemon
Fattet hummus Chick peas with yoghurt
Falafel Fried chick pea rissoles
Salata Mixed salad
Hummus bi Tahina Chick pea and sesame meal salad
Betingan Meshwi Aubergine (eggplant) purée
Laban Salateen Cucumber and yoghurt salad
Tabbouleh Cracked wheat salad
Salata Filfil bi Outa Tomato and pepper salad
Sabaneh bi Loubia Spinach with black-eyed beans (peas)
Mahshi Silq Stuffed chard leaves
Laban Yoghurt
Labna Fresh cheese
Gebna Meshwi Grilled (broiled) cheese
Eggah bi Korrat Leek omelette
Mujaddarah Lentils and rice
Zhug Yemeni relish
Roz Rice
Roz ou Ful Rice with broad (*fava*) beans
Roz bel Shaghria Rice with vermicelli
Burghul Pilaf Cracked wheat
Betingan Aubergines (eggplants)

Japan and South-East Asia
Tamagoyaki Japanese omelette
Nigiri Zushi Rice-balls
Nasu No Shigiyaki Aubergine (eggplant) with sesame
Horenso No Hitashi Spinach dressed with sesame seeds
Wakame To Kyuri No Sunomo Seaweed and cucumber salad
Dan Dan Mian Cold noodles with sesame sauce
Acar Campur Cooked mixed vegetable salad

Latin America and the Caribbean
Tortillas Flat corn breads
Tacos Fried corn tortillas
Chilaquiles Fried tortillas
Tamales Steamed pancakes with spicy fillings

Tortillas de Trigo Wheat tortillas
Arepa Tortilla pancake
Huevos Rancheros Ranch-style eggs
Guacamole Avocado sauce with tomatoes and coriander
Arroz a la Costa Ricana Costa Rican style rice
Arroz Guatemalteco Rice with vegetables
Arroz con Coco y Pasas Rice with coconut and raisins
Coo-coo Okra vegetable dish
Fried Ripe Plantains
Ensalada Mixta Mixed salad
La Salade de Leyritz Leyritz salad
Frijoles Red kidney beans
Frijoles de la Olla Beans in the pot
Frijoles Refritos Refried beans
Gallo Pinto Beans with rice and onions
Porotos Granados Cranberry beans with sweet-corn and pumpkin
Papas a la Huancaina Potatoes with cheese sauce

CHAPTER 7

BREADS OF T

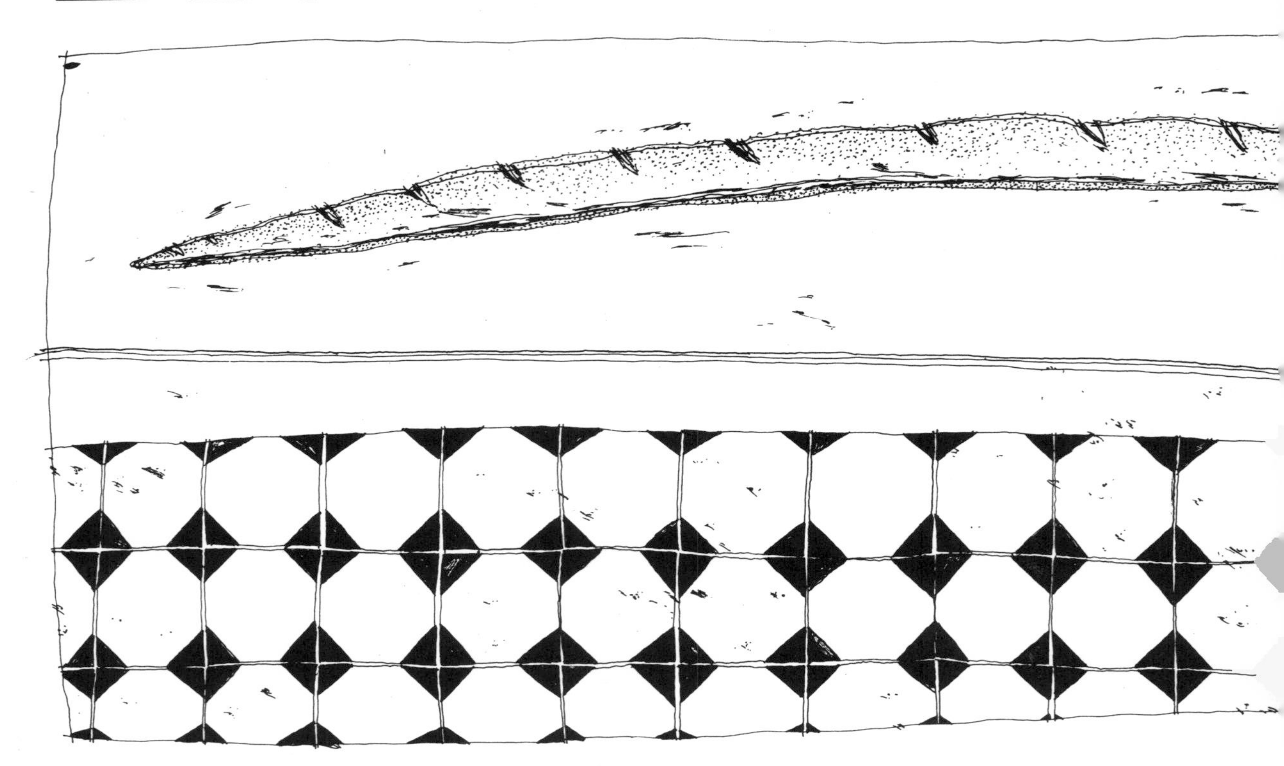

Bread has been the most important single item in the European and Middle Eastern diet for many thousands of years. It is not only the cheapest source of energy, it is also an excellent source of protein, vitamins and minerals. In some countries bread and other cereal products still provide more than half the energy and protein consumed every day.

In Britain and the United States grain provides between one-quarter and one-fifth of the energy required. This is much less than 50 years ago; the national decline in bread consumption has been associated with an increase in the consumption of meat, fat and sugar – with a corresponding increase in the number of people dying from heart disease. Too much meat and animal fat in the diet and too few cereals have been suggested as the cause.

In the countries we have selected for their healthy diet, much larger quantities of cereals are consumed. In wheat-eating countries, naturally, much is in the form of bread. The Spanish, for example, eat about 50 per cent more cereals than we do, either as bread or pasta. In the Middle East and Greece they eat twice the quantity of cereals we eat and in Yugoslavia, Rumania and Bulgaria three times as much. In the Far East and South America where rice or maize (corn) are staples they consume twice as much cereal as we do.

It is not really surprising that this large consumption of cereals is associated with good health, since man evolved from seed-eating apes and still has the teeth, jaws and digestive system associated with this diet. Our bodies are not adapted to the excessive quantities of fat and sugar which

HE WORLD

are now such a large part of Western diet. The calories provided by this excess of sugar and fat can be more sensibly obtained from bread, pasta, rice or other cereal products, with their bonus of protein, vitamins and mineral nutrients.

In most countries of the world, white bread is more popular than brown. Even in Greece and other Balkan countries where some coarser breads are eaten, most bread eaten is still white. In Italy and France the standard white flour used for bread-making is less refined than British and American white flour, and it contains more bran. In the Middle East much of the flour used to make bread still retains part of the wheat's bran and nutritious germ. In Spain, however, very little bread other than white is eaten and the flour used is as heavily refined as ours.

Wholewheat bread is now widely recommended by health experts because it contains more fibre, minerals and vitamins. They argue that the diet of pre-industrial man contained much more fibre and that he was much healthier. However, most of their evidence is derived from the study of people living in pre-industrial societies in Africa, where maize (corn) is generally the staple cereal rather than wheat. It is therefore interesting to note that the healthiest wheat-eating countries today are not large consumers of wholewheat bread – although their larger consumption of bread does provide them with more dietary fibre.

It may not matter much whether bread is wholewheat or not when comparatively large amounts of bread or other cereals are eaten. Bread substitutes for calories obtained from sugar and excess fats, and even white bread supplies substantial quantities of fibre, minerals, vitamins and protein. Eating larger quantities of bread and less sugar and fat is probably even more important than switching from white to wholewheat bread. Eating different types provides variety and adds interest.

As bread has become a smaller element of our diet, so has our knowledge of how to eat it and enjoy it. It is no longer customary in Anglo-Saxon cultures to use bread to mop up the juices on the plate; but these rich juices often contain valuable nutrients and should not be wasted. In India, nan and chapatis are a substitute for a knife and fork. They are used as a scoop for meat and vegetables and for taking up the juices. Pitta bread in the Balkans and the Middle East is used in the same way to mop up delicious spreads such as *hummus* and *tahina*; or it is opened up and stuffed with small pieces of cheese, tomato and lettuce, and sprinkled with olive oil.

In Latin American countries, bread is customarily used to mop up juices, and indeed the practice is related to the origin of soup, when the bread acted as a sop. In Spain and Italy today many soups contain bread; slices of yesterday's dry loaf are found in garlic soups, tomato soups and gazpacho, adding both flavour and texture.

Bread is the basis of the simplest of all meals: a slice dipped into a saucerful of olive oil. It is a favourite peasant snack in Greece, the equivalent of our bread and butter, and a healthier alternative. The bread might be eaten with a tomato salad dressed with oil and vinegar and a pinch of oregano. Good olive oil makes a pleasant substitute for butter and margarine in sandwiches – as the Spaniards and Southern Italians know. If you have good bread it is a very satisfying and easy habit to adopt.

There is a tradition of sourdough bread in almost all the countries represented in this book, and most particularly in the Balkans, the Middle East and South-West Europe. It is certainly the tastiest bread there is as well as being sustaining, and it generally keeps extremely well. In some parts of the world it is believed to prolong life and prevent tooth decay.

Leavening bread by the sourdough method is as ancient as the Babylonians, and is still the traditional method in countries where climate and the lack of communications hinder the use of baker's yeast. It is the interaction between the lactic acid bacteria (*Lactobacillus*) and yeasts present in most natural products which causes the spontaneous fermentation that sours and lightens the bread. It seems that a symbiotic relationship between *Lactobacillus* and yeast develops. When the sour mixture is used to make a dough, some of it is kept back each time as a leaven for the next batch of bread, and in this way a selection of organisms are present that are well adapted to living with each other, and it is those organisms that provide the correct sour but pleasant flavour.

Sourdough Starter

If you cannot obtain some sourdough from a bakery that uses it, then simply mix a cup of rye and whole-wheat flour with a cup and a half of water and leave it in a warm place, lightly covered, until it smells pleasantly sour (about 4 days). It must then be used with yeast as it will not provide enough leavening on its own. Alternatively, try the recipe used by Sharon Cadwaller, daughter of one of the best sour-bread bakers outside the Klondike.

- ½ oz/15 g fresh yeast or 1 tablespoon dried yeast
- 1 teaspoon brown sugar
- scant pint/575 ml/2½ cups warm potato water (unsalted water in which potatoes have been boiled)
- scant pint/575 ml/2½ cups water
- 12 oz/350 g/3 cups plain flour

Combine the yeast, brown sugar and potato water and place in a ceramic or glass dish. Cover lightly with muslin (cheese cloth) and allow to stand at room temperature, out of draughts, for 48 hours. You may have to stir it occasionally.

After 48 hours add to this mixture the water and the flour. Mix well. Cover lightly and let it sit for 8 hours. After this period you will have your basic starter. Refrigerate or use part of it in the following recipe.

Always keep your sourdough starter, and the ingredients for recipes you are making, in ceramic or glass containers, as metal can ruin the starter, and always refrigerate it. (Freeze it if you do not intend to use it for some months.) A starter sometimes darkens if it is not used regularly, but it is all right except when it turns black or green. It should always have a sour, crushed-apple smell.

Multi-grain Sourdough Bread

- scant ¾ pint/450 ml/1¾ cups sourdough starter
- 15 oz/420 g/3¾ cups unbleached flour
- 1 pint/575 ml/2½ cups lukewarm water

Put the starter and the flour in a mixing bowl and mix with the water. Cover the mixture and let it sit at room temperature overnight. In the morning remove nearly ¾ pint/450 ml/1¾ cups of the starter and return it to the starter jar in the refrigerator. The remainder will be used in the bread, with the following ingredients.

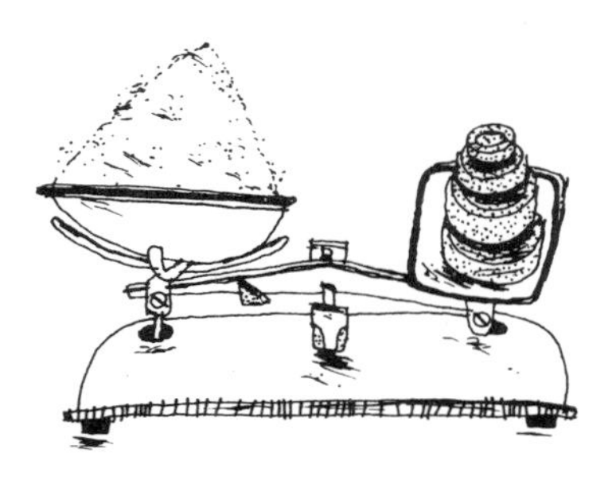

makes 2 small loaves

1¼ pints/725 ml/3⅛ cups milk
2 oz/50 g/¼ cup margarine or butter
7 fl oz/200 ml/⅞ cup honey
2 oz/50 g/4 tablespoons raw wheat germ
1 teaspoon bicarbonate of soda
1 tablespoon dried yeast
1 lb 14 oz/850 g/7½ cups mixed flours (any combination of wholewheat, corn, barley, soy, oat, rye or rice that includes wholewheat)
2 teaspoons salt
unbleached flour

Heat the milk until it is nearly boiling and mix with the margarine or butter and honey. Let it cool until it is lukewarm and then mix with the sourdough starter. Mix together the wheat germ, soda and yeast and add this to the starter mixture. Mix the other flours with the salt and stir into the starter mixture, adding enough unbleached flour to make a stiff dough.

Turn the dough out on to a floured board and knead until the dough is satiny, then fold into a ball and place in a large greased bowl. Cover with a damp cloth and allow to rise until it doubles in bulk. Punch down and divide into two loaves. Place in greased bread pans and allow to rise again. When the dough is again double in bulk put the pans in a pre-heated oven at 350° F/180° C/gas mark 4 for 10 minutes, then reduce heat to 325° F/170° C/gas mark 3 and bake until the loaves are a golden brown – about 40–45 minutes. Remove from the tins at once.

Cool the loaves on racks, and then cover and store or freeze.

Wholewheat Bread

People on a vegetable and grain diet become very adventurous with their cooking and make breads from all sorts of different grains and seeds; but, most important, they know that by using wholewheat flour, and preferably stone-ground wholewheat flour that has had the minimum of processing, they will be getting all the vitamins, minerals, bran and proteins that are found in wheat. This recipe is a plain wholewheat loaf, invented by Doris Grant.

makes 1 2 lb loaf or 2 1 lb loaves (1 900 g or 2 450 g loaves)

13 fl oz/375 ml/1½ cups hand-hot water
4 teaspoons Barbados or dark brown sugar
2 teaspoons dried yeast
1 lb/450 g/4 cups wholewheat flour
2 teaspoons salt

Grease the bread tin or tins. Put a third of the water into a jug and stir in ½ teaspoon of the sugar and the yeast. Leave on one side for 10 minutes to froth up. Put the flour into a large bowl and mix in the remaining sugar and the salt. Add the frothy yeast and the remaining water to the flour and mix well to a dough. It will be rather softer than ordinary bread dough. Squeeze and knead the dough with your hands for a few minutes – it will become smoother and less sticky – and then put the dough into the tin or tins. Cover with a cloth or place the tins in a large plastic bag and leave for 45–60 minutes, until the loaves have doubled in size. When the dough is nearly ready, pre-heat the oven to 400° F/200° C/gas mark 6. Bake a large loaf for 35–40 minutes, or two small ones for 25–30 minutes. Remove the loaves from the tins and cool on a wire rack.

This one-rise loaf, known as the 'Grant loaf', has a moist texture and good flavour. It will not keep for more than about 2 days, but it freezes well. It is essential to use 100 per cent wholewheat flour for a satisfactory result.

Bran-plus Wholewheat Loaf

This recipe was devised by Helen Cleave, wife of T. L. Cleave, whose book, *The Saccharine Disease*, pioneered the fibre story, pointing out the connection between the higher consumption of sugar and modern Western diseases. Cleave reasoned that it was important not only to return the bran lost in refining, but to add extra bran to compensate for what has been lost in jams and spreads, where sugar, too, has been refined.

The loaf has a dense texture; simply follow the Grant loaf recipe for wholewheat bread, adding a tablespoon of bran to each pound (450 g) of flour. You can mix the yeast with two teaspoons of sugar if you want to make the yeast work faster. The bran loaf should be kneaded rather longer than the Grant loaf and given more time to rise.

Poppy Seed Wholewheat Bread

Whole grain breads are the staple food of American vegetarians, many of whom make some of their bread at home even though there are many good wholefood bakeries in the United States. This recipe makes a bread that is particularly good toasted. Be sure to use hard wheat bread flour, known in the United States as hard red spring wheat flour. Hard wheat flour makes well-risen bread, while soft wheat flour is for pastry and cakes.

makes 2 loaves 9 × 5 in/ 23 × 13 cm

1 oz/25 g fresh yeast, or 1 tablespoon dried yeast
5 fl oz/150 ml/⅔ cup warm water
1 pint/575 ml/2½ cups hot water (or water from cooking potatoes)
4 tablespoons honey
2 teaspoons sea salt
about 2 lb/900 g/7¾ cups wholewheat bread flour
4 oz/110 g/½ cup poppy seeds
3 tablespoons corn oil, or sesame or safflower oil

Stir the yeast into the warm water in a small bowl. Leave to stand for about 10 minutes until it froths up.

Meanwhile combine the hot water, honey and salt in a large mixing bowl. Add 1 lb/450 g/4 cups of the flour and stir vigorously for about 2 minutes. Stir in the yeast until thoroughly blended, then put the dough in a warm place to rise for 1 hour.

Stir the dough again to develop the gluten, then mix in the poppy seeds. Work in the oil, then gradually add enough of the remaining flour to make a stiff dough. You may not need all the flour, or you may need a little extra.

Turn out the dough on to a lightly floured working surface and knead steadily for 10 minutes, or until the dough springs back when you press it in with your thumb.

Put the dough back in the cleaned and lightly oiled bowl and put to rise again for 1 hour, then punch it down. If you have time, put it to rise for a further hour and punch down again. The extra rising gives the yeast more time to work and makes a very springy dough.

Divide the dough in half and shape each half to fit a lightly oiled 2 lb/1 kg loaf tin. Put to rise in the tins for 30 minutes. Bake in a pre-heated oven at 350° F/180° C/gas mark 4 for 50–60 minutes. The loaves are ready when they are firm and sound hollow if tapped underneath.

You can vary the bread by shaping all the dough into one large round loaf and putting it on a lightly oiled baking tray to bake; it will take just a few minutes longer to cook. You can vary the flavour by using sunflower seeds or toasted sesame seeds in place of the poppy seeds.

Country Bread from the Abruzzi

This is a good basic white bread recipe from the Abruzzi district in Italy, and makes one large loaf.

2¼ lb/1 kg/8¼ cups unbleached strong white flour (or all-purpose flour)
1 oz/25 g fresh yeast or 2 tablespoons dried yeast
1½ pints/850 ml/3¾ cups warm water
2 tablespoons salt

Tip the flour into the middle of your working top or table. Mix the yeast with a little of the water and mix the salt into the remaining water. Make a well in the middle of the flour and pour in the yeast and the water a little at a time, mixing it in gradually with your fingers. When you have a manageable dough start kneading and continue to knead until the dough is springy – it may take 30 minutes. Leave the dough to rise in a warm place. Preheat the oven to 450° F/230° C/gas mark 8.

When the dough has doubled in size form it into a huge round loaf on a baking tray and allow to rise a second time until well puffed up and taut. Just before you put it in the oven on a baking shelf decorate with four light slashes in a diamond design. Bake for 10 minutes and then reduce the heat to 375° F/190° C/gas mark 5 and cook for a further 30 minutes. Turn the loaf round and turn the heat down to 300° F/150° C/gas mark 2 to complete baking – the loaf is done when it sounds hollow when you tap the bottom. It will take about 1½ hours, by which time it will have a good crust.

Italian Bread with Olive Oil, Rosemary and Garlic

This is a speciality of Castel di Lama in the Marches region of Italy, according to James Beard, who gives the recipe in his book *Beard on Bread*.

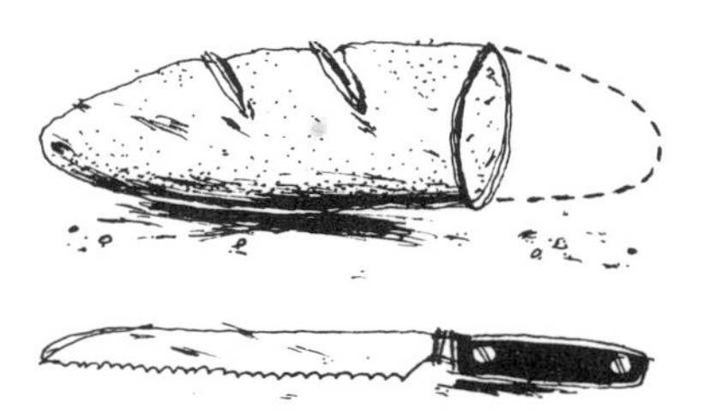

makes 1 small loaf

11–12 oz/300–350 g/3 cups unbleached white flour (or all-purpose flour)
½ teaspoon salt
½ oz/15 g fresh yeast or ½ tablespoon dried yeast
8 fl ozs/225 ml/1 cup warm water
3 sprigs fresh rosemary or 1 tablespoon dried (not ground)
2 cloves garlic, thinly sliced
3–4 tablespoons olive oil
coarse crystal salt

Mix the yeast and 4–5 tablespoons of the water together with 2–3 tablespoons of the flour. Leave in a warm place for about 30 minutes for the yeast to start working. Dissolve the salt in the remaining water. Put the flour in a bowl, and pour the yeast mixture into a well in the middle; add the remaining water and 1 tablespoon of olive oil. Mix to a dough, and then transfer to a floured board and knead well. When the dough is smooth and springy, form it into a ball, coat the outside with a little more oil, put it back into the cleaned bowl and cover with a sheet of plastic. Leave to rise until it has doubled in size (about 1–1½ hours).

When it is well risen, turn the dough on to a floured board and knead again, then put it back into the bowl and leave to rise a second time. When it has doubled in size again, put it back on the board, punch it down and form it into a round flat disc about ½ in/1.25 cm thick. Pre-heat the oven to 375° F/190° C/gas mark 5. Oil a large baking sheet and transfer the round of dough to it. Using a skewer or a nail, punch indentations all over the top of the bread and put a rosemary spike and a thin sliver of garlic into each indentation. Then pour olive oil over the top of the bread and smooth it over with your hand.

Sprinkle the top with coarse salt and leave to rise again for a few minutes; when it is taut and springy, bake for 15–20 minutes. Remove the slivers of garlic before serving the bread. Eat warm if possible. The loaf is also excellent without the garlic and the rosemary.

Pitta
Pitta Bread

Wheat bread is more than the staff of life in the Middle East; it is considered holy. Even if people find some lying in the street, they pick it up and kiss it. The most common bread is *shami*, bought fresh and warm, or home-made. People buy spice mixtures called *zahtar* in the street, in little cones of rolled-up newspaper, to dip their bread in. Those who cannot afford this dip it in salt. *Shami* is like the pitta bread sold in Britain and the USA, but coarser in texture from the wholewheat flour and made in rounds rather than ovals.

makes 8–10 pieces

about 10 fl oz/300 ml/ 1¼ cups cold water
½ oz/15 g/½ tablespoon fresh yeast, or ¼ oz/7 g/ ¼ tablespoon dried yeast
pinch of sugar
1 lb/450 g/4 cups unbleached strong white (unbleached all-purpose) flour or a mixture of ⅔ strong white flour and ⅓ wholewheat flour
½ teaspoon salt
oil

Warm a small glassful of the water and dissolve the yeast in it. Add the sugar and put in a warm place for about 10 minutes, until it becomes frothy.

Sift the white flour into a large bowl and mix in the salt, and the wholewheat flour if used. Work in the yeast mixture by hand, adding enough of the remaining water to make a firm, soft dough. Knead the dough vigorously in the bowl or on a floured board for about 15 minutes, until it is smooth and springy and no longer sticks to your fingers.

Sprinkle a little oil into the bowl and roll the ball of dough in it to grease it all over. This will prevent the surface from becoming dry and crusty. Cover with a dampened cloth and put in a warm, draught-free place for at least 2 hours, until nearly doubled in bulk.

Punch the dough down and knead again for a few minutes. Divide the dough into 8–10 pieces about the size of an egg. Flatten them on a lightly floured board with a floured rolling pin or the palm of your hand until about ¼ in/5 mm thick. Dust with flour and lay the rounds on a cloth sprinkled with flour. Put to rise again in a warm place.

Set the oven to heat to its maximum temperature, and while it is heating put in 2 large oiled baking sheets for 10 minutes to make them as hot as possible. When the bread has risen to double its size again, space out the rounds on the hot baking sheets, sprinkle them lightly with cold water and bake for 6 minutes. They should then be well puffed up but still white, and soft inside.

You can cook the pitta bread under a hot grill (broiler) if your oven does not get hot enough to make a good pouch. Lay the dough rounds in the oiled grill (broiler) pan and slide it on the lowest runner so that the bread does not come too near the grill (broiler) and burn when it puffs up. As soon as the rounds puff, turn them over and cook the other side for a minute or two.

Put the bread into a plastic bag while still warm; this will keep it warm and pliable until serving time. Pitta bread can quickly become dry and hard. To freshen it, moisten with a sprinkling of water and warm either in the oven, wrapped in foil, or under the grill.

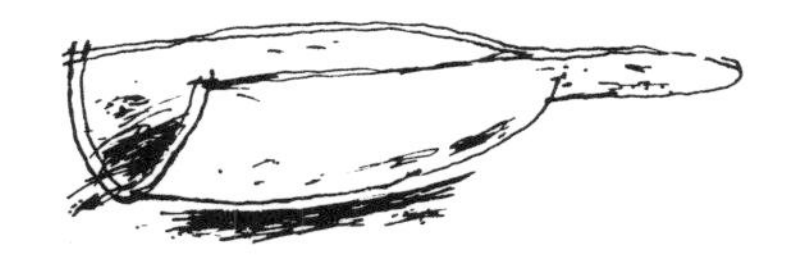

Tannour
Thin bread from the Middle East

This flat bread, slightly leavened with yeast, is delicious when eaten fresh. It makes a good alternative to pitta bread, and can be eaten with dips such as *hummus*†.

makes 4 pieces

- 5 fl oz/150 ml/⅔ cup warm water
- ¼ oz/7 g fresh yeast or 1 teaspoon dried yeast
- 2 tablespoons warm olive oil
- 1½ tablespoons salt
- 8–10 oz/225–275 g/2–2½ cups plain white flour

Put the warm water in a large bowl, dissolve the yeast in it and stir in the flour a little at a time, together with the olive oil and salt. Add enough flour to make a stiffish dough, knead it well on a floured board until it is smooth and springy, then coat the outside with oil and replace in the bowl, covered with a damp cloth until well risen, to double its original size. Remove the dough, knock it down, divide into four and form each ball of dough into a flat round disc by patting it out with four fingers and then stretching it until it measures 8–9 in/20–23 cm across.

Authentically, this bread should be cooked in an open-topped pit oven called a *tannour*. It can be cooked on a hot griddle. Cook first one side and, when the surface is covered with blisters, turn it quickly and cook the other side. The timing depends on the heat of the griddle but it should cook quickly and be a little blackened in places.

Pogača
Flat bread

This quick and easy bread recipe is enriched with eggs, milk and a little fat. The Yugoslavian recipe, common also in Bulgaria, demonstrates that a sweetening agent such as sugar or honey is not necessary when making dough with fresh yeast.

makes 1 loaf

12 oz/350 g/3 cups flour, either unbleached strong (or all-purpose) white or wholewheat, or a mixture of both
¾ oz/20 g/3 teaspoons fresh yeast
1 egg
1 teaspoon salt
2–3 tablespoons lukewarm melted lard, butter or oil
4 fl oz/125 ml/½ cup tepid milk or water
a little fat for brushing

Tip the flour into a large bowl, make a hollow in the middle and break the egg into it. Add the salt and fat. Cream the yeast to a thin paste with a little of the liquid and then pour it into the flour. Stir with a round-bladed table knife, adding the rest of the liquid gradually to form a fairly firm dough. You may need a little more liquid or a little less, because different flours absorb different amounts. Knead the dough vigorously for 5–10 minutes, until it is springy and no longer sticky, and then shape it into a ball.

Wash and dry the bowl and brush it round with oil. Put in the dough and roll it round until coated with oil, to prevent a crust from forming on the surface. Cover loosely and leave to rise for about 2 hours in a not too warm place; fresh yeast does not like too much heat. When the dough has doubled in size, knock out any bubbles, knead it lightly with a dusting of flour until it has an even texture again, then shape it into a flattened ball about the thickness of two fingers. Place on a greased baking sheet, or in a greased baking tin about 8 in/20 cm square. Brush over the top with fat and, if you like, prick the surface here and there with a fork. Leave to prove for 20–30 minutes, or until double in volume.

Bake the bread on a high shelf in a pre-heated oven at 375° F/190° C/gas mark 5 for 25–30 minutes.

Serve the bread warm. It is the perfect supplement to a modest supper of a meatless vegetable dish, or perhaps a large bowl of freshly made yoghurt. It also goes well with Feta cheese and a few spring onions and tomatoes.

Unleavened Bread

Bedouins and peasants in the Yemen, like those in other parts of the Arab world, still make bread as it was made in 1000 BC. They grind wheat, maize (corn) and other cereals in stone handmills like those found in Mesopotamian excavations. They pound the wheat in mortars first, winnowing off the husks. Then they put the cleaned grain in large hollowed-out stones and grind it into flour with smaller stones. They add water to the flour, knead it and flatten the dough by pulling it and patting it with their hands into very thin cakes. They dust it with flour and bake it on hot fire-blackened stones in the hearth, brushing off the ashes when it is ready. Although a leavening agent or 'starter' is sometimes used, such as a fermenting flour-and-water mixture which traps natural yeast from the air or a lump of dough from a previous batch, the bread usually consists only of flour and water.

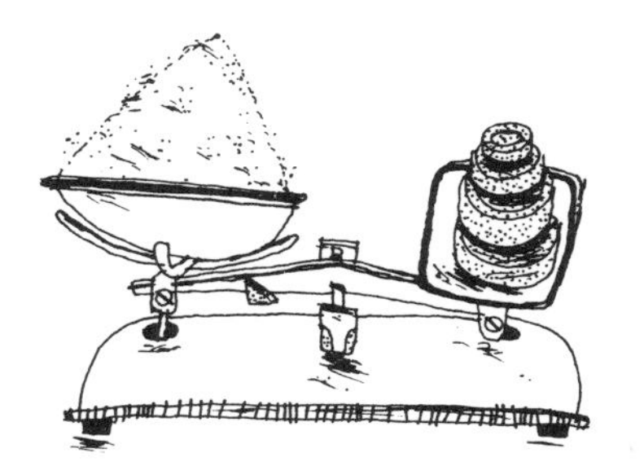

The best way of making this bread in a modern kitchen is under the grill (broiler). It is possible to make it over a flame on a griddle or metal sheet or in a frying pan, but under the grill (broiler) it puffs up perfectly. Make it with a mixture of wholewheat and strong white flour or with the fine maize (corn) flour available from Greek, Indian and Italian shops or a combination of maize (corn) and other flour. Using a bowl, for each 1 lb/450 g/4 cups flour, add just enough water, usually about 10 fl oz/300 ml/1¼ cups, to make it hold together in a firm dough. Knead vigorously for at least 8 minutes until it is elastic and resilient, and then leave it covered with a damp cloth for half an hour.

Take small lumps of dough (a little larger than a large egg), flatten with floured palms and pull out or roll out very thin. Turn on the grill (broiler) and put a tray underneath. When both are very hot, lay the thin cakes of dough on the tray. In 2–3 minutes the dough will puff up. When it begins to colour, turn it over and give the other side 2–3 minutes, until light brown spots appear.

Eat it hot with a soup or use it to dip in a stew, sauce or spicy relish, or brush it with melted butter and spread it with honey. A similar bread is fried in very little oil or clarified butter in a frying pan. Unleavened bread is rather bland to Western palates; you may prefer to add 2 tablespoons of oil and 1 teaspoon of salt to the water for extra flavour.

Cornbread

Maize (corn) is the native grain of America, where not surprisingly there are hundreds of recipes for cornbread. This one makes a light, quick bread, particularly good served hot from the oven with soup as a simple lunch, or with butter and honey for a snack.

makes 1 loaf 9 in/23 cm square

8 oz/225 g/2 cups yellow cornmeal
5 oz/150 g/1¼ cups fine-ground wholewheat flour
1 tablespoon baking powder
1½ teaspoons sea salt
2 eggs
5 tablespoons honey
1 tablespoon molasses (or black treacle)
12 fl oz /350 ml/1½ cups milk

Mix together the cornmeal, flour, baking powder and salt in a large bowl and make a well in the middle. Break the eggs into the well and beat them with a fork. Spoon the honey and molasses into the egg and beat together, then add the milk. Stir it into the egg mixture, then gradually draw in the cornmeal and flour. Mix until thoroughly blended, but no longer.

Pour the mixture into a lightly oiled loaf tin 9 in/23 cm square. Bake in a pre-heated oven at 350° F/180° C/gas mark 4 for 30–35 minutes, until the bread is well risen, firm and golden brown. Eat warm to enjoy it at its best.

Proja
Maize (corn) bread

The traditional breads of Yugoslavia were made with maize flour. After the Second World War, rapid urbanization and an increase in prosperity displaced rural customs and white wheat bread became a status symbol; however, maize bread is now returning to favour.

In Serbia, a simple boiled maize bread called *kacamak* was traditionally eaten; the flour was stirred with a wooden paddle into a copper pot of boiling water over the open fire for at least an hour; the dough was then left to set and eaten with melted pork fat or with butter made from the top of the milk. A poor man's *proja*, another maize bread, would be unleavened and have cooked, mashed potato added to the flour. The rich man's *proja* given here is raised with eggs and enriched with cottage cheese and sour cream to produce a flavoursome golden bread.

makes 2 2 lb/900 g loaves

2¼ lb/1 kg/7 cups maize (corn) flour
1 oz/25 g/2 tablespoons salt
18 oz/500 g/2¼ cups cottage cheese
about 5 tablespoons boiling water
6 eggs, beaten
7 oz/200 g/¾ cup sour cream

Combine the flour and salt in a very large mixing bowl. Mix the cottage cheese and water together and stir into the flour. Work in the eggs and sour cream until the mixture forms a dough of even texture.

Divide the dough between two 2 lb/900 g buttered loaf tins and bake in a pre-heated oven at 450° F/230° C/gas mark 8 for about 1 hour. Cool on a wire rack.

Lepinja
Flat brown bread

As Yugoslavia becomes more industrialized, fewer people bake their own bread and those who do buy their flour from the shops. But many people can remember how in their childhood the flour for these flat loaves of bread would be fetched from one of the numerous local mills where a water wheel turned the two huge mill-stones that ground the flour.

If you find this traditional bread a little bland, mix 3 teaspoons of salt into the flour.

makes 12 pieces

18 oz/500 g/4½ cups unbleached white flour
18 oz/500 g/4½ cups wholewheat flour
¾ oz/20 g/3 teaspoons fresh yeast or ½ oz/10 g/2 teaspoons dried yeast
pinch sugar
27 fl oz/800 ml/3½ cups warm water

Combine the flours in a large mixing bowl. Make a well in the middle and put in the yeast and sugar; pour on a little of the water and mix the yeast to a smooth, thin cream. Pour the remaining water little by little into the well, stirring to draw in the flour, and work up a smooth dough of even texture.

Cover the bowl with a cloth and put it in a warm place for 30 minutes for the dough to rise.

Turn out the risen dough and knead it quickly to knock out any bubbles and give it an even texture. Divide it into 12 equal pieces and form these into balls, then flatten them under your hand into thin discs. Lay the discs on a floured cloth and leave for 30 minutes to rise.

Prick the discs all over with a fork and lay them on baking sheets or directly on the bottom of the oven. Bake in a pre-heated oven at 450° F/230° C/gas mark 8 for 10–15 minutes.

Lichki
Maize (corn) and wheat bread

Yugoslavian peasants recommend maize bread as a cure for a variety of ills including general physical weakness. Whether it is for health reasons, or from nostalgia, or purely for the taste, the middle-class city dwellers are returning to maize bread. Bread of all kinds is important in the Yugoslav diet – the average daily consumption is 14 oz/400 g per person, with people in the less developed areas eating as much as 1½ lb/700 g a day.

In this recipe, the traditional maize is mixed with wheat flours to make a wholesome and substantial bread.

makes 2 large loaves

14 oz/400 g/3 cups maize (corn) flour
14 fl oz/400 ml/1¾ cups boiling water
11 oz/300 g/2¾ cups unbleached white flour
11 oz/300 g/2¾ cups wholewheat flour
¾ oz/20 g/1½ tablespoons salt
¾ oz/20 g/3 teaspoons fresh yeast
17½ fl oz/500 ml/2¼ cups lukewarm water

Put the maize flour into a very large mixing bowl and pour the boiling water over it. Combine the white flour, wholewheat flour and salt and mix them well into the maize and water. Mix the yeast to a smooth paste with a little of the lukewarm water, stir in the remaining water, and add this liquid to the dough. Mix thoroughly to work all the ingredients into a dough of even texture. Cover the bowl with a cloth and put it in a warm place for about 30 minutes for the dough to rise.

Turn out the risen dough, divide it into two equal pieces, and knead each lightly to fit a 2 lb/900 g greased loaf tin; or you can put the shaped loaves on to a baking sheet instead of into tins.

Leave the loaves in a warm place for about 10 minutes to rise again. Bake them in a pre-heated oven at 475° F/240° C/gas mark 9 for 30–40 minutes. Turn out on to a wire rack to cool.

Mamaliga
Cornmeal cake

The national dish of Rumania, and the staple food of the country people, has a name that means aptly 'bread of gold'; for *mamaliga* is cornmeal cooked to a firm mass. Like any staple food, it is combined with a wide range of other foods – eggs, sausages, small meatballs, bacon, sour cream, sauerkraut, grated cheese, chopped onions or thick sweetened cream.

serves 4–6

1¾ pints/950 ml/4¼ cups water
2 teaspoons salt
7 oz/200 g/1½ cups cornmeal

Heat the water and salt in a large saucepan until boiling furiously. Add the cornmeal a handful at a time, letting it trickle slowly through your fingers, like rain, into the boiling water. Stir all the time as you add it, using a long-handled wooden spoon because the boiling mixture may spit. Continue adding the cornmeal slowly until it is all in; if you add it all at once, it will form a hard mass.

When the mixture is smooth and thick, cover the pan, lower the heat and continue cooking gently for 30–40 minutes. You can then spoon it straight from the pan to combine with your chosen dish.

Alternatively, run a wet spatula round the sides of the pan to loosen the mixture from the sides and turn it out on to a wooden board. Shape it into a cake, either with a spoon dipped in water or with a wooden knife. Leave to cool, then cut into slices to serve like bread with stews and soups.

Buckwheat Bread

This dense, moist bread from America uses cooked buckwheat, which provides extra flavour and keeps the bread fresh longer. Rye adds a slightly sour taste – but you can use cornmeal instead. If you cannot get buckwheat, use cooked millet (sorghum), brown rice, oats or barley – or simply more wholewheat.

makes 2 loaves 9 × 5 in/ 23 × 13 cm

- 6 oz/175 g/1½ cups buckwheat groats (kasha)
- 1 pint/575 ml/2½ cups cold water
- knob of butter
- 1 oz/25 g fresh yeast, or 1 tablespoon dried yeast
- 5 fl oz/150 ml/⅔ cup warm water
- 1 pint/575 ml/2½ cups hot water (or water from cooking potatoes)
- 4 tablespoons honey
- 4 tablespoons molasses (or black treacle)
- 1 tablespoon sea salt
- about 2½ lb/1.1 kg/9 cups wholewheat bread flour
- 2 oz/50 g/¼ cup melted butter
- 8 oz/225 g/2 cups rye flour

Put the buckwheat, cold water and knob of butter in a pan, bring to the boil, then simmer until the grain is very soft and mushy. Kasha used in bread must be well cooked first or it will become rock-hard during baking. Dissolve the yeast in the warm water and leave for a few minutes to froth up.

Stir the hot water, honey, molasses and salt together in a large mixing bowl, then stir in 1 lb/450 g/4 cups of the wholewheat flour; stir it for 2 minutes. Mix in the yeast and then put in a warm place to rise for 1 hour.

Stir the mixture again for 1 minute, then mix in the buckwheat and the melted butter. Add the rye flour and mix in. Add the remaining wholewheat flour a little at a time, until the dough is stiff – you may need either a little less or a little more flour.

Knead the dough until it is springy with an even texture. Return it to the cleaned, lightly oiled mixing bowl and put to rise again for 1 hour, and then punch it down. Put to rise for another hour if you have time, and then punch it down again.

Divide the dough in half and shape each half to fit a lightly oiled (2 lb) loaf tin. Put to rise again in the tins for 30 minutes. Bake in a pre-heated oven at 350° F/180° C/gas mark 4 for 50–60 minutes, or until the loaves are firm and sound hollow when the underside is tapped.

Potato Bread with Caraway

This Central European recipe is especially good for dipping into stews and sauces, or makes a sustaining lunch with cheese. The bread keeps well.

makes 1 large loaf

3 potatoes, boiled
15 fl oz/450 ml/1¾ cups warm water plus 3 tablespoons
2 lb/900 g/8 cups unbleached strong white flour (or all-purpose flour)
1½ tablespoons salt
½ tablespoon caraway seeds
1 oz/25 g fresh yeast or ½ oz/ 15 g/1 teaspoon dried yeast
a little sunflower oil
1 tablespoon cornmeal

Mash the potatoes while still warm. Mix the yeast with 3 tablespoons of lukewarm water and stir in 3 tablespoons of the flour; leave in a warm place until the yeast starts to froth – about 20–30 minutes. Transfer to a large warm bowl, add the remaining lukewarm water and the salt, and caraway seeds. Gradually beat in the rest of the flour and the mashed potatoes until you have a softish dough. Turn the dough out on to a board and knead thoroughly until the dough is smooth and springy – not less than 10 minutes.

Shape the dough into a ball and coat it with the oil, then return it to the bowl. Cover with a sheet of plastic and leave to rise in a cool place until it has doubled in size – this will take several hours or it can be left to rise overnight.

Take out the dough, knead it again briefly and shape it into a large round loaf. Put it on to a baking sheet sprinkled with cornmeal. Let it rise again for 30 minutes, then slash the top of the loaf. In the meantime, pre-heat the oven to 375° F/190° C/gas mark 5.

When the loaf is well-risen and puffy, bake for about 1 hour until a good golden brown. It is done when the loaf sounds hollow when tapped on the bottom.

Orange Bread

A light, easily mixed and versatile bread. It is often on the Caribbean breakfast table, but it is also served as a dessert at lunch, sometimes with stewed fruit, fruit salad or ice-cream. This recipe is from Barbados, but versions of the bread are found in many of the Caribbean islands, especially the English-speaking ones.

makes 1 large loaf

8 oz/225 g/2 cups flour
1 tablespoon baking powder
4 oz/110 g/½ cup sugar
½ teaspoon salt
1 tablespoon grated orange rind
1 egg, well beaten
7½ fl oz/210 ml/1 cup orange juice
2 oz/50 g/¼ cup unsalted butter, melted

Sift the flour, baking powder, sugar and salt into a mixing bowl and add the orange rind. Combine the egg with the orange juice and butter and stir into the flour mixture to make a smooth batter.

Pour it into a greased loaf tin 9 × 5 in/23 × 13 cm and bake in a pre-heated oven at 350° F/180° C/gas mark 4 for 50 minutes, or until a skewer inserted in the middle comes out clean.

Turn out to cool on a wire rack, then slice and butter to serve.

Banana Bread

A light, tasty bread that is quick to mix. This is a Jamaican recipe, but banana bread is eaten throughout the Caribbean. It is served at breakfast to spread with butter and marmalade, jam or honey. It also makes an excellent sweet tea bread.

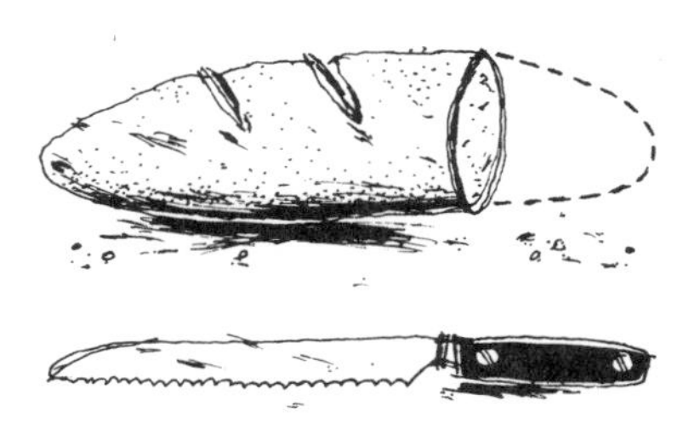

makes 1 large loaf

- 4 oz/110 g/½ cup butter
- 4 oz/110 g/½ cup sugar
- 1 egg
- 8 oz/225 g/2 cups flour
- 1 tablespoon baking powder
- ½ teaspoon salt
- ½ teaspoon grated nutmeg
- about 1 lb/450 g peeled ripe bananas
- 1 teaspoon vanilla extract
- 3 oz/85 g/⅓ cup seedless raisins, tossed in a little flour
- 4 tablespoons coarsely chopped pecans or walnuts

Cream the butter and sugar together in a mixing bowl until light and fluffy. Add the egg and beat thoroughly.

Sift in the flour, baking powder, salt and nutmeg and beat until thoroughly blended. Mash the bananas with the vanilla and beat into the mixture. Add the raisins and nuts and mix well.

Pour into a buttered 2 lb/900 g loaf tin and bake in a pre-heated oven at 350° F/180° C/gas mark 4 for 1 hour, or until a skewer inserted in the middle comes out clean.

Turn out to cool on a wire rack, then serve sliced and buttered.

KNOWING YOUR COOKING OILS

The kind of oil or fat used in cooking makes an important contribution to the character and flavour of a dish. The oil carries the flavour of each separate ingredient to the palate. Some oils have very little flavour of their own, while others have their own particular flavour and will evoke the feel of a country or region. Olive oil suggests the Mediterranean, and some connoisseurs can identify the olive oils of different regions by their aroma and flavour. Sesame seed oil calls to mind Japanese and Chinese cooking. Cottonseed oil has its own flavour reminiscent of the Middle East.

Regional and national barriers are breaking down, however, and improved transport means that mass-produced oils are readily available at lower prices than traditional oils. Corn oil is now as much used in Spain as olive oil, for example. However, traditional oils are still much prized for the flavour they impart to many national dishes which have been enjoyed for generations.

Corn (maize) oil, soya bean oil and olive oil are recommended for cooking. These are the oils most commonly used in the recipes we have selected from South-West Europe, South America and the Far East. In the Balkans and the Middle East they also have sunflower, cottonseed and sesame oils for cooking, and these are also good sources of polyunsaturated fats and essential fatty acids – in particular linoleic acid.

Butter, used for cooking in some parts of the Middle East, is a poor source of linoleic acid and polyunsaturates, and is not recommended except when it is needed in a dish because of its special flavour and character. Lard is used in some Balkan countries and in China, and is not a bad source of linoleic acid and polyunsaturates. It is recommended as an alternative when vegetable oil is not available or when its special flavour is needed. Beef dripping and suet (which may come from beef or lamb), however, are not recommended. They are poor sources of essential fatty acids and polyunsaturates.

Consumption of oils and fats in Japan is one-third of that in the United States or Britain, and in most countries with a low incidence of heart disease and cancer it is less than a half. In a few countries, such as Spain and Greece, over-all consumption of fats and oils approaches that of the United States and the United Kingdom. However, in both Spain and Greece, most of the oil consumed comes from the olive or from corn, which do not seem to be associated with the risk of heart disease. Butter was, until recently, a rarity on the family table in Spain and Greece.

Fats and oils are composed of fatty acids and glycerol, chemically joined together. Saturated fats contain their full quota of hydrogen atoms and are usually hard at room temperature. Butter and other animal fats are highly saturated. Fish oils are relatively unsaturated. Most vegetable oils, except for palm and coconut oils (not recommended for cooking), are also relatively unsaturated – that is, there are spaces left in the fat molecule where hydrogen atoms can be attached to them. If these oils are hydrogenated by a process commonly used in the food industry, they may be made into saturated fats. They then become harder at normal temperatures and can be spread like butter.

The unsaturated oils are of two types: mono-unsaturated and polyunsaturated. Most nut and vegetable oils, such as corn, soya, cottonseed, and particularly sunflower and safflower, are high in polyunsaturated fatty acids. Olive oil is high in mono-unsaturated fatty acids. The oils high in polyunsaturates have the effect of lowering blood cholesterol, whereas saturated fats raise cholesterol and so probably increase the risk of heart disease. Olive oil seems to be neutral in this respect. Although sunflower and safflower oils are particularly effective in lowering blood cholesterol, it may not be beneficial to health to use them exclusively. Communities which use them generally use other oils as well. There may be an advantage to health in using a range of vegetable oils in the kitchen since this provides the body with a variety of fatty acids and so reduces the burden put on the body by an unbalanced supply.

Another important distinction is whether the fatty acids in oil are 'essential' or not. The body needs to be provided with certain fatty acids, just as it must be provided with vitamins, because it cannot make them. These fatty acids belong to a family derived from linoleic acid. This is essential for the formation of prostaglandins which control the clotting reactions in the blood and prevent thrombosis. A shortage of this fatty acid makes the blood clot more readily and so makes the body more vulnerable to fatal thrombosis. If a blood clot forms in the heart or brain, death from a heart attack or stroke may follow.

Linoleic acid is also essential for the formation of nervous tissue. It may be significant that multiple sclerosis is commonest in industrialized countries such as Britain and America, where intake of linoleic acid in childhood, when nervous tissue is formed, may be deficient.

Unrefined oils

Olive oil is a natural unrefined oil which has its own special flavour and a rich colour which gives it taste and character. Other unrefined oils include sesame oil, safflower oil, corn oil, peanut (or groundnut) oil, wheatgerm oil and walnut oil. Traditionally they are extracted by cold-pressing of the oil-seed and do not undergo much more in the way of treatment or processing. However, nowadays they are often extracted using solvents which are then removed to leave the oil. This is a more efficient and economic process, but some countries have laws forbidding the use of this method which threatens traditional industry and may produce a different taste and quality of oil. Other oils are normally refined by such a process.

Refined oils will usually keep a year or more, but will lose some of their vitamins A and D, iodine, minerals and volatile acids, and in some cases their vitamin E. But the effect of refining, and removing all the particles of seed and juice, reduces the chance of the oil becoming rancid.

Without refined oils, however, there would be a drastic shortage of vegetable cooking oils. They are useful for frying, especially for deep-frying, but not so good for making dishes in which the flavour of the oil is an important factor, such as ratatouille, pasta, and most other Mediterranean or Middle Eastern dishes. So keep both kinds of oil: a refined oil such as sunflower or soya oil for frying, and a rich unrefined oil, olive, sesame or corn oil, for salads and dishes in which the oil is an integral ingredient.

How to use oils

Most oils start to smoke at 230° C and will flare up at about 325° C. Olive oil smokes at 170° C and flashes at 285° C. The correct temperature for deep-frying is between 165° C and 190° C. If overheated to very high temperatures the oil decomposes.

If the oil foams excessively or begins to smoke before reaching frying temperature then it has become decomposed and should be discarded.

Corn (maize) oil

Since maize (corn) is grown in hot climates, maize oil or corn oil is now widely used as a substitute for the traditional olive oil in many parts of the world. Although its flavour is bland it makes a good all-purpose kitchen oil. Although it can be used for salads, it is best kept for cooking. It is rich in linoleic acid and other polyunsaturates.

Rape seed oil

Known commercially as colza oil, this oil is made from the seeds of the bright yellow rape, or field mustard, a relative of the wallflower. It is used extensively in Europe in blended oils, mainly for frying. Until recently it was definitely not recommended because it contained erucic acid which is bad for the heart. A new variety now available contains little erucic acid. As this oil is a newcomer we have had insufficient experience of it to recommend it fully, but certainly it is a good source of linoleic acid and polyunsaturates.

Soya-bean oil

The soya bean is extremely rich in both oil and proteins. Its oil is one of the most widely used in the world: most blended cooking oils are soya based. It can be recommended as it is rich in linoleic acid and polyunsaturates. These make it difficult to store well because they can oxidize and develop off-flavours. However, they probably make it the best of all cooking oils from a health point of view.

Peanut (arachis, groundnut) oil

Is practically tasteless and therefore makes an excellent cooking oil. It is used extensively in the Far East, particularly Indonesia, and is popular in France and in the US. It is often used as a substitute for olive oil, both in salads and for cooking. Experiments with animals have found that this oil causes atheroma. Although it does not automatically follow that this happens in man, a question mark remains over it. However, it is quite a good source of linoleic acid and other polyunsaturates.

Sunflower oil

Extracted from sunflower seeds, this oil is becoming increasingly popular, as it has long been in Russia and Bulgaria where it is produced. It is a very pleasant, mild-tasting oil, particularly good for salads and slow-simmered dishes. It is also used by modern vegetarians for most purposes. It is rich in linoleic acid but not a good source of other polyunsaturates.

Olive oil

This is the traditional oil in Mediterranean countries and the Balkans and is also used widely in the Middle East. Olive oil is the most deliciously flavoured oil of all, but has become prohibitively expensive, so is now frequently used mixed with another vegetable oil, such as sunflower. It is a reasonable source of linoleic acid and other polyunsaturates and is therefore recommended.

Safflower oil

This oil is made from a yellow-flowered member of the thistle family, cultivated in India and the Middle East. The oil yielded by the seeds is sold in health-food shops and is used in diets since it has the highest linoleic acid composition of any oil, but is not a particularly good source of other polyunsaturates. It is rather strongly flavoured and not particularly pleasant.

Palm oil

Made from the nut-like fruits of the oil palm, a different species from the coconut palm, palm oil is widely used in West Africa and other parts of the tropics. It is not recommended from the point of view of good health, since it is rather high in saturated fats.

Sesame oil

This oil is popular in the Middle East, Mexico and Japan as well as in China and India. Sesame oil has a delicious flavour and is also supposed to contain large quantities of lecithin.

Lecithin is recommended by some diet enthusiasts but does not need to be added to the diet since the body makes its own supply. Sesame oil does not easily go rancid, which makes it useful in hot countries. It is expensive, but can be mixed with a tasteless vegetable oil, such as sunflower oil, without losing its flavour. A good source of linoleic acid, it is recommended especially for its flavour.

Cottonseed oil

This oil is produced on a large scale and is mainly used in the making of margarines and cooking fats. It has a distinctive flavour well-liked in certain parts of the Middle East and in the Far East. It is often used in canning. Rich in linoleic acid and other polyunsaturates, it is recommended.

Walnut oil

This oil is cold-pressed from fresh walnuts and is used raw for salads in parts of France. It is very expensive but can be mixed half and half with peanut or sunflower oil with good results. Rich in polyunsaturates, it is recommended as an indulgence for the palate – if you can afford it.

Coconut oil

This is one of the most highly saturated of vegetable oils and has a thick texture like margarine. It is used for cooking in South-East Asia, the West Indies and India, but it is not recommended since it contains 75 per cent saturated fatty acids and little linoleic acid. It is also indigestible.

Wheat germ oil

This oil is high in vitamin E and linoleic acid. It has a nutty flavour. As it is so expensive it is generally used only medicinally. It does not keep well. If you eat wholewheat bread then you will obtain it in your diet very cheaply.

CHOOSING THE RIGHT RICE

Rice can be divided into four kinds: *long grain*, which is thin and spindly, e.g. 'Patna' rice; *medium grain*, which is the same length but plumper, e.g. 'risotto' rice; *short* or *round grain*, which is shorter and much plumper, e.g. 'pudding' rice; and *glutinous* or *sticky* rice which is also round but used for Japanese and other Asian dishes. Brown rice, which is rice that has been de-husked but not polished, may be from any of these categories.

All these types of rice cook differently. Well cooked, *long grain* becomes light, dry and fluffy, with the grains separating easily; *medium grain* absorbs more liquid but retains a little 'bite' with the grains remaining separate; *short grain* absorbs even more liquid and cooks readily into a creamy mass; *glutinous* absorbs a lot of liquid, becomes very sticky and cohesive in a mass, but remains chewy.

Obviously it is best if the right sort of rice can be used for whatever it is you are cooking – long grain for pilafs, medium for risottos and so on. If you do have to make do with a different type, choose the sort nearest to what you should have and try to adjust the quantity of water, cooking time and method to give the result you want. Remember too that even within the categories outlined here, quality can vary. There are also several different strains within each group.

The Balkans

The rice grown and eaten in the Balkans is short round grained and very absorbent and is used in many savoury dishes. Fry it first, then add liquid and bake it in the oven rather than on top of the stove.

Italy

Italy is a big rice-growing country, most of it coming from the Po valley in Northern Italy. Long, medium and round-grained rice is grown, but the kind most used in Italian cookery is the medium grained. All three types are exported. The best is the yellow medium grained *Cristallo* or *Avorio* rice, which stays very firm when cooked and goes white. The next best is the white medium-grain rice sold as *Arborio*. This has less bite, becoming softer when cooked. It is used more for dishes such as Sicilian *arancini* which need to be moulded. Italian grocers and good supermarkets usually stock *Arborio* or a rice called 'risotto rice'. Short grain rice is not a good substitute (and not generally used in Italy itself, although grown for export).

Spain

Most of the rice eaten in Spain is grown there, in the lagoons around Valencia, and in the Marismas, but only in exceptionally good years is there enough for it to be exported as well. The best Spanish rice is from Pego and is similar to *Cristallo* and *Arborio* rice (Spain introduced rice to Italy in the first place); risotto rice can therefore be used for Spanish dishes like paella. The same sort of rice is grown in the Algarve in Portugal and the Camargue in France, but not on a sufficiently large scale to export.

The Americas

Some rice is grown in Guyana and Central America; most of it, however, is imported from the United States where a long grain 'Patna', the slightly softer medium grain 'Carolina' and a round grain are grown. 'Carolina' most resembles the Valencia rice brought over by the Spanish conquistadors. However, the rice usually used is long-grain. 'Carolina', which is not expensive, can sometimes be found in good grocers and some supermarkets in Britain.

The Middle East

Beautiful long grain rice is grown in Iran, but only for home consumption. It is far better than any rice imported to Britain, of which the Pakistani Basmati rice (grown in the Indus valley) is the best. Nowadays, the best Basmati rice is becoming increasingly easy to buy in Britain. If it is not obtainable in a good grocer's or supermarket, any shop specializing in Greek or Indian food will stock it.

Japan

The Japanese like a chewy rice that is easy to pick up with chop-sticks. The rice they grow fulfils these requirements and is known as sticky or glutinous rice. It is medium grained and slightly sweet. It can be bought in shops specializing in Japanese food. A similar sort of rice, *keng*, is sold in Chinese shops. Short grain rice, if cooked with care, can be used as a substitute for Japanese rice, which is best cooked in a patent rice steamer.

South-East Asia

All the rice eaten in this part of the world is grown here, most of it traditionally coming from Thailand, Vietnam and Kampuchea. The recent wars, however, have meant that only Thailand now has rice to export. Long and medium grain rice is grown there, the people of North-East Thailand and Laos favouring a rice that is even stickier than the sort liked in Japan. Long grain rice should be used for any dish not specifying 'sticky' rice. It is ideal for mopping up spicy sauces and curry juices. In terms of fluffiness, the fluffiest rice is liked in the tropics, less fluffy in Thailand and western Malaysia, and still less fluffy in the Philippines and Indonesia. As one brand of long grain can cook up fluffier than another it is best to experiment with whatever you can find.

Brown rice

Any sort of rice that has had the husk removed but not the bran (has not been polished) is called brown rice. Brown rice is available at all whole-food and health-food shops, and is beginning to appear in good supermarkets. When choosing the type of grain for a specific dish, therefore, the characteristics of brown rice are the same as white rice. The difference is that brown rice takes longer to cook, as the bran forms a cellophane-like skin which does not allow the cooking water to penetrate so quickly. The best way to cook it is to boil it vigorously at first, then let it simmer 30–40 minutes. It must not be stirred until it is cooked (when all the water is absorbed), and it should be left covered in the pan for 10 minutes before serving.

Rice: how to cook it

When rice is the staple food, providing possibly half the daily calorie requirement, then it must be properly cooked to provide its full nutritional value. Excessive milling of rice removes all the vitamin-rich scutellum of the grain. In particular it removes thiamin (vitamin B1). This is not crucial, provided the rest of the diet is sufficiently varied, but if it is not then overall lack of vitamin will cause beriberi – a disease marked by swelling of the body and paralysis.

When rice is milled in the traditional way with a pestle and mortar, enough of the scutellum remains with the grain to provide adequate thiamin. But mechanical milling polishes the grain more thoroughly, and beriberi becomes increasingly likely. In the Menam Delta of Thailand, most farmers were using the commercial mills and a high incidence of beriberi developed. So the Thai government invested in a programme of enriching rice by adding a small amount of specially treated rice grains to milled rice. These grains were impregnated with vitamins and sealed to make them resistant to losses in washing and cooking.

Washing rice before cooking and throwing away the water used for cooking causes important losses of thiamin. In some parts of India this is done, but in others people are careful to keep the water and use it as a drink or as the basis for soup. Such rice water is said to have been the base for the famous mulligatawny soup which is seasoned with chilli and garlic. During the colonial wars in Madras, British officers were besieged at Trichinopoly. Their loyal sepoys served the officers rice, while the sepoys subsisted on the water in which the rice had been cooked. The officers developed beriberi. The sepoys remained healthy.

A generation ago, when the Japanese were less affluent and indeed healthier than they are now, it was common to mix one part of barley or millet with two parts of rice and cook in the usual way. Hulled (Scotch) barley is a good extra source of the thiamin which may be missing from polished rice. It is also a useful source of other vitamins, energy, fibre and protein. Pearl barley is not quite so good because it is milled to remove the outer germ and bran and thus contains less fibre and vitamins; 70 per cent of the thiamin is lost. Millet is a useful source of energy and protein but it is deficient in vitamins C, A and B12 and so it is better mixed with a food like rice which does adequately supply these vitamins. Brown rice, rice which does not have the bran and germ removed by milling, was seldom eaten in Japan, but now health-conscious Japanese are beginning to eat it for the extra vitamins.

GLOSSARY: FLAVOURS AND FOODSTUFFS

Achiote oil (*annatto oil*) Cooking oil flavoured with annatto seeds and used for frying meat or fish, or for adding to stews and sauces. To make the oil, heat a cup of peanut or other vegetable oil with 1/4 cup of the seeds; cover the pan and cook over a low heat for 2–3 minutes, then strain off the oil. Keep it in a tightly sealed jar in a refrigerator.

Alfalfa The sprouted seeds provide a salad vegetable. The sprouts are quickly grown in the same way as lentil sprouts and are rich in vitamins, trace elements, and protein. Alfalfa is also used world-wide as a forage crop for livestock.

Annatto seeds Seeds of a small Central and South American tree. They are used as a colouring agent for foodstuffs and fabrics and also impart a mild but distinctive flavour to cooking oil. See *achiote oil*.

Bacalao (Spain), *bacalhau* (Portugal) Dried salt cod. Hard with a very distinctive smell, it has to be soaked well. The thickest part is the belly.

Bamboo shoot Ivory-coloured, conical, young shoot of the bamboo tree, used frequently in Oriental cooking but never eaten raw. Fresh young bamboo shoots are covered with sharp hairs which must be removed because they are very dangerous if swallowed. The canned shoots available are free of the hairs and pre-cooked. They will keep for up to a month after opening if put in a bowl of water in a refrigerator; the water should be changed every three days. The shoots can be used in hot dishes, or battered and deep-fried, or served cold with other vegetables.

Bonito Small species of tuna fish, which may be up to 30 in/75 cm long. It is available canned and can be used in the same ways as tuna.

Burghul Also known as *bulgur* in the Balkans and *pourgouri* in Cypriot shops, it is wheat which has been parboiled, then dried and cracked (in a mill) to various degrees of coarseness. It can now be found in most delicatessens, health-food shops and specialist grocers.

Calaloo (also *callaloo, calalou, callilu, callau*) Leaves of two distinct plants but used interchangeably: (i) leaves of the taro plant; (ii) Chinese spinach. It is sold as *hiya* in Japanese shops and as *bhaji* in Indian shops. It is also available in tins.

Carob powder Sweet, chocolate-flavoured powder prepared from the pulp of the pod of the carob, or locust, tree.

Chard Also called Swiss chard and seakale beet, these crinkly green leaves belong to the same family as spinach, but they are firmer and more resilient, with a broad white stalk which should be cooked separately.

Chayote (*vegetable pear, pepinello, choko*) A type of squash borne on a trailing vine; pear-shaped, ridged, and often covered with prickly hairs. The colour varies from creamy white to dark green; the dark green type is best. A chayote is the size of a large pear, contains one large seed, and has firm, delicately flavoured flesh which is often sliced and fried in batter. The young shoots of the plant are eaten as asparagus, the leaves are eaten as greens, and the large tuberous roots are eaten as yams. The fruit is available in West Indian markets.

Chilli peppers Fruits of several herbaceous plants of the *Capsicum* family; smaller than the sweet peppers. A green chilli is an unripe fruit; a red chilli is a ripe fruit. Fresh chilli peppers can be obtained in some markets and specialist shops. Some are obtainable in tins. Dried red chilli peppers are more generally available. Strength of flavour varies with the type of chilli. *Poblano* chilli – large, shaped like a spinning top, very dark green; since it has a mild flavour, a sweet green pepper makes a fair substitute. *Serrano* chilli – short and fat, mid-green to dark green, very hot flavour; usually only available tinned. *Ancho* chilli – this is a ripe *poblano* chilli and the most commonly used dried chilli in Mexico. It is dark brown but becomes red; when soaked; the flavour is mild and rich. *Mulato* chilli – wrinkled and dark brownish-red; sweet but very pungent. *Pasilla* chilli – long, thin and blackish-red; well-flavoured.

Chinese five spices A combination of aniseed, fennel, clove, cinnamon, and Szechwan pepper. Available in Chinese shops; allspice can be used as a substitute.

Chorizo (Spain), *chouriço* (Portugal) Hard sausage made with pork, garlic, paprika and other spices. Can be cooked or eaten raw. The Spanish and the Portuguese versions are similar, but not identical.

Clarified butter Butter that has been boiled and cleared of all the milk solids that cause it to burn brown and become rancid. It keeps for months in a jar without refrigeration. It has a strong taste and is used in much smaller quantities than ordinary butter. Its preparation is described in Chapter 3.

Coriander The leaves of the plant, which produces the round coriander seed long known as a spice, are now available throughout the year. They have a special and distinctive taste and are good raw in salads or cooked in stews or soups. They wilt quickly and must be used as soon as possible.

Daikon Giant or Oriental white radish which grows to 12 in/30 cm or more in length. It is pickled as a relish, cooked as a vegetable, or eaten raw grated in salads or sliced to dip in sauces. It is sold in many Oriental shops.

Doufu Chinese white bean curd. See *tofu*.

Fava beans Another name for broad beans. Use large lima beans as a substitute.

Fennel Feathery herb with an anise flavour (sometimes known as anise). Looks similar to dill and the stalks are excellent in fish sauces and salad dressing. The bulbs of sweet or Florence fennel can be cooked or eaten raw in salads.

Feta cheese A semi-soft, white, low-fat curd cheese originally from the Balkans. Fat content is 45–60 per cent; made from sheep's or cow's milk or both. It has a slightly sour and salty taste which increases as the cheese becomes older. It is eaten both fresh and cooked; when cooked it melts very slowly and keeps its shape more than other cheeses. It is available from Greek shops and from many delicatessens.

Funghi porcini (Italy) Dried fungi – the boletus or cep gathered in early autumn and dried for winter use. Be careful to buy them cream-coloured and brown, not black and gnarled as these have a very strong flavour. Stored in a tightly sealed box, they keep for a long time. Soak before use and never throw away the reconstituting water; use it in the recipe. Do not cook for too long or they may lose their flavour. Add dried fungi to rice dishes, soups, sauces and stews. They have a characteristic meaty flavour, so fresh mushrooms do not make an entirely successful substitute.

Green papaya Fruit of the same family as avocado and mango. It is pickled or used as a vegetable when unripe, and eaten like a melon when ripe. The skin is smooth and green and the ripe flesh is orange-yellow, soft and juicy. It is very rich because of its oil content. The centre of the fruit contains numerous brown-black seeds which can be used as a spice. It is available from West Indian markets.

Halumi A firm, white Greek cheese also produced in Israel and the Arab world.

Harusame Japanese vermicelli; transparent, thin noodles made from the starch of beans or sweet potatoes.

Jamon serrano (Spain) Serrano ham. A very fine, specially cured ham cut very thin and eaten raw. Can be substituted with Italian *prosciutto*.

Karmardine Sun-dried apricots sieved and pressed into thin sheets can be bought folded in Middle Eastern groceries. People tear off pieces from the dark orangy-brown sheets to nibble at. They can be soaked or boiled up in water to make an apricot drink or a cream.

Katsuobushi Dried bonito. In the piece it looks rather like a boomerang and is extremely hard, requiring a special implement to scrape off thin shavings. It is widely available as shavings sold in packets, and also in powder form.

Kemiri (*candlenuts, macadamia nuts*) Edible nuts from the South Sea Islands, used to thicken dishes and also cooked in coconut milk to serve hot with vegetables, meat and poultry. Available from Oriental food shops and specialist grocers.

Kombu An important seaweed in Japan; a type of kelp which is sold in large sheets.

Kona sanshu A spicy seasoning which gives a brown colour. A possible substitute is ground black pepper mixed with a pinch of sugar.

Labna Cream cheese made from yoghurt thickened considerably by draining off the whey through thin muslin (cheesecloth).

Lemon grass One of several grass-like oriental plants with stems as thick as a finger. Used as a herb to flavour dishes, but it does not have a lemon flavour.

Masa harina Special cornmeal flour used for making *tortillas*. The grains are slaked in lime-water before grinding, which gives a distinctive flavour.

Mexican green tomato A small green fruit related to the Cape gooseberry. It looks like a small green tomato with a husk. It has no flavour until cooked. Available in cans.

Mirin A sweet Japanese rice wine used only for cooking.

Miso Paste made from fermented bean curd. It is very rich in protein and vitamins.

Morcilla (Spain), *morcela* (Portugal) Blood sausage made with pork products and spices including cumin (Portugal), cinnamon and pine nuts. To be cooked. The Spanish version differs from the Portuguese.

Mozzarella (Italy) Cheese made from the milk of water buffalo or from cow's milk. Best eaten when dripping fresh, otherwise used for cooking. Keep it in a refrigerator or cool place in a bowl of milky water.

Nopalitos Very young cactus leaves or fruits, not available fresh but canned in vinegar, brine, or water.

Nori An important seaweed in Japan; it is the same as laver or Irish moss. It is sold in paper-thin sheets and is much used as a garnish, for wrapping round food during cooking, and for crumbling into foods as a seasoning.

Okra, gumbo, or *'ladies' fingers'* Green, pointed pod vegetable; both pod and seeds are eaten. Try to buy young pods the size of your little finger as older ones will be less tender. Young pods need 10–15 minutes' cooking, older ones two or three times longer. When using the pods whole in dishes, cut off the stems carefully without piercing the pods or they will release a sticky substance. In some dishes such care is not necessary because the sticky substance is intended to thicken the dish. Okra can be brought fresh in many markets and supermarkets when in season; it is also available tinned.

Orange blossom water The distilled essence of orange blossom petals is used to flavour puddings and sweet dishes. As with rose-water, the concentration varies. Though much weaker than those produced in parts of the Arab world, the types available here are a little more powerful than rose-water.

Pancetta (Italy) Same cut of pork as bacon – it is belly of pork and air-dried. Cured in salt and spices, it usually comes tightly rolled up like salami and is sliced to order. Keeps for up to three weeks in a refrigerator, when carefully sealed. Good quality *pancetta* can be eaten as it is, like *prosciutto*. Used as flavouring agent in sauces, fillings, vegetables and roasts. Wrapped round meat – like veal – it bastes as it cooks. *Prosciutto* is the nearest substitute.

Pecorino (Italy) A hard country-made ewe's milk cheese of the grana type; (Parmesan is another grana cheese, but it is made with cow's milk). It has a pungent, sometimes salty taste, good with the many strong flavours of Southern Italy. Eaten in chunks, and used for grating and cooking.

Phyllo pastry Paper-thin sheets of pastry made from flour, water, vegetable oil and salt. It is sold in packets in Greek food shops, where it is sometimes known as phyllo strudel pastry.

Pine nuts or *pignoli* The kernels from the cones of the stone pine have a very delicate almond flavour. They are used in puddings and biscuits, and are sometimes added to meat dishes.

Plantain A large member of the banana family. It is eaten both green and ripe (when the skin is black), but in either case it must be cooked before it is eaten. It is served as an appetizer, in soups, as a starchy vegetable, or as a dessert. It is sold in West Indian markets.

Quince Fruit closely related to the apple and pear. It is pear-shaped with a hard yellow skin when ripe. The hard flesh is golden yellow and highly aromatic. It adds a pleasant pungency to cooked fruit dishes and is excellent for jam-making because of its high pectin content. It is sometimes available in specialist greengrocers during October and November, but more often seen in private gardens.

Rice vinegar Vinegar made from rice. It has a more delicate flavour than wine or malt vinegar.

Ricotta (Italy) Soft fresh whey cheese made from ewe's milk or cow's milk. Usually unsalted. Real, fresh ricotta is very perishable and should be eaten within 24–48 hours even if it is refrigerated. Gervais, a passable substitute, which lasts a little longer is made from whole milk and can be found in most supermarkets. Do not substitute cottage cheese or cream cheese.

Rose-water The concentrated distilled essence of rose petals gives a delicate perfume to puddings and pastries. It can be bought in Middle Eastern stores as well as pharmacies (as it can also be used as a skin lotion). Very little is required.

Sake (*saké, saki*) Wine made from fermented rice. Served as a drink, usually warm, and also used in cooking.

Salchichon (Spain) Hard sausage which is eaten raw (rather like salami).

Samna See *clarified butter*

Stanbouli A hard, dry cheese which originates in Turkey.

Sweet potato A globular or elongated tuber, not related to the ordinary potato. The skin may be white, pink, red, or purple. The flesh is white to yellow, firm, and sweet. It is in season during the winter months.

Tahina An oily paste of ground sesame seeds bought ready-made in jars from Middle Eastern grocers and health-food shops.

Tocino (Spain), *touchinho* (Portugal) Salted pork fat. The nearest substitute is unsmoked speck. The Spanish and Portuguese versions are similar but not identical.

Tofu (*tau hoo, doufu*) Bean curd made from a purée of soya beans. It resembles soft but firm white cheese and is sold in cake form. It is available fresh from Oriental food shops and some wholefood shops. It will keep for up to two weeks in a refrigerator in an uncovered bowl of water which should be changed every two days.

Tree ears (*wood ears, black fungus*) Gelatinous edible fungus from China, where it grows wild on trees and is also cultivated on them. The dried form is available from Oriental food shops and specialist grocers. The dried ears look like large tea leaves; they must be soaked before use and then swell into gelatinous flakes.

Unto (Spain) Aged fat bacon. The nearest substitute is fat, smoked streaky bacon.

Vine leaves Young leaves of the grape vine. Fresh leaves should be picked while not too large and boiled for a few seconds to soften them before use. Leaves preserved in brine are widely available from Greek shops; they should be soaked for 2–3 hours, with frequent changes of water, before use. Vine leaves are used to wrap round meat fillings and as a base for salads. Swiss chard leaves, spinach leaves, or beet leaves are possible substitutes.

Wakame Dark green seaweed with lobed leaf. It is available in Oriental food shops dried and packeted; it is soaked before use in salads and soups. Sometimes it is boiled, drained, and served with a dressing as a first course.

Wasabe A green powder prepared from Japanese horseradish, often eaten with fish. To prepare, mix a level teaspoon of powder with a teaspoon of water in an eggcup and quickly turn upside down to exclude air. Leave for 5–10 minutes for the full flavour to develop. The full flavour will not develop if the paste is left exposed to the air. The powder may also lose flavour on storage, so it may be more reliable to buy it in a tube.

Wok Chinese frying pan in which foods can be cooked over intense heat with very little fat; this preserves the flavour, colour, and nutritional value of cooked foods. It is especially good for quick-fried vegetable dishes.

Zahtar A spice mixture containing thyme and salt.

N.B. Many delicatessens stock dried salt cod and other Spanish or Portuguese products. You can often buy fresh coriander at Indian or Greek food shops, and squid or cuttlefish at specialist Greek or continental fish shops.

INDEXES

Recipe titles

Acar Campur, 139
Agnello, al Forno, 47
con Finocchi e Pomodori, 48
Ají, Molido con Aceite, 160–1
Nitsuke, 128
All-i-oli, 49
Almendras Tostadas, 33
Amy's Orange Buttercream Torte, 197
Anchoïade, 29
Anticuchos, 175
Apricot Fool, 201
Arepa, 158–9
Arroz, a la Costa Ricana, 165
com Grelos, 41
con Carne de Cerdo, 40–1
con Coco y Pasas, 165–6
Guatemalteco, 165
Atole, 179
Aubergines Farcies, 27
August Garden Stir-fry, 193–4
Ayran, 111

Bacalhau com Pimentos e Tomates, 31
Bacon and Bananas, 180
Banana Bread, 225
Bapsetek Ikan, 140
Bar (ou Mulet) Grillé au Fenouil, 42
Beef Stew with Beans, Peas and Rice, 173
Belila, 110
Betingan, 109
Meshwi, 93
Biber Yoğurtlu, 58–9
Bibingkat Malagkit, 147
Bistec, 175
Blue Cheese Salad, 192
Bosanska Kalja od Kapusa, 69
Bosanski Lonac, 69
Bouillabaisse, 22
Bran-plus Wholewheat Loaf, 213
Brown Rice, 195
Buckwheat Bread, 223
Bulgur Pilâvı, 74
Burghul, bi Dfeen, 102–3
Pilaf, 109

Calamares a la Plancha, 32–3
Caldeirada de Peixe, 43
Caldo Gallego, 46–7
Caldo Verde, 21
Caponata alla Marinara, 25
Caponata alla Siciliana, 27
Carne en Jocón, 174
Carob Brownies, 196
Carrot, Cake, 198
Cashew and Ginger Quiche, 191
Ceviche, 164
Chaomian, 134–5
Chawan Mushi, 121
Cheese Fritters, 192
Chiaotse, 136
Chilaquiles, 158
Chilli, 196
Chillis Rellenos, 172
Chin Kou Yu Yu Ssu, 140–1
Chupe, de Camarones, 163
de Pescado, 163
Cocido Madrileño, 45
Coco Quemado, 177
Coelho em Vinho Verde, 48
Coo-coo, 166–7
Cornbread, 220
Country Bread from the Abruzzi, 214–15
Cream of Butternut Squash Soup, 186
Cream of Pumpkin Soup, 162
Curried Lentils and Vegetables, 194

Dan Dan Mian, 135
Dashi, 117
Date Slices, 200
Daube de Poisson, 164
Djaj Meshwi, 104
Dried Fruit Compôte with Ginger, 200
Dyo-M'Ena Pilafi, 75

Eggah bi Kouat, 106
Empanadas, 159
de Maiz, 137
de Platanos, 178
Ensalada, de Tomate y Cebolla, 26
Mixta, 168

Falafel, 91
Fasolado, 60
Fattet Hummus, 89
Faves con Butifarrones, 44
Flan, 177
de Leche, 51
Fresh Nut Butter, 203
Fried Ripe Plantains, 167
Frijoles, 168–9
de la Olla, 169
Refritos, 170
Ful Medames, 88

Gallo Pinto, 170
Gebna Meshwi, 105
Giraboix, 42–3
Guacamole, 160

Harissa, 91
Hoo Wan T'Heng, 131
Horenso No Hitashi, 125
Huevos Rancheros, 160
Hummus, bi Tahina, 93
Sandwich 188–9

Insalata di Verdure, 26
Italian Bread with Olive Oil, Rosemary and Garlic, 215

Jemput-jemput, 146

Kabuni, 79
Kahwa, 111
Kakitama-Jiru, 117
Kamaboko, 126–7
Karedok, 138–9
Kartofi sus Suene, 60
Khoshaf, 110
Kibbeh, bil Sanieh, 102
Nayyeh, 96
Kiritampo, 124
Kofta Kebab, 101
Köfte, 65
Kotopoulo Kapama, 70
Kousa Mahski, 100

Laban, 104–5
Salateen, 94
Labna, 105
Lahana Salata, 76
Lahma bi-ajeen, 97–8
Lahm Meshwi, 101
La Salade de Leyritz, 168
Lentil Spinach Soup, 185–6
Lepinja, 221
Liangmian Huang, 132–3
Lichki, 221–2

Maccarones a la Catalana, 36
Maccheroni al Funghi, 37
alla Pastora, 35
Mahshi Silq, 103
Mamaliga, 222
Felii Prajita, 73
Mamounia, 90
Mangoade, 189
Manjar Blanco, 179

Melanzane, al Funghetto, 28
Sott'Olio, 28–9
Melon Fresco, 180
Mero al Jerez, 44
Minestra di Pasta e Ceci, 21
Miso Shiru, 118
Udon, 120–1
Mole Poblana de Guajolote, 176
Mousaka s Patladzhani, 64
Muesli, 184
Mujaddarah, 107
Multi-grain Sourdough Bread, 211–12

Nasi Goreng, 137
Nasu No Shigiyaki, 124
Nigiri Zushi, 123
Nut Milk, 203

Ochazuke, 122–3
Orange Bread, 224–5
Orecchiette, 34–5
al Cavolfiore, 35

Pan Bagnato, 26
Pansit Molo, 133
Panzarella, 24
Papas a la Huancaina, 171
Pasta with Garlic and Fresh Herbs, 195
Pasteis de Bacalhau, 32
Pasticcio di Spaghetti e Peperoni, 34
Patlıcan, Salatas, 58
Tavası, 59
Pebre, 161
Pechena Tikva, 80–1
Pescado en Escabeche, 30
Petits Pois en Bouillabaisse, 24
Picadillo, 173
Picarones, 178
Pipérade, 39
Piri-Piri, 49
Pissaladière, 30–1
Pitta, 216–17
Pizza Calabrese, 38–9
Planatos Fritos, 167
Pogača, 218
Popara, 57
Poppy Seed Wholewheat Bread, 213–14
Porco com Feijao, 47
Porotos Granados, 170–1
Potato Bread with Caraway, 224
Prazheni Filii, 81
Prepelice s Pirinčem, 72
Proja, 220
Puchero, 46
Pui Gatit cu Vin si Masline, 70
Punjeni Paprike i Praradajz, 66–7

Rasol Čorba, 78–9
Ratza cu Varza Acra, 71
Raw Granola, 202
Riba s Kiselo Zele, 63
Rizogalo, 79
Rouille, 22
Roz, 107
bel Shaghira, 108
ou Ful, 108

Sabaneh bi Loubia, 95
Salata, 99–100
Fasolakia, 76
Filfil bi Outa, 95
od Praziluka, 77
Salsa, Cruda, 162
de Aji, 161
di Pomodori, 50
Verde, 161
Salsicce, 36
Samak Meshwi, 96
Samna, 88
Sashimi, 126
Staté Ayam, 144
Savanyú Káposzta, 77–8
Scrambled Tofu, 186–7
Sesame-Cauliflower Quiche, 190
Shio Yaki, 127
Shorba, 92
Shorbat el Adas, 92
Sinigang, 142
Şiş Kebap (Shish Kebab), 68
Sobrebarriga, 174
Sopa de Ajo, 23
de Lentejas, 23
Sourdough Starter, 211
Split Pea Soup, 184
Srit-Fried Sprouted Lentils, 203–4
Strawberry Pignoli, 204
Summer Salad with Russian Dressing, 204
Sunday Brunch Muffins, 198–9

Tabbouleh, 94
Tácos, 156
Taiwan Nuo Mi Fan, 138
Tamagoyaki, 122
Tamales, 157
Tannou, 217
Tarama Salata, 57–8
Tarator, 59
Tempura, 129
Tinola, 146
Tofu, 131–2
Tomato Bisque, 185
Torinabe, 130
Torta di Vermicelli e Pomodori, 38
Tortilla Española, 40
Tortillas, 155–6
de Trigo, 158
Toucinho do Céu, 50
Trahana, 74–5
Tsukimi Udon, 120
Ts'ui P'i Fei Chi, 143
Türlü Güveç, 61
Two-crust Pumpkin Pie, 199
Tyropitta, 62

Udang Bakar, 141–2
Unleavened Bread, 219

Vegetable Stir-fry, 193

Wakame To Kyuri No Sunomo, 125
Wholewheat, Bread, 212–13
Fruit Cake, 200–1
Piecrust, 189
'Wings of Life' Salad, 187

Xató, 25

Yahniya ot Spanak, 67
Yakni, 99
Yasaino Nimono, 128
Yoghurt, 72–3
-Tahina Salad, 188
Yu-Dofu, 118–19
Yumurta Çılbır, 63

Zaru Soba, 119
Zelena Salata s Kiselim Mlekom, 76
Zhug, 106

General

Abruzzi, 18
Acid, amino, 115
erucic, 229
fatty, 12, 227, 230
folic, 10
lactic, 11
linoleic, 227, 228, 230
'trans-fatty', 12
volatile, 228
Africa, diet in, 8
Aguardiente, 152, 153
Aji-no-moto, 116
Akita, 124
Albania, 79
Alentejo, 31
Allergy, 11
All-i-oli sauce, 42–3, 49
Almonds, toasted, 33
with meat and raisins, 173
America, bread, 213, 220, 223
cake, 196, 197, 198
chilli, 196
pie, 199
quiche, 191
salad, 187, 188, 192
soup, 186
vegetables, 193–4
Amino acids, 115
Amy's orange buttercream torte, 197
Anchovy, and bread salad, 25
and olive tart, 30–1
spread, 29
Andalusia, 33, 44
Apricot fool, 201
Apricots, 11
Apulia, 21
Arak, 86
Arborio rice, 231
Arepas, 159
Armeya chorba, 78
Artificial sweeteners, 13
Atherosclerosis, 82
Atole, 150, 153, 179
Aubergine, with yoghurt, 59
moussaka, 64
purée, 58, 93
Aubergines, 109
cooked like mushrooms, 28
in oil, 28–9
stuffed, 27

Aubergines, *contd.*
sweet-sour, 27
with sesame, 124
August garden stir-fry, 193–4
Avocado sauce with tomatoes and coriander, 160
Avorio rice, 231
Ayran, 54

Baba ghanouj, 93
Bacalhau, 17, 31, 32
Bacon, 13
and bananas, 180
Badkila, 88
Bagoong, 9
Baked caramel custard, 51
Baklava, 55, 56
Balkans, agriculture, 53
racial history, 53
yoghurt in diet, 11
Banana, bread, 225
cakes, fried, 146
Bananas and bacon, 180
Banica, 62
Banitza, 55, 59
Barbados, 166
Barley, 84, 233
Basmatic rice, 232
Basque, 39
Bean, curd, simmered, 118–19
fried, 132–3
green, salad, 76
paste with noodles, 120–1
soup, 60
soya, curd, 131–2
soya, paste soup, 118
Beans, and pork, 47
beef stew with, 173
black-eyed, with spinach, 95
bread, with rice, 108
brown, dressed in oil and lemon, 88
cranberry with sweet-corn and pumpkin, 170–1
dried, as source of protein, 18
in diet, 151
in the pot, 169
red kidney, 168–9
refried, 170
rice with broad (*fava*), 108
soy, 112
with rice and onions, 170
Beard, James, 215
Beef, and pork stew, 142
casseroled steak, 174
dripping, 227
ox heart cubes, 175
saturated fat content, 10
steak, 175
stew, 174
with beans, peas and rice, 173
Beefsteak, 175
casseroled, 174
Beriberi, 233
Bircher-Benner, Dr, 185
Birth defects, 8
Bladder cancer, and saccharin, 13
Blood, clotting, 10, 11, 12, 228
pressure, 7, 13, 116
vessel disease, 183
Börek, 55
Bosnian stew, 69
Boza, 56
Bran, in brown rice, 185, 232
in mixed flour bread, 54
in wholemeal bread, 12
loss in refining, 213
Bread, and anchovy salad, 25
banana, 225
bran-plus wholewheat, 213
buckwheat, 223
calcium in, 11
corn, 54, 220
and wheat, 221–2
country, from the Abruzzi, 214–15
eating habits, 209–10
flat, 218
brown, 221
importance in diet, 12
in South-West Europe, 18
in the Balkans, 53–4
in the Middle East, 82, 83, 85, 216
in Yugoslavia, 220, 221
Italian with olive oil, rosemary and garlic, 215
bacamak, 220
Khubz, 87
maize, 18, 220
and wheat, 221–2
multi-grain sourdough, 211–12
orange, 224–5
pain de campagne, 18
pan integrale, 18
pasta, rice and corn in diet, 12, 18
pitta, 210, 216–17
pogata, 61
poppy seed wholewheat, 213–14
potato with caraway, 224
proja, 220
protein in, 10, 11
rye, 18
shami, 84, 216
sourdough, 210
thin, from the Middle East, 217
unleavened, 219
wholewheat, 12, 209, 212–13
with egg salad, 26
Breakfast, Filipino, 147
in Japan, 114
in Latin America, 152, 153
in the Balkans, 55, 57
in the Middle East, 86, 88, 90
in the Yemen, 85, 219
South-West Europe, 19
Breakfast cereals, 202
Brinza, 55
Britain, dietary cancers, 8
heart disease, 8
life expectancy, 8–9
Broad beans with *butifarron* sausage, 44
Broccoli, 11
little ears with, 35
Brunch, 198
Brussels sprouts, 11
Buckwheat noodles on bamboo plates, 119
Buddhism, 112, 115
Bulgaria, 60, 61, 67, 72, 74, 80, 81
Bulgur, 74, 109
Bumbu Kacang, 144
Bumbu Kecap, 144
Buñuelos, 153
Burdock root, 124
Burekakia, 55
Burgers, fried, 65
Burghul, 84, 97, 102, 103, 109
Butifarron sausage, 44
Butter, 12, 18, 227
clarified, 88
fresh nut, 203

Cabbage, salad, 76
soup, 21
vitamin C in, 11, 54
white, casserole, 69
in Balkans, 54
Cadwaller, Sharon, 211
Calabecita, 151
Calabeza, 151
Calabria, 28, 34
Calcium, in bread, 12
in milk, 11
Calories, 209
in bread and grain foods, 12
in rice, 233
in sugar, 12
intake in different countries, 13
Canary Islands, 46
Cancer, 7, 8, 9
and vitamins, 11
bladder, 13
breast, 7, 202
colon, 202
diet-related, 8, 52, 82, 113
in Spain, 9, 17
lung, 11
stomach, 113
Cannelloni, 19
Canton, 143
Caramel custard, 177
Caraway with potato bread, 224
Caribbean, 224, 225
Carob, brownies, 196
powder, 196
'Carolina' rice, 232
Carrow, cake, 198
cashew and ginger quiche, 191
vitamin A in, 11
Cashew, carrot and ginger quiche, 191
Casserole, Greek chicken and tomato, 70
mixed vegetables, 62
white cabbage, 69
Castel da Lama, 215
Catalonia, 25, 30, 44, 49
Cauliflower, sesame-, quiche, 190
Celeriac, 54
Cereals, 208
Ceviche, 152
Chard leaves, stuffed, 103
Chayotes, 151
Cheese, and baked potatoes, 60–1
blue, salad, 192
brinza, 55
feta, 55, 57, 59
fresh, 105
fritters, 192
grilled (broiled), 105
in the Balkans, 55
low-fat, 11
parmesan, 37
pecorino, 35
protein in, 10
ricotta, 35
sir, 55

Cheese, *contd.*
  sirene, 55, 60
  with layered pastry, 62
Chica de jora, 152
Chicha de manzana, 153
Chick pea, and pasta soup, 21
  and sesame meal spread, 93
  fried rissoles, 91
  stew and cracked wheat, 102–3
Chick peas, as source of protein, 18
  with yoghurt, 89
Chicken, and mushrooms with rice-cakes, 124
  and papaya, 146
  crisp-fried, 143
  Greek, and tomato casserole, 70
  grilled, 104
  roasted in the sukiyaki style, 130
  saturated fat content, 10
  skewered grilled, 144
  with wine and olive sauce, 144
Chile, 159, 161, 163, 170, 179
Chilli, 151, 196
  hot sauce with turkey, 176
  peppers, stuffed, 172
  red, paste, 160–1
  sauce, 161
  very hot sauce, 161
Chinaque, 153
Cholesterol, 7, 10–11, 114
  and vegetable oils, 12, 228
  in eggs, 10
Chorizo, 23, 170
Chouriço, 21
Ciorba de praz, 78
Citrus fruits, 11
Cleave, Helen, 213
Cocido, 45
Coconut, cream with sticky rice, 147
  milk, 166
  oil, 228, 230
  pudding, 177
  to open, 166
  with rice and raisins, 165–6
Cod's roe, smoked, 57–8
Coffee, Turkish, 111
Colombia, 158, 165, 174
Condensed milk, paste of, 179
Constipation, 8, 12
Corn (maize), and wheat bread, 221–2
  bread, 18, 54, 220
  gruel, 179
  importance in diet, 12
  in Arab diet, 84
  in South American diet, 150
  oil, 18, 227–9
  protein in, 10
Cornmeal cake, 222
Costa Rica, 165, 168
Cottonseed oil, 88, 227, 228, 230
Courgettes, stuffed, 100
Couve, 21
Cristallo rice, 231
Cuba, 177
Cucumber, and seaweed salad, 125
  and yoghurt salad, 94
  soup, 59
Ćufte, 65

Daikon, 115, 122, 142
Damascus, 89, 90
Dashi, 114, 116, 117
Date slices, 200
Deep-frying, 129
De Langen, C. D., 114
Diabetes, 8, 12, 154
Diarrhoea, 9
Dietary disease in the Western world, 7–8
Dindendeng, 9
Diverticular disease, 8, 12
Donbrui, 120
Doufu, 131, 132–3
Dried fruit compôte with ginger, 200
Duck with sauerkraut, 71

Eating habits, in Chile, 152
  in Colombia, 153
  in Japan, 114–16
  in Mexico, 150
  in Nicaragua, 153
  in South-West Europe, 19–20
  in the Balkans, 55–6
  in the Fertile Crescent, 86–7
  The Yemen, 85–6
Egg, salad with bread, 26
  scrambled, soup, 117
Eggah bi sabaneh, 106
Eggplant, *see* Aubergine
Eggs, in diet, 10–11
  poached, with noodles, 120
    with yoghurt, 63
  ranch-style, 160
  scrambled with sweet peppers, 39
  Spanish omelette, 40
Empadas, 150, 173, 178
Enchiladas, 150, 153
Endive curly salad in hot dressing, 25
Energy, from bread, 208
  from milk, 11
  from vegetables and fruit, 11
Epazote, 169
Erucic acid, 229
Eskimos, 10

Falafel, 85
Fats and oil in diet, 10–11, 11–12, 17–18, 83, 112, 227
Fattet hummus, 105
Fatty acids, 228
  in vegetable oils, 12, 227, 230
Fatteh, 89
Fava, 88
  see also Beans, broad
Fennel, with grey mullet or sea-bass, 42
  with lamb and tomato, 48
Feta, 55, 57, 59
Fibre, 7, 11, 12, 13, 34, 209, 213
Fish, ball soup, 131
  balls, 131
  braised horse mackerel, 128
  cakes, Japanese, 126–7
  grilled, with Taratoor bi Tahina sauce, 96
  in diet, 10
  in Indonesian diet, 141
  in Japanese diet, 112, 115–16
  in Latin American diet, 152
  in West Indian diet, 154
  marinated, 30, 164
  oil, 227
  raw, 126
  salt-grilled (broiled), 127
  sausage with braised vegetables, 128
  soup, 22
  stew, 43, 163, 164
  with sauerkraut, 63
Flan, 19, 152
Flayfly, 97
Flour, hard red spring wheat, 213
  rye, 18
  white, 12, 209
  wholewheat, 12, 212
Folic acid, 10
Fool, apricot, 201
Fritters, 129, 178
  cheese, 192
  sweet-corn patties, 137
Fruit cake, wholewheat, 200–1
Fruit, compôte with ginger, 200
  dried, 110, 200
  importance in diet, 11
  in Arab diet, 85
  in Latin America, 151
  in the Balkans, 54, 55
  in West Indies, 154
  to sweeten dishes, 12
Funghi porcini, 37

Galicia, 18, 46
Gallstones, 8, 11
Game, 10
Garlic, and oil sauce, 49
  importance in diet, 11
  mayonnaise, 22
  soup, 23
  with pasta and fresh herbs, 195
Gibanica, 55
Gibanica sa sirom, 62
Ginger, carrot and cashew quiche, 191
  with dried fruit compôte, 200
Glycerol, 227
Gomashio, 116, 125
Gramigna, 21
Granola, raw, 202
Grant, Doris, 212
  loaf, 212–13
Greece, 79
  diarrhoea in, 9
  health record, 9
  life expectancy, 8
  mortality at birth and during infancy, 9
Green peppers with salt cod and tomatoes, 31
Grey mullet, grilled with fennel, 42
Grouper cooked in sherry, 44
Guadeloupe, 164
Guatemala, 158, 174, 178
Gumbo, 166
Gum disease, 8
Gyuvech (güveç), 55, 61

Haemorrhoids, 8
  (piles) due to lack of fibre, 12
Hallacas, 157
Halumi, 105
Halva, 56
Harusame, 130
Hawayij, 92, 100
Headaches, 116

Health record, Indonesia, 114
Japan, 112–13
Middle East, 82
Spain, 16–17
the Balkans, 53
Heart attack, 11, 183, 228
Heart disease, among Jews, 82
cholesterol in blood, 10–11, 228
in Indonesia, 114
in Japan, 113
in Spain, 8, 9, 17
in the Balkans, 52
related to diet, 7, 8, 9, 114, 148–9, 202, 208
Heavenly food, 50
Herbs with pasta and garlic, 195
High blood pressure, and salt, 13, 17
and sodium, 116
in Portuguese, 17
Hijiki, 116
Hilbeh, 85, 106
Honey, 12–13
Horse mackerel, braised, 128
Hoshi zakana, 114
Huajio, 135
Huevos rancheros, 153
Humitas, 157
Hummus sandwich, 188–9
Hydrogenation, 228

Iberian peninsula, 30
Id es Saidi, 90
Indonesia, 139, 141, 144
Infant mortality, 8
Iodine, in fish, 10
in oils, 228
in seaweed, 125
Iraq, 88, 90, 96, 104
Italy, 9

Jamaica, 180, 225
Japan, birth defects, 8
dietary cancers, 8
heart disease, 8
importance of fish in diet, 10
oil and fats in diet, 227
Japanese, omelette, 122
seasonings, 116
Java, 138
Jibna bi-ajeen, 97

Kacamak, 220
Kadaif, 55, 56
Kamaboko, 121
Kat, 86
Katsuobushi, 116, 117, 119, 122
Kebapche, 56
Keftes, 65
Kembong, 140
Kemiri, 139
Kencur, 138
'Keng', 232
Khubz, 87
Kibbeh, 84, 109
Kidney stones, 8
Kiselo zele, 77
Kiseo kupus, 77
Kissel, 55
Kofta kebab, 65
Köfte, 65
Kombu, 116, 117, 118, 127
Konasansho, 116
Kopoglu, 58
Kyufte, 65

Lactic acid, 11
Lactic acid bacteria, 210
Lactic bacteria, 11
Lactobacillus, 210
bulgarius, 54
Ladies' fingers, 166
Ladouban jiang, 132
Lahma bi-ajeen, 97, 98
Lajiao jiang, 132
Lajiao you, 135
Lamb, raw, paste of, 96–7
roast, 47
saturated fat content, 10
skewered, 101
skewered and grilled over charcoal, 68
with fennel and tomato, 48
with spinach, 67
Lard, 53, 227
Layered pastry with cheese, 63
Lebanon, 90, 94, 96, 102
Lecithin, 230
Leek, omelette, 106
salad, 77
Lentil, Madrid soup, 23
soup with rice, 92
spinach soup, 185–6
Lentils, and rice, 107
curried with vegetables, 194
stir-fried sprouted, 203–4
Lettuce, salad with yoghurt, 76
vitamin C in, 11
Leyritz salad, 168
Life expectancy, 8–9, 152
Linoleic acid, 227, 228, 229, 230
Lonac, 69
Low-fat cheese, 11

Macaroni, Catalonian, 36
country, 35
with mushrooms, 37
Macedonia, 66
Mackerel with potatoes in a hot red sauce, 140
Macrobiotic diets, 183
Madrid, 23
Main meal, in Japan, 114–15
in Latin America, 152–3
in the Balkans, 55
in the Fertile Crescent, 86
in the Yemen, 85
South-West Europe, 19
Maize, 150–1
and wheat bread, 221–2
bread, 220
gruel, 179
Majorca, 44
Malagkit, 147
Malaysia, 137, 146
Malformation, risks of, 8
Malunggay leaves, 9
Mamaliga, 54, 73, 79, 222
Mangoade, 180
Mankousha, 97
Margarine, 12
Martinique, 164, 168
Masa harina, 155, 157
Masgoof, 96
Mayonnaise, garlic, 22
Meat, and wheat stew, 90–1
canned, salt content of, 13
filling for Arab pizza, 97–8
in diet, 10, 18
in Indonesian diet, 144
in Japanese diet, 115
in Latin American diet, 152
in Middle Eastern diet, 84
in the Balkans, 55
minced and cracked wheat, 102
minced (ground) on skewers, 101
protein content of, 10
turnovers, 159
with raisins and almonds, 173
Mecca, 111
Melon, fresco, 180
vitamin A in, 11
Meshwi, 101
Methyl mercury poisoning, 10
Meze, 55, 62, 65, 86
Mexico, 161, 162, 176
beans, 169
beverage, 179
breakfast, 160
dessert, 177
peppers, 172
plantains, 167
snacks, 156
Spanish settlement in, 17
tortillas, 158
Middle East, agriculture, 82
bread consumption, 83
fat consumption, 83
health record, 82
meat consumption, 84
spices in diet, 85
sugar in diet, 85, 86
wheat consumption, 84
yoghurt in diet, 11
Midi, 29
Milk, hot breakfast dish, 57
in diet, 11
nut, 206
protein in, 10
Millet, 84, 233
Minerals, in bread, 208
in fish, 10
in honey, 13
in milk, 11
in oils, 2, 28
Minho, 41, 50
Mirin, 116, 119, 121
Miso, 115, 121
shiru, 114, 118, 124
Monosodium glutamate, 116
Mono-unsaturated oils, 228
Morcella, 45, 47
Mortality, 8, 9
Moussaka, aubergine, 64
Muesli, 184
Muffins, Sunday brunch, 198–9
Mullet, grey, grilled with fennel, 42
Multiple sclerosis, 228
Murcia, 40
Mushrooms with macaroni, 37

Naples, 38
Niacin, 151
Nicaragua, 168, 170, 180
Nice, 30
Nitrates, in processed foods, 13
Nitrites, in processed foods, 13, 113
Nitrosamines, 13

Noodles, buckwheat on bamboo plates, 119
cold with sesame sauce, 135
fried, 134–5
pork-stuffed in shrimp and chicken soup, 133
with bean paste, 120–1
with poached eggs, 120
Nopalitos, 151
Nori, 114, 116
Nut, fresh butter, 203
milk, 203

Ochra vegetable dish, 166–7
Offal, 18
Oil and garlic sauce, 49
Oils, coconut, 228, 230
corn (maize), 18, 227, 228, 229
cottonseed, 88, 227, 228, 230
fish, 227
in diet, 11–12, 17–18, 227
olive, 11, 12, 17, 88, 227, 229–30
palm, 228, 230
paprika, 57
peanut, 228, 229
rapeseed, 229
refined, 228
safflower, 228, 230
sesame, 88, 227, 228, 229, 230
soya-bean, 227, 228, 229
sunflower, 18, 227, 228, 229
to use, 229
unrefined, 228
unsaturated, 228
vegetable, 12, 17–18
walnut, 228, 230
wheat germ, 228, 230
Okra vegetable dish, 166–7
Olive, and anchovy tart, 30–1
oil, 229–30
sauce with chicken and wine, 70
Omelette, Japanese, 122
leek, 106
Spanish, 40
Onigiri, 115, 123
Onion and tomato salad, 26
Onions, beans with rice and, 170
importance in diet, 11
Orange bread, 224–5
Orecchiette, 34, 35
Overweight, 8, 12
Ox (beef) heart cubes, 175

Paella, 18, 19, 232
Pain de campagne, 18
Palermo, 27
Palm oil, 228, 230
Pancakes, steamed with spicy fillings, 157
tortilla, 158–9
Pancetta, 21, 35, 36, 47
Pancotto, 24
Pan integrale, 18
Pansit, 133
Papaya and chicken, 146
Paprika oil, 57
Parmesan cheese, 37
Pasta, 19
importance in diet, 12
in Portugal and Spain, 18
little ears of, 34–5
protein in, 10
shredded, 74–5
with garlic and fresh herbs, 195
Pasteis de bacalhau, 20
Pastry, layered, with cheese, 62
Patis, 142, 146
'Patna' rice, 232
Peaches, 11
Pea soup with eggs, 24
Peas, 18
Peanut, dressing with mixed salad, 138–9
oil, 228, 229
Pebre, 153, 171
Pecorino, 35
Pellagra, 151
Penang, 131
Pepper, and spaghetti gratin, 34
and tomato salad, 95
-flavoured salt, 143
Peppers, stuffed and tomatoes, 66–7
sweet, with scrambled eggs, 39
with yoghurt, 58–9
vitamin C in, 11
Peptic ulcers, 8
Perlis, 140
Peru, 17, 163, 175
Petmez, 80
Philippines, 17, 137, 142, 146, 147
Phosphorus, 10
Phyllo leaves, 62
Pickles, 13
Pignoli *see* Pine nuts
Pilaf, cracked wheat, 74
raisin, 79
two-in-one, 75
Piles, 12
Pine nuts, 27, 33, 204
Piri-piri suace, 49
Pisang rajah, 146
Pisco, 152
Pissaladière, 20
Pizza, 20
Arab, with a meat filling, 97–8
Calabrian, 38–9
Plancha, 32
Plantain, deep-fried pasties, 178
Plantains, fried ripe, 167
Pogača, 61
Polenta, 151
fried slices, 73
Polyunsaturated fats, in fish, 10, 140
in vegetable oils, 12, 227, 228, 229, 230
Popara, 57
Popcorn, 86
Poppy seed wholewheat bread, 213–14
Pork, and beans, 47
and beef stew, 142
and shredded squid, 140–1
and shrimp with Taiwan rice, 138
saturated fat content, 10
-stuffed noodles in shrimp and chicken soup, 133
with rice, 40–1
with soy sauce, 141–2
Portuguese, high blood pressure, 17
Potatoes, baked, and cheese, 60–1
in diet, 151
with cheese sauce, 171
with mackerel in a hot red sauce, 140
Pourgouri, 74
Prawn stock, 133
Prawns, grilled (broiled), 141
Processed foods, salt content, 13
Proja, 220
Prostaglandins, 228
Protein, in bread, 208
in Japanese diet, 112
in milk, 11
in pulses, 18
sources of, 10
Provence, 24, 42
Puchero, 46
Pui, 70
Pulque, 152
Pulses, in Arab diet, 84
in Balkan diet, 53
Pumpkin, 54
baked, 80–1
cream of, soup, 162
pie, two-crust, 199
with cranberry beans and sweet-corn, 170–1

Quarapo, 153
Quail with rice, 72
Quiche, carrot, cashew and ginger, 191
sesame-cauliflower, 190

Rabbit in *Vinho Verde*, 48–9
Raisin pilaf, 79
Raisins, with meat and almonds, 173
with rice and coconut, 165–6
Ramadan, 92, 110
Rape seed oil, 229
Ravioli, crescent-shaped, 136
Raw granola, 202
Refrescos, 152
Refritos, 151
Renkon, 115
Revane, 56
Rice, 107, 231–3
and lentils, 107
balls, 123
brown, 195, 232, 233
-cakes with chicken and mushrooms, 124
Costa Rican style, 165
fried, 137
importance in diet, 12, 18–19
in Italy, 231
in Japan, 232, 233
in South-East Asia, 232
in Spain, 231–2
in the Americas, 232
in the Middle East, 232
proetin in, 10
pudding, thick, 79
sticky, with coconut cream, 147
Taiwan, with shrimp and pork, 138
to cook, 233
types, 231–2
water, 146
with beans and onions, 70
with broad (*fava*) beans, 108
with coconut and raisins, 165–6
with green tea, 122–3
with lentil soup, 92

Rice, *contd.*
with pork, 40–1
with quail, 72
with turnip tops, 41
with vegetables, 165
with vermicelli, 108
Ricotta, 35
Risottos, 19
Rouille, 22
Russian dressing, 204
Rye flour, 18

Saccharin, and bladder cancer, 13
Safflower oil, 228, 230
Salad, anchovy and bread, 25
blue cheese, 192
cabbage, 76
cooked mixed vegetable, 139
cracked wheat, 94
cucumber and yoghurt, 94
curly endive in hot dressing, 25
dried fruit, 110
egg, with bread, 26
fresh vegetable from Sicily, 26
green bean, 76
leek, 77
lettuce with yoghurt, 76
Leyritz, 168
mixed, 99–100, 168
with peanut dressing, 138–9
seaweed and cucumber, 125
summer with Russian dressing, 204
tomato and onion, 26
and pepper, 95
'Wings of Life', 187
with vegetable oils, 12
yoghurt-tahina, 188
Salchichón, 25
Salsicce, 35, 37
Salt cod, croquettes, 32
in Portuguese diet, 17, 31
with green peppers and tomatoes, 31
with vegetables and all-i-oli sauce, 42–3
Salt, in diet, 8, 13, 17, 154
-pepper-flavoured, 143
Sambal ulek, 138–9
Samna, 85, 88, 89, 103
Sashimi, 123, 126
Satay powder, 144
Saturated fats, 10
in cakes and ice cream, 12
Sauce, all-i-oli, 42–3, 49
avocado with tomatoes and coriander, 160
chilli, 161
fresh Mexican tomato, 162
garlic and oil, 49
green tomato, 161
hot chilli, 176
piri-piri, 43, 49
soy, 115
Taratoor bi Tahina, 96
very plain tomato, 50
Sauerkraut, 77–8
juice soup, 78–9
with duck, 71
with fish, 63
Sausage, 36
butifarrones, 44
chorizo, 23, 25, 45, 46, 47, 170
fish, 128
Japanese fish, 126–7
meat, 36
morcella, 45, 47
salchichón, 25
salsicce, 35, 37
Savanyú káposzta, 77
Savoury custard, 121
Scutellum, 233
Sea-bass, grilled with fennel, 42
Seaweed, 116
and cucumber salad, 125
in Japanese diet, 125
Semki, 80–1
Semolina pudding, 90
Sesame, -cauliflower quiche, 190
meal spread with chick pea, 93
oil, 88, 227, 229, 230
sauce with cold noodles, 135
seed, 116, 125, 190
seeds with dressed spinach, 125
with aubergine, 124
Seventh Day Adventists, 202
Shami, 84, 216
Shaslik, 68, 101
Sherry, grouper cook in, 44
Shichimi togarashi, 116, 120
Shijtake, 121
Shish kebabs, 56
Shoga, 116
Shrimp, and pork with Taiwan rice, 138
soup, 163
Sicily, 25, 27, 47
Silq, 95
Sinigang, 142
Sir, 55
Sirene, 55, 57, 60
Slivova rakiya, 58
Smoked cod's roe purée, 57–8
Sodium, 116
Soffrito, 21
Sorghum, 84
Soup, basic stock, 117
bean, 60
cabbage, 21
chick pea and pasta, 21
cold tomato with bread, 24
cream of butternut squash, 186
cream of pumpkin, 162
cucumber and yoghurt, 59
fish, 22
fish ball, 131
garlic, 23
lentil spinach, 185–6
lentil, with rice, 92
Madrid lentil, 23
pea with eggs, 24
sauerkraut juice, 78–9
scrambled egg, 117
shrimp, 163
and chicken with pork-stuffed noodles, 133
soya bean paste, 118
split pea, 184
tomato bisque, 185
Yemeni, 92
Sourdough, 210
multi-grain bread, 211–12
starter, 211
Souvlakia, 75
Soya bean, curd, 131–2, 186–7
in Japanese diet, 112, 115, 118
oil, 11, 12, 227, 228, 229
paste soup, 118
Spaghetti and pepper gratin, 34
Spain, birth defects, 8
diarrhoea in, 9
health record, 9
heart disease, 8
life expectancy, 8
mortality at birth and during infancy, 9
Spices, Chinese Five, 142
hawayij, 92, 100
in Japan, 116
in Middle Eastern diet, 85
Spina bifida, 8
Spinach, 9
and lentil soup, 185–6
dressed with sesame seeds, 125
vitamin A in, 11
with black-eyed beans, 95
with lamb, 67
Split pea soup, 184
Spreads, anchovy, 29
chick pea and sesame meal, 93
Sprouting seeds, 203
Squash, cream of butternut, soup, 186
Squid, shredded, and pork, 140–1
tiny, cooked on a hotplate, 32–3
Srpski ajvar, 58
Starch, 12, 13
Stew, 99
beef, 174
and pork, 142
with beans, peas and rice, 173
Bosnian, 69
Canary Island, 46
cracked wheat and chick pea, 102–3
fish, 43, 163, 164
Galician, 46–7
Madrid, 45
meat and wheat, 90–1
Stir-frying, 193
Stock, basic soup, 117
Strawberry pignoli, 204
Streptococcus thermophilus, 54
Stroke, 7, 154, 228
Suchi, 114–15
Suet, 227
Sugar, brown, 12
in Arab diet, 85
in Balkan diet, 55
in Caribbean diet, 154
in diet, 12–13
in honey, 13
in South American diet, 152
refining of, 12
Sukiyaki pan, 130
Sultan's slices, 81
Sunday brunch muffins, 198–9
Sunflower oil, 18, 53, 227, 228, 229
Supper, in Japan, 115
in Latin America, 153
in the Balkans, 56
in the Fertile Crescent, 86
South-West Europe, 19

Sweet-corn, patties, 137
with cranberry beans and pumpkin, 170–1
Switzerland, 185
Syria, 90, 94, 96, 102
Syrup, wheat in, 110

Tabbouleh, 84, 109
Tacos, 150, 153, 156, 160, 173
Tahina, yoghurt-, salad, 188
Taiwan, 134, 135, 136, 138, 140, 143
Tamales, 150, 153, 157, 173
Tamarind, 142
Tannour, 217
Tapas, 20, 32
Taratoor bi Tahina sauce, 98
Tart, olive and anchovy, 30–1
Tasseia, 89
Tau hoo, 142
Tea, green, with rice, 122–3
Tempura, 124
Tepsi böreği, 62
Tequila, 152
Terasi, 139, 141, 144
Texas, 17
Thanksgiving, 199
Thiamin, 233
Thrombosis, 228
Tocino, 44, 45, 46
Tofu, 115, 118–19, 131–2, 186–7
Tomato, and Greek chicken casserole, 70
and onion salad, 26
and pepper salad, 95
and vermicelli gratin, 38
bisque, 185
cold soup with bread, 24
fresh Mexican sauce, 162
green, sauce, 161
very plain sauce, 50
with lamb and fennel, 48
Tomatoes, and stuffed peppers, 66–7
vitamin C in, 11
with salt cod and green peppers, 31
Tooth disease, 8
Tortas, 56
Torte, Amy's orange buttercream, 197
Tortillas, 40, 150, 151, 155–6, 160
fried, 158
pancake, 158–9
wheat, 158
Trahana, 74–5
Trahonya, 74
'Trans-fatty acids', 12
Tras-os-Montes, 48
Tree ears, 134
Trinidad, 173
Tsatsu mage, 128
Tsukemono, 115
Turkey, influence on Balkan cookery, 53
Turkey, in hot chilli sauce, 176
Turkish coffee, 111
Türlü, 61
Turnip tops with rice, 41
Two sides yellow, 132–3
Tyropitta, 62

Ulcers, peptic, 8
Umeboshi, 114
United States, dietary cancers, 8
heart disease, 8
life expectancy, 8–9
Unto, 46, 47

Valencia, 42
Varicose veins, 8, 12
Varza acia, 77
Vegetables, cooked mixed salad, 139
fresh salad from Sicily, 126
mixed casserole, 61
oils, 12, 17–18
stir-fry, 193
August garden, 193–4
Vegetables, and fruit in diet, 11
braised with fish sausage, 128
cooking of, 11
in Arab diet, 85
in Balkan diet, 52, 54
in Caribbean diet, 154
in Indonesian diet, 139
in Japanese diet, 115
in Latin America, 151
with curried lentils, 194
with rice, 165
with salt cod and all-i-oli sauce, 42–3
Venezuela, 158
Vermicelli, and tomato gratin, 38
with rice, 108
Vinho verde, 48
Vitamin A, and millet, 233
in refined oils, 228
in vegetables and fruit, 11
Vitamin B1, 233
Vitamin B2, 11
Vitamin B12, and millet, 233
in eggs, 10
in yeast extract, 183
Vitamin C, and millet, 233
and nitrosamines, 13
in chillies, 152
in sauerkraut, 77
in vegetables and fruit, 11
in white cabbage, 54
Vitamin D, in eggs, 10
in refined oils, 228
Vitamin E, 230
in unrefined oils, 228
Vitamins, in bread, 208
in eggs, 10
in fish, 10
in milk, 11

Wakame, 116, 118, 125
Walnut oil, 228, 230
Wasabi, 116, 119
paste, 123, 126
Western, diet, 8
diseases, 8
Wheat, and meat stew, 90–1
cracked, 109
and chick pea stew, 102–3
and minced meat, 102
pilaf, 74
salad, 94
in Arab diet, 84
in Balkan diet, 53–4
in syrup, 110
Wheat germ, in pasta, 34
loss of in refining of flour, 12
oil, 228, 230
Wholewheat, 12
bran-plus load, 213
bread, 212–13
fruit cake, 200–1
Grant loaf, 212–13
piecrust, 189
poppy seed bread, 213–14
Wine, 56
Wok, 132, 134, 139
World Health Organization, 8

Yahni, 55
Yemen, 85–6, 92, 106, 219
Yemeni relish, 106
Yerbe mate, 152
Yoghurt, 54, 72–3, 104–5
and cucumber salad, 94
and cucumber soup, 59
drink, 111
in diet, 11
lettuce salad with, 76
-tahina salad, 188
with chick peas, 89
with aubergines, 59
with peppers, 58–9
with poached eggs, 63
Yugoslavia, 69, 72, 76, 77, 78, 218, 220, 221

Zahtar, 84, 216
Zelen hajver, 58
Zhug, 85, 106
Zucchini, *see* Courgettes